Programming .NET
Web Services

Programming .NET
Web Services

Alex Ferrara and Matthew MacDonald

O'REILLY®

Beijing · Cambridge · Farnham · Köln · Paris · Sebastopol · Taipei · Tokyo

Programming .NET Web Services
by Alex Ferrara and Matthew MacDonald

Copyright © 2002 O'Reilly & Associates, Inc. All rights reserved.
Printed in the United States of America.

Published by O'Reilly & Associates, Inc., 1005 Gravenstein Highway North, Sebastopol, CA 95472.

Editors:	Nancy Kotary and John Osborn
Production Editor:	Mary Brady
Cover Designer:	Ellie Volckhausen
Interior Designer:	David Futato

Printing History:

September 2002:   First Edition.

ISBN: 0-596-00250-5

[M]

Table of Contents

Preface

Over the last few years, we've lived with an endless stream of web-related hype. Technology evangelists, columnists, and CEOs repeatedly proclaimed that the Internet was about to revolutionize everything from the social fabric of our entire society to grocery shopping. Some of these changes have taken place, but other radical predictions and ambitious new technologies now look—well, a little embarrassing.

One of the visions that has been conjured up time and time again that of a "programmable Internet," on which all sorts of applications and devices communicate continuously, sharing features and functionality openly and painlessly. The truth is, though we now have an unprecedented network that links computers across the globe, we haven't begun to realize its full potential. Despite ambitious technologies like COM/DCOM, CORBA/IIOP, RMI, and XML-RPC, the Internet is currently used primarily for sending email and retrieving HTML pages; programs on proprietary platforms remain unable to use each others services without costly customization.

Now Microsoft (and traditional rivals like IBM and Sun) have proposed a new "web services platform," based on XML and related technologies that aims to let applications share functionality over the Internet as easily as they can on a local computer. The potential is amazing, and the implementation is simple, elegant, and surprisingly open. XML is incorporated from the ground up, cross-platform support is inherent, and productivity tools are available from participating vendors to handle all the heavy lifting. Web services and simple web services directories are already spreading over the Internet, with everything from horoscope and translation services to Microsoft's own TerraService, which provides access to a 1.5-terabyte SQL Server database of satellite images. Companies like eBay and McAffee have been hard at work developing innovative web service solutions with .NET, and key sites such as Google and Amazon have already exposed some of their capabilities using web services interfaces.

The Microsoft .NET Framework is both an implementation of this platform and a means to easily build services that can interoperate on it. Microsoft has (at least to some degree) abandoned its traditional preference for closed technologies and proprietary standards. Java clients on Unix machines can consume .NET services, and .NET clients can interact with web services written in most other non-.NET languages just as readily, provided they adhere to emerging XML-based web services standard protocols like SOAP and WSDL. The complexity and headaches that have clouded distributed programming with COM and CORBA have been replaced with simple, lightweight XML-based standards. To sum it all up: XML-based web services in general, and .NET web services in particular, are a radically changed and improved attempt to reach a long-standing goal of universal connectivity.

What This Book Covers

This book explores Microsoft .NET web services from the developer's perspective. We explain how to create web services with the .NET Framework and its ASP.NET tools, but more importantly, we consider the best practices needed to design web services that are efficient, scalable, and robust. This book also sheds some light on the underlying plumbing for the .NET web service technology: the open standards like SOAP and WSDL that are at work behind the scenes. This understanding is not required to write a web service with .NET, but it can be quite useful when deciding how to use its features and how to deal with its limitations.

Throughout this book we'll also show you how to *extend* web services. One of the greatest features of web services protocols is their simplicity. Unlike earlier distributed object technologies, XML-based web services standards do not yet specify mechanisms for handling security, transactions, or object pooling. In order to provide these features, you need to design and implement your own solutions and leverage platform technologies like COM+ and ASP.NET. Throughout this book, you'll see the best ways to develop these homegrown solutions.

Audience

Just as important as what this book covers is what this book *doesn't* cover—the syntax of the C# programming language, the fundamentals of ASP.NET, or the basics of the .NET Framework. This book is targeted at the professional developer who already has some .NET experience. If you aren't already familiar with C# and .NET, there are plenty of other excellent .NET books available from O'Reilly to get you started, including titles like *Programming C#*, Second Edition, by Jesse Liberty (2002), *Programming ASP.NET*, by Liberty and Hurwitz (2002) *.NET Framework Essentials*, Second Edition, by Thai and Lam (2002), and *C# in a Nutshell*, by Drayton, Albahari, and Neward (2002).

On the other hand, if you are a seasoned .NET developer, you don't need to worry about wasting time revisiting the basics about types, metadata, and the Common Language Runtime. Instead, our discussion will focus exclusively on web service topics. For example, you'll see web services that work with disconnected DataSets, but we won't review the basics of ADO.NET. This concentrated focus makes this book unique among the current crop of .NET books, most of which try to teach the .NET Framework fundamentals, the C# or VB .NET programming language, and other programming basics in one muddled combination.

 If you are familiar with the .NET platform, you may have already realized that C# code can be converted to equivalent VB.NET statements on a line-by-line basis. Unfortunately, due to space limitations, the examples in this book are presented in C# code only. Any potential differences that could affect the VB.NET programmer are explained in the text, and VB.NET developers will still find this work to be an excellent reference for web service fundamentals and best practices for web service design. For additional information, see *C# and VB.NET Conversion Pocket Reference*, by Jose Mojica (O'Reilly, 2002).

What You Need to Use This Book

To make the best use of this book, you'll need the following software:

- Windows 2000 Professional or Windows XP (the minimum requirement for developing with the .NET Framework).

- The Internet Information Services (IIS) component of Windows. This feature is part of the standard Windows operating system, but it is not installed by default. Ideally, you should install it before you install the .NET Framework. To ensure that it is present, choose Windows Components from the Add or Remove Programs window.

- The .NET Framework, either in its redistributable (SDK) form or as a part of the Visual Studio .NET retail package. You can also work with the second beta of the .NET Framework, although the released version is recommended. The first beta, however, is not supported (or compatible with the examples presented here).

The web service features of Visual Studio .NET (VS.NET) are documented throughout the book, and you may well find that its automatic error-checking, integrated debugging, and IntelliSense statement completion are impossible to live without. However, .NET web services can be coded just as easily by hand and compiled with the command-line *csc.exe* compiler. This book describes this approach as well. For the most part, we focus on pure code and the technology behind web services. The development approach you use will be of secondary importance. If you do use VS. NET, we assume that you have it installed and set up correctly.

How This Book Is Organized

The book begins by describing web service basics: how they work, how to create them, and how to consume them in a client. Thanks to .NET development tools, writing a simple web service is not much more difficult than creating an ordinary class, once you know the rules and restrictions. The bulk of the book—the next six chapters—covers ways you can integrate commonly required advanced features into web services. Often, technology details are introduced to solve a particular problem, not up front when they may just cloud a discussion with additional details. For example, SOAP headers make an appearance as a powerful way to implement custom state management, and SOAP extensions appear as a way to perform automatic tracing.

The book ends by considering how web services can be published so they are easily accessible and how you can break down the boundaries between your web services and non-.NET code for truly cross-platform solutions.

This brief outline explains what each chapter contains:

Chapter 1, *Understanding Web Services*
> History is littered with failed web technologies, and Microsoft's contribution to the pile is far from modest, including such legacy approaches as ActiveX documents and Visual Basic web classes. With .NET, however, there's good reason to believe that Microsoft has learned from the disasters of the past. In this chapter, you'll learn why .NET XML web services should work where other technologies have stalled and what roles web services will play in the applications of the future. You'll also learn about the standards, like WSDL, SOAP, and HTTP, that underlie .NET web services.

Chapter 2, *Creating ASP.NET Web Services*
> This chapter starts with every developer's favorite example, the canonical Hello-World program—this time recast as a web service. Before the chapter is finished, you'll move up to a DNS lookup service and learn how to test your web methods using HTTP GET in Internet Explorer. Along the way, you'll learn about .NET's web service types, virtual directories and web service deployment, and how to develop a web service in Visual Studio .NET or compile it with the command-line compiler.

Chapter 3, *Consuming Web Services*
> Web service clients can be written in any language that provides an XML parser and any platform that supports the HTTP protocol. However, you're likely to find that the tools included with the .NET Framework make .NET applications the best choice. In this chapter, you'll learn how to generate a proxy class that handles web service communication automatically and allows any .NET application—including Windows Forms, ASP.NET pages, or even console utilities—to access a web service without worrying about the low-level details.

Chapter 4, *Working with Data Types*
> Sharing data between different languages, platforms, and operating systems opens up many new issues and considerations. This chapter provides an advanced exploration of web service data types and how they are encoded.

You'll learn what can be sent as a web method parameter or return value and how to work with arrays, DataSets, XML nodes, and custom structures. We'll also take an in-depth look at .NET's XML serialization architecture and you'll learn about custom data shaping.

Chapter 5, *Managing State*

The debate over the advantages of stateless versus stateful programs is alive and well with .NET web services. This chapter examines why web services won't support property procedures and explores the hard realities that cause many state-maintaining web service classes to fail. We'll consider state options on the client and server side, from the ASP.NET state service to custom cookies. We'll also look at how you can use tokens to track your own lightweight sessions and combine them with SOAP headers to provide an elegant solution for cases in which basic information must be retained.

Chapter 6, *Asynchronous Services*

.NET makes web methods behave like ordinary local functions, which are synchronous by default and wait for a response before allowing execution to continue. Though this is the default behavior, there's no reason to let it dictate how you use web services in a mature application This chapter shows how you can remove this requirement, unshackle your code, and use common optimization patterns to make your clients more efficient. These tricks include invoking multiple methods at once, using callbacks and event notifications, and creating multithreaded clients. We'll also look at how to create a web method that creates an asynchronous component, sets it to work, and returns immediately. This allows some advanced tricks, like automatic progress tracking and batch processing.

Chapter 7, *Caching and Profiling*

In order to create a successful web service, you need to code with performance in mind. This chapter shows the best practices for using output caching to speed up access and data caching to replace or supplement state management. We'll also look at how you can use performance counters and profile .NET web services. This allows you to study the results of attempted performance enhancements before a web service goes "live."

Chapter 8, *Debugging, Tracing, and Logging*

.NET web services may mimic traditional classes from the programmer's point of view, but they can't throw ordinary .NET exceptions. This chapter explores how you can take control of errors and notify the client with special SOAP exceptions. You'll also learn how to use Visual Studio .NET's integrated debugger, with its celebrated single-step execution with multiproject web service solutions, and how to use .NET Framework services for automatic logging and tracing. This chapter ends with an introduction to SOAP extensions and sample code that shows you how to use a custom extension to peer beneath .NET's object layer and examine or log raw SOAP messages en route.

Chapter 9, *Security and Authentication*

Web services standards don't currently provide any integrated security mechanism, but you have countless options, from transport-level security to IIS authentication to ASP.NET's own authentication services. In this chapter, you'll learn how you can secure your web service—and more importantly, what techniques work best.

Chapter 10, *Publishing and Discovery*

Now that you've created the perfect web service, how do you get the word out? This chapter looks at the technologies that allow clients to track down the web services they need, including everything from simple DISCO files to online web search engines and the UDDI registry that lets businesses share details about their internal processes. We'll consider static and dynamic discovery with DISCO files, which aggregate web services into simple groups. We'll also examine the UDDI registry, how to use it to register a business and add services, and consider whether it's ready for prime time.

Chapter 11, *Interoperability*

This chapter focuses on service interoperability. It discusses interoperability problems that can occur between SOAP implementations and what's currently being done to iron out discrepancies in SOAP implementations. It also covers some simple steps you can take to make sure your .NET web services are accessible by other implementations.

Appendix A, *Namespace Quick Reference*

This appendix provides an alphabetically organized reference to the key classes of the System.Web.Services namespace.

Appendix B, *Web Service Technologies*

This appendix offers a list by category of some of the most frequently mentioned web service standards and technologies, and where to look for additional information.

Conventions Used in This Book

The following font conventions are used in this book:

Italic is used for:

- Pathnames, file directories, and filenames
- Internet addresses, such as domain names and URLs
- New terms where they are defined

Constant width is used for:

- Code samples and commands
- Names and keywords in .NET programs, including method names, variable names, names, and namespaces

You should pay special attention to notes set apart from the text with the following icons:

 This is a tip, suggestion, or a general note. It contains useful supplementary information about the topic at hand.

 This indicates a warning or caution. It will help you solve and avoid annoying problems.

Comments and Questions

Please address comments and questions concerning this book to the publisher:

O'Reilly & Associates, Inc.
1005 Gravenstein Highway North
Sebastopol, CA 95472
1-800-998-9938 (in the United States or Canada)
1-707-829-0515 (international/local)
1-707-829-0104 (fax)

There is a web site for the book, which lists examples, errata, or any additional information. You can access this page at:

http://www.oreilly.com/catalog/prognetws/

To comment or ask technical questions about this book, send email to:

bookquestions@oreilly.com

For more information about books, conferences, Resource Centers, and the O'Reilly Network, see the O'Reilly web site:

http://www.oreilly.com

Acknowledgments

Writing a book about any part of the .NET Framework is a challenge. Bookstore shelves are swamped with .NET titles, but few reflect the real issues and challenges practicing developers face as they tackle the new platform. Digging into the low-level details is a task that's ideally suited for a publisher like O'Reilly, where everyone prizes technical integrity. This book couldn't have been written without the help of many folks at O'Reilly, including John Osborn, who saw our complementary styles and brought us together to cowrite the book, and Nancy Kotary, who kept the book on track through countless technical review and revision cycles (even if it required dozens of emails a day). We also owe a heartfelt thanks to the technical reviewers who submitted timely comments and tested our code creations, including Martin Gudgin, Chris Jones, and B. Robert Helm, as well as Brian Jepson, who, although not directly tied to this project, can always be counted on to provide helpful feedback or track down a Microsoft contact. Without the support of these people and many more at O'Reilly, the book would never have been written.

Alex

Several people deserve my sincere and deep-felt gratitude for their contributions and/or unwavering support during the writing of this book. In addition to writing half of this book, my coauthor Matthew contributed his technical expertise, attention to detail, and a continual enthusiasm for the subject matter throughout the course of this yearlong project. Matthew, working with you has been a great experience, and I owe you my thanks for all of your hard work. I'd also like to thank the U-inspire, Inc./Boston Technical team for their understanding in allowing me the time I needed to write. I owe special thanks to Matt from Boston Technical for all of the organizational and technical feedback he provided. Last, this book would not have been possible without the continuing love, understanding, and support of my wife. I love you, Tracy.

Matthew

First, I'd like to thank Alex, who not only wrote half the chapters but also offered technical, organizational, and philosophical feedback on my work from its initial conception to the final product. It's been a pleasure working with you, and I'm sure the final product is more than the sum of its two parts. Next, I'd like to recognize the contribution of a few people who were key to my web services work: Nora, Razia, Hamid, Paul. Finally, this book would never have been written without the endless support of my loving wife.

CHAPTER 1

Understanding Web Services

Web services are about sharing functionality across the boundaries of devices, networks, operating systems, and programming languages.

In this chapter, we'll consider four topics:

- Web services—what they are and where they fit into software development
- The technologies such as DCOM and IIOP that were the precursors to .NET web services and their limitations
- The underlying technologies and standards that support .NET web services, including SOAP, HTTP, WSDL, and UDDI
- Competing web service implementations and how they might work in harmony with .NET

These topics are covered in greater detail in later chapters.

Why Web Services?

Today, you can access the Internet via many different devices, connecting to a wide range of functionality beyond that available on the devices themselves. The early age of static web pages has given way to sophisticated applications for e-commerce, stock trading, team management, and a whole lot more.

The defining characteristic of the Internet is that information is transmitted (for the most part) in a pattern of requests and responses using open protocols like the pervasive HTTP. Currently, most of this information takes the form of HTML markup tags that build basic user interfaces in the form of web pages, which are viewed in a browser. Although platforms like ASP.NET use it to create applications with a wide range of features, HTML only scratches the surface of what enterprising programmers can really do with the Internet.

Web-Enabled Applications

Recently, the worlds of web and desktop application development have moved closer to each other. Desktop interfaces, like those of Windows XP, have started to resemble Internet browsers. Internet functionality has entered ordinary desktop applications, and Windows applications now interact with web servers over HTTP. For example, Microsoft Money can automatically download banking information; the Windows operating system can automatically notify you when operating system upgrades are available; and Visual Studio .NET allows you to search the MSDN library without leaving the development environment. You can even read Hotmail messages inside Microsoft Outlook and monitor eBay auctions with third-party desktop tools.

While the addition of such features is clearly an innovation, most are handcrafted, proprietary solutions. In order to add web-aware features to an application today, you must develop an infrastructure from scratch. For example, Microsoft Money needs code to interact with multiple web sources, each with its own protocols, in order to gather data from more than one bank for a user. Third-party eBay clients rely on screen scraping that will break whenever eBay updates its web site user interface. There is no web equivalent for prepackaged, reusable COM components.

Web applications are equally hobbled. Relatively clumsy methods like links, frames, and screen scraping must be used to integrate the functionality of different sites. The problem is that these applications are "monolithic": they exist as all-in-one packages, and there is no easy way to decouple a user interface from its functionality, to provide, for example, a stock quote or a package delivery lookup, without forcing the user to go through a browser.

This is where web services and .NET come into the picture. Web services protocols specify a framework for invoking functions over the Internet. They are based on open standards and adopt a loosely coupled and extensible design that can be used for the current generation of web-enabled applications, and much more. The .NET Framework is a highly optimized platform and set of tools for deploying web services.

What Is a Web Service?

A *web service* is an application or block of executable code that is hosted on a web server and whose functions are exposed through standard XML protocols. .NET Framework services make it easy to find this code, invoke it, and retrieve a result. In fact, calling a .NET web service is just as easy as calling a local function.

A .NET web service is *not* an object! At least, not in the traditional sense. A web method is essentially independent, stateless, and atomic. A web service is more like a library of functions in a DLL than a true object-oriented abstraction. This simplicity is a large part of the advantage of web services. Because web services aren't tightly bound to a specific technology for security, state management, or transport, they can be used in almost any development scenario. This is completely different than earlier technologies like COM and CORBA, as you'll see later in this chapter.

The Roles of Web Services

There's still some confusion about who actually *uses* a web service. Many have mistakenly assumed that web services are somehow like application service providers, which "rent" their software by the month and allow subscribers to use it over the Internet. This is far from either current reality or the .NET vision. Web services might enable some new business models but do not endorse or constitute any particular arrangement.

Instead, web services are a way to share programming functionality. You can think of them as "COM for the Web," even though the underlying technology is dramatically different.

Some of the ways you can use web services include:

To enable business-to-business transactions or to connect the internal systems of separate companies
> This is perhaps the most common way that web services will be used for the next year or two. Web services can enable document and knowledge sharing or the integration of related services. A web service could be used, for example, to help an e-commerce company interacts automatically with a shipping company to fill orders. In these cases, the web service consumer is probably software used internally in an organization.

As prebuilt modules for developers
> For example, a third-party developer could create a web service for authentication to be used by ASP.NET sites. If you chose to use this service, you might pay a monthly subscription fee based on usage, but the process would be completely transparent to the end user, who would see the functionality is an integrated part of your application. Such prebuilt components can easily be consumed by web, desktop, and mobile applications.

As value-added product features for client applications
> For example, since Microsoft wants IT departments to deploy the Windows operating system, the company has an incentive to build in technology that lets system administrators perform remote administration using web services. A bank that wants you to open an investment account has an incentive to provide a web service for downloading transaction information that can be used at no charge by financial software like Quicken. While end users don't directly consume the service, its availability in Quicken might motivate them to open an account at the bank that provides it.

As component DLLs for internal code reuse

For example, you might find that the easiest way to reuse certain functionality in ASP.NET applications is not to create a .NET assembly, but to design a web service that can be used by a variety of clients, including desktop applications, PDAs, and rich client browsers like Internet Explorer. You don't have to worry about where the web service and clients are located; you just need to make sure each client has an Internet connection.

As tools for connecting software packages within the same company

For example, web services can be used to connect specialized payroll software to accounting software over a secure corporate network (not the Internet).

You may already have a specific idea of how you want to use web services in your own organization. The important concept to remember is this: *web services are not end-user products!* Instead, they are component-based applications that allow you to reuse business logic in different environments and on different types of clients. The consumer of a web service is always another application.

The Origin of Web Services

If web services are such a remarkable, flexible tool for developers, why haven't we already started using them? The Internet has certainly been around for a long time, and concepts like business-to-business transactions and distributed computing are well known. Why haven't web services already been incorporated into modern development practices?

In fact, the concept behind web services is nothing new. You may already be familiar with other programming frameworks based on the idea that applications and functions should be distributed between computers on a network for greater efficiency and flexibility. So far, none has met with wide success because they've run up against two main problems: their own complexity and the heterogeneous nature of the Internet, which includes computers of all possible operating systems, networks, and development platforms.

A Brief History of Web Services

The history of programming is in large part the story of a shift from smaller, more isolated environments (like mainframes and standalone applications) to broader, more inclusive systems, first with networks and client/server programming and then with the Internet and distributed applications.

Sharing code between applications

In the early 1990s, two component technologies vied for developer interest: Microsoft's COM (Component Object Model Architecture) and the cross-vendor initiative

CORBA (Common Object Request Broker) introduced by OMG (Object Management Group). Both allowed units of functionality to be reused as binary objects and allowed software on the same computer to share code in a disciplined way.

As local area networks became more popular, however, it became increasingly important to allow different computers to talk together. Developers could create their own solutions using sockets, but that required the client and the server to handle most of the heavy lifting, as well as the low-level protocols for encoding and decoding messages. Not only was this unpleasant for the developer, but also cumbersome and error-prone.

Sharing code between computers

In the mid-90s, Microsoft extended its component model with DCOM (Distributed COM). DCOM didn't replace or alter COM—it was really just a wire protocol dictating how COM objects could communicate across machine boundaries. OMG also introduced a wire protocol of its own called IIOP (Inter-ORB Protocol), which was designed to allow different CORBA ORBs to work together over the Internet.

These standards allowed an application on one computer to invoke code hosted on another, but, because both were descendants of desktop programming solutions, they had several layers of complexity that made them difficult to use (DCOM in particular was frequently criticized for this). Experienced developers, however, found that these protocols did the job, enabling application resources and processing "weight" to be spread over several workstations, and allowing a shift from client/server software to a type of programming commonly called *3-tier* or *n-tier development*.

Sharing code between networks

Unfortunately, neither COM/DCOM nor CORBA/IIOP work well over the Internet. To start, the two standards are mutually exclusive. DCOM servers can interact only with DCOM clients, and the same restriction applies to CORBA over IIOP. DCOM is restricted to computers that run the Microsoft Windows operating system. CORBA, like COM, is a complex binary standard that doesn't work easily over firewalls. In short, much as COM and CORBA needed to be adapted for the network environment, another change was required before developers could easily design software for distributed applications on the Web.

In the next few sections, we will look at these two standards more closely, along with a third, Java RMI.

COM/DCOM

DCOM is a network protocol based on the DCE (Distributed Computing Environment) standard. The advantage of DCOM is its programming model. DCOM allows developers to use COM objects on remote computers in the same way they use COM objects on a local computer (see Figure 1-1). DCOM simply replaces local interprocess communication with a network protocol. Calls become a little slower, but neither the client nor the component needs to know that it's communicating across a network. Figure 1-1 shows the multilayered protocol that allows COM to work over the network.

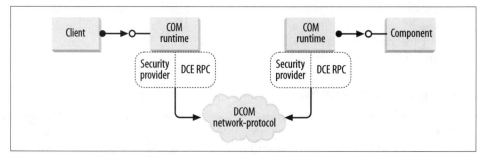

Figure 1-1. COM/DCOM architecture

Unfortunately, DCOM just isn't suited for distributed networks. Consider this sentence from an old Microsoft white paper about DCOM:

> Network connections are inherently more fragile than connections inside a machine. Components in a distributed application need to be notified if a client is not active anymore, even—or especially—in the case of a network or hardware failure.*

Few would argue today that network communication is much more fragile than interprocess communication on the same machine. But the solution employed by DCOM—constant pinging or keep-alive messages—adds too much overhead and just don't make sense in the stateless world of the Internet. As the number of clients in a DCOM network increases, the amount of network traffic required to handle the constant pinging begins to have a serious detrimental effect. This design (which is also known as distributed garbage collection) is a large part of the reason that DCOM is fundamentally unscalable for serving a large number of clients. These limitations also make it impossible to use a DCOM component over an unreliable or periodic connection.

 Keep-alive messages are required in DCOM because it's designed, like CORBA, to be a stateful protocol. Without keep-alive messages, the server could become clogged up with dozens of objects that were never properly released by their clients. As you'll see, web services neatly sidestep this problem because they don't maintain state and thus don't need to perform this sort of distributed garbage collection. In this case, features have been traded for a more robust, rational protocol.†

---

* DCOM Technical Overview, Microsoft Corporation, November, 1996.

† DCOM Technical Overview, Microsoft Corporation, November, 1996.

For more information about DCOM, refer to *http://www.microsoft.com/com/tech/dcom.asp*. Be warned that some of these links aren't working these days, betraying Microsoft's shift away from DCOM as an enabling technology for distributed applications.

 Web services don't completely replace the DCOM way of doing things, which can still be useful for distributed objects systems in a .NET-centric environment. Instead, the .NET platform introduces new remoting features that allow .NET objects to be used across machine boundaries in a reliable network environment. These are found in the System.Runtime.Remoting namespaces of the .NET Framework.

CORBA/IIOP

CORBA is, at its simplest, a broad standard for creating ORBs, or Object Request Brokers. ORBs play the same role that COM does on the Microsoft platform—they allow objects to communicate with each other. In the early days of CORBA, most developers expected DCE (distributed computing environment) to be the network protocol of choice, as it was for DCOM. Instead, IIOP was created. IIOP defines how ORBs communicate over a network. Figure 1-2 shows the different layers of communication in a CORBA-based system.

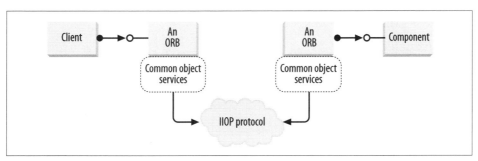

Figure 1-2. CORBA/IIOP architecture

In many ways, CORBA seemed like the ideal solution for distributed objects—and to many developers it still does. For one thing, CORBA is supported by an impressive group of more than 500 member companies. However, this diversity has also contributed to CORBA's downfall. There are countless CORBA implementations, and each one is subtly unique. No commercial ORB has ever been able to claim the widespread adoption or performance of Microsoft's proprietary COM standard.

For more information about CORBA, refer to *http://www.corba.org/*. Real history buffs may be interested in the white papers at *http://www.omg.org/news/whitepaper/*, which compare the COM and CORBA technologies.

Java RMI

CORBA quickly gained a reputation for being complex and difficult to program. Partly in response to this, Sun created its own native ORB, called RMI (Remote Method Invocation). RMI is a natural choice for Java programmers and conveniently integrated into the language. However, this comfortable integration is also a disadvantage. RMI depends on many of the unique features of Java, like object serialization and interfaces, neither of which are supported by popular languages like C++. In fact, Java isn't even CORBA-compliant.

More information about RMI can be obtained from Sun. One starting point is *http://java.sun.com/products/jdk/rmi*.

Problems with Existing Standards

Perhaps the most surprising observation to be made about COM/DCOM and CORBA/IIOP is that, despite their differences, they share most of the same limitations, shown in the following list:

Reliance on binary communication
> This reliance makes these existing standards difficult to use over firewalls, which may restrict binary data over most ports. Even when a firewall is configured to allow access over the appropriate port, changing its settings—a common occurrence—will break the object communication.

Difficulty scaling
> With COM and CORBA, it is possible to design components that can handle hundreds of clients as easily as they handle a dozen. However, this requires a great deal of experience and discipline on the programmer's part. The typical component doesn't fare as well.

Platform or programming language dependence
> COM is closely tied to the Windows platform. There is no easy way to create and host a COM component on another operating system, such as Unix. CORBA doesn't suffer from this limitation, but it has not been widely adopted in non-Java languages. The end result is that both standards are "closed in," limiting their possible audience and the ways that they can be used.

Complexity
> COM and CORBA include a wealth of built-in services, such as transactions, security, and encryption. Each of these features increases the potential for problems, adds extra overhead, and opens the possibility for incompatibilities. Web services protocols don't currently provide or specify APIs for any of these high-level services. That makes them considerably easier to implement, but also means that you need to add these features on your own, as we'll explain in later chapters of this book.

Lack of a universal standard for data representation

Our discussion has focused on the evolution of code sharing across boundaries but ignored another important series of developments: the evolution of a universal standard for encoding information. Quite simply, there was no standard for sharing structured data when COM and CORBA were created. Since then, we've seen the introduction of SGML, then XML, and finally SOAP, which tackles data type representation head-on.

Of course, despite the web service hype, both COM and CORBA are mature technologies that are used every day. They have problems, but they are far from unworkable. In fact, in some respects they don't compete directly with web services and may be an ideal solution for distributed components in a heterogeneous network environment.

The Promise of .NET Web Services

Web services are designed to overcome the limitations of these earlier technologies. With .NET, Microsoft has set out to build the best possible programming framework for creating and consuming web services. Amazingly, Microsoft has abandoned its traditional "embrace and extend" approach, which often replaced open standards with proprietary solutions.

.NET web services differ from existing distributed application technologies in several ways:

Open standards

There is no hidden or locked-in part with web services. Every aspect of the technology, from web service discovery to web service description and communication, is defined by public standards that Microsoft does not own. This openness of information can only help developers extend the technology and learn how to master it.

Cross-platform capabilities

Any programming language that can create an XML document and send information over HTTP can interact with any web service. You can consume a non-.NET web service in a .NET client, or consume a .NET web service in a non-.NET client, as you'll see in the final chapter of this book. Best of all, you never need to rely on a special "compatibility layer"—.NET web services are built on open standards from the ground up.

Simplicity

Once you sort through the various standards used to implement web services, you'll realize that they're simple, elegant, and straightforward. This means that there are far fewer opportunities for developer error. It also means that developers must develop some of their own strategies for security, state management, and transactions. The bulk of this book is aimed at giving you the knowledge you'll need for this task.

Human-readable messages

The shift away from the binary standards used in COM and CORBA to XML text allows for easier debugging and lets web services communicate over ordinary HTTP channels, sending messages through firewalls effortlessly. This change does bring along a few potential disadvantages, however. One obvious shortcoming is that web service messages require more bytes to transmit the same amount of information.

The .NET Web Service Architecture

Microsoft's implementation of web services is designed to make it just as easy to invoke a remote web service as to call a method on a local class. To achieve this, the .NET Framework provides tools that hide the often-tedious details of standards like SOAP and WSDL. The process works like this (note that the steps in italic—steps 1, 3, 5, and 8—are the only steps that are performed manually):

1. *You design a web service as a .NET class with attributes that identify it as a web service with exposed functions.*
2. .NET automatically creates a WSDL document that describes how a client must communicate with the web service.
3. *A client finds your web service and decides to use it. The client adds it as a web reference to a Visual Studio .NET project (or runs the* WSDL.exe *utility).*
4. .NET automatically inspects the WSDL document and generates a proxy class that allows the client to communicate with the web service transparently.
5. *The client calls one of the methods of your web service class. From the client's perspective, it seems no different than calling a method in any other class, but in reality, the client is interacting with the proxy class, not the web service.*
6. Behind the scenes, the proxy class converts the supplied parameters to a SOAP message and sends it to the web service.
7. A short time later, the proxy class receives a SOAP reply, converts it to the appropriate data type, and returns it to the client as an ordinary .NET data type.
8. *The client uses the returned information.*

The process is pictured in Figure 1-3.

.NET web services make use of the ASP.NET technologies that are part of the .NET Framework. They also require the services of Microsoft Internet Information Server. Visual Studio .NET provides many tools and a sophisticated IDE to simplify the tasks required to get a web service up and running.

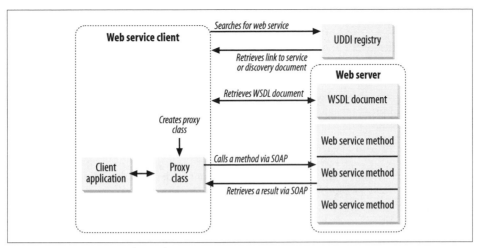

Figure 1-3. Interacting with a web service

The Underlying Technologies

In order to create or use a web service, you don't need to know much about its underlying technology. But, as is often the case, in order to design web services that exploit the best features of the platform and artfully avoid common pitfalls, it helps to understand the underlying foundation.

Web services use a combination of different open standards, which are described in Table 1-1.

Table 1-1. Web service technologies

Technology	Role
WSDL	An XML-based format that describes a web service, listing its methods, the data types used for all parameters and the return value, and the supported methods of communication (or "bindings").
HTTP	The communication protocol used to send web service requests and responses over the Internet. It's also the familiar standard used for retrieving web pages in a web browser.
SOAP	An XML-based format used to encode the information in web service request and response messages before sending them over the Internet. For example, SOAP defines how values of different data types should be represented.
DISCO	An optional Microsoft specification that allows clients to find (or "discover") web services. A DISCO file is essentially a list of uncategorized web service links. Slated to be replaced by the WS-Inspection standard, which is not yet natively ingrained into the .NET Framework.
UDDI	A directory that allows clients to find the web services exposed by a specific company. UDDI is the youngest of the web service standards.

WSDL is the only standard that is tightly bound to .NET web services. SOAP is strongly recommended (and required for compatibility with other web service development platforms), but "no-frills" HTTP POST and HTTP GET transmission is also supported. DISCO and UDDI are both optional extensions that make it easy to publish and discover web service information, but neither is required. And while HTTP communication is the most logical way to transport information, there is no reason to assume this will remain the case. In fact, the low-level communication protocol is transparent to the web service programmer.

 In some cases, it *does* matter what communication protocol you are using. For example, if you design a web service that requires cookies, your web service will depend on the HTTP protocol. In this book, you'll be warned when certain extensions or designs create this sort of tight coupling.

Along with the standards listed in Table 1-1, several web service standards haven't graduated into the .NET world. One of these is WS-Inspection, a specification for discovery documents that list groups of web services and their endpoints. WS-Inspection has been developed by a joint Microsoft-IBM effort, and is slated to replace DISCO as the native discovery mechanism used by the .NET platform. However, the current version of .NET still uses the older DISCO standard.

In addition, there are competing specifications to tackle some of the limitations inherent in web services, including transactions, authentication, licensing, and encryption. None of these specifications has reached the level of an established standard or been incorporated into .NET. However, for an overview of these possible future directions, refer to Appendix B.

WSDL

Every .NET web service provides a WSDL (Web Service Description Language) document that describes everything a client needs to know about it. The WSDL document performs the same role that an IDL (Interface Definition Language) file does for a CORBA or COM component: it defines the web service's interface. Essentially, the WSDL document is a contract between the client and service that declares "if you invoke this method with these parameters, you will receive this data type as a return value."

In many respects, web services are simpler than the components you create for COM or CORBA. For example, web services do not support multiple interfaces—every web service class provides exactly one set of public methods. On the other hand, the WSDL document is quite a bit more complex than the equivalent COM or CORBA IDL, because it is designed to be platform-independent and to support communication protocols other than SOAP and HTTP. That means that every WSDL file for a .NET web service contains a large amount of boilerplate code needed to provide support for the basic level of communication (SOAP, HTTP GET, and HTTP POST).

In .NET programming, you don't have to spend much time thinking about WSDL, and you certainly won't need to write your own WSDL. Every .NET web service automatically generates its WSDL document. In fact, you can view this document for any web service with an XML-enabled browser, as you'll see in Chapter 3.

Some have argued that the WSDL standard is not required for web services, because SOAP messages are self-describing and clearly specify the data types of any values they contain. However, WSDL documents provide a straightforward and consistent way for you to determine the calling syntax of any web method. Even better, WSDL documents allow you to use automatic proxy generation tools, like those included with Visual Studio .NET and the .NET Framework. As you'll see in Chapter 3, these tools make consuming a web service as easy as using a local class.

The WSDL document uses an XML-based format that divides its information into five main groupings. The first three are abstract definitions, which are independent of any specific platform, network, or language details. The last two types are concrete descriptions.

The WSDL document itself is fairly lengthy. For a more detailed look at WSDL, refer to Chapter 3, which examines the automatically generated WSDL document for a sample web service.

SOAP

Web services communicate with their clients via XML-formatted messages. SOAP (Simple Object Access Protocol) is the messaging protocol of choice for web services. The "O" in the SOAP acronym is a bit of a misnomer, because SOAP messages do not correspond to objects. The core idea at the heart of the SOAP standard is that messages should be encoded in a standardized XML format. SOAP has found an ideal niche with RPCs (remote procedure calls) in mind, in which case the SOAP message contains the parameters sent by the client or the return value sent by the service. It's worth noting that other products (like Microsoft's own BizTalk server) use SOAP to transfer other types of information. Similarly, SOAP messages are not restricted to HTTP transmission and could be used just as easily with sockets, named pipes, or even an email message over SMTP.

A simple SOAP message is shown in the following code sample. It's a request message to the GetIPForHostname web service introduced in the next chapter. Its payload is enclosed in a special <soap:Envelope> tag. In this case, one parameter (hostName) is being sent; it contains www.oreilly.com as a string.

```
<?xml version="1.0" encoding="utf-8"?>
<soap:Envelope xmlns:xsi=http://www.w3.org/2001/XMLSchema-instance
               xmlns:xsd=http://www.w3.org/2001/XMLSchema
```

```
                 xmlns:soap="http://schemas.xmlsoap.org/soap/envelope/">
  <soap:Body>
    <GetIPForHostname xmlns="http://www.bostontechnical.com/webservices/">
      <hostName>www.oreilly.com</hostName>
    </GetIPForHostname>
  </soap:Body>
</soap:Envelope>
```

SOAP isn't the only way to encode information in a .NET web service. You can also send data through HTTP POST or HTTP GET. In theory, HTTP POST transmission could still use the SOAP format, but in practice it's easier to send data as a simple, untyped name/value collection.

Why You Will Use SOAP with .NET

In this book, almost all of the examples assume that you are interacting with .NET web services using SOAP messages. This is the default choice in .NET, and the most powerful. The other alternatives are HTTP GET and HTTP POST, which will typically be used only when testing a web service through the automatically generated Internet Explorer test page.

Really, there's no reason *not* to use the SOAP message format, as .NET supports its use transparently. Some of the advantages of SOAP include:

More flexible data types
> SOAP allows data structures and DataSets to be encoded in XML just as easily as simple data types like integers and strings.

Support for headers and extensions
> When you use SOAP messages, you have additional tools that allow you to easily add features like tracing, encryption, and security.

True cross-platform support
> If you need to consume your .NET service in a non-.NET client, SOAP is the best option. SOAP toolkits are available for many other programming languages (and earlier versions of Microsoft C++ and Visual Basic). To communicate with a web service using HTTP GET or HTTP POST, you will probably need to construct the request string and parse the response manually—hardly an elegant solution.

DISCO

DISCO is a simple way to refer to discovery files, which provide some basic means for you to group together web service links. Since a primary goal of web services is business-to-business interaction, a business needs a tool that not only allows it to create useful functionality, but also allows it to easily share that functionality with other organizations. Communicating information about a single web service might be easy, but if you have a complex combination of web services that reside in different ASP. NET applications and are targeted to different clients, it becomes much more complicated to make sure the appropriate people have the required information.

One good approach would be to create an HTML page that provides links to the various web services. However, this approach is not standardized, requires the creation of a basic user interface, and might confuse customers who are browsing the site for retail information. Other ways to exchange information, like automated emails or telephone messages, are possible, but are slow and bound to introduce inefficiency and unforeseen problems. DISCO provides a simple alternative.

A DISCO file is little more than a list of web services and their associated links, presented in a special XML format. DISCO files can include files from multiple web servers and can support "dynamic discovery," which automatically searches a directory in a server for web service files. Discovery files are also recognized natively by .NET tools like Visual Studio .NET and offer an easy way to browse through or add a group of related services to a client.

Following is a sample DISCO file that references a single service:

```
<disco:discovery  xmlns:disco="http://schemas.xmlsoap.org/disco"
                  xmlns:wsdl="http://schemas.xmlsoap.org/disco/wsdl">
  <wsdl:contractRef
        ref="http://www.bostontechnical.com/webservices/DNSLookupService.asmx" />
</disco:discovery>
```

WS-Inspection files use a similar syntax, ensuring that the transition from DISCO to WS-Inspection will be easy, when it occurs:

```
<?xml version="1.0"?>
<inspection xmlns="http://schemas.xmlsoap.org/ws/2001/10/inspection/">
 <service>
  <description
    referencedNamespace="http://schemas.xmlsoap.org/wsdl/"
    location="http://www.bostontechnical.com/webservices/DNSLookupService.asmx" />
 </service>
</inspection>
```

UDDI

In order to use a web service, the client still needs to know the appropriate company's web site address or the URL of the discovery file. Discovery files are useful, because they consolidate multiple web services into a single list, but they don't allow clients to search for types of web services without knowing about the company ahead of time.

UDDI (Universal Description, Discovery, and Integration) aims to fill this gap by providing a repository where businesses can publish information about the web services they provide. UDDI is (like CORBA) an industry initiative led by more than 100 companies (the full list can be found at *http://www.uddi.org/community.html*), including archrivals Sun and Microsoft. The goal of this industry consortium is to develop a draft UDDI specification and then, after 18 months, turn it over to a standards body. Of course, the actual information in this repository must be maintained manually. The solution is to allow various "node operators" to run instances of the UDDI registry, each with an identical copy of the repository. Currently, IBM and Microsoft provide this service, and Hewlett-Packard is preparing to do the same. These businesses host this repository for free in order to help promote the adoption of web services. In addition, Microsoft includes an enterprise version of UDDI with Windows .NET server specifically for use on corporate intranets.

The UDDI registry stores information about businesses, the services they offer, the type of each service, and links to information and specifications related to these services. One of the most interesting aspects of UDDI is that its interface is itself a web service. In order to register a business or search for a service, you need to send SOAP messages. The steps to do this are covered in Chapter 10.

As promising as it is, UDDI is just one piece of the puzzle. Even if you can find the web services you need to use in a UDDI registry, you may still end up with little more than a collection of method definitions, with some minimal documentation—the equivalent of a rather terse API reference. Understanding how to use individual web methods may not explain the overall logic of the services themselves—and it can't substitute for the serious relationship a typical business will want with the service provider.

Competing Web Service Technologies

Fortunately, Microsoft is not the only provider of web service developer tools—if it were, the technology could never achieve widespread adoption. Instead, there are web service tools available for a wide variety of languages and platforms, and basic SOAP and XML toolkits for many more. Some of the options are listed here:

- IBM provides its own Web Service Development Kit, which is a runtime environment complete with numerous examples.
- Oracle provides a Web Integration Development Language and its own web service offerings.
- Sun Microsystems has played a bit of catch-up with its Sun ONE (Open Net Environment) offering, which now supports web services written in the Java language.
- Microsoft's SOAP Toolkit allows you to call web services with the previous generation of Microsoft Visual Studio products (like Visual Basic and C++).
- Internet Explorer 5 and later allows web services to be invoked in web pages through simple scripting code. This technology goes by the name WebService Behavior.
- Perl provides a SOAP::Lite kit for basic SOAP functionality.

This book focuses on the .NET tools for creating web services, which offer an elegant implementation and are some of the most powerful tools. In the final chapter of this book, we'll consider some possible interoperability issues between web services written in other languages and .NET clients and how to resolve them.

Other Technologies

To conclude this chapter, we'll consider some of the other technologies that are associated with, complementary to, or sometimes confused with .NET web services.

.NET MyServices

.NET MyServices (originally code-named HailStorm) is a set of user-centric web services developed by Microsoft. MyServices is built on top of the .NET web service framework and is meant to provide some fundamental services that applications will need to access and share user information.

.NET MyServices tackles issues like maintaining information, supporting authentication, and providing notification for a single individual. As with all web services, even though these services revolve around the end user, the end user doesn't interact with them directly. Instead, various applications rely on these services to retrieve basic information and provide higher-level features. In fact, most .NET MyServices are really little more than a standardized web service interface to an online data store. This data can include anything from a business calendar with meeting times to financial account information.

Originally, Microsoft planned to be the exclusive host for every user's MyServices data. Potential partners, however, were skeptical of the arrangement and wanted the freedom to create custom-tailored data stores. In its final incarnation, MyServices is expected to allow organizations to host their own MyServices with proprietary (but possibly linked) data stores.

Currently, the best-known (and most mature) part of .NET MyServices is the Passport authentication system. Passport began life as Hotmail's native authentication system, which was used to verify passwords for email access. Passport later became a full-fledged web service and is now used by a number of companies for client authentication. In fact, it's even available for custom web sites through the ASP.NET Framework and can be used in any situation in which you need a lightweight means to verify that users are who they claim to be.

.NET MyServices is not described in this book, because its services are of more interest to application developers (or web service consumers) than to web service developers.

.NET Remoting

.NET remoting is the distributed component technology that replaces DCOM in the .NET world. It's still ideal for many situations in which .NET web services aren't suitable, including internal applications that need to share high volumes of information or need the fastest possible response times. Unlike web services, however, .NET remoting is not designed for sharing services with other businesses and the rest of the world, and there is no dedicated technology for sharing and publishing services (like DISCO files and UDDI).

To make things even more interesting, .NET remoting now is extensible and can support a wide range of transmission protocols for communication, *including* HTTP and SOAP. Once again, that might make them appear to compete with web services, if it weren't for the fact that .NET remoting lacks support for UDDI publication and uses a custom .NET-centric serialization format.

.NET remoting deserves consideration if you are creating a distributed system that works in a fairly homogenous environment and doesn't need to interact with a wide range of clients. In other words, it's best for homegrown solutions and least suited to the standards-based development that's needed to ensure broad compatibility with other organizations. You might find it at work on a company LAN or with a controlled set of known clients over the Internet. The advantage of .NET remoting is sheer performance—because you have the flexibility of binary communication, a remoting component will often outperform a web service. Remoting also provides more flexibility for stateful services. However, the performance difference isn't always in favor of remoting. Because web services have intrinsic support for performance-enhancing features like caching, they can outperform a remoting-based solution with a similar amount of code. Unlike .NET web services, remoting doesn't require ASP.NET or IIS (Internet Information Server) to host components.

The .NET remoting technologies are not described in this book. For an introduction, see *Programming C#*, Second Edition, by Jesse Liberty (O'Reilly, 2002).

XML-RPC

XML-RPC is a simple but widely used protocol that preceded SOAP and .NET web services. RPC provides remote procedure calls (RPCs) by sending XML documents that encode parameters in the request and a return value in the response. This is exactly what .NET web services do, without SOAP.

XML-RPC suffers from some limitations, especially its lack of support for data typing. The .NET web service technology incorporates the best of XML-RPC—its insight that programs can communicate if they agree on a standard message format—and adds to it a powerful industry standard that has been designed with the thorny problems of cross-platform data type representation in mind.

Message Queuing

Microsoft, Sun, and many other companies also provide messaging systems that allow store-and-forward communication. This type of model isn't appropriate for scenarios in which an immediate response is required, but it can provide a compelling option for one-way communication like logging. These server-based messaging products, like MSMQ (Microsoft Message Queuing), provide a rich set of features, including transactions, and complement rather than compete against web services. Web services, however, are a more broadly useful technology and a much easier model for implementing remote function calls, not just one-way messages. Web services can also work asynchronously, as described in Chapter 6.

BizTalk Server

BizTalk Server aims to allow developers to integrate business processes, both inside a single organization and between trading partners. Although the current version of BizTalk Server is built on COM technology, there is a wide range of ways that it can be enhanced with .NET add-ins and integrated with .NET web services. Microsoft provides an overview of these options in a white paper at *http://www.microsoft.com/biztalk/techinfo/development/wp_XMLFrame.doc*.

Under the hood, BizTalk Server is essentially a host for additional high-level services that you can use to integrate business processes. For example, with BizTalk Server you can create interfaces that allow different processes to interact, even when one requires data in a format different than the other provides. You can also configure long-running distributed transactions, design a document workflow using a visual designer, enforce business rules, and exchange SOAP-formatted messages. BizTalk Server requires a book of its own, but it is primarily of interest to developers who are working with business-to-business interaction.

In the next few chapters of this book, we'll take a closer look at the core standards, including SOAP and WSDL and the tools .NET provides, to make web service development easy.

CHAPTER 2

Creating ASP.NET Web Services

Using the .NET Framework, it's easy to get a basic service up and running. In just a few minutes and fewer lines of code, you can put together a simple "Hello World" service without any understanding of HTTP, SOAP, WSDL or any of the several technologies that form the basis for web services. In fact, if you're a Microsoft Visual Studio .NET user, all you need to do to create a simple "Hello, World" service is to open a new Visual C# or Visual Basic ASP.NET Web Service project and uncomment the sample code provided by the template.

In this chapter, you'll learn about ASP.NET, the new Microsoft technology for building web applications and services, and how to use the .NET platform and Visual Studio .NET to create some simple web services. We'll also talk about some of the features of .NET that will get you on the road to developing well-documented scalable web service applications. By the end of this chapter, you'll have a solid understanding of how .NET supports web services and how to use the .NET platform to create them. We'll start with the ubiquitous "Hello, World" example exposed as a web service.

Creating a Web Service: "Hello, World"

In this section, you'll create a simple web service in the "Hello, World" tradition. Through this brief example, you'll see how easy it is to use ASP.NET to create a working web service (with a text editor or with VS.NET) and learn about the basic technologies behind .NET web service.

Creating a Web Service with Inline Code

While Visual Studio .NET provides a feature-rich integrated development environment for .NET development, it's not required to create .NET web services. Applications can also be created using your favorite text editor and the command-line tools that ship with the .NET Framework SDK. Here, we use Notepad as a text editor, but you should feel free to use whatever editor you're most comfortable with (Emacs or vi).

If you chose to develop with a text editor, you must place all of your code in one or more text files, assign them each the file extension *.asmx* and place them in an IIS folder on a server or workstation that has the .NET Framework installed. Once you save the code to a folder served by the IIS web server, it's ready to run—that's it! How you get the file to your web server is your business. If you're running IIS locally on your workstation (and you've installed the .NET Framework), this is as simple as saving the file to a suitable location on your local drive (e.g., *c:\inetpub\wwwroot*). If you're using a remote server (in which case there's no need to have the .NET Framework installed locally), you might have to use FTP or a network share instead (more about this later).

Once you've chosen a text editor and file location, all that's left is to write the code.

Example 2-1 lists the code for a C# version of the ubiquitous "Hello, World" application; unlike the classic desktop version, this one delivers its familiar message over the Web through an exposed method called `HelloWorld()`. To identify the class and method as a web service to the compiler, this code uses some special notation. It also includes an ASP.NET directive at the head of the file.

To create a C# version of the *HelloWorld* web service, enter the code from Example 2-1 exactly as it appears, and save the file to your web server under the *c:\ inetpub\wwwroot* folder (or whatever folder is the web root folder for your system) with the name *HelloWorld.asmx*.

Example 2-1. HelloWorld: C# web service

```
<%@ WebService Language="C#"
Class="ProgWS.Ch02.HelloWorldService" %>
using System.Web.Services;
namespace ProgWS.Ch02
{
  public class HelloWorldService: WebService
  {
    [WebMethod]
    public string HelloWorld()
    {
      return "Hello World";
    }
  }
}
```

In the following sections, we'll explain the standard elements of this web service source file and then show you how to test it.

The WebService directive

Example 2-1 begins with a *WebService directive*, an ASP.NET statement declaring that the code that follows is a web service:

```
<%@ WebService Language="C#" Class="ProgWS.Ch02.HelloWorldService" %>
```

The `WebService` directive is similar to the `Page` directive that begins most *.aspx* pages.

For the *HelloWorld* web service to work, you must assign values to two `WebService` directive attributes: `Language` and `Class`.

The required `Language` attribute lets .NET know which programming language the class has been written in. As you might guess, the acceptable values for the language attribute are currently `C#`, `VB`, and `JS` for JScript.NET.

The `Class` attribute, also required, tells ASP.NET the name of the class to expose as a web service. Because a web service application can comprise multiple classes, some of which may not be web services, you must tell .NET which class to expose, a step analogous to declaring a `Main()` method to indicate the entry point of a .NET console application or component. Note that even if your web service contains only one class, setting this attribute is required.

The using directive: importing .NET namespaces

The next line in the example is a `using` statement that tells the compiler to alias the `System.Web.Services` namespace to the local namespace. For C#, this directive is:

```
using System.Web.Services;
```

This directive allows you to refer to objects in the `System.Web.Services` namespace without having to fully qualify the request. This statement is optional, but if it is not included, every reference to an object in this namespace must be fully qualified. An example is the next line, which is our class declaration. With the `using` statement, it looks as follows in C#:

```
using System.Web.Services;
public class HelloWorldService: WebService
```

Without the `using` statement, it would have to be written fully qualified:

```
public class HelloWorldService: System.Web.Services.WebService
```

Importing a namespace does not give you access to any of the additional namespaces that *appear* to be nested in that namespace. In other words, if you were to import the `System.Web` namespace, you would not be able to refer to the `System.Web.Services.WebService` class as `Services.WebService`. While a namespace like `System.Web.Services` may "appear" to be nested in the `System.Web` namespace, that is not the case. They are implemented as two different assemblies that bear little relation to each other aside from a partial name sharing. The apparently hierarchical nature of the .NET Framework's namespaces exists in name only as an organizational convenience and has no bearing on class structure.

The namespace keyword

.NET allows you—and Microsoft encourages you—to put the classes of an application into a unique namespace. In C#, this is done with the namespace keyword and the following syntax:

```
namespace name
{
... type declaration ...
}
```

In Example 2-1, the HelloWorldService class is placed in the ProgWS.Ch02 namespace with the following statement:

```
namespace ProgWS.Ch02
{…
}
```

Namespaces can contain definitions for classes, interfaces, structs, enums, and delegates, as well as other namespaces. In addition, the source code for objects in a namespace does not have to be stored in the same file—it can span multiple files.

> For Java programmers: a namespace is similar to a package. However, unlike a package, in a namespace there are no directory structure requirements, because all of the source code is presumed to be in the same directory or a global assembly cache.

Namespaces provide a means of grouping pieces of code that might be written and maintained by other developers. When the class definitions of your web service exist within a namespace, you must specify the namespace along with the class name in your WebService directive as in Example 2-1:

```
<%@ WebService Language="C#" Class="ProgWS.Ch02.HelloWorldService" %>
```

This line tells ASP.NET to look for the class HelloWorldService in the namespace ProgWS.Ch02.

The WebService class

At the heart of Example 2-1 is a class called HelloWorldService. This class is a subclass of System.Web.Services.WebService. By inheriting from the WebService class, a web service gains direct access to the ASP.NET intrinsic objects, such as Application and Session, just like any other ASP.NET application.

> While inheriting from the WebService class is a common approach for creating a .NET web service, it is by no means necessary. You can rewrite the previous examples without this inheritance, and your service will run just fine. However, if you need access to the Application and Session objects without inheriting from WebService, you'll need to use the System.Web.HttpContext object explicitly, as we'll explain in a later chapter.

The WebMethod attribute

The `HelloWorldService` class exposes a single method, the public method `HelloWorld`, which takes no arguments and returns a string containing the text "Hello World". To expose a method as a part of a web service, you must decorate it with the `WebMethod` attribute, which tells the compiler to treat it as such. Any method marked with the `WebMethod` attribute must be defined as `public`. Class methods exposed as web services follow the same object-oriented rules as any other class, and therefore methods marked `private`, `protected`, or `internal` are not accessible and will return an error if you attempt to expose them using the `WebMethod` attribute. For additional details, see "The WebMethod Attribute" later in this chapter.

The neat thing about this simple example is that you've created a full-blown web service out of an arbitrary method. You could just as easily have substituted a method that retrieves a record from a data store or a method that wraps a COM object. Additionally, you could have used any of the languages supported by the .NET Framework for this implementation and, then, as you will see later, used any .NET or non-.NET language in a client application. By inheriting from the `System.Web.Services.WebService` class, you are able to take advantage of an API that insulates you from the underlying SOAP/XML message exchanges.

To put this web service to work, all you need to do is copy it to the web server just as you would any other resource, whether it's an image, HTML file, ASP page, or another resource. Once you've done that, the web service is ready to be used by a consumer application, a process we'll look at in detail in Chapter 3. This ease of deployment is the main benefit of inline coding; perhaps the biggest drawback is that your presentation code and business logic are lumped into the same file, which can make working with large projects difficult to manage. Let's take a look at how Visual Studio .NET can be used to create and deploy this web service without stepping outside its Integrated Development Environment by using the so-called code-behind approach.

Assemblies

We said that a namespace is a container for types such as classes, interfaces, structs, and enums. We also said that the source code for objects in a namespace does not have to be stored in the same file, but can instead span multiple files. When the set of source code constituting a namespace is compiled into a library, this library is called a *managed DLL*, or, more commonly, an *assembly*. Assemblies are the building blocks of .NET applications and the fundamental unit of deployment. They comprise a collection of types and resources that provide the CLR (Common Language Runtime) with the information it needs to be aware of type implementations. Their contents can be referenced and used by other applications using Visual Studio .NET or a .NET command-line compiler.

Creating "Hello, World" with Visual Studio .NET

While Notepad is an adequate tool for creating simple services, Microsoft's new development environment, Visual Studio .NET (VS.NET), provides a world of features to aid you in creating complex web services. Visual Studio .NET also provides the quickest path to getting a web service up and running, apart from the time it takes to install all or part of the more than 1.8 GB (compressed) of installation files required to run Visual Studio .NET. This section takes you through the process of creating the "Hello, World" service using Visual Studio .NET.

Setting up VS.NET for the web service project

To make use of the automation in VS.NET, you must first configure it to communicate with your web server. You can use either FrontPage Extensions or Universal Naming Convention (UNC) file shares. To keep things simple, we'll assume you have installed IIS on your local workstation. Here's what you need to do to set up VS.NET for your first web service. We go into detail on FrontPage Extensions and UNC file shares later in this chapter (see "Deploying a Web Service")

Microsoft FrontPage Server Extensions are the easiest to configure and a good choice for the simple web services in the next two chapters. FrontPage Extensions can be installed as a part of IIS, or alternatively downloaded for free from the MSDN site at *http://msdn.microsoft.com*. For this example, we're using a Windows 2000 workstation, IIS 5, and FrontPage 2000 Server Extensions, version 4.0.2.4426. While any version of the Extensions will work, the configuration process varies greatly among them and the steps outlined here may not work with your version.

Once you've installed FrontPage Server Extensions on your local workstation (i.e., the workstation hosting IIS), open the Internet Services Manager from the Start → Programs → Administrative Tools menu so that you can configure a FrontPage web. Right-click on Default Web Site and select All Tasks → Configure Server Extensions from the dialog box. You will be taken through a brief configuration wizard that asks you configuration questions. Once the server extensions have been installed, you're ready to create a web service project in Visual Studio .NET.

 With Windows XP, you reach Administrative Tools and the IIS Manager through he Control Panel.

Creating a C# web service project

Visual Studio 6.0 users will find the layout of Visual Studio .NET familiar enough that they can get working without much assistance. We'll help users who are new to Visual Studio. Users new to Visual Studio .NET can also rely on its extensive built-in Help feature.

To create a new web service, fire up Visual Studio .NET and either select the New Project button on the default Start Page or click File → New → Project on the main Visual Studio .NET menu bar. The Visual Studio project model is the same as earlier versions, in that a file can be part of a project, and a project part of a solution. A solution is the outermost container, containing zero or more projects. After selecting an option to create a new project, you'll see the screen in Figure 2-1.

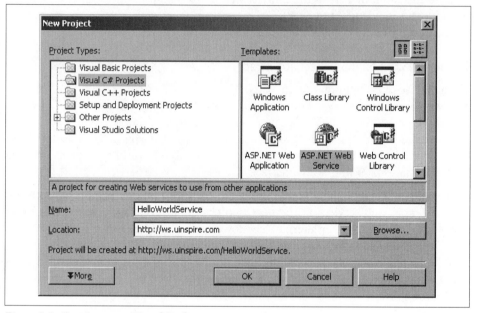

Figure 2-1. Creating a new Visual Studio project

Here you have the option to create a variety of project types from templates. Under Visual C# Projects, one template option creates an ASP.NET web service, while our examples use the C# language, the same option also available as a Visual Basic project, and similar options for Managed C++ exist as well. In addition to selecting a project language and template, you must specify a project name and location. The location fior the HelloWorldService should be the URL of the IIS web server you just configured to work with FrontPage Extensions (e.g., *http://localhost*). For this example, we'll use the project name "HelloWorldService."

Once you click OK, the IDE (Integrated Development Environment) creates a new solution and project and automatically populate the project with several files. The IDE will also create a virtual folder under IIS with the same name as the project name, which, in this case, is HelloWorldService.

Exploring the solution and project

The contents of your new project are displayed in the Solution Explorer window, which should appear on the right side of the VS.NET IDE, as shown in Figure 2-2.

Figure 2-2. The Visual Studio .NET Solution Explorer

If the Solution Explorer is not visible, you can open it by selecting Solution Explorer from the View menu (or pressing Ctrl-Alt-L).

When you create a new project without specifying the name of an existing solution, VS.NET creates a new solution whose name is the same as the one you chose for your project. You can see in Figure 2-2 that, in this case, a solution named HelloWorldService has been created; it contains one project, also called HelloWorldService.

Visual Studio .NET also automatically creates several assembly references and files, which are also displayed in the Solution Explorer, as shown in Figure 2-3. In this example, VS.NET has included assembly references to the System, System.Data, System.Web, System.Web.Services, and System.XML namespaces. (The System.Data and System.XML assembly references are not necessary for this example, so you can remove them if you'd like, but there's no real benefit to doing so other than simplicity.)

The five other files that appear in Figure 2-3 are *AssemblyInfo.cs*, *Global.asax*, *HelloWorldService.vsdisco*, *Service1.asmx*, and *Web.config*. The only file you really need to create the web service is the *.asmx* file, which we'll discuss in the next section. The four other files provide additional features and functionality that will help you as you build more complex services, but none of them are necessary for this example. In fact, you can delete all of the non-*.asmx* files and the service will run just fine (we don't recommend this). Here's a brief explanation of of each of these.

AssemblyInfo.cs
   An information file that provides the compiler with metadata (name, version, etc.) about the assemblies in the project.

Global.asax
   Customizable to handle application-level events (e.g., Application_OnStart).

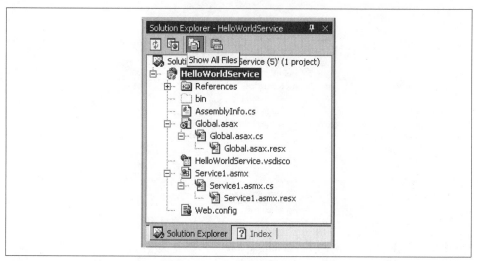

Figure 2-3. Displaying all files in VS.NET Solution Explorer

HelloWorldService.vsdisco

An XML file used for dynamic discovery of web services. The DISCO specification has been superseded by WS-Inspection and is discussed in Chapter 10.

Web.config

An XML file containing configuration information for the application.

Exploring the .asmx file and service design view

The most important file in our example is the sample service page named *Service1. asmx*. If you open the page by double-clicking it, Visual Studio .NET displays a blank design page in its main window. If we were dealing with an *.aspx* ASP.NET web application, this design page could be used to design the user interface for the page, but since we're developing an *.asmx* web service that will be consumed by a machine rather than a person, this design view is not as useful to us. If you try to add a Windows form component, you'll get an error ("Object reference not set to an instance of an object"), because the web service design view doesn't know what to do with the component. Unlike an ASP.NET web form project, an ASP.NET web service project doesn't include the plumbing to support Windows form components.

You can use the design view to add preprogrammed components to your service from the Visual Studio .NET Toolbox, but you can't do much beyond adding these items, which is just as easily done directly through the code view page (*Service1. asmx.cs*). Perhaps Microsoft or another vendor will provide more powerful support for drag-and-drop web service design using business-logic components at some point, but as of today, the design view is not very useful. Instead, you can view the source code of your service by right-clicking on the *Service1.asmx* file in Solution Explorer and selecting View Code. At this point, you'll also want to rename the

Service1.asmx file to something more appropriate to the project. You can do this by right-clicking the file in Solution Explorer and selecting Rename from the menu. Change the name to *HelloWorldService.asmx*.

Displaying all files in Solution Explorer

The *.asmx.cs* file is not displayed by default in Solution Explorer. To see it, select Show All Files from the Project menu tab (there's also an icon at the top of Solution Explorer to do this). The Solution Explorer view will change to look like Figure 2-3.

This new view displays all of the files associated with the HelloWorldService project. Notice that the *Service1.asmx* file now has a tree expander icon to the left of it. Click on the icon, and you'll see another file beneath the *Service1.asmx* file called *Service1.asmx.cs*. Elsewhere, you'll also notice a folder called *\bin*, which is used to store the project's compiled assemblies generated by Visual Studio .NET.

Understanding the autogenerated service code

When you create a new ASP.NET web service project, Visual Studio .NET generates some boilerplate code to get you started. The contents of the source file *HelloWorldService.asmx.cs* should resemble that reproduced in Figure 2-4.

This boilerplate code begins by importing several namespaces generally required for web services and by automatically generating namespace and class definitions. In this example, the namespace and class definitions are `HelloWorldService` and `Service1`, respectively.

The namespace definition is generated based on the project name, but you will probably want to change to something more suitable (in this case, we're going to continue to use *ProgWS.Ch02*) depending on your application. The service name is always autogenerated as *Service1*. Change this to something more appropriate for your application (in this case, we're using *HelloWorldService*), but you should also remember to change the name of the *.asmx* page to mirror your service name. Your service will run just fine if the names don't match up, but keeping the naming consistent can help make managing your service easier, particularly if you have a project with a large number of services.

The imported namespaces at the beginning of the code are provided as a convenience, and some of them are unnecessary. Specifically, the `System.Data`, `System.Collections`, and `System.Diagnostics` namespaces are not used at all. The classes of the `System.ComponentModel` namespace are used only by the web service designer methods, `InitializeComponent()` and `Dispose()`, which work in conjunction with a private member variable of type `IContainer` called `components`. To see these methods, you need to expand the Component Designer Generated Code region. Since you're most likely not going to need the (limited) features of the web service design view,

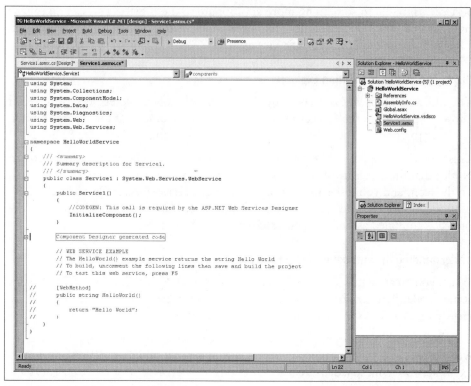

Figure 2-4. Visual Studio .NET boilerplate code

you can clean house by deleting the entire region. You will be left with code that looks like the following (some comments have been removed to shorten the listing).

```csharp
using System;
using System.Web;
using System.Web.Services;

namespace ProgWS.Ch02
{
  public class HelloWorldService : System.Web.Services.WebService
  {
    public HelloWorldService() {}
    // WEB SERVICE EXAMPLE
    // The HelloWorld() example service returns the string Hello World
    // To build, uncomment the following lines, then save and build the project
    // To test this web service, press F5

    //[WebMethod]
    //public string HelloWorld()
    //{
```

```
        //return "Hello World";
        //}
    }
}
```

This code should look familiar since it is nearly identical to the code shown in Example 2-1. All you need to do to make it look like the earlier example is to remove the comments in front of the HelloWorld() method and [WebMethod] attribute.

Notice, however, that the WebService directive that was present in the inline code example is missing:

```
<%@ WebService Language="C#" Class="ProgWS.Ch02.HelloWorldService" %>
```

Recall that this directive is required to tell the compiler which class file to use as the entry point for the web service. So where is it? When you wrote the inline code example, you included both the directive and the source code for the HelloWorld class in the same file. By contrast, when Visual Studio .NET creates web service code, it separates the WebService directive and the source code using an approach known to ASP.NET developers as *code-behind*.

Understanding the code-behind model

The *code-behind* approach to programming web services (as well as ASP.NET web applications) involves separating the WebService directive from the supporting C# code. In this model, the *.asmx* page contains only one line, the WebService directive, while the supporting source code is placed on its own page, which, in the case of C#, has the file extension *.asmx.cs*, as in the preceding example. This page must be compiled into an assembly and placed in the \bin directory of your web service before the service can be used. Visual Studio .NET takes care of this process for you automatically when you build your project.

When you send a request to your web service for the first time, ASP.NET reads the WebService directive to find out the name of the class file containing its supporting logic. ASP.NET knows to look for the compiled class in an assembly in the \bin directory of the project. If there are multiple assemblies in the \bin directory, ASP.NET will look through each of them until it finds the appropriate class.

One of the advantages to storing your code in a compiled form is that source code is not left lying around on your production web servers. A malicious user who gains access to the server hosting your application will not easily be able to steal your code (we say "easily" because there are tools for decompiling MSIL). The disadvantage to using the code-behind model is that deployment requires an additional step—compiling the source code—which is not necessary for inline code.

The CodeBehind Attribute

If you find and view the *.asmx* page that VS.NET automatically generates and places on your server, you'll notice that the WebService directive includes an additional attribute called CodeBehind. (Unfortunately, you cannot view this *.asmx* page from Visual Studio .NET; instead, you'll need to look at the file placed on your web server in the *c:\inetpub\wwwroot\HelloWorldService* folder). In our example, it looks like this (except it's all on a single line):

```
<%@ WebService Language="c#"
       Codebehind="HelloWorldService.asmx.cs"
       Class="ProgWS.Ch02.HelloWorldService" %>
```

This unfortunate choice for an attribute name often confuses developers new to ASP. NET, who often assume that it is used in some way by ASP.NET to locate the code-behind file (indeed, the Microsoft Visual Studio documentation would lead you to believe this to be the case). In fact, this is not the case. This attribute is a Visual Studio .NET–specific attribute and is used by VS.NET to match the *.asmx* page to the associated source code file. This attribute has nothing to do with ASP.NET. In fact, ASP.NET completely ignores this attribute when processing a page request.

Visual Studio .NET is not designed to support the inline coding model. It's possible for you to use it, but we certainly do not recommend it: you cannot directly create an inline web service in Visual Studio .NET, because when you create a new web service, by default, Visual Studio .NET creates separate *.asmx* and class files.

To create an inline service using VS.NET, you must create a new text file and change its extension to *.asmx*. Creating an *.asmx* page in this manner forces you to write your code in the Visual Studio .NET HTML editor, not the code editor, which does not provide support for color coding, Intellisense, or many of the debugging features. In addition, because the code in the page is not compiled into the project assembly, compile-time errors are not caught until the page is run.

Building the service

Because Visual Studio .NET uses the code-behind model, simply posting the source pages to the server as in the inline example will not work. If you do so, you will get an error when you try to access the service. Instead, it's necessary to save your *.asmx* page to the server and compile your source code, saving it to the project's *bin* directory. VS.NET automates this process for you through its build feature. Once your application is complete, select Build Solution from the Build menu (or press Ctrl-Shift-B) and VS.NET will compile your web service and transfer the *.asmx* page and associated compiled assembly to the web server for you. If any errors result from the compile, VS.NET will display them in a panel labeled Output at the bottom of the IDE. Once you have successfully built the web service, it's ready to be used.

Testing the Service

Unlike Active Server Pages, web services are not designed to be viewed in a browser. Instead, web services are consumed by a client application using protocols such as HTTP GET/POST, SMTP, or SOAP over HTTP (see Chapter 3 for more information on consuming web services). Some of these protocols, such as SOAP, are more appropriate for server-to-server communication, while others, such as HTTP GET, are more frequently associated with the model of traditional web page access.

A web service that uses HTTP GET as a transport protocol can be accessed in much the same way as a regular web page. All that is necessary to access such a page is to point a web browser to the service endpoint. In our example, the endpoint comes is an *.asmx* page. But how do you know which protocols HelloWorldService will support, since there is no mention of HTTP or SOAP in the example code? The answer is that, by default, all .NET web services try to support HTTP GET, HTTP POST, and SOAP. We say "try," because in many cases the web service may be too complex for HTTP GET support. Additionally, because web services are applications that expose functionality to web service clients, and as a result have no required graphical user interface, .NET provides a canned web service test page that is displayed when you point your browser to an *.asmx* page. If you open a browser and type in the URL of the *.asmx* web service you just created, you'll see the IE test page shown in Figure 2-5.

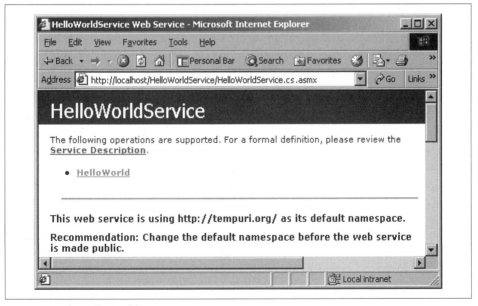

Figure 2-5. The HelloWorldService test page

The page in Figure 2-5 is generated by the .NET HTTP runtime each time it receives a request for an *.asmx* page. The page template is itself an ASP.NET *.aspx* page named *DefaultWsdlHelpGenerator.aspx* and is stored in the *\WINNT\Microsoft.NET\ Framework\[version]\Config* directory on the server that hosts the web service. This page operates just like any other *.aspx* page (remember that this is the extension for ASP.NET pages) and can be easily customized.

The test page displays the HelloWorldService service name along with the HelloWorld() method and a link to the service description. The service name and any additional information about this service are retrieved through a process called *reflection*, which uses the System.Reflection namespace to reveal information about existing types via metadata. In fact, if you look at the Page_Load function for the *DefaultWsdlHelpGenerator.aspx* page (again, in the *\WINNT\Microsoft.NET\ Framework\[version]\Config* directory on the hosting server), you'll see how this process works. If our service contained additional methods that were callable via HTTP, they would be listed as links here as well.

Viewing the Service Description

The runtime also automatically creates a *service description* from the *.asmx* page, an XML document that conforms to a specification called *Web Service Description Language*, or WSDL (pronounced "Wiz-Duhl"). If you click the service description link, you'll see the WSDL page. This page can also be viewed in a browser by appending *?WSDL* to the page URL, as in *HelloWorldService.cs.asmx?WSDL*. The service description for our service is shown in Figure 2-6.

You can see that the WSDL document includes information about the service namespaces, protocols supported, data types used, and web methods exposed in an XML-based format. This type of information is particularly important for an application looking to use our service, as you'll see in the next chapter.

The WSDL specification is a linchpin of sorts for the various web service development platforms. As you'll see in Chapter 11, where you'll learn about web service interoperability, web service development platforms must all abide by the same version of WSDL as well as the same version of SOAP if they are to work together (actually, WSDL is not an absolute requirement, but it is necessary for automatic proxy generation, as you'll see in Chapter 3). The version of WSDL we discuss in this book, 1.1, is currently supported by .NET and most other web service implementations (e.g., SOAP::Lite, Apache Axis).* The .NET Framework currently implements SOAP 1.1.

---

* If you're interested in learning more about WSDL, you can view the current spec at *http://www.w3.org/TR/ wsdl.html*. Be forewarned that reading this document, while an excellent way to learn the intricacies of WSDL, is a sure cure for insomnia. Alternatively, you can read Chapter 3, in which we discuss the parts of the WSDL specification.

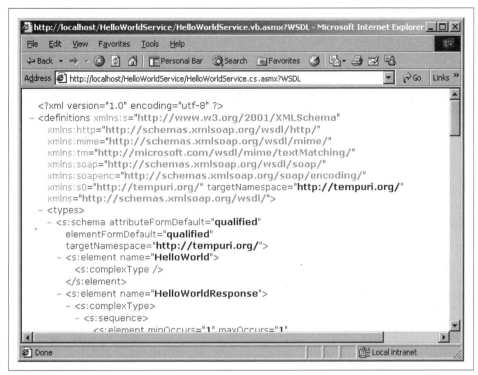

Figure 2-6. The HelloWorldService description

Getting back to the service test page: if you mouse over the HelloWorld link, you'll see the destination URL:

http://localhost/HelloWorldService.cs.asmx?op=HelloWorld

By clicking this link, you call the *.asmx* page, passing a parameter called op (standing presumably for operation) along with the name of the service. This action is the same as calling the HelloWorld web method of the web service using HTTP GET. The output page is shown in Figure 2-7.

Here you'll see the name of the service and method along with a button to test the service. Through reflection, the logic in the *DefaultWsdlHelpGenerator.aspx* test page is able to determine the signature of our HelloWorld method. Because our web method takes no arguments, the page need provide only a button for invocation. If our method had a different signature—for example, if it reads a string of text—the *.aspx* help page would also provide a text box to capture this string and pass it, using HTTP GET, to the web method when the form was submitted. This text box method works fine for simple data type arguments, but if the web method were to require an object, this approach would not work.

Beneath the Invoke button, there are also sample service interactions for SOAP, HTTP GET, and HTTP POST. We'll talk about some of the other methods of

Figure 2-7. The HelloWorldService invocation page

consuming web services in Chapter 3, but for now, note that on the source, the page is still using HTTP GET to invoke our service.

```
<form
 action='http://localhost/HelloWorldService/HelloWorldService.cs.asmx/HelloWorld'
 method="GET">
...
</form>
```

Invoking the Web Method

You can invoke the web method using the IE test page by opening a web browser and navigating to the service's URL. You will see a page listing the service's operation, which should be HelloWorld. Click the HelloWorld operation to navigate to the web method invocation page. This is a page that allows you to test the operation by clicking a button labeled Invoke. Click the button to invoke the service.

Invoking the example service produces the results shown in Figure 2-8.

Figure 2-8. HelloWorldService output

You know that web services are a means of communicating between servers using XML, so it should come as no surprise that the output of our service is nothing more than an XML document—and a short one at that! Had you used SOAP to access the service, you would have received a message in SOAP format; however, since IE isn't designed to either write or read SOAP messages by itself, you're limited to using HTTP GET and POST.

The response document begins with the following XML declaration:

```
<?xml version="1.0" encoding="utf-8" ?>
```

which identifies the document as an XML document and identifies the encoding of the document to be UTF-8 Unicode. While the encoding type may vary, all XML processors are required to support UTF-8 and UTF-16 Unicode encodings.

The first and only element in the output document is an element called string, which contains the output of our method and has one attribute called xmlns:

```
xmlns="http://tempuri.org"
```

This namespace declaration specifies that all unprefixed elements in this document come from the namespace tempuri.org.

The WebService Attribute

One of the features missing from our HelloWorld web service is information about what it does. To tell a client about the functionality provided by our service, we need some mechanism for documenting it. .NET provides an attribute for this purpose, WebServiceAttribute (a member of the System.Web.Services namespace), which you can use to let clients know where to find information about a web service. As with other attribute types, the WebServiceAttribute class inherits from System.Attribute. For convenience, the compiler will let you omit the Attribute part of the class name in most usage contexts, allowing you to use just WebService instead (not to be confused with the WebService directive in an *.asmx* page). For simplicity, we'll leave off the Attribute part as well throughout this text. The WebService attribute has two properties, described next.

Namespace
   Sets the XML namespace for the service

Description
   Adds a text/HTML description of the service that becomes part of the service description (WSDL) document

As discussed earlier, XML namespaces are important in the XML world for uniquely identifying the elements and attributes of an XML document. XML namespaces have nothing to do with the .NET's namespaces, which are used to organize classes.

Example 2-2 uses the `Namespace` and `Description` properties of the `WebService` attribute to document a web service named `DNSLookUpService`, which we introduce here for the first time. `DNSLookUpService` takes a hostname as a string argument and uses a class called `Dns` from the `System.Net` namespace to resolve and return the associated IP address.

Example 2-2. DNS LookupService

```
using System.Web.Services;
using System.Net;
[WebService(Namespace="http://www.bostontechnical.com/webservices/",
    Description="<b>A web service which performs Domain Name Lookups.</b>")]
public class DNSLookupService : System.Web.Services.WebService
{
        [WebMethod]
        public string getIPforHostname(string strHostname)
        {
                IPHostEntry hostInfo = Dns.GetHostByName(strHostname);
                return hostInfo.AddressList[0].ToString();
        }
}
```

In Example 2-2, the namespace for our web service is set to *http://www. bostontechnical.com/webservice/*. The web service will use this namespace as the source for definitions for all of the XML documents it returns in response to calls to its method. Remember that the purpose of XML namespaces is to avoid naming collisions among XML elements and attributes. Namespace URIs such as this one are commonly used because the domain name (e.g., *www.bostontechnical.com*) is guaranteed to be unique by a registration authority (e.g., Network Solutions). It is then the organization's responsibility (in this case, the owner of *www.bostontechnical. com*) to ensure uniqueness among the elements */webservice* domain of the namespace.

We've also added a description for our service. As you can see, HTML tags are permitted in the service description, making the resulting IE test page appear as shown in Figure 2-9.

The namespace and description are also included in the WSDL page for programmatic access, as shown in Figure 2-10.

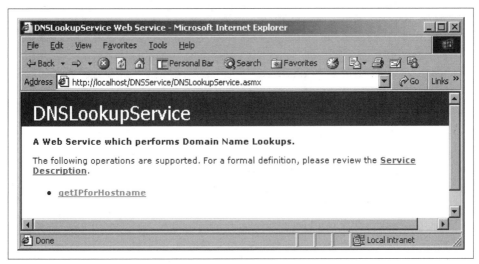

Figure 2-9. Adding a service description

The XML output in Figure 2-10 has been collapsed to improve readability, but notice the <service> element that appears toward the bottom of the listing and which contains our customized service name. Because the WSDL page is the contract for all web service consumers, the custom name is now available as part of the service identification.

The WebMethod Attribute

The WebMethod attribute, first used in Example 2-1, tells .NET that a particular public method should be exposed as a web-callable method. The WebMethod attribute has six associated properties to document and change the behavior of your web method. They are:

- Description
- MessageName
- EnableSession
- CacheDuration
- TransactionOption
- BufferResponse

The first two properties are used to document a web method, while the others affect its behavior. In the following sections, we'll introduce each briefly. Each property is described in greater detail in a later chapter.

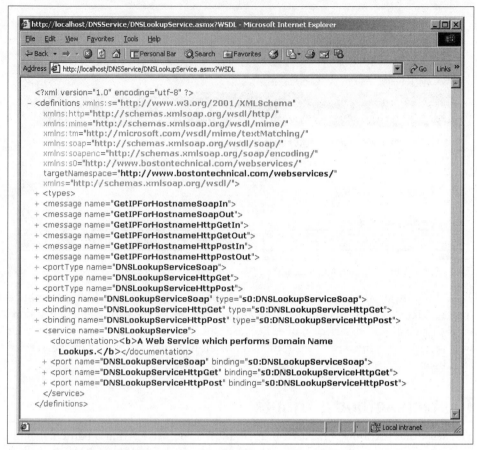

Figure 2-10. WSDL with custom service name

The Description and MessageName Properties

To avoid forcing your consumers to guess at what a web method does based on its name, include a description for each of your web methods, just as you should for the service itself. This is particularly necessary when a web service contains overloaded web methods. For example, the following code fragment declares two methods named Add(), one that accepts parameters of type Integer and one that accepts parameters of type Floating:

```
...
[WebMethod]
public int Add(int a, int b)
{
  return a + b;
}
[WebMethod]
public float Add(float a, float b)
```

```
{
return a + b;
}
...
```

In fact, if you try to access a web service containing two methods with the same name but different method signatures (an overloaded method) through the IE test page, you get a runtime exception when you view the page. The error for the previous example is as follows: "Both Single Add(Single, Single) and Int32 Add(Int32, Int32) use the message name "Add". Use the MessageName property of the Web-Method custom attribute to specify unique message names for the methods."

The procedure for commenting web methods is very similar to that for commenting a service. Start each method declaration with a WebMethod attribute. Use its Description property to add a description of your web method and its MessageName property to change its name:

```
[WebMethod(MessageName="<name>", Description="<desc>")]
```

In our DNSLookupService example, the descriptive code would look like this:

```
[WebService(Namespace="http://www.bostontechnical.com/webservices/",
    Description="<b>A web service which performs Domain Name Lookups.</b>")]
public class DNSLookupService : System.Web.Services.WebService
{
  [WebMethod(MessageName="LookupDNS",
            Description="Get an IP address for a given hostname string")]
  public string GetIPForHostname(string strHostname)
  {
    IPHostEntry hostInfo = Dns.GetHostByName(strHostname);
    return hostInfo.AddressList[0].ToString();
  }
}
```

The WSDL service description reflects these changes, as shown in Figure 2-11.

Notice that the WSDL document includes a <portType> tag for each of the supported access protocols (POST/HTTP GET and SOAP). Each of the <portType> tags contains an additional XML documentation element, which itself contains the textual explanation for the web method. In addition, the name attribute of each of the input and output elements now contains the value of the names that we've assigned to the method: getIPForHostname. Because this documentation is now part of the WSDL page, it is programmatically accessible to a calling application. You will see why this documentation is particularly useful to the consumer in the next chapter when we talk about .NET proxy classes.

The EnableSession Property

ASP.NET web services (classes that derive from System.Web.Services.WebService) exist within the context of an ASP.NET application and therefore have access to the Application and Session objects of the ASP.NET application within which they

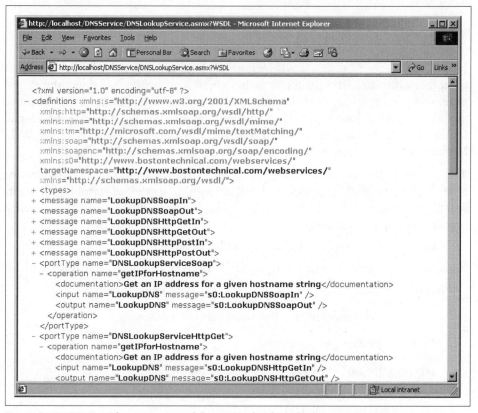

```
 http://localhost/DNSService/DNSLookupService.asmx?WSDL - Microsoft Internet Explorer
File   Edit   View   Favorites   Tools   Help
← Back  ▼  →  ▼  ⊗  ⊘  ⌂  | Personal Bar  Search  Favorites  ⊗  |  ⊟▼  ⊜  ⊠  ⊟
Address    http://localhost/DNSService/DNSLookupService.asmx?WSDL                          ▼  ⊘Go  Links »

    <?xml version="1.0" encoding="utf-8" ?>
  - <definitions xmlns:s="http://www.w3.org/2001/XMLSchema"
      xmlns:http="http://schemas.xmlsoap.org/wsdl/http/"
      xmlns:mime="http://schemas.xmlsoap.org/wsdl/mime/"
      xmlns:tm="http://microsoft.com/wsdl/mime/textMatching/"
      xmlns:soap="http://schemas.xmlsoap.org/wsdl/soap/"
      xmlns:soapenc="http://schemas.xmlsoap.org/soap/encoding/"
      xmlns:s0="http://www.bostontechnical.com/webservices/"
      targetNamespace="http://www.bostontechnical.com/webservices/"
      xmlns="http://schemas.xmlsoap.org/wsdl/">
    + <types>
    + <message name="LookupDNSSoapIn">
    + <message name="LookupDNSSoapOut">
    + <message name="LookupDNSHttpGetIn">
    + <message name="LookupDNSHttpGetOut">
    + <message name="LookupDNSHttpPostIn">
    + <message name="LookupDNSHttpPostOut">
    - <portType name="DNSLookupServiceSoap">
      - <operation name="getIPforHostname">
          <documentation>Get an IP address for a given hostname string</documentation>
          <input name="LookupDNS" message="s0:LookupDNSSoapIn" />
          <output name="LookupDNS" message="s0:LookupDNSSoapOut" />
        </operation>
      </portType>
    - <portType name="DNSLookupServiceHttpGet">
      - <operation name="getIPforHostname">
          <documentation>Get an IP address for a given hostname string</documentation>
          <input name="LookupDNS" message="s0:LookupDNSHttpGetIn" />
          <output name="LookupDNS" message="s0:LookupDNSHttpGetOut" />
```
    Done   Local intranet
```
```

Figure 2-11. WSDL with namespace and documented web methods

reside. While an ASP.NET application has only one Application object, it can have multiple session objects, which can be used to store data on a per-client basis. This state management mechanism is disabled by default and can be enabled by setting the EnableSession property to true. Enabling session management can decrease performance, so leave it disabled if you don't plan on using it.

If session state is enabled, the server manages client state using a unique HttpSessionState object for each client. In order to differentiate between each client's Session, a unique identifier is assigned to each Session object when the client first interacts with the server. On subsequent interactions, the client must present its unique identifier in order for the server to retrieve any client-specific data that has been stored in session state. The unique identifier can be stored in a cookie on the client or can be included as part of the URL. In a typical ASP.NET application, which is accessed via a web browser, this state management system occurs behind the scenes. If cookies are enabled on the web browser, it will automatically present the appropriate cookie to the server along with each request. Because a web service is not accessed in the same manner, if you choose to enable session management, you must programmatically set the cookie each time you call your web service. (You'll learn more about this and other state management approaches in Chapter 5.)

The CacheDuration Property

Implementing proper caching in your web services can increase scalability and performance. One of the easiest ways to implement caching systems is with the CacheDuration property of the WebMethod attribute. .NET implements this type of caching, called *output caching*, by system by storing matching pairs of requests and responses in a hashtable in memory for the specified amount of time. During this time, any incoming request that matches a request already in cache forces the server to output the cached response. Use the CacheDuration property to set the number of seconds (integer) a request/response pair will be held in cache. The default is 0, meaning that the response is not cached.

This caching mechanism is often ideal for web methods that involve processor-intensive or other expensive queries where the results change infrequently. An example of this type of functionality is a web method that queries a database for news headlines that change daily. For a system like this, we might set the CacheDuration property for our web method to five minutes or more to reduce the number of round-trips to the database. Because the caching system is based on request/response pairs, it uses few server resources in situations like this in which the web method's range of expected input parameters is small. If, however, you have a wide range of expected input parameters (and therefore request strings), the cache hashtable can quickly grow to consume a great deal of memory or can cause valuable items to be deleted from the cache. This can be further aggravated if the output of your method (which is stored in cache) is sizable. An example of a web method that would not lend itself well to caching with CacheDuration is the GetIPForHostname method of our DNSLookupService. It meets the first part of the requirement, in that it involves a fairly expensive network operation to retrieve a reasonably static small result; however, this type of service receives a wide range of inputs. Using a high cache duration setting for this method would cause the hashtable to grow in memory as unique lookup requests were made to the service.

We discuss output caching in detail in Chapter 7, along with data caching.

The TransactionOption Property

If you've ever programmed MTS or COM+ components, you're probably comfortable with the idea of developing transaction-based services. A transaction can be thought of as any set of procedures (e.g., events, function calls) that collectively result in a change of state such as a success or failure. One example is a credit card processing system that authenticates a credit card number, charges the card, and triggers a fulfillment process. If any of these three steps fails (e.g., the card is declined), the transaction as a whole will fail, and each of the individual processes must be returned to its original state (e.g., cancel a fulfillment process if it has been started). All three steps are part of a transaction.

Microsoft includes support in the .NET platform for MTS or COM+ style transactions through the System.EnterpriseServices namespace. We're not going to get into the details of developing transacted services in this book; however, it is important to understand the difference between .NET-style transactions and what we'll call *distributed web service transactions*.

.NET transaction support is set through the TransactionOption property of the WebMethod attribute. The five possible settings for this property are:

- Disabled
- NotSupported
- Supported
- Required
- RequiresNew

By default, transactions are disabled. If you decide to use .NET transactions, your web method will be able to participate only as the root object in a transaction. This means that your web method may call other transaction-enabled objects, but may not itself be called as part of a transaction started by another object. This limitation is due to the stateless nature of the HTTP protocol. As a result, the Required and RequiresNew values for TransactionOption are equivalent (and both declare a RequiresNew method that will start a new transaction). Disabled, NotSupported, and Supported all disable transactions for the web method, despite what their names imply.

We discuss the TransactionOption property in more detail in Chapter 5.

The BufferedResponse Property

The default behavior for a web method is to store a response in a memory buffer until either the buffer is full or the response is complete. This storage process is called *serialization*. In most scenarios, this behavior is preferred, because buffering results in improved performance by reducing the number of transmissions to the client. However, if your web method returns a large amount of data or takes a long time to run, you might want to disable buffering by setting the BufferResponse property to false. This setting causes .NET to send the response back to the client as it is serialized, but can reduce performance for smaller result sets.

For all practical purposes, there's no reason that you should ever need to change this property's value. For an *.aspx* page, the output of which is meant to be displayed to a user, it can make sense to disable buffering for long-running pages such as a search page, so that the user can start viewing the data before it's completely returned. Because web services are designed for host-to-host communication, this type of scenario rarely occurs. and the default value for this setting does not need to be changed.

Deploying a Web Service

The process you use to deploy your web services will vary depending on whether you use inline coding or code behind to write them and whether you use an IDE like Visual Studio .NET. As you've seen, deployment for web services written using the inline approach is a snap. Once you have written and tested a web service on your development machine, all you have to do is to save the raw source to a server running the .NET SDK and IIS 5.0 or later. .NET compiles the service and caches a copy of the compiled class for you. If the source page changes, .NET will automatically recompile and cache the new page. This process is handled by .NET using some of the classes found in the System.Web.Caching namespace. You'll learn more about these classes in Chapter 7.

If you're using the code-behind approach, the deployment process is more involved. Let's take a closer look at what you need to do in order to be able to deploy your web services using the code-behind approach, first with and then without the help of Visual Studio .NET.

Deploying a Web Service with VS.NET

The deployment process in Visual Studio .NET is as simple as choosing the Build Solution option from the Build menu item (or pressing Ctrl-Shift-B). But, in order to take advantage of this two-click deployment, you first need to properly configure Visual Studio .NET to be able to deploy to your instance of IIS. Earlier we mentioned that there are two ways for Visual Studio .NET to communicate with IIS: Microsoft FrontPage Server Extensions, and UNC file shares. In the earlier example, we used FrontPage Extensions because they are easier to configure (or at least easier to explain). Let's take a closer look at the differences between Frontpage Extensions and UNC.

FrontPage Extensions and UNC

Visual Studio .NET offers you two methods of connecting to the web server. You can use either FrontPage Extensions or UNC. FrontPage Extensions is a technology that allows Visual Studio .NET to transfer files to and from the web server over HTTP. In order to use this method of file transfer, you must install and configure the FrontPage Server Extensions to the web server as we discussed in the earlier "Creating "Hello, World" with Visual Studio .NET" section.

The other way Visual Studio .NET can communicate with the web server is via UNC, or Universal Naming Convention file or folder shares. A file or folder share is just a file or folder on the network that is configured to be shared by one or more users. UNC provides a naming convention for identifying network resources, in this case the web server. UNC names consist of three parts: a server name, a share name, and a file path, separated by backslashes (\) as follows:

\\servername\share\file_path

This format is called a *UNC path*. The server name portion of the UNC path is either a network address (IP address) or a hostname that can be mapped to a network address using a naming service like DNS. The share can be either a custom share configured by a system administrator or one of several built-in shares. An example of a built-in share is the *admin$* share, which typically maps to *c:\winnt*, or the *c$* share, which maps to *c:*. The file path allows you to specify the subdirectory below the specific share. For example, the following path:

> *\\myserver\c$\inetpub*

points to the *c:\inetpub* folder on a server called *myserver*.

If you choose UNC access for your project, it's important to make sure that the UNC path corresponds to the URL specified in the creation dialog box; otherwise, VS.NET will return an error.

Locally and remotely hosted projects

There are no configuration differences between web service projects hosted locally (i.e., on your workstation) or remotely (i.e., on a remote web server). Regardless of whether your projects are hosted locally or remotely, you should still use either FrontPage or UNC access. Of course, if you choose to use UNC access for your projects, you must make sure to configure a share to the appropriate IIS folder so that VS.NET can transfer files. For local workstation development, VS.NET takes care of some of the work for you automatically.

VS.NET UNC support

When VS.NET is installed, it creates an empty "VS Developers" user group and a share on the *\inetpub\wwwroot* folder called *wwwroot$* (which we'll discuss shortly). VS.NET then grants the newly created group read and write permissions on that share. This VS Developers group is created without any members, so unless your user account has administrative privileges on your workstation, you will need to add yourself to this group.

By default, Visual Studio .NET is configured to use UNC access for projects. When you specify the URL for a new project, such as *http://ws.uinspire.com/HelloWorldService* in the earlier example, Visual Studio .NET attempts to create the project using the UNC path:

> *\\ws.uinspire.com\wwwroot$\HelloWorldService*

If Visual Studio .NET is unable to connect using this UNC path, you get an error message asking you either to retry using a different UNC path or to try to open the project using FrontPage Server Extensions. If you are hosting your project on your local workstation, the fact that Visual Studio .NET automatically creates the *wwwroot$* share upon install can make your life easier (assuming you've added yourself to the VS Developers group). However, if you want to host your project on a remote server, you will need to make sure this *wwwroot$* share is properly config-ured or manually specify another path. You also have the option of installing the Visual Studio .NET Server Components to the remote server on which you wish to do your development.

FrontPage and UNC performance

UNC is the preferred access method primarily because it performs much better than FrontPage Extension's access. This shouldn't come as much of a surprise consider-ing that FrontPage file transfers are done over the slower HTTP. As a result, if you have a choice between using UNC and FrontPage Extensions, it's preferable to use UNC. Another reason to choose UNC is that FrontPage Extensions have tradition-ally had security problems. If, however, you need to change Visual Studio .NET's default access method, you can do so. This option can be changed via Tools → Options → Projects → Web Settings, then setting the Preferred Access Method to FrontPage.

 While you have the option to use either a UNC file share or FrontPage Extensions for your project, FrontPage Extension's access is slower.

Even if you intend to use Visual Studio .NET (which does much of the deployment automatically) for web service development, it's still important to understand how this process works so that you can troubleshoot your web services. Let's start by tak-ing a closer look at how IIS must be configured to support ASP.NET web services.

Deploying a Web Service Directly to IIS

An ASP.NET web service consists of a collection of resources (*.asmx* web services, *global.asax*, configuration information, compiled components stored in the *\bin* directory, and so on) that run as a so-called IIS *virtual application*. IIS allows you to divide an instance of a web server into multiple separate virtual applications. Each of these virtual applications has its own set of application mappings, debugging options, and configuration options like script timeout duration and session state tim-eout. This separation, particularly separation of the application mappings, makes vir-tual directories good containers for ASP.NET applications. When you create a web service project using VS.NET, this virtual application configuration can be done automatically, but if you're developing without VS.NET, you'll need tools like the Microsoft Management Console (MMC) snap-in or the command-line scripts included with IIS, as explained next.

The most common way to create a new virtual application is to create a new instance of a web site in IIS. By default, the root folder of the new web site will be configured as a virtual application, known as the application root, which can contain other vir-tual applications.

Another way to create an application root is to mark a folder (virtual or physical) within an IIS web site as an application. This will define the folder as the root of an application.

The most common way to create a virtual application in IIS is through the Internet Services Manager, a snap-in for the Microsoft Management Console. To create a virtual application from an existing directory, follow these steps:

1. Locate the folder you wish to convert in the Internet Services Manager snap-in. We used a folder called *DNSService* in Figure 2-12.

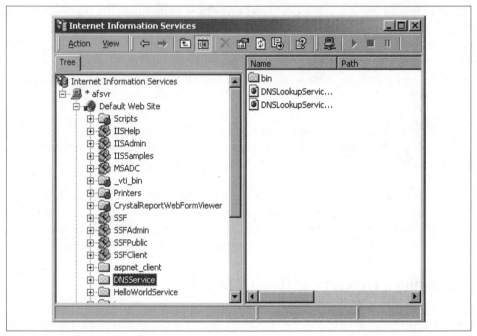

Figure 2-12. The IIS Management Console

2. Right-click the folder and select Properties.
3. Mark the folder as an application by clicking on the Create button of the Directory tab of the folder's Property dialog. (See Figure 2-13.)
4. Click OK to accept the change.

The folder is now configured as an IIS virtual application. You can now manually add a *bin* directory.

The *bin* directory is the first place that .NET looks for compiled assemblies, and so every ASP.NET web service should have a *bin* directory located directly beneath the application root folder. If one is not automatically created for you by a tool like VS.NET, you can create one manually by using Windows Explorer to navigate to

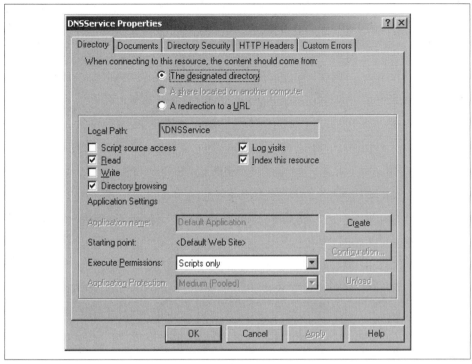

Figure 2-13. Configuring the virtual directory

the application's root folder (called *DNSService* in the previous example) and creating a new folder called *root*.

Remember that the location of the *bin* directory is always relative to the virtual application root. Because IIS allows you to have nested virtual applications, sometime figuring out which *bin* directory goes with which application can be confusing. For example, consider Figure 2-14, and let's assume a code-behind *.asmx* page resides in the folder named *dir2*. If the virtual directory named *store* is configured as a virtual application, then .NET will attempt to find the associated code-behind assembly in the *bin* directory associated with the *store* virtual application (*www.yyz.com\store\bin*). If, however, the *store* virtual directory *is not* configured as a virtual application, .NET will look in the *bin* directory located at *www.yyz.com\bin*.

.NET always looks for the *bin* directory located directly underneath the application root. If you start seeing .NET error messages like "Could not create type 'xxx'", it's probably due to a problem with the way you've configured your virtual application.

Example deployment

To take advantage of the compiled code model for our *DNSLookupService* example, create an *.asmx* page with the following single line:

```
<%@ WebService Language="C#" Class="DNSLookupService"%>
```

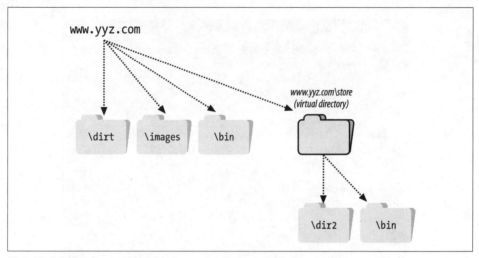

Figure 2-14. \bin directory locations

and save it as *DNSLookupService.asmx*. When this page is accessed, .NET looks through the assemblies in the *\bin* subdirectory of the virtual application for one containing the class `DNSLookupService`. If an application makes use of multiple assemblies in the *\bin* directory, you need to specify the assembly that contains the `DNSLookupService` by adding its name to the `Class` attribute value as follows:

```
<%@ WebService Language="C#" Class="DNSLookupService, MyAssembly"%>
```

This line tells .NET to search the assembly `MyAssembly` for the class `DNSLookupService`. This *.asmx* page will return an error, however, until you compile the assembly and copy it to the *\bin* directory. Do this by putting the C# code into another file; for this example, call it *DNSLoupService.asmx.cs*, using the same naming convention that Visual Studio uses by default. We can then compile this source code from the command line using a command like the following:

```
csc.exe /out:bin\DNSLookupService.dll /target:library /r:System.Web.Services.dll
DNSLookupService.asmx.cs
```

Using the .NET Compilers

If you develop your web service code as inline code, you will eventually need to compile it. The .NET SDK comes with a command-line compiler for each of the .NET languages that ships with the SDK. The .NET compilers, located in the *\WINNT\Microsoft.NET\Framework\[version]* directory, where [version] is the version number of your instance of the .NET Framework (mine is v1.0.3705), are listed in the following table.

.NET Language	Compiler
C#	*csc.exe*
VB.NET	*vbc.exe*
JSCRIPT.NET	*Jsc.exe*

There are several options for compiling a C# program into an assembly. If you're using Visual Studio, select "Build Solution" from the Build menu or use the shortcut Ctrl-Shift-B. Visual Studio .NET will compile your application into an assembly and place it into the *bin* directory, usually under a subdirectory called *debug* or *release* depending on your settings. If you're compiling from the command line, use the *csc.exe* compiler to create your assembly, as shown in the following command:

```
csc.exe /out:bin\DNSLookupService.dll /target:library /r:System.Web.Services.dll
DNSLookupService.asmx.cs
```

 This command assumes that you are running the compiler from the directory on your web server that contains your C# source file, and that you have created a *bin* subdirectory. For this command to work properly from any folder, include the compiler in your PATH environmental variable. In Windows 2000, this is done via Control Panel → System Properties → Advanced tab → Environment Variables → System Variables, and adding \\WINNT\\Microsoft.NET\\Framework\\[version] to your PATH variable. Alternatively, if you have Visual Studio .NET installed, there is a menu option under Start → Programs → Visual Studio .NET → Visual Studio .NET Tools called Visual Studio .NET Command Prompt, which will open a command prompt window with the proper variables set for running the VS.NET tools.

The output from the previous command is shown in Figure 2-15.

Figure 2-15. Compiling from the command line

The compilation command tells the compiler to compile our source file *DNSLookupService.asmx.cs* into an assembly called *DNSLookupService.dll*. The /out: switch allows you to specify the output name and location for the compiled assembly. The /target: switch (which can be abbreviated as /t:) allows you to specify whether the output should be a console executable, Windows executable, library (DLL), or module. In our example, we want to build a DLL, so we've specified the library option, which forces the compiler to build our assembly to the \bin subdirectory (as specified with the /out switch).

The .NET compilers have a number of command-line switches. Some of the more useful ones are listed Table 2-1.

Table 2-1. .NET command-line compiler switches

Switch	Description
/out:*<file>*	Specifies the name and location for the output file. The default action is for the compiler to derive the output name from the source filename.
/target:*<type>*	The target switch (short form, /t:) specifies the type of output file (types include exe, winexe, library, module).
/define:*<symbol list>*	Defines conditional compilation symbols; similar to using the #define *xx* statement in your program.
/doc:*<file>*	Specifies the output XML documentation that is created using any XML comments in your source code.
/recurse:*<wildcard>*	Specifies the names and locations of files to compile. For example, /recurse: dir1\dir2*.cs compiles any files in and below *dir2*.
/reference:*<file list>*	The reference switch (short form, /r:) specifies a list of assemblies (which must contain assembly manifests), separated by commas or semicolons, which will be made available for use at compile time. If you reference a file that itself references another file, both files must be included in the reference file list. This is also true for assemblies that contain classes that inherit from classes in other assemblies.
	To import metadata from a file that does not contain an assembly manifest, such as a module, use the /addmodule switch.
/addmodule:*<file list>*	Same as /reference, but used for modules. Modules do not contain assembly manifests.
/win32res:*<file>*	Adds a Win32 resource file to your output file. A Win32 resource can contain version information that helps to identify your application to the Windows Explorer.
/win32icon:*<file>*	Allows you to specify an icon to be used by the Windows Explorer for the output file.
/debug[+|-] or: /debug:[full|pdbonly]	Specifying + forces the compiler to write debugging information to a program database (.pdb) file. Specifying - causes no debug information to be written.
	The /debug:full switch enables attaching a debugger to the running program. The /debug:pdbonly switch displays the assembler only when the program is attached to the debugger.
/optimize[+|-]	The optimize option (short form, /o) enables or disables compiler optimization for smaller and faster code. By default, optimization is enabled.
/incremental[+|-]	The incremental option (short form, /incr), incremental compilation compiles only those methods that have been modified since the last incremental compile. Information about the state of the previous compilation is stored in the *<output_file_name>.dbg* and *<output_file_name>.incr* files. These files are created the first time this option is used and henceforth are used for incremental builds.
	In an incremental build, the /doc option is ignored.
	Output files created with the incremental option may be larger than those created without.

Like most Windows command-line tools, the .NET compilers display a complete list of available options with the following command:

```
csc.exe /?
```

Once the source code has been compiled into an assembly and copied to the \bin directory, it's ready to be used by .NET. Unlike COM objects, which must be registered using *regsvr32.exe* before they can be used, .NET requires no such explicit registration.

In the next chapter, we cover some of the different ways of consuming web services using .NET applications.

CHAPTER 3

Consuming Web Services

Web services were designed as a method for intermachine communication, which is typically done by implementing a client/server model in which requests by a consumer client are made through a broker or proxy object to a web service on a remote server. This is the model used by most developers of .NET web services and of non-Microsoft web services as well.

In this chapter, you'll learn the techniques commonly used to consume web services. We'll talk first about the three most popular methods used to consume web services and then move on to describe the techniques you will use to work with SOAP-enabled web services. Though it is always possible to call a web service directly, it is more common to communicate through an intermediary proxy client. In later sections of this chapter, you will learn how to create and manage proxies using Visual Studio .NET or command-line tools. We will also introduce you to the Web Service Description Language (WSDL) and WSDL documents, which can be used by .NET tools (and other web services toolkits) to automatically generate proxies for consumers.

The Web Service Consumer Model

One of the goals of the web services architecture is to create a service framework that allows service providers and consumers to interact with one another without their having to know about one another ahead of time. Because service providers and consumers may not know about one another, it is often necessary to use an intermediary registry that service providers can publish to and service consumers can use to locate services. In order to achieve this goal, a consumer model called the publish/find/bind process is commonly used.

Publish/Find/Bind Consumer Model

Three requirements must be met before you can use a web service. First, the service must be made available to you or to the public in general. Second, you must have some way to locate this service. Third, you need to be able to have some (preferably automated) way of binding to the service so that you can consume it. This typical consumer model for a web service is commonly referred to as the *publish/find/bind* process. This process, which involves a service provider, a service registry, and a service consumer, is shown in Figure 3-1.

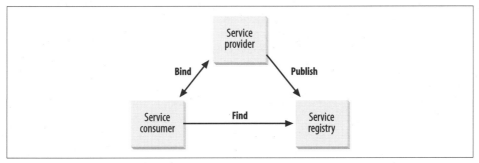

Figure 3-1. The publish/find/bind consumer model

The *service provider* is the person or organization hosting the service. In order for the service provider to make its service available to the public, it must have a means of publishing information about where the service is located, what protocols and interfaces it supports, and what prerequisites are required for communicating with it (e.g., whether you need to setup an account with the provider before you can use the service). The service provider will typically publish some or all of this information to a service registry in the form of a Web Service Description Language (WSDL) document (examples of which are UDDI and ebXML). Service consumers, of course, must know about this registry ahead of time, and when they do can use it to locate services for consumption, a process known as *service discovery*, the gathering of the information necessary to communicate with the service (usually a WSDL document). Once the service consumer has acquired the necessary service information, it can attempt to bind to the service (and use) it.

This chapter deals with the binding process, whereby a service consumer communicates with a service provider by creating a client-proxy from a WSDL document. The publishing and finding (locating) process is covered in Chapter 10, which discusses UDDI in detail. You should realize that while the publish/find/bind process is one of the commonly accepted approaches to consuming a web service, it is by no means necessary. In many cases a service consumer will know the service provider with whom it is to communicate ahead of time, in which case a service registry is bypassed altogether. In situations in which a service registry is unnecessary, the binding process remains the same.

Client/Service Model

In the .NET service consumer model, a .NET client application communicates with a web service through a proxy. This proxy is nothing more than a .NET assembly that is created from the service's WSDL. You'll see in this chapter that this proxy can be generated either automatically for you by Visual Studio .NET or manually by you using the *wsdl.exe* tool that comes with the .NET Framework SDK. Once the proxy is created, you can use it to access the methods and properties of a remote web service just as easily as you would a local assembly. Figure 3-2 outlines the communication process.

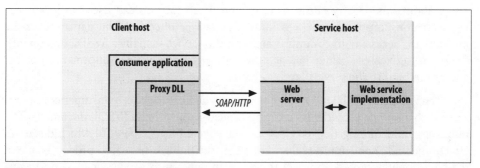

Figure 3-2. Client/service communication

The proxy takes care of the communication with the remote service, converting the native C# data types of your consumer application to XML messages (a process called *serialization*, discussed in Chapter 4), sending the XML to the web service using whatever message format and transport protocol you have chosen (typically SOAP/HTTP) and then converting the response message back to C# data types that are returned to your application (a process called *deserialization*). The advantage of this proxy approach is that it decouples your .NET consumer application from the distributed call process, which is handled in the proxy. This means that, if the underlying messaging format or transport protocol changes (e.g., the service provider moves to a newer version of SOAP), all you need to do is rebuild the proxy to use the new message format and transport as opposed to having to recode your consumer application (of course, drastic changes in the underlying communication semantics usually require an application recode anyway). From the point of view of the consumer application, the proxy is just another assembly that exposes the interface of the remote service.

Of course, while a proxy makes the process of consuming a service significantly easier, you don't need to use a proxy to consume a web service. If the web service supports HTTP as the transport protocol, you can communicate with it directly from the command line on most Windows machines. The next few sections will take you through this process, comparing and contrasting HTTP GET, HTTP POST, and SOAP as access methods. Next you'll learn how to create proxies in Visual Studio .NET and then how to do so using the command-line tools of the .NET Framework SDK. Finally you'll learn about consuming web pages as services, a process called *screen scraping*, using Microsoft's WSDL extensions.

Accessing Web Services: HTTP

Once you've created a web service (see Chapter 2) or found one you want to work with on the Web, the next thing you'll want to do is access it so that you can do something useful. There are three common protocols for accessing .NET web services: HTTP GET, HTTP POST, and SOAP. Each of these access methods uses HTTP as its underlying transport protocol. Although web services can operate over just about any Internet protocol, including SMTP, Jabber, FTP, or even directly over TCP (which is an option with .NET remoting), HTTP is the preferred transport protocol for .NET web services for at least four reasons:

- HTTP is simple, consisting of a request and a response encoded in plain text. This simplicity makes HTTP a protocol that is easy to understand and therefore easy to implement.

- HTTP is stateless. Once an HTTP message is sent, the connection between client and server is typically released (HTTP 1.1 uses pipelining to allow multiple messages to be sent over a given connection, but overall, HTTP is not a connection-oriented protocol). This stateless approach helps to minimize usage of server resources, which, in turn, allows web service applications to scale more readily.

- HTTP runs over port 80 by default, a well-known port that is open to public access on most firewalls for existing web servers.

- HTTP has gained common industry approval, having been endorsed by the IETF (RFC 2068 in case you're interested) and, more importantly, put into practical use in web servers all over the Internet. It is an ubiquitous Internet transport protocol.

HTTP does have its drawbacks, however, chief among them a lack of support for asynchronous messaging. It's not hard to imagine that a protocol originally designed for synchronously transferring hypertext documents lacks this feature. There are some ways of emulating asynchronous messaging at the web service application layer (we'll look at one approach in Chapter 6), but the lack of any standard makes interoperability an issue. Other transport layer protocols, notably Jabber, provide support for asynchronous messaging, but lack of widespread support makes them poor alternatives to HTTP.

Another limitation of HTTP is that is it not reliable. By "reliable" we mean that it does not guarantee delivery of a message. HTTP does not support message receipt confirmation (e.g., there are no ACKs or NACKs) and as a result does not provide any mechanism for retransmitting messages. This limitation is not a big deal for web browsing—you may be annoyed if your page doesn't load properly, but you can always hit reload. But, depending on the nature of a web service, reliability can be a significant problem. We'd like to think that in a banking system using web services, all of the messages get to their destination. There are ways of implementing reliability at the application layer, but as with asynchronous approaches, lack of standardization makes interoperability a problem, defeating one of the main goals of web services.

Internet Information Server (IIS)

Despite its limitations, the HTTP protocol is a mature technology (it's been in use since about 1990), supported by every commercial and open source web server on the Internet. Web server technology has had a decade to evolve, resulting in improvements in performance, scalability, and reliability. Organizations like Microsoft, Apache, and Netscape have gone through multiple iterations of their web server products, improving them with each successive release. The time and effort put into developing web servers like Apache and IIS have made them stable, reliable, high-performance HTTP servers that are good candidates for implementing the transport layer of the web services stack.

Recognizing the benefits of using HTTP for web services, Microsoft chose IIS as the default transport layer. This IIS integration allows you to leverage the scalability, performance, and security of Microsoft's IIS web server rather than having to get involved with unpleasant socket programming or reinventing a higher-level communications server. This integration also means that if you want to use a web server other than IIS, you're on your own. ASP.NET is designed to work in conjunction with IIS only and doesn't provide support for other web servers.

Working with HTTP

Because HTTP GET, HTTP POST, and SOAP all run over HTTP, it's possible for you to interact with a web service using Telnet and a plain text query or message. Telnet is both a protocol and an application. The Telnet protocol provides a standard way of making a connection with a remote machine. The Telnet application, which ships as part of the TCP/IP suite included in most operating systems (including Windows 2000 and Windows XP), is a tool for making remote connections. You can access Telnet by typing **telnet** at the command prompt in Windows.

In the following sections, you'll use Telnet to make HTTP GET, HTTP POST, and SOAP calls to the DNSLookupService. In the process, you'll become familiar with the query and response formats of each method.

To see the message exchanges with the DNSLookupService from Chapter 2, you will need to open a Telnet session to the web server hosting the DNSLookupService web service. You can do this in most versions of Windows by doing one of the following:

- Invoke the command prompt window (Start → Programs → Accessories → Command Prompt) and type:

      telnet your_servername 80

   The Microsoft Telnet program that's available from the command prompt in some versions of Windows may not display the characters you type, which can lead to errors (and doesn't bode well for illustrations). To change this setting, type **Ctrl-]** (once you're connected) to call up the connection setup screen, then type **SET LOCAL_ECHO**, followed by a carriage return, which returns you to your Telnet session.

- Open Internet Explorer and enter **telnet://<your_servername>:80** into the Address text box.

If you wish, you can also telnet from a Unix machine. Telnet on a Unix machine will echo characters back to you as you type them.

Using HTTP GET

Let's first explore the interaction that occurs when you call a web service using HTTP GET. You'll begin by viewing once again the IE test page that we discussed in Chapter 2. Using the DNSLookupService that we created in Chapter 2, view the GetIPForHostname web method in the IE test page. You'll see a form for executing the method and helper text that gives examples of the various requests and responses for the three communication methods supported. You'll see three sections (assuming you haven't customized the page to remove them): HTTP GET, HTTP POST, and SOAP. Remember that these three access methods are automatically included as web service bindings by .NET.

The HTTP GET section should look something like this:

```
HTTP GET
The following is a sample HTTP GET request and response. The placeholders shown need
to be replaced with actual values.
GET /DNSService/DNSLookupService.asmx/GetIPForHostname?strHostname=string HTTP/1.1
Host: localhost
HTTP/1.1 200 OK
Content-Type: text/xml; charset=utf-8
Content-Length: length
<?xml version="1.0" encoding="utf-8"?>
<string xmlns="http://www.bostontechnical.com/webservices/">string</string>
```

This text is an example of the request and response messages that are exchanged when you invoke a web service using HTTP GET. The *length* field is a placeholder for the number of characters (including whitespace) in the message. The string field is a placeholder that represents input or output data of type string. To consume a web service with HTTP GET, you must send a request in the format of the top of the section (from HTTP GET to Host: localhost) to receive the HTTP and XML response in the format of the bottom section (from HTTP/1.1 200 OK on).

Figure 3-3 shows a Telnet session between a client and a local web server running the DNSLookupService web service. In this example, the client issues a request to the GetIPForHostname web method using the GET method, and receives a response formatted in XML.

The session reproduced in Figure 3-3 begins with a Telnet command to open a connection with port 80 on the server named *isa.bostontechnical.com*:

```
fas% telnet isa.bostontechnical.com 80
```

Once connected, the web method is accessed using HTTP GET. (The following code would be on a single line, but is broken here due to printed page width.)

```
GET /DNSService/DNSLookupService.asmx/GetIPForHostname?strHostname
=www.oreilly.com HTTP/1.1
```

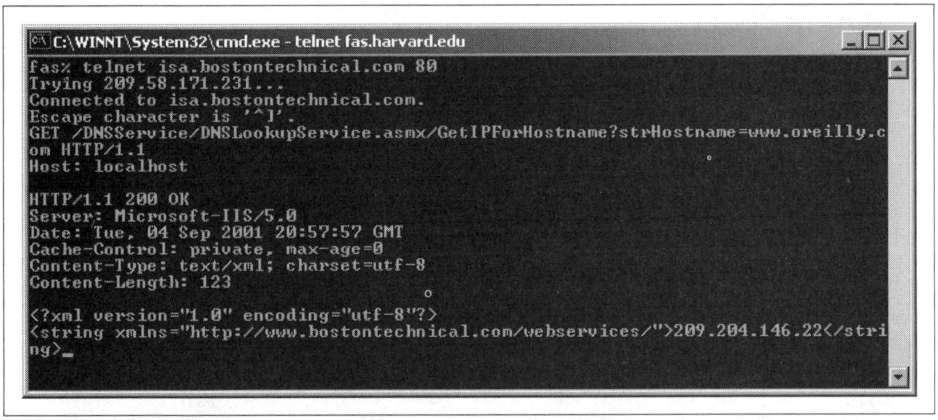

```
C:\WINNT\System32\cmd.exe - telnet fas.harvard.edu
fas% telnet isa.bostontechnical.com 80
Trying 209.58.171.231...
Connected to isa.bostontechnical.com.
Escape character is '^]'.
GET /DNSService/DNSLookupService.asmx/GetIPForHostname?strHostname=www.oreilly.c
om HTTP/1.1
Host: localhost

HTTP/1.1 200 OK
Server: Microsoft-IIS/5.0
Date: Tue, 04 Sep 2001 20:57:57 GMT
Cache-Control: private, max-age=0
Content-Type: text/xml; charset=utf-8
Content-Length: 123

<?xml version="1.0" encoding="utf-8"?>
<string xmlns="http://www.bostontechnical.com/webservices/">209.204.146.22</stri
ng>_
```

Figure 3-3. Telnet access to the DNSLookupService using HTTP GET

In this example, the HTTP/1.1 is supplied because we need to provide the web server with a host header. This additional text, which is not boldfaced in the code sample, is not part of the web service call and may not be necessary depending on your server's configuration. In addition, this example will work with HTTP 1.0, in which case you can leave out the host header information entirely.

Host Headers

Host headers are supported starting with version 1.1 of HTTP and provide a means for hosting multiple web sites at a single IP address. They are commonly used by ISPs for hosting hundreds of domains using only a few IP addresses.

In order to take advantage of host headers, you need to tell the web server that you're using HTTP 1.1. Do this by supplying the HTTP/1.1 after your HTTP GET request. Otherwise, the web service will assume version 1.0 and will not give you the opportunity to specify a host header.

You can see that we've passed the input hostname www.oreilly.com as the parameter called strHostname in the query string. Next we provide the host header information required by our server and press the Enter key twice to see the response:

```
Host: localhost
```

The response to our request begins with an HTTP 1.1 header telling us that the request was OK (code 200), followed by the XML response.

The response to our HTTP GET request is an XML document. In Figure 3-3, the Content-Type of the returned document is set to text/xml, with a character set of UTF-8. The XML response contains one element, string, which holds the result of the query.

Using HTTP POST

Accessing a web service using the HTTP POST method is similarly straightforward. Assuming that the service is set up to support HTTP POST requests, the only difference is that, with the POST method, request parameters are passed in a different part of the HTTP header called the entity body, the same part of the header that is used for passing form information, which is why the Content-Type must be set to application/x-www-form-urlencoded. Figure 3-4 is an example of a Telnet session that uses HTTP POST with the DNSLookupService.

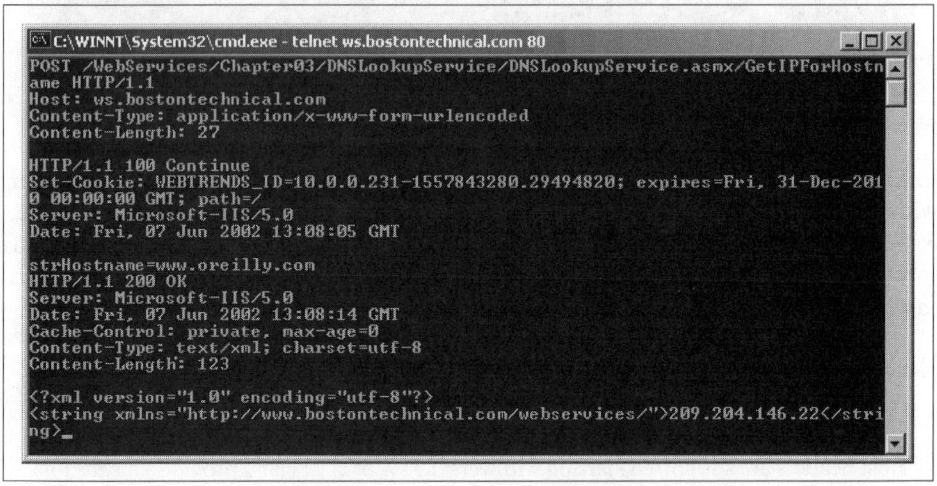

Figure 3-4. Telnet access to the DNSLookupService using HTTP POST

The session displayed in Figure 3-4 again begins with a Telnet command to port 80 of a web server called *ws.bostontechnical.com*:

```
C:\> telnet ws.bostontechnical.com 80
```

Once the session has been established, the POST verb is issued for the GetIPForHostname web method of the DNSLookupService web service. Notice that in this example no parameters are passed in the query string.

```
POST /WebServices/Chapter03/DNSLookupService/DNSLookupService.asmx/GetIPForHostname
HTTP 1.1
```

HTTP version 1.1 is also specified at the end of the command, as was done in the HTTP GET example, followed by the host header on the next line:

```
Host: ws.bostontechnical.com
```

The next two lines provide information about the encoding and length of the data we're POSTing, respectively. Unlike HTTP GET, where the content is part of the query string, the HTTP POST method sends the content separately after the HTTP header. Because the content is not part of the query string, we need to provide the web server with encoding and length information; otherwise, it won't know how to interpret the content or where the content ends and the next HTTP request begins. The next two lines specify this information. The content type of the request is set to application/x-www-form-urlencoded, which is the default encoding for forms submitted using HTTP POST. The content length is set to 27, the number of characters in the content we're sending, which is strHostname=www.oreilly.com.

```
Content-Type: application/x-www-form-urlencoded
Content-Length: 27
```

At this point, the appropriate header information has been provided and we're now ready to send the content. The end of the header information is signified by two carriage returns and results in an HTTP/1.1 100 Continue message from the web server:

```
HTTP/1.1 100 Continue
Set-Cookie: WEBTRENDS_ID=10.0.0.231-1557843280.29494820; expires=Fri, 31-Dec-201
0 00:00:00 GMT; path=/
Server: Microsoft-IIS/5.0
Date: Fri, 07 Jun 2002 13:08:05 GMT
```

Next the content is submitted:

```
strHostname=www.oreilly.com
```

The response is an HTTP header and XML document that contains the result of our method call, similar to the one seen in the HTTP GET example.

Using SOAP

SOAP is essentially a specialized version of HTTP POST that introduces some additional HTTP headers and abides by a special XML message format. Because SOAP runs over HTTP POST, you can access the DNSLookupService the same way you do with HTTP GET or POST. To call the GetIPForHostname web method using SOAP, telnet to the web service and send it the proper HTTP headers and SOAP message. The HTTP header for this example is as follows:

```
POST /WebServices/Chapter03/DNSLookupService/DNSLookupService.asmx HTTP/1.1
Host: localhost
Content-Type: text/xml; charset=utf-8
Content-Length: length
SOAPAction: "http://www.bostontechnical.com/webservices/GetIPForHostname"
```

The first two lines tell the web server that we're going to use the POST method to send data to the web service.

The third and fourth lines specify the type and length of the information we're going to post, just like the previous HTTP POST example. However, since SOAP messages follow XML formatting rules, we specify text/xml as the Content-Type rather than application/x-www-form-urlencode as was done in the HTTP POST example. The Content-Length field lets the web server know how much content to expect, which is the number of characters in the SOAP message including whitespace. If we set the Content-Length to a value smaller than the length of our SOAP message, only part of the message will be interpreted, resulting in an error. For this example, you can copy the SOAP message found when viewing the service using the IE test page, replacing the *string* placeholder argument with www.oreilly.com. The length of this message should be 296 characters, but it's a good idea to use a text editor such as Word to double-check that this is correct. You can cut and past the message into Word and select Tools → Word Count to get the number of characters including whitespace. This is the value you should use for Content-Length.

The last line of the header, SOAPAction, is specific to SOAP over HTTP and identifies the following text as a SOAP message. For our DNSLookupService example, the text of the SOAP request message is as follows:

```
<?xml version="1.0" encoding="utf-8"?>
<soap:Envelope xmlns:soap="http://schemas.xmlsoap.org/soap/envelope/">
  <soap:Body>
    <GetIPForHostname xmlns="http://www.bostontechnical.com/webservices/">
      <strHostname>www.oreilly.com</strHostname>
    </GetIPForHostname>
  </soap:Body>
</soap:Envelope>
```

The SOAP message is an XML document, the schema for which is defined at *http:// schemas.xmlsoap.org/soap/envelope/*. This book does not go into much detail on the SOAP schema, since it's not really necessary for .NET Web Service development;* however, as shown in the previous example, SOAP follows a hierarchical pattern. Drilling down to the soap:Body element, we see that it contains an element that corresponds to our web method's name (GetIPForHostname). This element contains another element, strHostname, which holds our parameter. It's easy to see the structure used to pass the parameter information.

Now telnet to the web server and post the header and SOAP message from the IE test page. You should get something similar to the following in return:

```
HTTP/1.1 200 OK
Server: Microsoft-IIS/5.0
Date: Wed, 05 Sep 2001 22:13:16 GMT
Connection: close
Cache-Control: private, max-age=0
Content-Type: text/xml; charset=utf-8
Content-Length: 446
<?xml version="1.0" encoding="utf-8"?>
<soap:Envelope xmlns:soap=http://schemas.xmlsoap.org/soap/envelope/
xmmlns:xsi=http://www.w3.org/2001/XMLSchema-instance
xmlns:xsd="http://www.w3.org/2001/XMLSchema">
  <soap:Body>
    <GetIPForHostnameResponse xmlns="http://www.bostontechnical.com/webservices/">
      <GetIPForHostnameResult>209.204.146.22</GetIPForHostnameResult>
```

---

* For more information, see *Programming Web Services with SOAP*, by Tidwell, Snell, and Kulchenko (O'Reilly, 2001).

```
    </GetIPForHostnameResponse>
  </soap:Body>
</soap:Envelope>
```

The response is a SOAP message containing the results of our call to GetIPForHostname.

SOAP provides a much more tailored solution to the problems associated with distributed method calls (more about this in the next section) and parameter passing than HTTP GET and POST, but translating each web method call to SOAP and then translating the results back to a native format is time-consuming and error-prone. To insulate the developer from part of this process, various groups (including Microsoft) have released SOAP SDKs, which are sets of objects or scripts that automate much of the grunt work of sending and interpreting SOAP messages.

The Microsoft SOAP Toolkit 2.0 is an API and a set of tools for creating web services and web service consumers using Visual Studio 6.0. Specifically, the Toolkit offers the following features:

- Both high-level and low-level COM interfaces for creating and reading SOAP messages
- A SOAP Message Object interface supporting document-schema–based message exchanges
- Support for WSDL 1.1 and a WSDL file generator
- A number of sample applications

With the .NET implementation of web services, Microsoft has gone one step further by taking care of all of the SOAP details for you. For the web service developer, .NET adds yet another layer of abstraction atop a SOAP API through the WebService and WebMethod directives discussed in Chapter 2. For the web service consumer, .NET provides similar abstraction through proxy classes and WSDL.

Comparing HTTP GET, HTTP POST, and SOAP

In the previous example, we were able to pass an argument to our web method and get an XML document returned as a result without using SOAP. At this point, you might be wondering why SOAP is at all necessary for web service communications if the HTTP GET and POST methods do the trick by themselves. Although the HTTP GET and POST methods have been used in many applications for the past decade, both suffer from serious drawbacks when used without SOAP.

First, in an HTTP GET call, the request parameters are appended to the URL as a sequence of key/value pairs that are part of the query string. Information passed as part of the query string is restricted to a certain maximum length by both web browsers and web servers. For browsers, this limit varies depending on the browser and operating system (IE supports a maximum of 2,048 characters, whereas Netscape's limit is an operating system–dependent number usually around the same). For web servers, this value also varies but is usually not more than 64K or 128K. This makes the HTTP GET request a poor candidate for use in web service systems that require the passing of large data sets. This restriction is also the primary reason HTTP GET is not commonly used as a transport for SOAP messages.

The HTTP POST method doesn't suffer from the same length limitations as GET; however, because POST was designed to support user fields on web forms, a POST request must pass its arguments as name/value pairs. This mechanism works well for passing simple data types associated with the elements on, say, an input form, but it was not designed to support complex data types. This is not to say that complex data types cannot be passed using HTTP POST, but because it is only a transport mechanism, HTTP POST does not define any semantics or rules that could be used to characterize the structure of the data it carries. When it comes to passing complex data using HTTP POST, you're the one responsible for defining how to represent that data and which type system to use. Suppose, for example, you wished to change the method signature of the web method GetHostnameForIP of the DNSLookupService in order to pass it an IP address as a series of 4 bytes. First, you would need to redefine the input argument; a struct would be an obvious choice:

```
public struct IPAddress
{
  public byte IPByte1,IPByte2,IPByte3,IPByte4;
  public IPAddress(byte a1, byte b1, byte c1, byte d1)
  {
    IPByte1 = a1;
    IPByte2 = b1;
    IPByte3 = c1;
    IPByte4 = d1;
  }
}
```

Once you've decided on a format for the input parameter, you need to modify the GetHostNameForIP method signature to accept an IPAddress type and also rewrite its logic. The following is the revised code:

```
[WebMethod]
public string GetHostnameForIP(IP IPAddress)
{
  string strAddress = IPAddress.IPByte1.ToString() + "." +
      IPAddress.IPByte2.ToString() + "." +
      IPAddress.IPByte3.ToString() + "." +
      IPAddress.IPByte4.ToString();
  IPHostEntry hostInfo = Dns.GetHostByAddress(strAddress);
  return hostInfo.HostName.ToString();
}
```

Now that you've rewritten the DNSLookupService, you need to specify a way to send an IPAddress from client to server as part of the POST message. You may think that something like XML would be a good choice for this process. In XML, we might represent an `IPAddress` in the following manner.

```
<ipaddress>
  <IPByte1>unsignedByte</IPByte1>
  <IPByte2>unsignedByte</IPByte2>
  <IPByte3>unsignedByte</IPByte3>
  <IPByte4>unsignedByte</IPByte4>
</ipaddress>
```

Now we can pass this XML message to the server using HTTP POST as we would any other simple type.

At first glance, the use of XML as a data representation format seems to solve the problem of representing complex data; it does solve a good part of it, but this increased flexibility also brings an entirely new set of potential problems related to interoperability. For example, XML can be used to implement a variety of type systems and encoding styles. Which definition of an `unsignedByte` data type should the destination presume we used? If we need to pass multiple complex data types, should we send them as separate messages in separate name/value pairs or should we use one message containing both types? It's probably better to send one message to reduce overhead, but then how do we organize it? Now we begin to see that passing a more complex type such as this `IPAddress` becomes difficult to do using HTTP POST alone, because in order for the source and destination to be able to understand how to interpret the data, they must first agree upon some rules related to its structure. Furthermore, as we start to use XML as a format for passing complex data types in a distributed computing system, other issues (such as state and transaction management, security, and error management) arise. These problems are not new—for years, separate development groups in many companies have been spending a great deal of time designing their own custom in-house solutions to address these problems. Unfortunately, a lack of collaboration between groups means that none of these systems can interoperate.

This is where SOAP comes in handy. SOAP is a protocol that codifies the process of sending XML documents over HTTP (or any other transport protocol for that matter). It also introduces rules that solve the problem of distributed method calls across heterogeneous systems, such as an XML vocabulary for parameters and return values and rules for exception handling. SOAP alone does not solve all of the problems listed earlier. For example, the SOAP specification does nothing to address issues such as transaction management and security (although other specifications—such as WS-Security, WSTx, etc.—tackle these issues). But most developers agree that the SOAP specification constitutes a step in the right direction. Overall, SOAP is a protocol designed specifically to address the types of problems that result from making distributed method calls over the Internet.

Two other reasons for choosing SOAP over HTTP are interoperability and security. While most non-Microsoft web service development tools support some version of

SOAP, not all of them support HTTP GET or POST for web service communication. For example if you want your ASP.NET web service to interact with SOAP::Lite or Apache Axis (the successor to Apache SOAP), which are two of the more popular kits for developing web services, HTTP GET is not an option since neither supports it. Furthermore, using HTTP GET for web service communication can result in security problems. This vulnerability occurs because web browsers like Internet Explorer also use HTTP GET and POST for communication, and users could therefore be "tricked" into executing web services by clicking a link on a site that has been set up by a malicious user. Consider the following example of ASP code adapted from a Microsoft security alert:

```
<%
Response.Redirect "http://intranetserver/401K.asmx/ChangeWithholding" & _
                  "?PreTax=0&PostTax=0"
%>
```

With a properly crafted redirect, this link could cause a user to unwittingly execute an HTTP GET–enabled web service on his local intranet. Because of this potential vulnerability, Microsoft has gone so far as to issue a security recommendation for disabling the HTTP GET and HTTP POST access methods in production web services (*http://msdn.microsoft.com/library/en-us/dnnetsec/html/dishtt.asp*). Since SOAP messages require special formatting, this type of attack is not possible on a web service supporting only SOAP, making SOAP a much better alternative. Realistically, this specific attack may be somewhat far-fetched, but it shows some of the potential for problems when using HTTP GET or POST.

Exposing Web Services: WSDL

While SOAP provides a communication or message protocol for calling remote methods and passing complex data types, the Web Service Description Language specification, or WSDL, provides a means to expose the details of how to interact with the service and its methods. These details include information about the communication protocols supported, methods exposed, data types involved, and location of the service. In this manner, the SOAP and WSDL standards work together to provide a means of accessing remote objects or functions across the Web. WSDL gives us a standard way to programmatically learn about a web service interface and allows us to use automatic proxy-generating tools to easily consume a web service without having to get involved in the SOAP messaging you saw in the last example. SOAP, using XML as its language and HTTP as its transport protocol, gives us a standard mechanism for this interaction. It is true that a web service may not support SOAP—and if that were the case this information would be part of the WSDL document—however, for the majority of web service applications, SOAP is the standard, and we will use it as the default access method through the rest of this book.

REST

SOAP/HTTP is the most popular model for creating web services, but it's not the only one available. Another model, called REpresentational State Transfer (REST) recently spurred some interest when Amazon.com chose it as a web services model over the more common SOAP/HTTP.

REST tries to simplify the process of distributed computing. It is a communication model that is based on the paradigm of using a small set of verbs (e.g., the GET, POST, and DELETE verbs that are already part of the HTTP specification) to act on a potentially infinite set of nouns (which are URIs). For example, every time you enter a URL into your browser, you're using the HTTP GET verb to retrieve the contents of the URL you specify. This is the basic idea behind REST, except that with REST the data returned is XML. So you can see that REST is really all about HTTP verbs acting on the URIs of XML data. One big advantage to this type of system is that HTTP and URIs are in use all over the web today, supported by every web server in existence. Another advantage is that there's no need for advanced coordination to interact using HTTP and URIs—you can make an HTTP GET request to any active URI and you know you'll get a response. In theory, this provides for scalability since every node in a REST system is not required to "learn" a new interface for every other node, as is the case with a system based on SOAP/HTTP. We say "in theory" because issues such as security can cause this truth to break.

Whether REST is more suitable than SOAP/HTTP as a distributed computing model is the subject of some debate. At this point the outcome of that debate remains to be seen, but one thing is clear: SOAP/HTTP is much further along than REST in tackling issues like message security, state management, asynchronous transactions, and so on. Many proponents of REST feel that it is a more natural model for distributed computing, but without some enhancements and significant industry backing, it will be difficult for REST to compete.

Web services developers are not required to provide WSDL documents since, as you saw in the message exchange section, WSDL is not necessary to use web services. In fact, many web services don't have associated WSDL documents. A quick search through some of the web services found in web services directories such as the Xmethods directory (*http://www.xmethods.com/*) shows that many web services do not have associated WSDL documents (.NET conveniently creates a WSDL document automatically). But support for WSDL is found in virtually all of the major web service development packages, and that support is growing monthly.

The WSDL specification was created jointly by Microsoft and IBM and was submitted to the W3 Consortium in March of 2001 as a suggestion. The suggestion has not yet been endorsed by the W3C, but many feel that its current widespread use makes it a good candidate for reaching recommendation status.

The W3C Specification Approval Process

There are several steps in the W3C specification approval process:

- W3C receives a Submission.
- W3C publishes a Note.
- W3C creates a Working Group.
- Working Group creates a Working Draft.
- W3C publishes a Candidate Recommendation.
- W3C publishes a Proposed Recommendation.
- W3C publishes a Recommendation.

The approval process can take several years. The WSDL specification is currently a W3C Note. A good summary of this process is available at *http://www.w3schools.com/w3c/w3c_process.asp*.

WSDL is an attempt to create a standardized way to describe the interfaces exposed by web services. Some of the goals of the WSDL specification are as follows:

- Provide a structured means for describing the web methods, data types, location, and binding information (protocols and message formats supported) that make up a web service
- Support arbitrary messaging formats and network protocols (HTTP GET, SOAP, etc.)
- Facilitate the automatic generation of proxy code, which we'll discuss shortly

You saw an example of the first goal when you added descriptions and namespace associations to our web service in Chapter 2. Any modifications made to our service using the WebService and WebMethod directives were automatically propagated to the WSDL document by .NET.

We also talked about how the wire protocol support for web services is extensible, allowing us to use protocols such as SOAP over HTTP as well as any other transport protocol we might desire to use. A web service's protocol support is declared in its associated WSDL document through a list of bindings. This particular concept of a binding (within the context of web services) is defined by the WSDL specification and is the source of this network protocol extensibility.

The third goal—enabling the automatic creation of proxy code—is something that we discuss in this chapter. As you'll see in the following section, the .NET web service communication model makes use of a proxy for communication between client and service. This proxy is created based on the information contained in the WSDL document. Furthermore, because this information is stored in XML format, it can be easily manipulated programmatically.

WSDL Elements

A WSDL document has six major elements: definitions, types, message, portType, binding, and service. There are two other new elements called port and operation. These eight elements together constitute the complete definition of the web service and—as you'll see—they're all closely linked. Four of the elements—types, message, portType, and operation—collectively make up the abstract part of the WSDL called the Service Interface Definition. These elements describe the service in a general manner but don't say anything about how or where to find an instance of the service. Three other elements—service, port, and binding—make up the concrete portion of the service definition and are called the Service Implementation Definition. These three elements specify the information needed to access an instance of the given service. The abstract and concrete portions of the document are linked by the binding element. Let's take a closer look at each of these eight elements and then you can continue creating a consumer application:

Definitions

> The definitions element must be the root element of a WSDL document. It optionally declares the name of the web service, declares the namespaces used to define the elements found throughout the remainder of the document, and acts as the container for the service elements of the WSDL document.

Types

> The types element declares custom type definitions for the data types used by the service. Our example uses XML Schema notation, which, while not mandatory (other type systems may be added via extensibility elements), is the most widely used. This means that the types element is just an embedded XML Schema in which the complex data types used in the message section are defined. When using SOAP, typically, each of the methods of the web service has two types: one named according to the web method name used to define any input parameters and one named similarly but with Response appended to it, used to define any returned data. If a web method uses the same argument for both input and output, the argument appears in both sections. In the previous example, the input and output parameters to our GetIPForHostname web method are declared as complex types (named GetIPForHostname and GetIPForHostname-Response) containing primitive string types. These custom defined types are used later on in the document.

Message

> The message element is an abstract type definition for all messages communicated by the service. A WSDL document contains a list and definition of all of the messages the web service is capable of sending and receiving. Our example web service consists of one web method that takes an input request and returns output data. This communication involves two SOAP messages, GetIPFor-HostnameSoapIn and GetIPForHostnameSoapOut, which are defined in the message

sections. For simplicity, we've removed = references to the two other protocols that are automatically supported by .NET, HTTP GET, and POST. The full WSDL document includes a set of message elements for each supported protocol. In the full version of our example, there are six message elements: three sets (one for each protocol, HTTP GET, HTTP POST, and SOAP) and two messages (one for each message, input, and output) for a total of six message elements.

Operation

The operation element is a description of a web method in terms of the messages that are sent and received. There will be one operation for each web method/message format (e.g., SOAP, GET, POST). In our example, there is only one operation exposed—our web method GetIPForHostname. Other types of operations might involve getting or setting properties. Because our operation involves two messages, one to pass the request and another to return the response, the operation can be defined in terms of these two messages. If we look at the example web method, we see that the operation element within the portType element is defined in terms of the two previously defined messages in elements called input and output.

Port type

A portType element is just a grouping of operations. The portType element says nothing explicit about the message format (e.g., SOAP, GET, etc.) used by the operations (that's left to the binding element), but since the messages and types that make up an operation will typically differ depending on the message format, there will be a different portType element for each set of operations supported by the service. In our example, we included only one of three portType elements, the SOAP portType, for simplicity. Because our example contains only one operation—our web method—the portType element contains only one operation. If our web service exposed multiple methods, there would be an operation listed for each of them.

Binding

The binding element describes the transport protocols, message formats, and message styles supported by a given web service. Because a web service can support multiple transport protocols and message formats, the WSDL document can contain multiple binding elements. Our example displays the SOAP binding called DNSLookupServiceSOAP. Because SOAP supports two common message styles, document-style and RPC, the binding element also must specify the appropriate one. By default, all .NET web service applications are set up to support document-style SOAP message formats. The binding element is used to match this specific message format and style to an abstract portType element. In this way, we bridge the gap between conceptual web services and the concrete details (protocol and format) of a particular implementation.

Port

As the binding element defines the protocol and message format for an implementation of the web service, a port maps a binding to a network location. In our example, the port element, which is a child of the service element, associates the URL of our service (*http://localhost/DNSService/DNSLookupService. asmx*) to a binding. The binding and network address together are known as an *endpoint*.

Service

The service element defines the address for invoking the specified service. Most commonly, this includes the URL for invoking the web service.

Deconstructing a WSDL Document

The rules and descriptions of WSDL documents are codified by an XML grammar that is outlined by a W3C XML Schema Definition (XSD) schema defined at *http:// www.w3.org/TR/wsdl*. The purpose of this schema is to describe the format of a WSDL document.

An example of a WSDL document is the one that is autogenerated by .NET for the DNSLookupService we created in the first chapter. That WSDL is displayed here as Example 3-1 (slightly abbreviated for clarity).

Example 3-1. WSDL document (edited) for DNSLookupService

```
<?xml version="1.0" encoding="utf-8" ?>
  <definitions xmlns:s=http://www.w3.org/2001/XMLSchema
  xmlns:http=http://schemas.xmlsoap.org/wsdl/http/
  xmlns:mime=http://schemas.xmlsoap.org/wsdl/mime/
  xmlns:tm=http://microsoft.com/wsdl/mime/textMatching/
  xmlns:soap=http://schemas.xmlsoap.org/wsdl/soap/
  xmlns:soapenc=http://schemas.xmlsoap.org/soap/encoding/
  xmlns:s0=http://www.bostontechnical.com/webservices/
  targetNamespace=http://www.bostontechnical.com/webservices/
  xmlns:wsdl="http://schemas.xmlsoap.org/wsdl/">

<wsdl:types>
    <s:schema attributeFormDefault="qualified" elementFormDefault="qualified"
    targetNamespace="http://www.bostontechnical.com/webservices/">
      <s:element name="GetIPForHostname">
        <s:complexType>
          <s:sequence>
            <s:element minOccurs="1" maxOccurs="1" name="strHostname"
            nillable="true" type="s:string" />
          </s:sequence>
        </s:complexType>
      </s:element>
      <s:element name="GetIPForHostnameResponse">
        <s:complexType>
          <s:sequence>
```

Example 3-1. WSDL document (edited) for DNSLookupService (continued)

```
          <s:element minOccurs="1" maxOccurs="1" name="GetIPForHostnameResult"
          nillable="true" type="s:string" />
        </s:sequence>
      </s:complexType>
    </s:element>
  </s:schema>
</wsdl:types>

<wsdl:message name="GetIPForHostnameSoapIn">
  <wsdl:part name="parameters" element="s0:GetIPForHostname" />
</wsdl:message>
<wsdl:message name="GetIPForHostnameSoapOut">
  <wsdl:part name="parameters" element="s0:GetIPForHostnameResponse" />
</wsdl:message>

<wsdl:portType name="DNSLookupServiceSoap">
  <wsdl:operation name="GetIPForHostname">
    <wsdl:input message="s0:GetIPForHostnameSoapIn" />
    <wsdl:output message="s0:GetIPForHostnameSoapOut" />
  </wsdl:operation>
</wsdl:portType>

<wsdl:binding name="DNSLookupServiceSoap" type="s0:DNSLookupServiceSoap">
  <soap:binding transport=http://schemas.xmlsoap.org/soap/http
  style="document"/>
  <wsdl:operation name="GetIPForHostname">
    <soap:operation
    soapAction=http://www.bostontechnical.com/webservices/GetIPForHostname
    style="document" />
    <wsdl:input>
      <soap:body use="literal" />
    <wsdl:/input>
    <wsdl:output>
      <soap:body use="literal" />
    <wsdl:/output>
  </wsdl:operation>
</wsdl:binding>

<wsdl:service name="DNSLookupService">
  <wsdl:documentation><b>A Web Service which performs Domain Name
  Lookups.</b>
  </wsdl:documentation>
  <wsdl:port name="DNSLookupServiceSoap" binding="s0:DNSLookupServiceSoap">
    <wsdl:soap:address location="http://localhost/DNSService/DNSLookupService.asmx" />
  </wsdl:port>
</wsdl:service>
</wsdl:definitions>
```

Several elements have been excluded for simplicity, most notably the binding elements for non-SOAP protocols such as HTTP GET and POST, as well as their port type protocols. In addition, we've added extra spacing and indentation for clarity.

The document starts with a definitions element that aliases the various schema references employed in the document to abbreviations (e.g., xmlns:http=http:// schemas.xmlsoap.org/wsdl/http).

```
<?xml version="1.0" encoding="utf-8" ?>
<definitions xmlns:s=http://www.w3.org/2001/XMLSchema
xmlns:http=http://schemas.xmlsoap.org/wsdl/http/
xmlns:mime=http://schemas.xmlsoap.org/wsdl/mime/
xmlns:tm=http://microsoft.com/wsdl/mime/textMatching/
xmlns:soap=http://schemas.xmlsoap.org/wsdl/soap/
xmlns:soapenc=http://schemas.xmlsoap.org/soap/encoding/
xmlns:s0=http://www.bostontechnical.com/webservices/
targetNamespace=http://www.bostontechnical.com/webservices/
xmlns:wsdl="http://schemas.xmlsoap.org/wsdl/">
```

Next, the wsdl:types element contains schema for the GetIPForHostname and GetIPForHostnameResponse types, which are used later in the document as part of the request and response messages. You can see that each of these types is defined in terms of a complex type wrapping a string type. This makes sense since both the input and output of the web method in our DNSLookupService example are of type string.

```
<wsdl:types>
  <s:schema attributeFormDefault="qualified" elementFormDefault="qualified"
  targetNamespace="http://www.bostontechnical.com/webservices/">
    <s:element name="GetIPForHostname">
      <s:complexType>
        <s:sequence>
          <s:element minOccurs="1" maxOccurs="1" name="strHostname"
          nillable="true" type="s:string" />
        </s:sequence>
      </s:complexType>
    </s:element>
    <s:element name="GetIPForHostnameResponse">
      <s:complexType>
        <s:sequence>
          <s:element minOccurs="1" maxOccurs="1" name="GetIPForHostnameResult"
          nillable="true" type="s:string" />
        </s:sequence>
      </s:complexType>
    </s:element>
  </s:schema>
</wsdl:types>
```

Each of the wsdl:message elements that follow describes a one-way message. The service contains one web method that takes a string as an argument and returns a string as output. This constitutes two one-way messages, which is why there are two elements. Each message element contains a wsdl:part element that describes the message parameters and return values in terms of the types defined in the wsdl:types element.

```
<wsdl:message name="GetIPForHostnameSoapIn">
  <wsdl:part name="parameters" element="s0:GetIPForHostname" />
```

```
    </wsdl:message>
    <wsdl:message name="GetIPForHostnameSoapOut">
      <wsdl:part name="parameters" element="s0:GetIPForHostnameResponse" />
    </wsdl:message>
```

The `wsdl:portType` element combines the one-way messages into operations. You can see that the GetIPForHostname web method is described as a `wsdl:operation`, consisting of a parameter and return value—`wsdl:input` and `wsdl:output` messages, respectively.

```
    <wsdl:portType name="DNSLookupServiceSoap">
      <wsdl:operation name="GetIPForHostname">
        <wsdl:input message="s0:GetIPForHostnameSoapIn" />
        <wsdl:output message="s0:GetIPForHostnameSoapOut" />
      </wsdl:operation>
    </wsdl:portType>
```

The `wsdl:binding` element describes the concrete details of how the service messages should be implemented (e.g., SOAP, HTTP GET, HTTP POST). This service uses SOAP, so the `wsdl:binding` element includes SOAP bindings.

```
    <wsdl:binding name="DNSLookupServiceSoap" type="s0:DNSLookupServiceSoap">
      <soap:binding transport=http://schemas.xmlsoap.org/soap/http
      style="document"/>
      <wsdl:operation name="GetIPForHostname">
        <soap:operation
        soapAction=http://www.bostontechnical.com/webservices/GetIPForHostname
        style="document" />
        <wsdl:input>
          <soap:body use="literal" />
        <wsdl:/input>
        <wsdl:output>
          <soap:body use="literal" />
        <wsdl:/output>
      </wsdl:operation>
    </wsdl:binding>
```

Finally, the `wsdl:service` element defines the address for invoking the service, which in this case is the URL of the *.asmx* page implementing the service:

```
    <wsdl:service name="DNSLookupService">
      <wsdl:documentation><b>A Web Service which performs Domain Name
      Lookups.</b>
      </wsdl:documentation>
      <wsdl:port name="DNSLookupServiceSoap" binding="s0:DNSLookupServiceSoap">
        <wsdl:soap:address location="http://localhost/DNSService/
            DNSLookupService.asmx" />
      </wsdl:port>
    </wsdl:service>
  </wsdl:definitions>
```

Several elements have been excluded for simplicity, most notably the `binding` elements for non-SOAP protocols such as HTTP GET and POST, as well as their port type protocols. In addition, we've added extra spacing and indentation for clarity.

A service is a collection of related endpoints. In our example, the service element contains a set of port elements (remember, port = endpoint) that are all part of the same web service (our example has only one endpoint for simplicity). Figure 3-5 displays the relationships between the seven elements of the WSDL document. Note

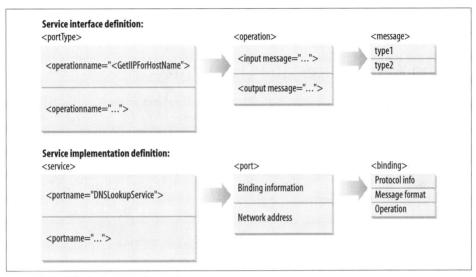

Figure 3-5. WSDL element relationships

that the contents of the <types> element appear within the <message> element.

As we mentioned earlier, the WSDL elements can be broken out into a service interface definition and a service implementation definition. The interface definition contains the abstract elements of the WSDL document (i.e., portType, operation, message, types) that are used to describe the service in a general manner—it defines the service's interface.

The implementation definition elements are used to define an instance of this abstract service definition. The implementation definition contains information regarding a specific implementation or example of this service (i.e., service, port, binding).

Another useful element not displayed in Figure 3-5 is the import element, which is used within a WSDL document to import other WSDL documents or XML Schemas. The import element is commonly used in situations in which one party has defined the service interface and another has defined the implementation. For example, the members of a standards body or trade organization might work together to define the service interface for a given operation, say credit card processing. Once the service interface had been agreed upon, each of the members can implement its own service and create a WSDL document containing its own service implementation and a reference (using import) to the service interface created by the group. There would be one abstract service definition and many implementations referencing that abstract definition. This is part of what UDDI is all about, and we'll explore it more in Chapter 10.

In the next section, we'll explain proxy classes, and then we'll move on to use what we've learned to create a proxy class for our DNSLookupService.

Calling Web Services: the Client Proxy

The .NET web service consumer model makes use of client *proxies*, .NET types that encapsulate for a client the process of making SOAP calls to the web service. A proxy class for a given service is typically created from its WSDL document. Once this proxy class has been created, all you need to do is reference it in your project as you would any other assembly or COM object. All calls to the web service are then handled through an instance of the proxy object, which takes care of the SOAP conversation with the server. The process is shown in Figure 3-6.

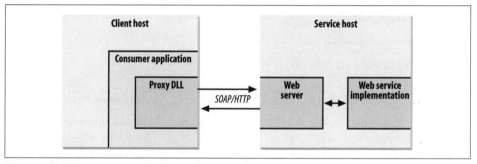

Figure 3-6. Calling a web service through a proxy class

The process shown in Figure 3-6 begins when the consumer application on the client instantiates an instance of the proxy object and performs method calls, passing it native .NET types and classes as it would with any other class. The proxy object then converts the native .NET type to an XML format and performs the remote method call to the web method on the server using SOAP. The SOAP message is transmitted over HTTP, received by the web server, and then dispatched to the appropriate ASP. NET web service.

 Any server platform and web service implementation is allowed as long as it supports the same SOAP—and WSDL for automatic proxy creation) specification—e.g., SOAP::Lite, Apache SOAP, .NET, or the client).

The web service then converts the SOAP message into a native type, performs the necessary processing, and returns the results to the proxy, again converted into an XML/SOAP format. The proxy deserializes the SOAP message to a .NET type and returns this type as the result of the initial method call. By operating in this fashion, the proxy DLL hides all of the implementation details of the underlying SOAP calls.

The process described here is idealized to some extent because it assumes that there are no interoperability issues between the client and server. In reality, this is often not the case, because different SOAP implementations such as Apache Axis and SOAP::Lite have minor differences in the way they implement the SOAP specification. These differences are a result of the SOAP specification being somewhat vague in some areas, and the people creating SOAP servers have had to make design decisions on their own. In some cases, this has led to interoperability problems between different implementations. These variations in implementation can mean the difference between a properly functioning system and days spent popping Advil. We'll discuss interoperability at greater length in Chapter 11.

The .NET classes needed to create a web service proxy are located in the System.Web. Services namespace, as we'll see a bit later. For most simple web services, the creation of a proxy class is fairly straightforward; however, the .NET platform ships with special tools that completely automate this process. Users of Visual Studio .NET can take advantage of this process by using the Add Web Reference option on the Project menu. Alternatively, you can use a utility called *wsdl.exe*, discussed later in this chapter, to generate the source code for your proxy class. You can then compile the proxy as you would any other class and add it to your project. This *wsdl.exe* utility uses a WSDL document (explained in the previous section) to automatically create the proxy.

Creating a Client Proxy

Visual Studio .NET makes the process of accessing a web service easy. Web service access is done through a proxy stub that is automatically created for you by the Add Web Reference feature of the Visual Studio .NET IDE. Add Web Reference feature. This automation makes working with web services through proxies as straightforward as working with other local assemblies.

Using VS.NET

To illustrate proxy creation, let's create a new project in VS.NET. For this example, we'll use the C# Console Application template to create a new project that makes use of our DNSLookupService. VS.NET automatically includes the skeleton code and references necessary to compile a basic console application.

The Add Web Reference option is listed under the Project tab in Visual Studio .NET. Once you select this option, you'll get a window prompting you to enter the address of the web service you want to reference. You can enter the address of any .*asmx* page, valid WSDL document, or DISCO file; if VS.NET is able to correctly parse it, the Add Reference button on the bottom-right part of the screen becomes active, allowing you to add this service as a web reference. You'll also see links to two web service directories, the Microsoft UDDI Directory and the Microsoft Test UDDI Directory. (UDDI, which stands for Universal Description Discovery and Integration, is a project supported by several industry heavyweights such as Microsoft, IBM, and HP, and involves creating a directory of web services. We'll talk more about UDDI and web service discovery using DISCO in Chapter 10.)

Entering the URL of the web service we created in the previous chapter brings up the screen shown in Figure 3-7.

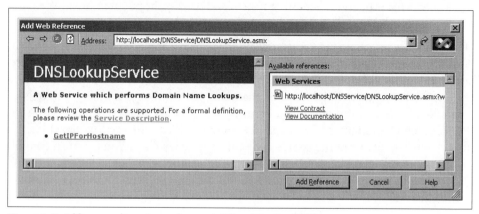

Figure 3-7. Adding a web services reference in Visual Studio .NET

In the left pane of this screen is the IE test page discussed in the previous chapter. The right pane shows a list of available references. Since our web method is available, the Add Reference button is enabled; otherwise, it would be grayed out. If we add our DNSLookupService as a web reference, VS.NET adds a Web References folder with the new web reference entry to our project beneath the References folder, as shown in Figure 3-8.

The new web reference to DNSLookupService has been added and assigned the server name (localhost) specified in a previous step. (This name can be easily changed by right-clicking on the Web References entry.) Notice that two files with a .*wsdl* and .*disco* extension have been added under the *localhost* reference entry as well. The .*wsdl* file is a copy of the service description that was created automatically by .NET when we created our service. .NET uses this file to generate the proxy object and its associated properties and methods. The .*disco* file contains additional information about the location and schemas associated with the service description.

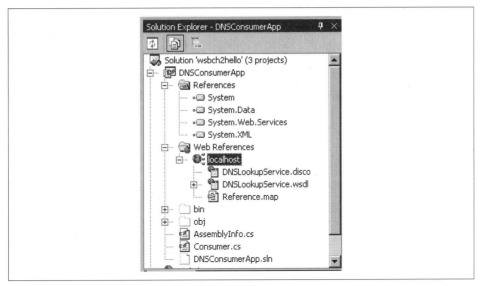

Figure 3-8. The web reference in the Solution Explorer

Now that the reference has been added, we have access to it in our code as we would any other local assembly or COM object. Example 3-2 uses DNSLookupService to look up IP addresses for hostnames.

Example 3-2. Consuming a web service using a web reference

```
using System;
namespace DNSConsumerApp
{
  class Consumer
  {
    static void Main(string[] args)
    {
      localhost.DNSLookupService objDNS = new localhost.DNSLookupService();
      string strIPAddress = "";
      strIPAddress = objDNS.GetIPForHostname(args[0]);
      Console.WriteLine("Hostname: " + args[0] + " IP Address: " + strIPAddress);
    }
  }
}
```

You can compile DNSConsumerApp and run it from the command line by typing:

> DNSConsumerApp *www.yahoo.com*

Figure 3-9 displays its output.

Using wsdl.exe

There are many reasons why you might not want or be able to use Visual Studio . NET for developing .NET applications. Perhaps you have another favorite IDE that

Figure 3-9. Running DNSConsumerApp.exe

you're used to using instead, or perhaps you just don't want to shell out the dough for a Visual Studio .NET license. In Chapter 2 we noted that you don't need Visual Studio .NET to create ASP.NET web services, and the same goes for creating .NET applications that use web services. In this section, you'll learn how to use the *wsdl. exe* tool that comes with the .NET SDK to generate .NET proxy source code and the *csc.exe* compiler to create proxy assemblies.

The *wsdl.exe* tool is part of the .NET SDK and is located in the *[Install Dir]\ Microsoft.NET\FrameworkSDK\Bin* directory. Given the URL of a service description document (WSDL document), the *wsdl.exe* utility automatically generates source code that can be compiled into a proxy DLL. The source WSDL does not have to be WSDL generated by .NET—any properly formed WSDL should work. In addition, if you don't append *?WSDL* to the *.asmx* filename, the utility is smart enough to process the file correctly, but it's important to remember that *wsdl.exe* uses the WSDL file to create the proxy class and not the service itself.

To generate proxy source code for accessing our DNSLookupService using *wsdl.exe*, issue the following command all on one line (don't forget to add the location of the utility to your PATH statement first):

```
wsdl.exe /language:cs /namespace:DNSConsumerApp /out:DNSLookupServiceProxy.csc http:/
/localhost/DNSService/DNSLookupService.asmx?WSDL
```

This command tells the *wsdl.exe* utility to compile the WSDL file located on our server. Going in reverse order, we've also specified the name of the output file, *Proxy.csc*, to which *wsdl.exe* should write, along with a namespace that should be used. Finally, the command also specifies that the language should be C#. Valid language options are: cs (C#—default), vb (VB.NET), and js (JScript.NET).

Example 3-3 is the C# source code that *wsdl.exe* generates for the DNSLookupService consumer proxy. Class names have been abbreviated for clarity (e.g., System.Web. Services.Protocols.SoapHttpClientProtocol is displayed as SoapHttpClientProtocol).

Example 3-3. C# source code generated by wsdl.exe for DNSLookupService proxy

```
namespace DNSConsumerApp {
    using System.Diagnostics;
    using System.Xml.Serialization;
    using System;
    using System.Web.Services.Protocols;
```

```
using System.Web.Services;


[System.Web.Services.WebServiceBindingAttribute(Name="DNSLookupServiceSoap",
Namespace="http://www.bostontechnical.com/webservices/")]
public class DNSLookupService : SoapHttpClientProtocol {

    public DNSLookupService() {
        this.Url = "http://localhost/DNSService/DNSLookupService.asmx";
    }
    [SoapDocumentMethodAttribute("http://www.bostontechnical.com/webservices/
GetIPForHostname", RequestNamespace="http://www.bostontechnical.com/webservices/",
ResponseNamespace="http://www.bostontechnical.com/webservices/", Use=System.Web.Services.
Description.SoapBindingUse.Literal, ParameterStyle=System.Web.Services.Protocols.
SoapParameterStyle.Wrapped)]
    public string GetIPForHostname(string strHostname) {
        object[] results = this.Invoke("GetIPForHostname", new object[] {
                    strHostname});
        return ((string)(results[0]));
    }

    public System.IAsyncResult BeginGetIPForHostname
    (string strHostname, System.AsyncCallback callback, object asyncState) {
        return this.BeginInvoke("GetIPForHostname", new object[] {
                    strHostname}, callback, asyncState);
    }

    public string EndGetIPForHostname(System.IAsyncResult asyncResult) {
        object[] results = this.EndInvoke(asyncResult);
        return ((string)(results[0]));
    }
  }
}
```

Looking beyond the various attributes and metadata, the source file also contains one class called DNSLookupService, which is part of the DNSConsumerApp namespace. In addition to the constructor method, this class contains three additional methods: GetIPForHostname, BeginGetIPForHostname, and EndGetIPForHostname. One of the methods, GetIPForHostname, exposes synchronous access to the proxy just like any ordinary method. Most of our examples makes use of synchronous methods that don't require callbacks, such as this one. The other two methods, BeginGetIPForHostname and EndGetIPForHostname, are used in conjunction by consumers that require asynchronous access to the web service proxy. It's important to realize that the synchronous and asynchronous methods of the proxy use virtually the same underlying mechanism to communicate with the remote web service. This is done through a method called invoke that you can see in the preceding GetIPForHostname method. The difference between the synchronous and asynchronous call methods is in the way the client code interacts with the proxy, not in the way the proxy interacts with the web service. Regardless of which call method you use, a proxy that uses SOAP over HTTP will always communicate with the remote web service synchronously. This is to say that the proxy cannot register a callback with the web service. (We'll discuss synchronous versus asynchronous access in detail in Chapter 5, but for now we're primarily concerned with synchronous access.)

The line preceding our class definition is called a *binding declaration*. The service contract (WSDL) for our DNSLookupService supports three types of access methods: SOAP, HTTP GET, and HTTP POST. These protocols are listed as bindings in the WSDL document in the following form:

```
<binding name="DNSLookupServiceSoap" type="s0:DNSLookupServiceSoap" />
<binding name="DNSLookupServiceHttpGet" type="s0:DNSLookupServiceHttpGet" />
<binding name="DNSLookupServiceHttpPost" type="s0:DNSLookupServiceHttpPost" />
```

The binding declaration identifies the particular binding our proxy class will use. Our proxy class is using the DNSLookupServiceSoap binding, which, unsurprisingly, uses SOAP as the transport protocol. A proxy class must support one or more bindings.

All proxy classes must also inherit from System.Web.Services.Protocols. WebClientProtocol or a derivative thereof. Our proxy class inherits from SoapHttpClientProtocol, which is a grandchild of WebClientProtocol. As you might imagine, the SoapHttpClientProtocol class includes logic specific to classes that make calls over SOAP, such as ours. If our class were to use a non-SOAP binding such as HttpGet, it would inherit from a different communication class.

We'll discuss some of the other attributes as we go through the examples, particularly when we talk about web service interoperability. For now, let's go ahead and compile the proxy class.

Compile the proxy source code to an assembly, using the *csc.exe* compiler discussed in Chapter 2. For the example, compile it to an assembly named *DNSLookupProxy. dll*. Use the following command:

```
csc.exe /t:library /out:DNSLookupProxy.dll Proxy.csc
```

This command creates a proxy DLL that you can then use in any of your .NET applications (regardless of whether they're written in C#, VB.Net, Jscript.NET, etc.) by referencing it just as you would any other assembly. This includes console applications, windows applications, windows services, ASP.NET applications, and so on. If you want to use it in an ASP.NET application, all you have to do is place it in the \bin directory of the application or the global assembly cache (however, the global assembly cache is not recommended). The proxy takes care of all the necessary SOAP marshaling necessary for communication with the web service. It is important to realize that, should the underlying web service interface change, it will break our proxy DLL, requiring us to recompile.

The *wsdl.exe* utility provides several configurable command-line options or switches. While you'll probably never need most of them, it's still good to know what options are available. The format for using the utility is:

```
wsdl [options] {URL | path}
```

The utility takes an input document as either a URL or a path on the local machine or shared network. This document can be a *.wsdl*, *.xsd*, or *.disco* document (the latter two will be discussed in Chapter 4 and Chapter 10, respectively). We'll talk more about DISCO later—for now, we'll use a WSDL file as input. Table 3-1 summarizes the *wsdl.exe* command-line options.

Table 3-1. Command-line options for the wsdl.exe utility

Option	Description
/username: `<username>` or /u:	Specifies a username for servers that require authentication.
/password: `<password>` or /p:	A password option for servers that require authentication.
/domain: `<domain>` or /d:	Specifies the domain on which the username and password should be authenticated.
/out: `<filename>` or /o:	Specifies the filename for the output source code. The default is generated from the name of the web service.
/namespace: or /n:	Specifies the namespace for the output proxy code.
/language: `<language>` or /l:	In most cases, the *wsdl.exe* utility outputs a source file for a proxy class. This option allows you to specify the language that should be used for this source code. Valid language options are CS (C#—the default), VB (VB.NET), and JS (JScript.NET). Another interesting feature of this option is the ability to specify the fully qualified name of a code-generating or compiling class that implements System.CodeDom.Compiler.CodeDomProvider. This feature allows you to use the *wsdl.exe* utility with custom compilers.
/nologo	Suppresses the Microsoft banner displayed by default when the utility is run.
/protocol: `<protocol>`	Specifies the protocol the proxy class will use for communication (the proxy class can run over several protocols—SOAP (default), HttpGet, or HttpPost. You can also specify custom protocols. Naturally, the web service must support the protocol set here or an error will occur.
/proxy: `<URL>`	Specifies a proxy server for the proxy class to use for HTTP requests. By default, the proxy class uses the proxy setting used by IE.
/proxyusername: `<username>` or /pu:	Specifies the username, if required by the proxy server, that will be used for authentication.
/proxypassword: `<password>` or /pp:	Specifies the password, if required by the proxy server, that will be used for authentication.

Table 3-1. Command-line options for the wsdl.exe utility (continued)

Option	Description
`/proxydomain: <domain>` or `/pd:`	Specifies the domain on which the proxy username and password should be authenticated.
`/server`	By default, *wsdl.exe* generates source code for a proxy class. The `/server` option forces the utility to generate skeleton source code for an abstract class based on the input contract(s).
`/appsettingsurlkey:key` or `/urlkey:key`	The input contract specifies a URL for the web service. Rather than using this URL, this option substitutes a URL specified in the `<appSettings>` configuration file. This option specifies the key associated with the value of the URL in the configuration file.
`/appsettingsbaseurl: <url>` or `/baseurl:`	With `/appsettingurlkey`, specifies a substitute base URL.
`/?`	Causes the utility to display command-line syntax and all supported options.

Using a Proxy Class

Once you have generated a compiled proxy DLL, you can make calls to the remote web service as though its logic were stored in a local assembly. In Example 3-4, the DNSConsumerApp console application uses the *DNSLookupProxy.dll* proxy assembly we just created to call the DNSLookupService. The DNSConsumerApp is used to retrieve the IP address of a host, writing it to the console.

Example 3-4. Consuming a web service using a proxy dll

```
using System;
namespace DNSConsumerApp
{
 class DNSLookup
 {
  static void Main(string[] args)
  {
   DNSLookupService objDNS = new DNSLookupService();
   string strIPAddress = "";
   strIPAddress = objDNS.GetIPForHostname(args[0]);
   Console.WriteLine("Hostname: " + args[0] + " IP Address: " + strIPAddress);
  }
 }
}
```

This class takes as input a string array, which is used for the DNS query. The first line of our Main method creates a new instance of our proxy object, which we then use to call the web method. Save this source code as *DNSLookup.csc* to the same folder containing our proxy assembly, *DNSLookupProxy.dll*, and then compile it by typing the following at the command line:

```
csc.exe /out:DNSLookup.exe /target:exe /r:DNSLookupProxy.dll DNSLookup.csc
```

You're now able to run basic hostname-to-IP queries from the command line using the executable as shown in Figure 3-10.

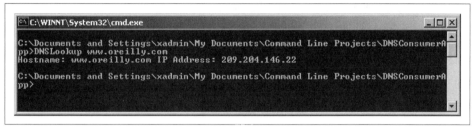

Figure 3-10. Using the DNSLookupProxy in an application

DNSConsumerApp uses the proxy class to make remote calls to the DNSLookupService web service using SOAP as the transport. This example should give you an idea of just how easy it is to create distributed web service applications using the .NET platform. Of course, using a development environment such as Visual Studio .NET makes this process even easier.

Working with the Proxy Class

From the point of view of our consumer application, the proxy class is the main access point to the web service in which we're interested. In addition to the methods and properties exposed by the web service, the proxy class has several other features that can be useful for managing the interaction between itself and the web service. In this section, we explore some of these classes, methods, and properties that enable greater control over the proxy/web service interaction.

WebClientProtocol

All .NET proxy classes must inherit from the abstract class WebClientProtocol (or a descendant thereof), which is found in the System.Web.Services.Protocols namespace (see Appendix A for details regarding this namespace). By using Visual Studio .NET or *wsdl.exe*, you are unlikely to ever create a proxy class manually by extending WebClientProtocol or a derivative thereof. However, because all proxy classes are children of WebClientProtocol, it makes sense for you to familiarize yourself with its properties and methods.

Among the most useful methods and properties of WebClientProtocol are Url, Credentials, and Timeout. The Url property allows you to change the destination URL of the service without having to regenerate and recompile the proxy. The Credentials property provides an easy way for you to supply security credentials to the remote service. Finally, the Timeout property lets you specify how long the proxy should wait for a response from the service. Table 3-2 provides details.

> Web services proxies also inherit several properties and methods from the Component class, which is the parent class of WebClientProtocol; we're going to skip these, since they don't really relate to web services. For the full list of Component members, review the .NET documentation. All of the properties are read/write.

Table 3-2. Frequently used WebClientProtocol members

Element	Description
`Credentials` property	Passes username, password, and other authentication information to verify access credentials for your proxy object. This property is set with an instance of an object that implements the `ICredentials` interface. Two of the built-in .NET classes that implement this interface are `NetworkCredential`, which provides storage for user/password-based credentials, and `CredentialCache`, which can store multiple credentials.
`Preauthenticate` property	Setting this Boolean property to `true` results in the proxy object sending any associated credential information to the web service each time a request is made. If this property is set to `false`, the first request made by the proxy object does not pass any credential information. If the web service is configured to accept anonymous access, business continues as usual; however, if the web service is configured with Basic Authentication, NTLM, or another type of security, it returns a 401 security error to the proxy, at which point the proxy will send another request with any associated credential information. Setting this property to `false` can minimize the number of times the credentials are sent over the wire.
`ConnectionGroupName` property	Creates additional connection groups for your web service access. Defaults to a `null` reference. By default, each proxy has one connection group. Setting this property to a string creates a new set of connections associated with that string.
`RequestEncoding` property	Specifies explicitly an encoding to use for message transfer, such as UTF-8 or ASCII. For a detailed list of encoding types, see the MSDN documentation for `System.Text.Encoding`.
`Timeout` property	Specifies in synchronous calls the amount of time in milliseconds that the proxy should wait for the web service to complete. The default is −1, which is infinity.
`Url` property	Your proxy can interact with any web service that obeys the WSDL contract from which the proxy was created using the `Url` property, which changes the base URL the proxy class uses to make requests. The default value is an empty string, which forces the proxy to use the URL specified in the original WSDL document.
`Abort` method	Aborts the request for asynchronous calls.

Example 3-5 shows how some of these properties and methods are typically used, using a modified version of our DNSConsumerApp. The following code is similar to the previous example, but now specifies a URL for the target proxy class, sets credential information, sets the encoding type, and adds a timeout. In a real-world setting you might have a scenario that includes a pool of web services, hosted at different locations by different organizations, each exposing identical web services (identical WSDL). In that case, you might want to be able to dynamically choose one of these services based on metrics such as availability, response time, cost, and so on. You could extend this example to use the `Url` and `Timeout` properties to select the appropriate service from the pool based on these metrics.

Example 3-5. Setting proxy properties that inherit from WebClientProtocol

```
using System;
using System.Net;
namespace DNSConsumerApp
{
```

Example 3-5. Setting proxy properties that inherit from WebClientProtocol (continued)

```
class Consumer
{
  static void Main(string[] args)
  {
    DNSLookupService objDNS = new DNSLookupService();
    //  Change the URL to the local machine
    objDNS.Url = "http://localhost/DNSService/DNSLookupService.asmx";
    //  Set the proper authentication credentials for IIS
    objDNS.Credentials = new NetworkCredential("tracy", "opensesame", "home");
    //  Send credentials only if necessary
    objDNS.PreAuthenticate = false;
    //  Make sure the encoding is properly set
    objDNS.RequestEncoding = System.Text.Encoding.UTF8;
    //  If the call takes longer than 2 seconds, time out
    objDNS.Timeout = 2000;
    string strIPAddress = "";
    try{
      strIPAddress = objDNS.GetIPForHostname(args[0]);
      Console.WriteLine("Hostname: " + args[0] + " IP Address: " + strIPAddress);
    }
    catch(System.Net.WebException e)
    {
      Console.WriteLine("Request timed out!");
      Console.WriteLine(e.Message);
    }
  }
}
```

This example executes the same GetIPForHostname function that you invoke in Example 3-2, but here we use proxy class properties to explicitly set some of our connection properties. After instantiating the proxy class, the first property set is Url, telling the proxy to use the web service located on our server as its endpoint. Next, an instance of a NetworkCredential object is assigned to the Credentials property to provide authentication information. The next line specifies that the credentials should be sent only if necessary, using the PreAuthenticate property. (The encoding for HTTP/SOAP is UTF-8, as mentioned earlier, but for discussion purposes is set explicitly here via the RequestEncoding property.)

The Timeout property is useful for limiting the wait time for web services. This can be particularly problematic for applications such as our DNSLookupService, which themselves may make distributed network calls. If, for example, the web service needs to query all the way up to a root DNS server to resolve the request, the response could take a considerable amount of time. This delay might be unacceptable in client applications that are themselves synchronous applications, such as ASP.NET pages. (You'll see some more examples of this type of problem and some solutions when we talk about asynchronous clients and servers in Chapter 6.)

In the previous example, we wrap the web service call in a try block and execute the catch code if the timeout expires while making the request. You can force this situation by adding the following line to the DNSLookupService and recompiling:

```
using System.Threading;
...
  public string GetIPForHostname(string strHostname)
  {
    string strReturn = "";
    try{
      IPHostEntry hostInfo = Dns.GetHostByName(strHostname);
      strReturn = hostInfo.AddressList[0].ToString();
      Thread.Sleep(4000);
    }
    catch(System.Net.Sockets.SocketException e)
    {
      strReturn = "0.0.0.0";
    }
    return strReturn;
  }
...
```

Now the web service will sleep for four seconds before returning the result, thus triggering a timeout, causing the code in the client's catch block to execute.

HTTPWebClientProtocol

While the WebClientProtocol class exposes generic properties for connection management, the abstract class HTTPWebClientProtocol extends WebClientProtocol with properties and methods specific to HTTP—examples of HTTP properties are cookies and user agents. These are two of the configurable properties, as you'll see shortly. Since this class extends WebClientProtocol, all of the properties from the previous section are also available. In that respect, HTTPWebClientProtocol sits on top of the basic functionality exposed by the WebClientProtocol class. Conceptually, this appears as shown in Figure 3-11.

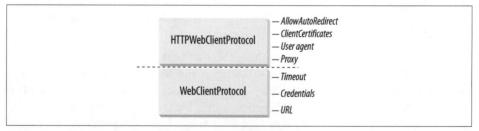

Figure 3-11. The abstract class HTTPWebClientProtocol

Table 3-3 lists all of the properties that are *introduced* by the HTTPWebClientProtocol class. All of the properties are read/write, with the exception of the ClientCertificates property, which is read-only.

Table 3-3. Public properties introduced by HTTPWebClientProtocol

Property	Description
AllowAutoRedirect	Web servers can be configured to redirect requests to other servers using a 302 redirect response. Most web browsers are configured to take care of this redirection automatically. When accessing a web service, however, you may not want your request to be redirected to another server, particularly if you've included authentication information, such as a username and password, in your request.
ClientCertificates	This property allows you to add an X.509 certificate collection to the proxy. This is useful for taking advantage of .NET certificate authentication, which can be linked with Active Directory. However, there is currently no widespread standard for using X.509 certificates within SOAP, so this will not work across platforms. We'll discuss this more in Chapter 9.
CookieContainer	One of the ways of overcoming the stateless nature of the HTTP protocol is through the use of cookies. This property allows you to manipulate any cookies associated with the proxy. (As you'll see in Chapter 5, this ability is particularly useful for managing state in a web service application.)
Proxy	Web service clients running behind a firewall may need to go through a proxy to access a web service. The Proxy property allows you to specify the appropriate URL and port of your proxy server using a class such as System.Net.WebProxy. Because different proxy servers may require different information, this property can be set with an instance of any class that implements the System.Net.IwebProxy interface.
UserAgent	One of the headers presented by the client when using the HTTP protocol is the User Agent string. The User Agent lets the web server know the client type (e.g., IE, Mozilla, webbot), and occasionally the web server may be configured to behave differently depending on the User Agent that is presented. This property allows you to modify the User Agent string that is presented to the server. The default is MS web services Client Protocol *xxx*, where *xxx* is the version of the CLR user by the proxy.

Proxies that inherit from the HttpWebClientProtocol class can take advantage of these properties for more fine-grained control over the HTTP communication between the proxy class and web service. Even though proxy classes that inherit from WebClientProtocol default to HTTP as the transport protocol, they will not have the same capabilities for interaction with HTTP. Some of these capabilities—notably, state management through cookies—prove very useful in web service applications. Example 3-6 shows how some of these additional properties can be used to access our DNSLookupService.

Example 3-6. Setting properties that inherit from HttpWebClientProtocol

```
using System;
using System.Net;

namespace DNSConsumerApp
{
  class Consumer2
  {
    static void Main(string[] args)
    {
```

```
        localhost.DNSLookupService objDNS = new localhost.DNSLookupService();
        //  Change the URL to the local machine
        objDNS.Url = "http://ws.bostontechnical.com";
        //  Set the proper authentication credentials for IIS
        objDNS.Credentials = new NetworkCredential("tracy", "opensesame", "home");
        //  Send credentials only if necessary
        objDNS.PreAuthenticate = false;
        //  Don't allow redirects (present authentication information) to other servers
        objDNS.AllowAutoRedirect = false;
        //  Set the proxy information
        objDNS.Proxy = new WebProxy("myproxy.bostontechnical.com");
        //  Customize the user agent
        objDNS.UserAgent = "DNSConsumer Client";
        string strIPAddress = "";
        strIPAddress = objDNS.GetIPForHostname(args[0]);
        Console.WriteLine("Hostname: " + args[0] + " IP Address: " + strIPAddress);
    }
  }
}
```

This example again starts by setting the appropriate authentication information. Unlike the previous example, here we set `AllowAutoRedirect` to `false` to prevent the proxy from presenting the security information to any server other than the one we've specified with the `Url` property. We also use the `Proxy` property to set the address of a proxy server to use for this request. It is interesting that there are several constructors available for the `WebProxy` class that allow you to specify one or more addresses that should be accessed directly without going through the proxy. In this way, clients running behind a proxy can be selective about when to use the proxy server and when to skip it in favor of a direct connection. Last, we modify the user agent of our proxy object to use a custom string.

Other Proxy Class Implementations

So far, both of the proxy classes discussed have been abstract classes that you can use as templates for creating your own proxy class implementations, though they are more likely to be used by Microsoft to create proxy types to support future message formats (and the contentious debate over standards guarantees that this functionality will be used). Several additional proxy types are already included in the .NET Framework and used by *wsdl.exe* to create proxy classes. As you can probably imagine, the .NET Framework ships with implementations for the three access methods we've been discussing: SOAP, HTTP GET, and HTTP POST. The classes for these implementations are members of the `System.Web.Services.Protocols` namespace:

- `SoapHttpClientProtocol`
- `HttpGetClientProtocol`
- `HttpPostClientProtocol`

The first of these classes, SoapHttpClientProtocol, inherits directly from the abstract class HttpClientProtocol and maintains the same interface without exposing any additional properties, methods, or events. On the other hand, the two HTTP classes inherit from another class called HttpSimpleClientProtocol, which is a child of the HttpWebClientProtocol (discussed in the previous section). This class is a base class that provides support for calling web services over HTTP. Proxy classes generated with *wsdl.exe* always extend one of the three classes listed previously.

Each of these classes contains logic specific to the particular type of access method used. For example, the SoapHttpClientProtocol class encapsulates the logic for using SOAP as the data transfer language (over HTTP) between the proxy class and a web service. Interestingly, because SOAP can be used over a variety of transport protocols in addition to HTTP, we would not be surprised if later versions of the framework provide additional classes that can be used for SOAP communication over other protocols like SMTP, TCP, and so on. The other two classes implement the same type of logic for communication using HTTP URIs. The proxy code generated earlier is an example of a class that inherits from the SoapHttpClientProtocol:

```
namespace DNSConsumerApp {
    using System.Diagnostics;
    using System.Xml.Serialization;
    using System;
    using System.Web.Services.Protocols;
    using System.Web.Services;


    [WebServiceBindingAttribute(Name="DNSLookupServiceSoap",
    Namespace="http://www.bostontechnical.com/webservices/")]
    public class DNSLookupService : System.Web.Services.Protocols.
SoapHttpClientProtocol {

        public DNSLookupService() {
            this.Url = "http://localhost/DNSService/DNSLookupService.asmx";
        }
    ...
```

Consuming a Web Site Using a Screen Scraper Service

The growth in popularity of the Web over the past several years has resulted in an enormous increase in the amount and variety of data available online. The evolution of development tools that are more powerful and easier to use has created an environment in which virtually anyone, with or without technical knowledge, can put his data up on a web site. The time-honored tradition of *screen scraping* is the process of programmatically pulling this data from a web site so that it can be used in another system (or often on another web site). In this scenario, you are in effect consuming a web site as a web service. This practice, which has come to be considered shady by some due to sporadic abuse, has its roots in the world of legacy systems in which it was often used to pull data from mainframes. We hope that the growth in popularity of web services will make screen scraping obsolete as sites continue to make their data available in a structured manner using web services rather than poorly formatted (and frequently changing) HTML. Regardless, screen scraping can be thought of as a primitive form of web service consumption, and this section explores it in more detail. .NET also introduces several features that make screen scraping considerably easier than in either ASP or VB, such as support for regular expressions (as part of the WSDL) as well as WSDL extensions that allow us to pull data from a web page using the web service proxy.

Traditional Screen Scraping

In the worlds of ASP and VB, screen scraping is usually performed using a COM object that allows your code to make an HTTP request to a web server, pulling the web page into a string variable for parsing. Examples of such components are AspHTTP from ServerObjects (*http://www.serverobjects.com/*) and the ServerHTTP library that is part of Microsoft's MSXML parser.

The same process is simplified in .NET, as you don't need to use third-party COM components, thanks to the classes in the System.Net namespace. The following example can be used to pull data from a web site into a string variable:

```
public String ScreenScrape(string url)
{
    String result;
    WebResponse objResponse;
    WebRequest objRequest = System.Net.HttpWebRequest.Create(url);
    objResponse = objRequest.GetResponse();
    using (StreamReader sr =
        new StreamReader(objResponse.GetResponseStream()) )
    {
        result = sr.ReadToEnd();
        sr.Close();
    }
    return result;
}
```

Given a target URL, this function returns a string variable containing the contents of the target. You can then parse that variable to retrieve any data you're interested in. This step of parsing the data can often be difficult when the data is in HTML, because HTML allows a great deal of variance in its syntax, such as unbalanced tags, that XML does not. In earlier versions of VBScript, this difficulty was further compounded by the fact that the only built-in parsing capability came in the form of the VBScript string functions. Fortunately, .NET provides support for regular expressions, similar to that found in VBScript version 5.0 and higher. Through the WSDL extensions, regular expressions can also be built into WSDL documents, as you'll see shortly.

Regular Expressions

For many years, regular expressions have been supported in various Unix utilities, such as grep (which stands for *global regular expression print*) and emacs, as well as in languages such as Perl and Java. Invented by American mathematician Stephen Kleene, regular expressions provide a powerful tool for pattern matching, which is needed for operations such as text parsing and substitution. Regular expressions found their way into version 5.0 of VBScript and are also supported by .NET through the System.Text.RegularExpressions namespace. This namespace contains two classes that are worth discussing:

Regex

> This class represents a regular expression and exposes a method called Match, which searches a string for the given regular expression. This class is designed to support the same regular expressions found in Perl 5.0.

Match

> This class represents the first matching result for a regular expression search. There is also a MatchCollection class that represents a set of successful matches.

Using these classes, we can locate the position of a given text pattern within a string, as well as retrieve text fragments of interest. Consider the following HTML fragment:

```
<td align=left>Lucent Technologies</td>
```

The following regular expression instruction parses this string and extracts the "Lucent Technologies" text from within the <td> tags:

```
using System.Text.RegularExpressions;
...
Regex r = new Regex("<td.*?>(?<TextOfInterest>.*?)</td.*?>");
Match m = r.Match("<td align=left>Lucent Technologies</td>");
if (m.Success)
{
  Console.WriteLine(m.Result("${TextOfInterest}"));
}
```

When run from the command line, this code snippet writes out the text "Lucent Technologies". The first thing to notice is the regular expression we're using:

```
<td.*?>(?<TextOfInterest>.*?)</td.*?>
```

As you can see, one of the problems with regular expressions is that they're rather difficult to read (and sometimes not much of a pleasure to write either!). We're not going to talk about the regular expression syntax in detail, but for a good in-depth discussion, check out *Mastering Regular Expressions*, Second Edition, by Jeffrey E. F. Friedl (O'Reilly, 2002). In this example, the ?<TextOfInterest> string tells the regular expression engine what we're trying to extract. This string is used in the second-to-last line of the code snippet to write out the data of interest.

Regular expressions come in handy for screen scraping applications in which you want to pull pieces of data from an HTML page containing repetitive HTML tags. An advantage that regular expressions offer over string function indexing approaches is that regular expressions can be used to look for a pattern without regard to where it is located in the page. This means that if the page changes, the regular expression won't, as long as the pattern still holds. Not only has Microsoft provided support for regular expressions in the .NET Framework, it has also added support for regular expression to WSDL, as we'll discuss in the next few sections.

WSDL Extensions for Regular Expressions

Version 1.1 of the WSDL specification doesn't make any mention of regular expressions, but in a pattern that should by now be familiar to many developers, Microsoft has added its own "extensions" to the specification in order to support regular expressions. The benefit of these additions is that they make WSDL useful for screen scraping applications. The disadvantage is that few, if any, other web service development tools support these extensions, so if you choose to use them, your WSDL document will be useful only to .NET clients. It's important to remember, however, that the WSDL specification was created by both IBM and Microsoft, so there's a reasonable chance that these extensions will be supported in later versions of WSDL. Let's take a look at how they can be used in a screen scraping application.

Scraping the Web Service Way

Web data is often organized in a table, so it's useful to look at an example of web scraping data from an HTML table. Consider the web page shown in Figure 3-12, which contains stock quote information.

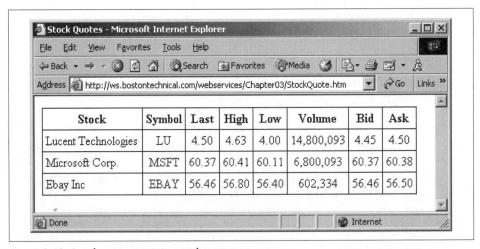

Figure 3-12. A web page containing stock quotes

The following is an abbreviated example of the HTML for the page shown in Figure 3-12:

```
<BODY>
<table bgcolor='black' cellpadding='4' cellspacing='1' width=500 align=left>
  <tr bgcolor='white' align='center' class='size13'>
    <th><b>Stock</b></th>
    <th><b>Symbol</b></th>
    <th><b>Last</b></th>
    <th><b>High</b></th>
    <th><b>Low</b></th>
    <th><b>Volume</b></th>
    <th><b>Bid</b></th>
    <th><b>Ask</b></th></tr>
  <tr bgcolor='white' align='center' class='size13'>
    <td align=left>Lucent Technologies</td><td>LU</td><td>4.50</td>
    <td>4.63</td>
    <td>4.00</td>
    <td>14,800,093</td>
    <td>4.45</td>
    <td>4.50</td>
  </tr>
```

Let's say that, for whatever reason, we were interested in pulling this stock quote data from this site. One approach would be to use the classes of the System.Net namespace as we did in an earlier example to retrieve the HTML from the web site, and then use the regular expression classes to extract the relevant data. Another way to extract the data is by using the text-matching features that Microsoft has added to WSDL.

Here is some WSDL code that incorporates text-matching elements and regular expressions that .NET can use to perform data extraction. Under the hood, much of the extraction process is done via XSL.

```
<?xml version="1.0" encoding="utf-8"?>
<definitions
...
xmlns:tm=http://microsoft.com/wsdl/mime/textMatching/ >
  <types>
    <s:schema elementFormDefault="qualified" targetNamespace="http://www.
bostontechnical.com/">
      <s:element name="GetQuotes">
        <s:complexType />
      </s:element>
      <s:element name="GetQuotesResponse">
        <s:complexType>
          <s:sequence>
            <s:element minOccurs="0" maxOccurs="1" name="Result" type="s:string" >
          </s:sequence>
        </s:complexType>
      </s:element>
      <s:element name="string" nillable="true" type="s:string" />
    </s:schema>
```

```
      </types>
      <message name="GetQuotesHttpGetIn" />
      <message name="GetQuotesHttpGetOut">
        <part name="Body" element="s0:string" />
      </message>
      <portType name="ScreenScrapeHttpGet">
        <operation name="GetQuotes">
          <input message="s0:GetQuotesHttpGetIn" />
          <output message="s0:GetQuotesHttpGetOut" />
        </operation>
      </portType>
      <binding name="ScreenScrapeHttpGet" type="s0:ScreenScrapeHttpGet">
        <http:binding verb="GET" />
        <operation name="GetQuotes">
          <http:operation location="" />
          <input>
            <http:urlEncoded />
          </input>
          <output>
<tm:text>
<tm:match name='Quotes'
               pattern='&lt;/th.*?&gt;&lt;/tr.*?&gt;(.*)&lt;/table.*?&gt;'
               ignoreCase='1' >
<tm:match name='Rows'
               pattern='\s*&lt;tr.*?&gt;(.*?)&lt;/tr.*?&gt;' ignoreCase='1'
               repeats='*' group='1'>
<tm:match name='Fields'
               pattern='\s*&lt;td.*?&gt;(.*?)&lt;/td.*?&gt;'
               ignoreCase='1' repeats='*' group='1' />
</tm:match>
</tm:match>
</tm:text>
          </output>
        </operation>
      </binding>
      <service name="ScreenScrape">
        <port name="ScreenScrapeHttpGet" binding="s0:ScreenScrapeHttpGet">
          <http:address
location="http://ws.bostontechnical.com/webservices/Chapter03/StockQuote.htm">
        </port>
      </service>
    </definitions>
```

We've excluded the standard namespaces and the SOAP- and HTTP POST–related
elements to save space. Notice the following namespace declaration at the top:

```
xmlns:tm="http://microsoft.com/wsdl/mime/textMatching/"
```

The extensions used are members of this text-matching namespace. The part of the
document in which we're interested is the output element of the binding section,
which is highlighted in the previous example. Instead of the MIME element that is
found by default, this section contains a set of named match elements, each of which

has an attribute called pattern containing a regular expression. The last match element in our example looks like the following:

```
<tm:match name='Fields' pattern='\s*&lt;td.*?&gt;(.*?)&lt;/td.*?&gt;' ignoreCase='1'
repeats='*' group='1' />
```

Looking closely at the regular expression in the pattern attribute, you can see that it's very similar to the regular expression used in an earlier example to extract data from <td> tags. One difference is that, because the expression is used within an XML document, the greater-than (>) and less-than (<) tags have been replaced with encoded equivalents (i.e., > and <). The ignorecase, repeats, and group attributes are optional and are described in detail in the MSDN documentation under "Creating XML Web Services That Parse the Contents of a Web Page."

Another thing to notice is the relation of the match elements to one another. The elements form a parent-child chain and, as you'll see, apply three different regular expressions at different points in the chain. Each successive subelement applies the regular expression to the result of the previous expression. The first element is used to locate the table containing our data. The second element extracts the table's rows by applying its regular expression to the result of the first element (the HTML comprising the table). Finally, the third element extracts the data from the <td> tags by applying its expression to the row result from the previous operation. This relationship is mirrored in our proxy object. We can see this by using VS.NET to generate a proxy from this WSDL document as usual.

Proxy Source Code

When you use the WSDL text matching features for a web service, the regular expression matching is done using XSL within the proxy object through .NET's match attribute. If you're interested, you can review the source code output from the *wsdl.exe* utility.

Accessing the service after adding a web reference to the WSDL document, you can use the generated proxy to access the contents of the stock quote table. The following code is an example of how this is done using a web reference called Proxy:

```
static void Main(string[] args)
{
  Proxy.ScreenScrape objProxy = new Proxy.ScreenScrape();
  Proxy.GetQuotesMatches qm = objProxy.GetQuotes();
  Proxy.Rows [] rows = qm.Quotes.Rows;
  Proxy.Rows r = rows[Convert.ToInt32(args[0])];
  foreach (Object o in r.Fields)
  {
    Console.WriteLine(o.ToString());
  }
}
```

Given a row number, this example will write out the information for a given stock. If we pass it an argument of 0, it returns the following:

```
LU
4.50
4.63
4.00
14,800,093
4.45
4.50
```

Since we're using the WSDL text-matching features, the process for accessing our data through the proxy is slightly different from the way we usually do it when we access a web service. The main difference is that we get the text matches through an object that is named by concatenating the operation name, in this case, GetQuotes with the word Matches—in this example, it's GetQuotesMatches. We then retrieve the data through the properties exposed by this object. Those properties get their names from the name attribute of the match elements in the WSDL document and their organization in relation to one another mirrors the organization of the match elements in the WSDL document. Since the WSDL document used a parent-child relationship with the attribute named Quotes at the top, Rows in the middle, and Fields at the bottom, we access the proxy's properties in the same way.

Bear in mind that if you want to use the text-matching features of Microsoft's WSDL extensions, you'll need to code the WSDL document by hand, since there are currently no tools to automate its creation. This can make using the WSDL screen scraping approach much more time-consuming than using the classes of the System. Net namespace, as we showed you in an earlier example. The main advantage to using the WSDL screen scraping approach is that you can post a WSDL document containing the regular expression logic used to extract data from a web site, and then anyone using .NET will be able to easily generate a proxy as they would for any other web service. This makes it very useful for current site operators to expose their data to the .NET-enabled masses 7in a structured way without having to create classical web services of their own. But remember, only consumers using .NET will be able to use this WSDL.

Working with Data Types

Because the hardware architectures of competing computer vendors often differ in the ways they store and handle data, passing data between proprietary platforms has long been a problem for developers of distributed applications. Some architecture use 32 bits to store an integer, while others use only 16; some store the most significant bits of a number on the left, while others store them on the right. In either case, when systems that differ in such fundamental ways try to "talk," they find they are unable to understand each other

In recent years, XML and XSD (the W3C XML Schema Definitions) have become popular tools for enabling the exchange of information between systems and are natural choices for the grammar used by SOAP and web services.

In this chapter, we'll look more closely at some of the problems that can occur when trying to return primitive and complex data types from a web service or to pass them as arguments as part of a web method call. We'll also explore some of the ways XML and SOAP can solve these problems.

We'll begin by taking a closer look at how XML Schemas are used to represent the built-in primitive data types supported by .NET web services. We'll look at the ways both structs and arrays can be used to handle collections of primitive types and how they are represented in XML. We'll also explain how you can create and code your own complex data types so that they can be passed as arguments and returned as values via serialization.

Working with Simple Data Types

Although Visual Studio .NET makes it possible to create and use simple web services without ever viewing a WSDL file or a SOAP message, sooner or later, you're likely to find yourself looking under the hood to customize an application or overcome an obstacle. In the following sections, we'll take a look at the XML that .NET uses to exchange simple and complex data types (roughly equivalent to the primitive and custom types available through the .NET CLR).

XML Schema

XML documents, including WSDL files and SOAP messages, and go hand in hand with XML Schemas. Schemas are themselves XML documents and can usually be identified by their *.xsd* (for XML Schema Definition) file extensions. XML Schemas provide, among other things, information about the syntax and properties of the types used in the XML documents that they describe. Any data type used in an XML document must be defined in an associated schema document.

Because .NET web services are written in a variety of languages and communicate using XML messages, web methods must have a way to translate their input arguments and return values to and from their equivalent data types in XML. Fortunately, a schema that defines many of the simple types routinely used by web services is available on the Web from the W3C at *http://www.w3.org/2001/XMLSchema.xsd* (or XML Schema, as we'll refer to it). For more complex types, however, you must create your own, as you'll see in a later section.

An XML Schema document defines the rules or semantics that apply to a particular data type. The W3C XML Schema supports two kinds of data types: *simple types* and *complex types*. A complex type can have child elements and attributes, while a simple type cannot. Simple types are typically used to represent the primitive types supported on most platforms, such as integers and strings, while complex types are used to represent arrays, collections, and custom types.

The XML Schema requires that any new type you create be based on some existing data type. You modify the base type by either extending or restricting it. Consider, for example, the Int16 primitive type of the .NET CLR, also known as a short in the C# language. An Int16 can represent values ranging from –32,768 to 32,767. Since some variation of this data type is found on most platforms, the XML Schema defines an integer type with the same range of potential values. See Example 4-1.[*]

Example 4-1. The short data type schema

```
<xs:simpleType name="short" id="short">
  <xs:annotation>
    <xs:documentation source="http://www.w3.org/TR/xmlschema-2/#short" />
  </xs:annotation>
  <xs:restriction base="xs:int">
    <xs:minInclusive value="-32768" id="short.minInclusive" />
    <xs:maxInclusive value="32767" id="short.maxInclusive" />
  </xs:restriction>
</xs:simpleType>
```

---

[*] This example is taken directly from the XML Schema for XML Schemas at *http://www.w3.org/2001/XMLSchema.xsd*. Whitespace has been added for clarity.

This definition uses of a number of XML Schema elements and attributes, some of which are beyond the scope of this book. For further information, see the O'Reilly books *XML in a Nutshell*, Second Edition, by Harold and Means (2002) or *Learning XML*, by Erik T. Ray (2001). In this listing, xs is an alias for the URL that points to the W3C XML Schema.

The simpleType element identifies the data type that follows as a simple type and the name attribute assigns it the name short. Like all XML data types, this one is a derived XML type and created by imposing restrictions on a base type, in this case the XML int type. The restriction base element identifies the type from which short is derived. The syntax shown here effectively creates the short type by restricting the range of the int type to values greater than −32,768 and less than 32,767, inclusive. If you follow the restriction bases up the chain, you'll find that the int type is a restriction of long, which is in turn a restriction of integer, all the way up to the anySimpleType type. With each successive type definition, the set of acceptable values is reduced. anySimpleType does not actually exist in the schema and is just a placeholder.

Now that we've covered the basics of XML Schemas, let's take a look at the primitive types of the .NET Common Language Runtime (CLR) and the XML types used to represent them.

.NET Primitive Data Types

We've already talked about how a web service is described in terms of the types of messages it accepts and returns. You saw in Chapter 3 that these messages are defined in the WSDL document that describes the service. Both the messages and the WSDL document itself are formatted using XML. With SOAP, and a little extra work, web methods can accept and return almost any type of data. If our web service is set up for HTTP GET, however, our options are considerably restricted, since a result can be returned only as a string (as we saw in previous chapters). This limitation is one of the reasons that SOAP—which is based on XML and provides for complex data types—is currently the most common communication language for web services.

The primitive types of the CLR can be accepted and returned by a web method using any transport protocol. But the primitive types of the CLR are *not* synonymous with those of programming languages such as C#, VB.NET, or Java, which have their own primitive data types: the int type might be 16 bits long in one language and 32 bits long in another. Therefore a communication system using different languages (one for the server and one for the consumer) must be able to specify which representation of an int to use.

The CLR addresses this problem by providing the Common Type System (CTS). The CTS extends language compatibility and interoperability by mapping the primitive types of .NET languages to common CLR types. For these languages (which must implement the CTS), primitives such as int are mapped to the appropriate system class—in this case, the System.Int32 class. The CTS is one of the reasons .NET is able to support multiple programming languages. Table 4-1 lists some of these CLR types along with the appropriate C# primitive and its XML representation and description.* (Don't worry too much about knowing which primitive types map to which CLR types—the point is that there is a difference.)

Table 4-1. Mapping of CLR primitive types to C# and W3C XML types

CLR primitive type	C# keyword	XML Schema type name	Description
Boolean	bool	boolean	Either true or false
Byte	byte	byte	One byte of data
String	string	string	Character strings
Int16	short	short	16-bit signed integer
Int32	int	int	32-bit signed integer
Int64	long	long	64-bit signed integer
Single	float	float	Single-precision 32-bit floating-point number
Double	double	double	Double-precision 64-bit floating-point number
Decimal	decimal	decimal	Arbitrary precision numbers

Notice also that each of the types has an XML Schema representation.

Structs

When a web service accepts or returns a single variable, a simple type will often suffice. But when more than one variable must be exchanged in a single message, a more complex type is required. A useful .NET type for exchanging lists of simple types is the struct. The PrimitiveTypesService web service shown in Example 4-2 is a service that returns a struct containing nine of the CLR primitive types listed in Table 4-1.

Example 4-2. The PrimitiveTypesService

```
using System;
using System.Web.Services;
using System.Xml;

[WebService(Namespace="http://www.bostontechnical.com/webservices", Description="Primitive
Type Example")]
public class PrimitiveTypeService: System.Web.Services.WebService
```

---

* In addition, each of the integer types in Table 4-1 has an unsigned version (for example, UInt16), left out here for brevity. The full list can be found in the .NET Framework documentation.

Example 4-2. The PrimitiveTypesService (continued)

```
{
  public PrimitiveTypeService()
  {
  }

  public struct Primitives
  {
    public Boolean myBoolean;    // Same as bool in C#
    public Byte myByte;          // Same as byte in C#
    public String myString;      // Same as string in C#
    public Int16 myInt16;        // Same as short in C#
    public Int32 myInt32;        // Same as int in C#
    public Int64 myInt64;        // Same as long in C#
    public Single myFloat;       // Same as float in C#
    public Double myDouble;      // Same as double in C#
    public Decimal myDecimal;    // Same as decimal in C#
  }

  [WebMethod]
  public Primitives ReturnPrimitives()
  {
    Primitives p = new Primitives();
    p.myBoolean = true;
    p.myString = "Hello World";
    p.myInt16 = 32000;
    p.myInt32 = 123456789;
    p.myInt64 = 123456789123456789;
    p.myFloat = 123456789;
    p.myDouble = 3.12345678912345678912345678912345678912;
    p.myDecimal = 3.12345678912345678912345678912345678912M;
    return p;
  }
}
```

The PrimitiveTypesService web service first declares a struct named Primitives for use as a container in which to return nine variables, whose data types match the nine CLR primitives listed in Table 4-1. The corresponding C# types are named in the comments that follow the declaration of each variable. An instance of Primitives is then created, and the value of each of its typed variables is assigned a value (with the exception of the Byte type, which is left null).

Executing PrimitiveTypesService returns the XML document shown in Example 4-3, formatted as a SOAP response message within the body of a SOAP envelope (whitespace added for clarity).

Example 4-3. PrimitiveTypesService response message

```
<?xml version="1.0" encoding="utf-8"?>
<soap:Envelope xmlns:xsi="http://www.w3.org/2001/XMLSchema-instance" xmlns:xsd="http://
www.w3.org/2001/XMLSchema" xmlns:soap="http://schemas.xmlsoap.org/soap/envelope/">
  <soap:Body>
```

Example 4-3. PrimitiveTypesService response message (continued)

```
  <ReturnPrimitivesResponse xmlns="http://www.bostontechnical.com/webservices">
    <ReturnPrimitivesResult>
      <myBoolean>true</myBoolean>
      <myByte>0</myByte>
      <myString>Hello World</myString>
      <myInt16>32000</myInt16>
      <myInt32>123456789</myInt32>
      <myInt64>123456789123456789</myInt64>
      <myFloat>123456792</myFloat>
      <myDouble>3.1234567891234568</myDouble>
      <myDecimal>3.1234567891234567891234567891</myDecimal>
    </ReturnPrimitivesResult>
  </ReturnPrimitivesResponse>
  </soap:Body>
</soap:Envelope>
```

The Body element of the message contains a ReturnPrimitivesResponse, which in turn contains a ReturnPrimitivesResult, the element that holds the web service response. Each of the primitives assigned a value by PrimitiveTypesService (myBoolean, myByte, etc.) appears as an element of the resulting SOAP message, but the document contains no information regarding their type. The names of these elements correspond, as you'd expect, to the variable names within the Primitives struct of the web service. But to determine their types, you must look at the WSDL document that Visual Studio .NET generates for the PrimitiveTypesService when you build and deploy it. The first few lines of the document, including the types element, are included in Example 4-4 for discussion.

Example 4-4. PrimitiveTypesService WSDL fragment

```
<?xml version="1.0" encoding="utf-8" ?>
<definitions xmlns:s="http://www.w3.org/2001/XMLSchema" xmlns:http="http://schemas.
xmlsoap.org/wsdl/http/" xmlns:mime="http://schemas.xmlsoap.org/wsdl/mime/" xmlns:tm="http:
//microsoft.com/wsdl/mime/textMatching/" xmlns:soap="http://schemas.xmlsoap.org/wsdl/soap/
" xmlns:soapenc="http://schemas.xmlsoap.org/soap/encoding/" xmlns:s0="http://www.
bostontechnical.com/webservices" targetNamespace="http://www.bostontechnical.com/
webservices" xmlns="http://schemas.xmlsoap.org/wsdl/">

<types>
  <s:schema attributeFormDefault="qualified" elementFormDefault="qualified"
          targetNamespace="http://www.bostontechnical.com/webservices">
  <s:element name="ReturnPrimitives">

    <s:complexType />
  </s:element>

  <s:element name="ReturnPrimitivesResponse">
    <s:complexType>
      <s:sequence>
        <s:element minOccurs="1" maxOccurs="1" name="ReturnPrimitivesResult"
                  type="s0:Primitives" />
```

Example 4-4. PrimitiveTypesService WSDL fragment (continued)

```
      </s:sequence>
    </s:complexType>
  </s:element>

  <s:complexType name="Primitives">
    <s:sequence>
      <s:element minOccurs="1" maxOccurs="1" name="myBoolean" type="s:boolean" />
      <s:element minOccurs="1" maxOccurs="1" name="myByte"
                 type="s:unsignedByte" />
      <s:element minOccurs="1" maxOccurs="1" name="myString" nillable="true"
                 type="s:string" />
      <s:element minOccurs="1" maxOccurs="1" name="myInt16" type="s:short" />
      <s:element minOccurs="1" maxOccurs="1" name="myInt32" type="s:int" />
      <s:element minOccurs="1" maxOccurs="1" name="myInt64" type="s:long" />
      <s:element minOccurs="1" maxOccurs="1" name="myFloat" type="s:float" />
      <s:element minOccurs="1" maxOccurs="1" name="myDouble" type="s:double" />
      <s:element minOccurs="1" maxOccurs="1" name="myDecimal" type="s:decimal" />
    </s:sequence>
  </s:complexType>

  <s:element name="Primitives" type="s0:Primitives" />
  </s:schema>
</types>
```

Let's take a closer look at this document. The `definitions` element is the required root element that starts all WSDL documents, and includes several namespace declarations that are used throughout the document. Two notable namespace declarations are:

```
xmlns:s="http://www.w3.org/2001/XMLSchema"
xmlns:s0="http://www.bostontechnical.com/webservices"
```

The first declaration assigns the alias name `s` to the URL for the W3C XML Schema. Remember that the alias name, `s` in this case, is arbitrary and can just as easily be a string of text such as "w3cxmlschema", "xsd", or "xs". `xsd` is the most common alias for the W3C XML Schema namespace, but for some reason Visual Studio .NET uses `s` instead.

Most of the elements found in this section of the WSDL document—such as `schema`, `element`, and `complexType`—are prefixed with the namespace alias `s`, signifying that they are described by the XML Schema located at *http://www.w3.org/2001/ XMLSchema.xsd*. This XML Schema document includes definitions for each of these types, including their facets and attributes.

The second namespace declaration assigns the alias name `s0` to the namespace for this book (*http://www.bostontechnical.com/webservices/*). As with the XML Schema alias named `s`, Visual Studio .NET breaks with convention in choosing the alias name `s0` for the current namespace rather than the more common `tns` (which stands for "this namespace"). Any element or attribute in the WSDL file prefixed with this shorthand (e.g., `s0:Primitives`) will be regarded as part of our namespace, and .NET will look there for its associated schema. In this case, the schema is contained within this document.

The `targetNamespace` is an optional attribute that defines the containing namespace for all of the newly defined elements found in this WSDL document. Examples are the `service`, `port`, `message`, `bindings`, and `portType` definitions discussed in Chapter 3. The `targetNamespace` allows other WSDL documents to reference the definitions in this document using an import statement. It also allows the current document to refer to its own definitions using the `s0` alias defined in the header. This is why both the `s0` alias and `targetNamespace` refer to the same URL. The `targetNamespace` says that all of the definitions are members of the `http://www.bostontechnical.com/webservices` namespace. The `s0` alias, also set to `http://www.bostontechnical.com/webservices`, allows definitions in the document to refer to other definitions in the same document.

The `types` element, required whenever complex data types are used, specifies the types used in the request and response messages for the `PrimitiveTypesService` and also defines the complex `Primitives` type used as the return value of the response. The request message, `ReturnPrimitives`, isn't particularly interesting, since our web method doesn't take any arguments. The response message, `ReturnPrimitives-Response`, specifies that the return type for our web method is a complex type called `ReturnPrimitivesResult`. The WSDL sequence element is used to spell out the order of the subelements of a complex type. A response message can return only one element, so only one is listed in the sequence for `ReturnPrimitivesResponse`. The details of that element are specified as follows:

```
<s:element minOccurs="1" maxOccurs="1" name="ReturnPrimitivesResult"
        type="s0:Primitives" />
```

The `minOccurs` and `maxOccurs` attributes are set to 1, since only one element is returned. Since the default value for both attributes is 1, it needn't be set, though doing so improves readability. The `name` attribute is used to name the element `ReturnPrimitivesResult` and to identify its type as `Primitives`. The `s0` alias locates the specification for `Primitives` in the namespace for this book.

Finally, type `Primitives` is defined as a `complexType` that's a sequence of nine elements, each corresponding to one of nine types predefined by the XML Schema located at *http://www.w3.org/*.

Arrays

While structs are a useful means of passing a sequence of simple data types in a single message, arrays are useful for passing multiple instances of either a simple or a complex type. Here's a web method that returns an array of type `Primitives`:

```
...
[WebMethod ]
public Primitives[] ReturnPrimitives()
{
  Primitives[] pa = new Primitives[3];
  for (int i = 0; i < 3; i++)
```

```
    {
      Primitives p = new Primitives();
      p.myBoolean = true;
      p.myString = "Hello World";
      p.myInt16 = 32000;
      p.myInt32 = 123456789;
      p.myInt64 = 123456789123456789;
      p.myFloat = 123456789;
      p.myDouble = 3.123456789123456789123456789123456789;
      p.myDecimal = 3.123456789123456789123456789123456789M;
      pa[i] = p;
    }
    return pa;
  }
  ...
```

In this example, the ReturnPrimitives method now returns an array of three objects of type Primitives. The resulting WSDL schema looks like this:

```
<s:element name="">
  <s:complexType>
    <s:sequence>
      <s:element minOccurs="1" maxOccurs="1" name="ReturnPrimitivesResult"
                 nillable="true" type="s0:ArrayOfPrimitives" />
    </s:sequence>
  </s:complexType>
</s:element>

<s:complexType name="ArrayOfPrimitives">
  <s:sequence>
    <s:element minOccurs="0" maxOccurs="unbounded" name="Primitives"
               type="s0:Primitives" />
  </s:sequence>
</s:complexType>

<s:complexType name="Primitives">
... same as previous example ...
</s:complexType

<s:element name="ArrayOfPrimitives" nillable="true" type="s0:ArrayOfPrimitives" />
```

The ReturnPrimitivesResponse element is still restricted to one subelement, but this subelement is no longer of type Primitives, but rather of a new type called ArrayOfPrimitives, which is defined in the next section of the document. The complex type ArrayOfPrimitives is defined as a sequence, which is essentially the XML representation of an array. Unlike the ReturnPrimitivesResponse, which was defined in terms of a sequence element with exactly one subelement, ArrayOfPrimitives can have zero or more subelements, each of type Primitives. This is the definition of an array.

What we've essentially done in the last two sections is create our own custom type in .NET in the form of a struct, which is made up of a set of primitive types. Web services use XML as a language for communication, and all XML documents require an associated schema, containing the metadata, or rules to be used for interpreting the document. Because our custom type is not predefined in the XML Schema located at *http://www.w3.org/2001/XMLSchema.xsd*, we're required to create our own definition. Because this data type is used as a return type for our web service, its schema needs to be located, or referenced, in the WSDL document. Fortunately, as seen through this example, .NET takes care of the creation of this schema.

But what happens if you're not satisfied with the schema that .NET chooses? What if a different schema is necessary in order to communicate with a non-.NET web service? Fortunately, you can change it by using the built-in XML classes of the .NET Framework. Let's look at an example with a more complex data type and examine how to modify the XML/SOAP messages.

Working with Complex Data Types

There are many situations in which you'll need a web service to accept or return a more complex data type than a struct or an array. So far, you've seen that the .NET Framework can automatically convert its primitive data types to an XML representation and can also create schemas for structs of primitives and for arrays. But what about more complex data types in the form of class structures? We'll take up that subject in this section.

Consider the VideoService web service shown in Example 4-5, which uses a class named Video to return information about the movie *Braveheart*.

Example 4-5. The VideoService web service

```
using System;
using System.Collections;
using System.Web.Services;

public class Video
{
  public string strTitle;
  public string strDescription;
  public decimal decPrice;
  public arrArrayList Producer = new ArrayList();
}

[WebService(Namespace="http://www.bostontechnical.com/webservices",
Description="Video Class Example")]
public class VideoService : WebService
{
  [WebMethod]
  public Video GetVideos()
  {
    Video v = new Video();
    v.strTitle = "Braveheart";
    v.strDescription = "One of the greatest movies of all time.";
```

Example 4-5. The VideoService web service (continued)

```
    v.decPrice = 19.99M;
    v.arrProducer.Add("Mel Gibson");
    v.arrProducer.Add("Bruce Davey");
    v.arrProducer.Add("Alan Ladd Jr.");
    return v;
  }
}
```

The Video class consists of several primitive types and an object of type ArrayList, which is used to store an array of producer names. The XML representation of ArrayList is the same as that of an array.

The GetVideos web method creates and populates an instance of the custom class and then returns the instance. If you fire up the IE test page and take a look at the output from this web method, the response message will look something like Figure 4-1.

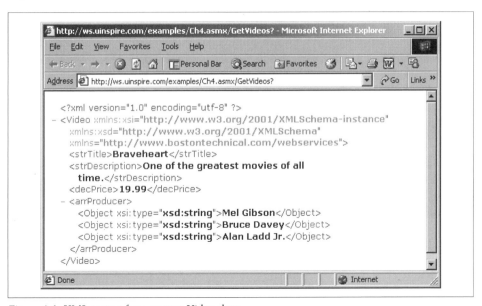

Figure 4-1. XML output for a custom Video class

The resulting XML document is exactly what you should expect, based on the results from our struct example. .NET has taken our C# class and automatically converted it into an XML representation through a process called *XML serialization*. However, the structure of the XML created by .NET may not be exactly what you want. First, the names you've chosen for the variables in your C# program may not be the names you want to display in the returned XML document or show to a customer. Moreover, you may need to format the return data to conform to a predetermined structure. For example, you might need to return the film title as an attribute rather than an element. Fortunately, you can tell .NET how you'd like the data type to be serialized. But before diving into that topic let's take a closer look at how the serialization process works.

Serialization

Serialization is the process of converting objects into a byte stream that can be stored to disk or transmitted over a wire. The goal of serialization is to be able to convert an object and all of its associated state information to a format that can be saved to disk or sent across a network and then deserialized back to an object at a later time. Some common serialization formats are binary, SOAP, and XML. The serialization format used for web services is XML, which as you'll see in the next section, isn't as thorough as other types of serialization supported by .NET. Web service serialization is managed by the XmlSerializer class, which is part of the System.Xml.Serialization namespace. Conceptually, the serialization process looks like the diagram shown in Figure 4-2.

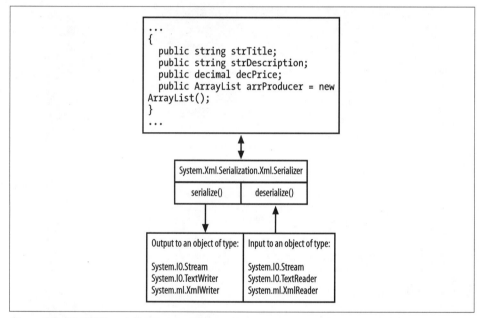

Figure 4-2. The XML serialization process

As depicted in Figure 4-2, serialization is a two-way process. Serialization and deserialization are performed by an instance of the XmlSerialization class. An instance of an object can be serialized to an object of type Stream, TextWriter, or XmlWriter as shown in the figure (the downward path) using the Serialize method of the XmlSerializer class. Conversely, objects of type Stream, TextReader, and XmlReader containing serialized data can be deserialized (the upward path) back to an object using the Deserialize class method.

This logic is performed automatically by .NET behind the scenes, but the process is straightforward. Example 4-6 is a console application that performs serialization manually for an instance of the Video class.

Example 4-6. ConsoleSerializer

```
using System;
using System.Collections;
using System.IO;
using System.Xml.Serialization;

namespace ConsoleSerializer
{
  public class Video
  {
    public string strTitle;
    public string strDescription;
    public decimal decPrice;
    public ArrayList arrProducer = new ArrayList();
  }

  class Serializer
  {
    static void Main(string[] args)
    {
      Video v = new Video();
      v.strTitle = "Braveheart";
      v.strDescription = "One of the greatest movies of all time.";
      v.decPrice = 19.99M;
      v.arrProducer.Add("Mel Gibson");
      v.arrProducer.Add("Bruce Davey");
      v.arrProducer.Add("Alan Ladd Jr.");
      XmlSerializer xs = new XmlSerializer(typeof(Video));
      TextWriter writer = new StreamWriter(args[0]);
      xs.Serialize(writer, v);
      writer.Close();
    }
  }
}
```

This console application takes a filename as an argument and writes the serialized version of the Video class to a text file. The content of the file looks like this:

```
<?xml version="1.0" encoding="utf-8"?>
<Video xmlns:xsi="http://www.w3.org/2001/XMLSchema-instance" xmlns:xsd="http://www.
w3.org/2001/XMLSchema">
  <strTitle>Braveheart</strTitle>
  <strDescription>One of the greatest movies of all time.</strDescription>
  <decPrice>19.99</decPrice>
  <arrProducer>
    <Object xsi:type="xsd:string">Mel Gibson</Object>
    <Object xsi:type="xsd:string">Bruce Davey</Object>
```

```
      <Object xsi:type="xsd:string">Alan Ladd Jr.</Object>
    </arrProducer>
  </Video>
```

This XML output is the same output from our web method in an earlier example. You can confirm this by comparing this output with that in Figure 4-1.

Shaping XML Output

Sometimes you may need to manipulate the structure of the XML document returned by a web method. For example, the standard XML generated by .NET may not properly conform to the schema expected by your client (e.g., the client expects an attribute in place of an element). Or you might want to use your own element and attribute names rather than the variable-based names generated by .NET for purely stylistic reasons. You can make these changes through a process called *XML Shaping*, which involves decorating elements of your serialized classes with attributes from the .NET System.Xml.Serialization namespace. This namespace contains two sets of attributes—XML attributes and SOAP attributes—for shaping XML. These attributes conform to one of the following two naming conventions:

- Xml<item>Attribute (e.g., XmlElementAttribute, XmlArrayAttribute, etc.)
- Soap<item>Attribute (e.g., SoapElementAttribute, SoapAttributeAttribute, etc.)

The XML attributes set includes attributes for manipulating the XML document that is returned when a client uses the HTTP GET or POST access method. The second set contains SOAP attributes that control SOAP-specific properties of the message when using SOAP Section 5 encoding, also known as RPC-style SOAP, which is another messaging format discussed in Chapter 11. Example 4-7 uses XML attributes to modify the names and positions of several members of the Video class.

 The term "XML Shaping," coined by Microsoft, should not be confused with XSL or any other XML transformation technology. This process, which is done for us by .NET under the hood, may make use of stylesheets, but we do not discuss them in this text. For more information on XSL and stylesheets, see *XSLT: Mastering XML Transforms,* by Doug Tidwell (O'Reilly, 2001), or *Professional XSL,* by Cagle, Corning, et al. (Wrox, 2001).

Example 4-7. Shaping the XML of the serialized Video class

```
using System;
using System.Collections;
using System.Web.Services;
using System.Xml.Serialization;

public class Video
{
  [XmlAttribute("Title")]
  public string strTitle;
```

Example 4-7. Shaping the XML of the serialized Video class (continued)

```
    [XmlElement("Description")]
    public string strDescription;
    [XmlElement("Price")]
    public decimal decPrice;
    [XmlArray("Producers")]
    public ArrayList arrProducer = new ArrayList();
}
... // The rest is the same as the previous example.
```

In this example, we've imported the System.Xml.Serialization namespace, which contains the attributes needed to modify the structure of the XML document that's generated when the Video class is serialized. These attributes include XmlAttribute, XmlElement, and XmlArray, and we use them, like the WebService and WebMethod attributes, to give .NET directions on how to properly represent the Video class structure in XML. Each of these directives is placed on the line immediately preceding the variable declaration (in VB.NET, they're on the same line), and each includes the name of the element or attribute that should be used. Figure 4-3 shows the resulting XML document.

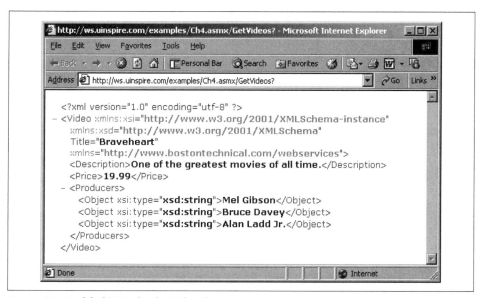

Figure 4-3. Modified XML for the Video class

In Figure 4-3, the title element of Figure 4-2 has been converted to an attribute, and the names of the items have been changed to remove their three-letter prefixes. By using XML attributes to decorate the members of your classes, you gain a great deal of control over the structure of the returned XML document. Table 4-2 lists some of the more commonly used XML attributes. Each of the attributes can be applied to a public property or field unless specified otherwise. (For the complete list, see the XmlSerializer documentation in the .NET Framework Class Library.)

Table 4-2. Commonly used XML attributes

XML attribute	SOAP attribute	Behavior
XmlAttribute	SoapAttribute	Returns the item as an XML attribute.
XmlElement	SoapElement	Returns the item as an XML element.
XmlArray		Specifies that the item should be represented as an XML array.
XmlAnyAttribute		Can be applied only to a field that returns an array of XmlAttribute objects; can be used to paste XML attributes into the output document.
XmlAnyElement		Can be applied only to a field that returns an array of XmlElement objects; can be used to paste XML elements into the output document.
XmlIgnore	SoapIgnore	Specifies that the item should be ignored when serializing.
XmlRoot		Can be applied only to a public class declaration. Denotes that the class represents the root of an XML document.
XmlText		Specifies that the item's value should be serialized as straight XML text rather than as an XML element.
XmlEnum	SoapEnum	Used to name the members of an enumeration differently from the name used in the enumeration.
XmlType	SoapType	Can be applied only to a public class declaration. Specifies that the class should be serialized as an XML type.

Shallow and Deep Serialization

The Video class used in Example 4-7 is a good example of a straightforward complex data type; however, most real-world .NET classes contain not only public instance members, but also accessors (property get methods), mutators (property set methods), constructors, static members and methods, and more. Unfortunately, if we try to return class instances containing some of the more traditional class functionality that we're accustomed to as object-oriented developers, such as accessor methods, private member variables, and static variables or methods, we'll quickly encounter some of the limitations of the XML/SOAP web services model. This is because the serialization model used by .NET web services is based on the System.Xml. XmlSerializer class, which employs a shallow form of serialization, as do the SOAP toolkits currently available from all other vendors. Unlike deep serialization, which is used to completely serialize objects into binary or other formats, shallow serialization ignores nonpublic information.

Private instance variables, public static variables, and functions are not converted to XML representations by .NET. The exclusion of private member variables is pretty much what you'd expect, since these member variables are not normally accessible parts of a class instance. The lack of static member variables, however, may come as a shock, considering that they play such a major role in object-oriented development. While static member variables are important, in principle, they run contrary to the definition of web services as a loosely coupled distributed system. In order to support static variables in a distributed system, you would need to keep track of and have communication between all instances of the object so that an update to the static variable in any instance could be communicated to all other instances. Given the nature of the web service architecture we've discussed so far, which is characterized by a stateless communication system over a potentially unreliable communication medium, this type of communication and tracking is not possible. Some argue that, even in a stateful system, it's poor design.

Class methods, accessors, and mutators are also ignored by the shallow XML serialization. This is also to be expected when you consider that web services typically pass data, not functionality. However, there will be times when you want to design custom types that restrict data values. For example, it would make sense to restrict a data type representing degrees Celsius to values greater than or equal to –273. In .NET languages, you can model such a data type using mutator methods that will prevent anyone from setting a Celsius temperature to a value less than this amount. But when you try to return an instance of a class that contains accessor or mutator methods, these methods will be ignored. This is because .NET web services pass only the object's public data, not its internal state. This behavior is found in most other web services toolkits as well. If you need to pass the internal state of an object, you can use .NET remoting, which is more powerful and stateful but is slower and not as interoperable with other web services platforms.

The Temperature class in Example 4-8 contains accessor and mutator methods that get and set the values of the DegreesCelsius and DegreesFahrenheit properties. While these properties can be accessed through their methods within the program and while instances of types that contain them can be returned by a web method, the properties themselves cannot be exposed as public web methods.

Example 4-8. The TemperatureService web service with accessors and mutators

```
using System;
using System.Web.Services;

public class Temperature
{
  decimal _DegreesCelsius;  // Nonpublic method is not serialized
  decimal _DegreesFahrenheit;  // Nonpublic method is not serialized
  public Temperature()  // Constructor is not serialized
  {
    _DegreesCelsius = 0;
  }

  public decimal DegreesCelsius
  {
    get
    {
      return _DegreesCelsius;
```

Example 4-8. The TemperatureService web service with accessors and mutators (continued)

```
  }
  set
  {
    if(value < -273)
    {
      _DegreesCelsius = -273;
    }
    else
    {
      _DegreesCelsius = value;
    }
    _DegreesFahrenheit = (9/5)*_DegreesCelsius + 32;
  }
}

public decimal DegreesFahrenheit
{
get
{
  return _DegreesFahrenheit;
}
set
{
  if(value < -459)
  {
    _DegreesFahrenheit = -459;
  }
  else
  {
    _DegreesFahrenheit = value;
  }
  _DegreesFahrenheit = (_DegreesCelsius - 32) * 5/9;
}
}
}

[WebService(Namespace="http://www.bostontechnical.com/webservices",
 Description="Accessor / Mutator Example")]
public class TemperatureService : System.Web.Services.WebService
{
  [WebMethod]
  public Temperature GetTemp()
  {
    Temperature t = new Temperature();
    t.DegreesCelsius = -500;
    return t;
  }
}
```

In Example 4-8, calling the GetTemp web method creates an instance, t, of the Temperature class and attempts to set its DegreesCelsius property to –500. Since this value is less than –273 (absolute zero in the Celsius system), the DegreesCelsius mutator will set the value of DegreeCelsius to –273 and also set the DegreesFahrenheit property to –241. Once these operations are complete, GetTemp returns t in a serialized response. With a few changes, the service could be altered to accept a Celsius or Fahrenheit temperature from a client and to return its value expressed in both Celsius and Fahrenheit degrees.

The output from the web method appears in Figure 4-4.

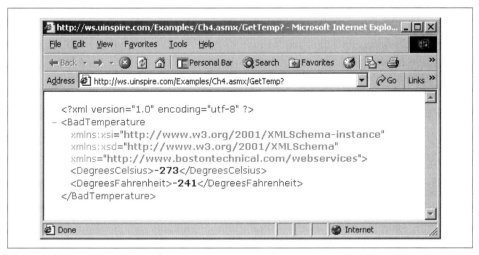

Figure 4-4. Temperature example output

If a .NET consumer attempts to deserialize this SOAP response message back into a .NET class, the class definition will look something like the following:

```
public class Temperature
{
  decimal DegreesCelsius;
  decimal DegreesFahrenheit;
}
```

Notice that the accessor and mutator are no longer present. This is because, as you've seen, only data—not functionality—can be passed in your return data types. Functionality will not be serialized as XML in the SOAP message and will therefore not be part of the consumer's deserialization process.

Using Complex Data Types as Arguments

So far we've discussed the various data types that can be returned as output by web methods, including the primitive types, arrays, structs, and classes. We've also talked about the XML Schema used within WSDL to define complex output types and have seen how XML output documents can be manipulated to rearrange their XML using the classes from the System.Xml.Serialization namespace. We have not, however, talked in very much detail about the data types that can be accepted by a web method as arguments. This section examines supported argument types and the access methods that are required to use them.

Accepting Complex Types: Service View

While the HTTP GET and POST access methods are fine for many web service applications, these methods limit the types of data that you can pass as arguments to a web method. Most of the examples we've discussed so far have been web methods that take either arguments that are primitive types, returning anything from a primitive to a complex type, or no argument at all. You've seen by using the IE test page generated for a service, which can be set to use either HTTP GET or POST (but not SOAP) as its access method, that returning complex data isn't a problem. Because IE is able to interpret the XML response, you've been able to verify it with your own eyes. So far, the web method input arguments that we've used have been so simple that they could easily be submitted using an HTML text box. But what happens when we publish a web method that takes a more complex type as an argument? Consider the `PaymentProcessor` credit card processing service in Example 4-9, which takes a `PurchaseOrder` object as an argument.

Example 4-9. PaymentProcessor web service

```
using System;
using System.Web.Services;

public enum CreditCard {Visa = 1, Mastercard = 2, Amex = 3, Discover = 4};
public class PurchaseOrder
{
  public string FirstName;
  public string LastName;
  public string Address;
  public string City;
  public string State;
  public string Zip;
  public CreditCard CardType;
  public long CardNumber;
  public double Amount;
}
[WebService(Namespace="http://www.bostontechnical.com/webservices",
 Description="Complex Argument Example")]
public class PaymentProcessor : WebService
{
  [WebMethod]
  public string ChargeCustomer(PurchaseOrder po)
  {
    string strStatus = "";
    int iChargeCode = Charge(po);
    if ( iChargeCode == 0 )
    {
```

Example 4-9. PaymentProcessor web service (continued)

```
    strStatus = "Charged " + po.FirstName + " " + po.Amount.ToString();
    }
    else
    {
      strStatus = "Failed with error code " + iChargeCode.ToString();
    }
    return strStatus;
  }

  private int Charge(PurchaseOrder po)
  {
    // Insert validation & payment processor logic here
    return 0;
  }
}
```

We start as usual by importing two of the namespaces that we expect to use:

```
using System;
using System.Web.Services;
```

Our payment processing web method takes an instance of a `PurchaseOrder` object as an argument and returns a string telling us whether the transaction was a success. This is fairly typical design: we're encapsulating the various pieces of information that we want to pass as one object, as opposed to a bunch of separate arguments (e.g., nine parameters). In the code for the `PurchaseOrder` class, notice the use of the enum type for the different credit card types. The enum datatype, like other .NET primitives, can also be represented in XML; that is, a representation for enumerations exists in XML Schema.

The `PaymentProcessor` service contains one web method named `ChargeCustomer`, which takes an instance of a `PurchaseOrder` object as an argument. The web method calls another private method called `Charge`, which would contain any validation or payment-processing logic, and returns a status code of 0 for success or the error code if a failure has occurred. The web method returns a message indicating whether the credit card authorization and charge was successful.

If we copy this code out to our web server (or build the code in VS.NET) and then view it in IE, we get the results shown in Figure 4-5.

Figure 4-5 displays the `ChargeCustomer` web method description page. (This particular IE test page has been customized for Boston Technical; yours will be different.) The most important thing to note about this page is that the Test section, which usually includes text fields for any arguments and a Submit button, instead contains the text: "No test form is available as this service or method does not support the HTTP GET protocol."

In addition, the sample SOAP request and response messages are listed further down on the page; however, the HTTP GET and POST messages are missing. The reason for this is that once we code our web method to accept a complex type such as the

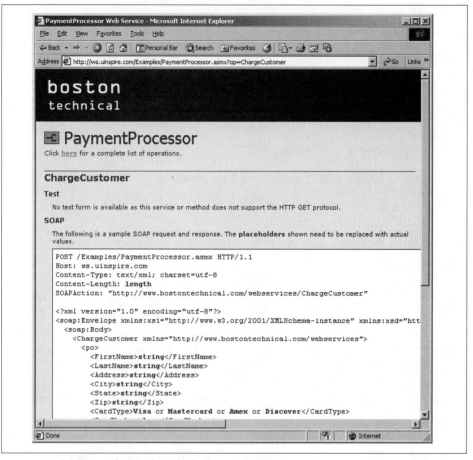

Figure 4-5. IE test page for a web method taking a complex type

PurchaseOrder one we've used here, we can no longer use either HTTP GET or POST for making requests. This makes sense considering that the argument must be represented in XML, there isn't any standard way of submitting XML via HTTP GET, and the standard way of submitting XML via a POST is by using SOAP. Both HTTP GET and POST are limited to using key/value pairs when passing information. This means that they're fine for passing the primitive types we defined in an earlier section, but they cannot be used to pass complex types like arrays, structs, and classes.

Passing Complex Arguments: Consumer View

Using SOAP to pass data solves the problem mentioned earlier by allowing us to pass complex data types to a web service. But coding our consumer application brings on another problem: how to determine the structure of the data type to pass. Take our ChargeCustomer web method as an example. As you just saw, it takes an object of type PurchaseOrder as its only argument. The class definition for the PurchaseOrder object resides on the server. How can our client application pass an instance of this object without knowing its definition? The answer, unsurprisingly, is that the schema for the class definition and any other associated types (in this case, the CreditCard enum type) is available as part of the types element of the WSDL document. .NET converts this schema to a language-specific definition as part of your proxy class when you either use the *wsdl.exe* tool or add a web reference from your VS.NET project (see Chapter 3). This means that any class definition required by a web method is included as part of the proxy class. We can confirm this by creating a simple consumer for our ChargeCustomer web method.

---

xsd.exe

The .NET SDK ships with *xsd.exe*, another tool that can generate language-specific type definitions from an XSD document.

Because this web service can be accessed only via SOAP calls, you'll need to set up a consumer application to test it out. We like console applications for their simplicity. Let's start by generating the code for, and compiling, a proxy DLL that we'll use to access this example web service. If you're using Visual Studio .NET, add a web reference to a new project based on the Console Application template. For this example, we'll use VS.NET, because the built-in Intellisense features are handy. As always, the same example can be put together just as easily using your favorite text editor.

In the following example, a web reference named Commerce has been added to our PaymentProcessor web service, allowing reference to the contents of the proxy DLL through the Commerce prefix. This addition is shown in Figure 4-6.

The Intellisense feature shows that the web service Proxy class contains one enum type and two public classes. They are:

- CreditCard
- PaymentProcessor
- PurchaseOrder

Remember that the CreditCard enum type contains information about the different types of credit cards supported by our PurchaseOrder object. PaymentProcessor is the proxy class that we'll need to use to access the web services, and the PurchaseOrder class is a definition of the argument to the ChargeCustomer web method. The following code is a consumer console application for this web method:

```
using System;

class ConsoleConsumer
{
```

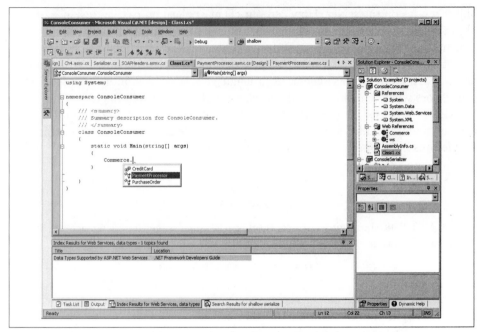

Figure 4-6. A proxy class for a web service that requires complex arguments

```
static void Main(string[] args)
{
    string strResult = "";
    // Create our PO object
    Commerce.PurchaseOrder po = new Commerce.PurchaseOrder();
    po.FirstName = "Alex";
    po.LastName = "Ferrara";
    po.Address = "27 Melcher St.";
    po.City = "Boston";
    po.State = "MA";
    po.Amount = 19.95;
    po.CardType = Commerce.CreditCard.Visa;
    po.CardNumber = 4111111111111111;
    // Create our Proxy
    Commerce.PaymentProcessor objProxy = new Commerce.PaymentProcessor();
    // Call the charge web method
    strResult = objProxy.ChargeCustomer(po);
    Console.WriteLine(strResult);
}
}
```

Compiling and running this application from the command line produces the results shown in Figure 4-7.

Using the type definitions generated for us by .NET (via *wsdl.exe* or VS.NET), we can create an instance of our data type, manipulate it as we would any other class in C#, and pass it as a parameter to a web method. To summarize:

Figure 4-7. Output from ConsoleConsumer

- Complex data types can be passed as arguments to web methods, but only using SOAP (essentially just XML of HTTP POST).

- By default, the type definitions, in XSD format, for all required data types are listed (or linked to) in the types section of the associated WSDL document for the web service.

- When a proxy class is created, .NET automatically creates a definition for any necessary data types. These types can be accessed via the proxy DLL.

The ability to pass complex data types to a web service and receive a complex data type as output in a standardized XML-based fashion is one reason web services have such great potential for cross-platform communication. You can craft an arbitrary object or graph of objects and easily pass their data between server and client, thanks to standards like XML and SOAP. In each of the examples, it's been necessary to communicate the structure of the object using the WSDL document. Without the data type definition stored within the WSDL or other XSD document, this communication isn't possible. Any data type we pass must have an associated XSD.

Now that we've covered the basics of passing and returning complex data, let's take a look at one of the more useful .NET data types for data transfer: the DataSet.

Passing Data with DataSets

ADO.NET is Microsoft's latest data access technology, the successor to ADO. The key component of ADO.NET is the DataSet class, equivalent to a disconnected portable database, providing many of the querying capabilities available in ADO.NET itself.

Throughout .NET, XML is the preferred format for storing and transmitting data, as is evident in our web service examples, in which custom data types are serialized to XML documents and defined using the XML Schema. So it's not surprising that DataSets, which are central to Microsoft's ADO.NET, can easily be converted to and from XML and can therefore be passed to and returned from .NET web services. As you'll see, this XML capability adds considerable functionality.

Unlike the complex types used in the previous example, however, the number and types of DataSet properties can vary. A DataSet object can contain multiple tables, columns, their relationships, and their constraints. The structure of a DataSet instance is highly variable and dependent on the data it contains. As a result, the XSD description of the DataSet varies as well, which was not the case for the other complex types we've discussed so far. But we know that the WSDL document for a web service is static. After all, the WSDL document is what we'd use to publish our web service to the outside world, so how is the dynamic structure of the DataSet represented in a static WSDL document? The answer is that it isn't. Instead, the WSDL document holds a reference to a variable XSD that is generated at runtime. Let's take a look at an example in order to get a better understanding of how this works.

Using a DataSet

The process for returning a DataSet is straightforward. The following example returns the contents of the products table from the NorthWind database that ships with SQL Server. (You don't need an SQL or other database to use the DataSet. You can just as easily create an instance of a DataSet object and manually populate it.) Let's take a look at the code, as shown in Example 4-10.

Example 4-10. The DataSet service

```
using System;
using System.Web.Services;
using System.Data;
using System.Data.SqlClient;

[WebService(Namespace="http://www.bostontechnical.com/webservices",
 Description="Untyped DataSet Example")]
public class DataSet : System.Web.Services.WebService
{
  [WebMethod(Description="Returns the contents of the Northwind.products
             table as a DataSet.")]
  public System.Data.DataSet GetProducts()
  {
    string strQuery = "SELECT * FROM products";
    SqlConnection myConnection = new
    SqlConnection("server=10.0.0.10;database=northwind;user id=sa;password=xxxxx");
    SqlDataAdapter myCommand = new SqlDataAdapter(strQuery, myConnection);
    System.Data.DataSet ds = new System.Data.DataSet();
    myCommand.Fill(ds, "Products");
    return ds;
  }
}
```

This code exposes a single web method called GetProducts, which retrieves the contents of the products table from the Northwind database. We could have just as easily stored the contents of several other tables in the DataSet in addition to relationship information—the structure of the DataSet is variable. We're interested in figuring out how the DataSet is returned, so let's take a look at the XSD portion of the WSDL document for this service; see Example 4-11. (We've left out some lines to save space.)

Example 4-11. DataSet service WSDL document

```xml
<?xml version="1.0" encoding="utf-8" ?>
<definitions xmlns:s="http://www.w3.org/2001/XMLSchema" targetNamespace="http://www.
bostontechnical.com/webservices" xmlns="http://schemas.xmlsoap.org/wsdl/">
<types>
  <s:schema attributeFormDefault="qualified" elementFormDefault="qualified"
          targetNamespace="http://www.bostontechnical.com/webservices">
    <s:import namespace="http://www.w3.org/2001/XMLSchema" />
    <s:element name="GetProductsResponse">
      <s:complexType>
        <s:sequence>
          <s:element minOccurs="1" maxOccurs="1" name="GetProductsResult"
                     nillable="true">
            <s:complexType>
              <s:sequence>
                <s:element ref="s:schema" />
                <s:any />
              </s:sequence>
            </s:complexType>
          </s:element>
        </s:sequence>
      </s:complexType>
    </s:element>
...
```

The `GetProductsResponse` element from the WSDL document is where you'd normally expect to see the definition for the returned data type. From the highlighted text, we can see that the complex type definition for this result is a reference to the XML Schema. So what's going on? Where is the type definition? The answer is that this WSDL document is telling us that the XSD is included with the result. This makes sense, since the object we're returning is of type `DataSet`, which dynamically takes on the structure of the data it contains. An easy way to verify this is to take a look at the sample request and response messages provided by the IE test page. Viewing the `GetResults` operation in a browser displays the following sample return message:

```xml
<?xml version="1.0" encoding="utf-8"?>
<soap:Envelope xmlns:xsi="http://www.w3.org/2001/XMLSchema-instance" xmlns:xsd="http:
//www.w3.org/2001/XMLSchema" xmlns:soap="http://schemas.xmlsoap.org/soap/envelope/">
  <soap:Body>
    <GetProductsResponse xmlns="http://www.bostontechnical.com/webservices">
      <GetProductsResult>
        <xsd:schema>schema</xsd:schema>xml
      </GetProductsResult>
    </GetProductsResponse>
  </soap:Body>
</soap:Envelope>
```

The highlighted lines make it pretty clear that the return type of this web method is an XSD Schema. The final confirmation comes from executing the web method, which yields the output in Example 4-12 (notice the XSD).

Example 4-12. DataSet service response message

```
<DataSet xmlns="http://www.bostontechnical.com/webservices">
  <xsd:schema id="NewDataSet" targetNamespace="" xmlns=""
   xmlns:xsd="http://www.w3.org/2001/XMLSchema"
   xmlns:msdata="urn:schemas-microsoft-com:xml-msdata">
    <xsd:element name="NewDataSet" msdata:IsDataSet="true">
      <xsd:complexType>
        <xsd:choice maxOccurs="unbounded">
          <xsd:element name="Products">
            <xsd:complexType>
              <xsd:sequence>
                <xsd:element name="ProductID" type="xsd:int" minOccurs="0" />
                <xsd:element name="ProductName" type="xsd:string" minOccurs="0" />
                <xsd:element name="SupplierID" type="xsd:int" minOccurs="0" />
                <xsd:element name="CategoryID" type="xsd:int" minOccurs="0" />
                <xsd:element name="QuantityPerUnit" type="xsd:string"
                             minOccurs="0" />
                <xsd:element name="UnitPrice" type="xsd:decimal" minOccurs="0" />
                <xsd:element name="UnitsInStock" type="xsd:short" minOccurs="0" />
                <xsd:element name="UnitsOnOrder" type="xsd:short" minOccurs="0" />
                <xsd:element name="ReorderLevel" type="xsd:short" minOccurs="0" />
                <xsd:element name="Discontinued" type="xsd:boolean"
                             minOccurs="0" />
              </xsd:sequence>
            </xsd:complexType>
          </xsd:element>
        </xsd:choice>
      </xsd:complexType>
    </xsd:element>
  </xsd:schema>
  <diffgr:diffgram xmlns:msdata="urn:schemas-microsoft-com:xml-msdata"
                   xmlns:diffgr="urn:schemas-microsoft-com:xml-diffgram-v1">
    <NewDataSet xmlns="">
      <Products diffgr:id="Products1" msdata:rowOrder="0">
        <ProductID>1</ProductID>
        <ProductName>Chai</ProductName>
        <SupplierID>1</SupplierID>
        <CategoryID>1</CategoryID>
        <QuantityPerUnit>10 boxes x 20 bags</QuantityPerUnit>
        <UnitPrice>18</UnitPrice>
        <UnitsInStock>39</UnitsInStock>
        <UnitsOnOrder>0</UnitsOnOrder>
        <ReorderLevel>10</ReorderLevel>
        <Discontinued>false</Discontinued>
      </Products>
...
```

This truncated output has two main parts. The first is the XSD definition for the NewDataSet data type, dynamically generated by .NET and necessary (one could argue that some clients can infer the schema, obviating the need for the XSD) for the client to be able to interpret the second part of the message (starting with the NewDataSet element) that contains the actual data. Both the type definition and the data have been included in the results, allowing the web method to return a dynamically structured data type.

Not all DataSet structures are returned in this manner. A web service coded to return an object of type System.Data.DataSet returns what is known as an untyped DataSet. This is exactly what we've just done, returning a DataSet that has no fixed structure or "type." We can, however, create typed DataSets that do have a fixed structure and therefore don't require the dynamic generation of the XSD. The next section explores the differences between typed and untyped DataSets.

Returning Typed and Untyped DataSets

Typed DataSets are instances of DataSets that have a predetermined structure. This structure is usually supplied by an XSD document, as you'll see shortly. Other than that, typed DataSets behave similarly to untyped ones—anywhere you use an untyped DataSet, you can substitute a typed one without a problem (but the opposite is not true).

As we've mentioned, by default, any DataSet you create will be untyped, meaning that its structure is variable. This default is convenient for many situations; however, there are some compelling advantages in certain situations to using typed DataSets; that is, DataSets that have a set structure or schema. The biggest advantage is that typed DataSets are "first-class" objects, with respect to the object model, in .NET, meaning that their attributes can be navigated using a more direct notation than that of an untyped DataSet. The following is an example of untyped DataSet navigation:

```
// This accesses the ProductName column in the first row of
// the products table.
string s = (string) dsProducts.Tables["Products"].Rows[0]["ProductName"];
```

And this example shows typed DataSet navigation:

```
// The same thing with a typed DataSet
string s;
s = dsProducts.Products[0].ProductName;
```

The second example uses a much more elegant method for navigating the DataSet's object model, which is possible only with a typed DataSet.

For VS.NET users, another advantage to using a typed DataSet is that there are several built-in Visual Studio features that make working with typed DataSets easier and less error-prone, one of which is the ability to visually model the structure of the DataSet. We're not going to talk about these features here, but you can view the online documentation for more information about working with typed DataSets in VS.NET.

Creating a typed DataSet from the command line

There are several ways to create a typed DataSet; here, we'll cover two of them. Either way, it's essentially a two-step process. The first step is to subclass the

System.Data.DataSet class. The second step is to apply an XSD to the DataSet. Fortunately, .NET ships with a utility called *xsd.exe*, which automates this process. Given an XSD document, the *xsd.exe* utility can automatically generate a typed DataSet with the following command-line instruction:

```
xsd.exe myDataSet.xsd /d /l:CS
```

In this command, myDataSet.xsd is a text file containing the XSD file from which the typed DataSet should be created. The /d switch specifies that source code for a DataSet should be created, and the /l switch specifies that the utility should use the C# language (also the default). We can use slightly modified output XSD from a previous example as the input file for this example. The XSD document in Example 4-13 can be used to create a typed DataSet following the structure of the products table.

Example 4-13. Schema document for a products table DataSet

```
<?xml version="1.0" encoding="utf-8" ?>
<xsd:schema id="myDataSet" targetNamespace="" xmlns="" xmlns:xsd="http://www.w3.org/2001/
XMLSchema" xmlns:msdata="urn:schemas-microsoft-com:xml-msdata">
  <xsd:element name="myDataSet" msdata:IsDataSet="true">
    <xsd:complexType>
      <xsd:choice maxOccurs="unbounded">
        <xsd:element name="Products">
          <xsd:complexType>
            <xsd:sequence>
              <xsd:element name="ProductID" type="xsd:int" minOccurs="0" />
              <xsd:element name="ProductName" type="xsd:string" minOccurs="0" />
              <xsd:element name="SupplierID" type="xsd:int" minOccurs="0" />
              <xsd:element name="CategoryID" type="xsd:int" minOccurs="0" />
              <xsd:element name="QuantityPerUnit" type="xsd:string"
                           minOccurs="0" />
              <xsd:element name="UnitPrice" type="xsd:decimal" minOccurs="0" />
              <xsd:element name="UnitsInStock" type="xsd:short" minOccurs="0" />
              <xsd:element name="UnitsOnOrder" type="xsd:short" minOccurs="0" />
              <xsd:element name="ReorderLevel" type="xsd:short" minOccurs="0" />
              <xsd:element name="Discontinued" type="xsd:boolean" minOccurs="0" />
            </xsd:sequence>
          </xsd:complexType>
        </xsd:element>
      </xsd:choice>
    </xsd:complexType>
  </xsd:element>
</xsd:schema>
```

When run through the *xsd.exe* utility and compiled, this XSD document outputs a typed DataSet class that can be instantiated and used as any other DataSet. In the following section, the next example does the same thing using the built-in capabilities of VS.NET.

Creating a typed DataSet in VS.NET

To create a typed DataSet in VS.NET, just add a new item using the DataSet template, double-click the new item to activate it, select the XML tab on the bottom of the window, and paste in the XSD document. The resulting screen is shown in Figure 4-8.

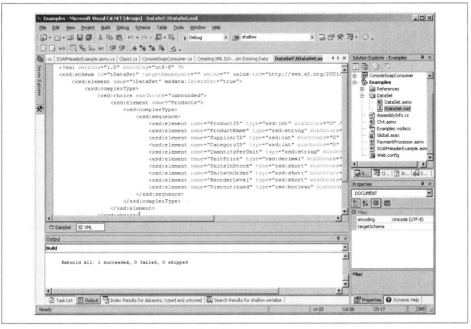

Figure 4-8. Creating a typed DataSet in VS.NET

Click on the DataSet tab to the left of the XML tab; VS.NET attempts to compile the XSD file into a typed DataSet. Behind the scenes, the process is similar to using the *xsd.exe* and *csc.exe* tools. If you select the Show All Files view in the Solution Explorer, you'll see that a class file with the same name as the DataSet has been created. If the XSD code is valid, your result will look something like that in Figure 4-9. In the previous example, we've used the XSD output from the earlier untyped DataSet example.

You can now reference this typed DataSet in your web service (and other) applications. You can also use the DataSet display shown in Figure 4-9 to modify your DataSet by changing types and adding relationships. Let's look just briefly at a web method you could use to do this. The following example returns an instance of a typed DataSet, called tDataSet, created in Figure 4-9:

```
[WebMethod(Description="Returns the contents of the Northwind.products table
 as a DataSet.")]
public tDataSet GetProducts()
```

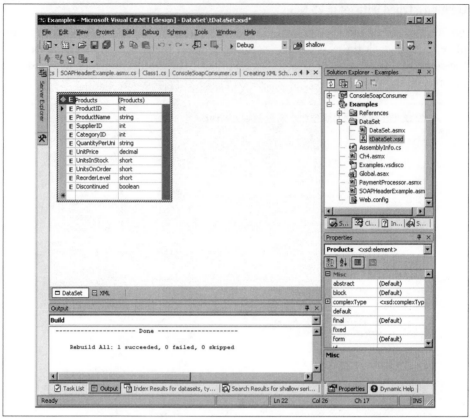

Figure 4-9. The compiled typed DataSet

```
{
  tDataSet ds = new tDataSet();
  //  Do some population here.
  return ds;
}
```

Because this is a typed DataSet, the resulting WSDL document contains a reference to the associated schema. If you were to look at the WSDL, you'd see a definition similar to the following:

```
<import namespace="" location="http://ws.uinspire.com/Examples/DataSet/DataSet.
asmx?schema=tDataSet" />
```

This line imports the schema for our typed DataSet so that the consumer can gather the format ahead of time.

Using Binary Data

Web services can be used to transmit any file type (images, office documents, mp3 files, etc.) as binary data. Sending and receiving binary data in a web service is straightforward. The easiest way to accomplish this is to send the data as an array of bytes. The following is an example of a web service containing web methods to send and receive binary data:

```
using System.IO;
. . .

[WebMethod]
public string PostDocument(byte[] bFile)
{
  System.Guid myGUID = System.Guid.NewGuid();
  System.IO.FileStream fs = new
  System.IO.FileStream("c:\\temp\\" + myGUID.ToString() + ".doc",
  System.IO.FileMode.Create);
  fs.Write(bFile, 0, bFile.Length);
  fs.Close();
  return myGUID.ToString();
}


[WebMethod]
public byte[] GetDocument(string strFilename)
{
  FileStream objFile = new
  FileStream("c:\\temp\\" + strFilename + ".doc", System.IO.FileMode.Open);
  byte[] myData = new byte[objFile.Length];
  objFile.Read(myData, 0, (int)objFile.Length);
  objFile.Close();
  return myData;
}
```

The PostDocument() method accepts as an argument an array of bytes that is converted to a file and saved to a folder on the server. A GUID (Globally Unique Identifier) is used for the filename to ensure uniqueness, and this GUID is returned to the client as a string. You would obviously want to add string validation for this method so that a client could not overwrite any important files on the server.

The GetDocument() web method takes a GUID in string format and returns the associated file, which has been stored on the server. There's no error trapping, so if the file doesn't exist things get ugly.

The Windows application in Figure 4-10 can be used to test the PostDocument() web method.

```
private void btnUpload_Click(object sender, System.EventArgs e)
{
  btnUpload.Enabled = false;
  FileStream objFile = new FileStream(textBox1.Text, System.IO.FileMode.Open);
  byte[] myData = new byte[objFile.Length];
  objFile.Read(myData, 0, (int)objFile.Length);
  label1.Visible = true;
  label2.Text = objProxy.PostDocument(myData);
  textBox1.Text = "";
  btnUpload.Enabled = true;
}
```

Figure 4-10. Posting binary data to a web service

The btnUpload_Click method posts the file as binary data to the PostDocument web method. The SOAP message returned from a call to GetDocument looks something like the following:

```xml
<?xml version="1.0" encoding="utf-8"?>
<soap:Envelope xmlns:xsi="http://www.w3.org/2001/XMLSchema-instance" xmlns:xsd="http:
//www.w3.org/2001/XMLSchema" xmlns:soap="http://schemas.xmlsoap.org/soap/envelope/">
  <soap:Body>
    <GetDocumentResponse xmlns="http://tempuri.org/">
      <GetDocumentResult>PD94bWwgdmVyc2lvbjOiMS4wIiBlbmNvZGluZzOidXRm
LTgiID8+DQo8eHNkOnNjaGVtYSBpZDOibXlEYXRhU2VOIiBoYXJnZXROYW1lc3BhY2U9Ii
IgeG1sbnM9IiIgeG1sbnM6eHNkPSJodHRwOi8vd3d3Lm9yZy8yMDAxL1hNTFNjaGVt
YSIgeG1sbnM6bXNkYXRhPSJ1cm46c2NoZW1hcy1taWNyA8eHNkOmVsZW1lbnQgbmFtZTOi
UXVhbnRpdHlQZXJVbmlOIiBOeXBlPSJ4c2Q6c3RyaW5nIiAN </GetDocumentResult>
    </GetDocumentResponse>
  </soap:Body>
</soap:Envelope>
```

In the next chapter, we'll change focus and look an important design decision you'll face when developing a web service—namely, whether to retain any information in memory. We'll consider the different types of state management available as well as the advantages and drawbacks of different stateful designs.

Managing State

One of the most important decisions you'll make when designing a web service is how—and whether—to retain *state*, or information, about the client and work done by the service, between requests. A short-sighted state management strategy can cripple your web service, making it nearly impossible to scale to a large number of clients or extend with additional features. On the other hand, well-planned state can simplify your life, provide a quick path to sophisticated features, and even (occasionally) improve performance. And just to make life interesting, state considerations are deeply intertwined with a web service's overall design—meaning that once you've chosen a state management strategy, it's difficult or impossible to change it.

This chapter starts by examining when stateful designs are useful and when they might be more trouble than they are worth. It also takes a high-level look at the different state models you can use. The bulk of the chapter, however, is spent exploring common techniques for state management. We focus on two topics: state maintaining information on the server, and automating the submission of repetitive information from the client (such as a user identifier or security token) so you don't have to. You'll learn how to integrate ASP.NET's built-in state facility into a web service and how to manage state on your own with custom cookies and ticket systems. You'll also learn how to use SOAP headers to make stateless web services run more smoothly.

The Great State Debate

State management is always a hotly debated topic in newsgroups and programming circles, especially when dealing with web applications. The problem is that HTTP is a stateless protocol, and connections are rarely maintained for longer than a couple of minutes. Developers are generally left with the following three state options in any web application.

- Abandon all the information about a client and its session as soon as its connection is broken.
- Maintain information on the client side. This technique has a higher transmission cost (it increases network traffic because the information needs to be continually shuttled back and forth) but does not use any extra memory on the web server.
- Maintain information on the server side. This approach tends to have a lower transmission cost but uses valuable memory on the web server.

From a performance perspective, the first approach is usually the best solution. From a developer's perspective, however, the last approach is best, because it simplifies coding and allows you to design a web service in the same way you would design a local class. The problem is that any memory requirement, no matter how minute, can quickly grow to a significant, scalability-destroying size when multiplied by hundreds or thousands of clients.

Ultimately, state decisions always involve compromise. There is no single perfect state management solution. The important fact to remember when designing a web service is that state decisions are also performance decisions.

Stateless Versus Stateful Design

The .NET Framework makes remote web service communication so transparent that you may be tempted to design web services in the same way that you would design local data objects. As you'll discover, this approach isn't realistic.

An ideal web service should function like a static utility class, which is to say that it should provide a collection of useful, well-encapsulated functions. If you've ever designed components for Microsoft Transaction Server or its successor, COM+, you are familiar with this style of coding. Some developers even recommend considering a web service as an endpoint for sending and receiving data and never as a true participant in object-oriented designs.

In most cases, this limitation is the trade-off involved in using web services well. Unlike in desktop or client/server development, the overhead in creating multiple object instances, performing multiple distinct calls to set properties, and retaining memory to store state is not trivial.

 When possible, web services should be stateless. If you decide that a web service should retain state, organize it in such a way to reduce the number of calls and the amount of memory that must be used. Finally, you should realize that property procedures *always* represent a poor way to implement stateful designs.

In the next section, we'll discuss an example that underscores what can go wrong if you try to design a web service in the same way that you code a local class.

Web Services and Property Procedures

Here's an example of why you need to consider state decisions carefully. Example 5-1 provides a perfect example of how not to design a web service. In the rest of this chapter, we'll discuss specific answers to the problem it poses.

Example 5-1. A web service with no means of maintaining state

```
class CustomerInfo : System.Web.Services.WebService
{
    string name;

    public string Name
    {
        get
        {
            return name;
        }
        set
        {
            name = value;
        }
    }
}
```

On the outside, `CustomerInfo` looks like a perfectly reasonable class containing a single property procedure that wraps a simple string variable. After creating this sort of class, you would probably expect to use it like this:

```
// Create the CustomerInfo web service.
localhost.CustomerInfo customer = new localhost.CustomerInfo();

// Attempt to set the Name property.
customer.Name = "Bill";
```

Unfortunately, the `Name` property is not part of the public interface of the web service. As a result, it won't be part of the automatically generated proxy class and it won't be accessible remotely.

To correct this problem, you need to flag the accessor and mutator (get and set) methods with the `WebMethod` attribute, as shown in Example 5-2.

Example 5-2. A web service with property procedures exposed as web methods

```
public class CustomerInfo : System.Web.Services.WebService
{
    string name;
```

Example 5-2. A web service with property procedures exposed as web methods (continued)

```
    public string Name
    {
        [WebMethod]
        get
        {
            return name;
        }
        [WebMethod]
        set
        {
            name = value;
        }
    }

}
```

This change still doesn't resolve the problem, because web services don't support property procedures. In fact, methods are the only code construct that you can use in a web service. Thus, when you create a proxy class that uses properties, the get and set portion of a property are interpreted as separate methods and renamed.

Your client must then use the following, slightly less intuitive syntax. (Note that we're assuming, in this case, that the client is a Windows application; a Console or ASP.NET client couldn't use the MessageBox class.)

```
    // Create the CustomerInfo web service.
    localhost.CustomerInfo customer = new localhost.CustomerInfo();

    // Set and retrieve the Name "property".
    customer.set_Name("Bill");
    MessageBox.Show("Name: " + customer.get_Name());
```

Unfortunately, this technique still falters. If you build and test this service, you'll find that you can call both methods and verify with the Visual Studio .NET debugger that the appropriate web service code successfully executes. However, when you try to retrieve the value of the Name property, you'll receive a null reference instead. The problem is that the property procedures you wrote are treated as ordinary methods. Unless you take extra steps to store and retrieve the internal state of the CustomerInfo class, it won't persist from one client request to another.

To solve this problem, you must make several changes:

*   Enable the ASP.NET session state facility for your property procedures using the EnableSession property of the WebMethod attribute.
*   Explicitly store the Name variable in the Session collection.
*   Create a default cookie collection for the proxy class, so that it will retain the ASP.NET session cookie.

We'll explore each of these steps in more detail later in this chapter. For now, consider the remodeled CustomerInfo web service shown in Example 5-3. State is now maintained, but at what cost?

Example 5-3. CustomerInfo web service, with state maintained

```
public class CustomerInfo : System.Web.Services.WebService
{
    string name;

    public string Name
    {
        [WebMethod(EnableSession = true)]
        get
        {
            return (string)Session["name"];
        }
        [WebMethod(EnableSession = true)]
        set
        {
            Session["name"] = value;
        }
    }

}
```

The client code can successfully set and retrieve the Name property, provided it creates an empty cookie collection to hold ASP.NET's session cookie:

```
// Create the CustomerInfo web service.
localhost.CustomerInfo customer = new localhost.CustomerInfo();

// Create an empty cookie collection.
customer.CookieContainer = new System.Net.CookieContainer();

// Set and retrieve the Name "property".
customer.set_Name("Bill");
MessageBox.Show("Name: " + customer.get_Name());
```

This solution should leave you feeling anything but triumphant. We've considered several failed attempts at state management in order to underscore one important point: state management is available for .NET web services, but that doesn't mean it's seamless or natural. In fact, using property procedures in web services is never a good design decision.

Our CustomerInfo class, as it stands, suffers from several problems:

- Using individual properties requires multiple calls over the Internet. Every time you set or retrieve a single property, a separate remote method call is required. This approach can dramatically slow a web service, because the majority of the time spent waiting for a web method to return from a simple operation is spent transmitting the request and response over the Internet.

- Values in the session state collection are not, by default, tied to the lifetime of the class. When the class is abandoned, state information will remain, occupying valuable server memory until the session times out.

- Values in session state are not specifically tied to a particular class instance. Instead, they are bound to a specific session ID, which is contained in the session cookie. Depending on how you use the class, you may need to manage this cookie separately. For example, if you have a stateful Account web service that models a bank account, you'll probably need to create two proxy classes to work with two separate accounts.

The last two problems are inherent in session state but can be alleviated with good design practices, as you'll discover later in this chapter. The first problem is an unacceptable consequence of using property procedures. It's also usually the result of ignoring the difference between stateless and stateful design.

Transactional Web Services

Transactions present another reason to think twice about using a stateful design. For example, consider a web service account object, as shown in Example 5-4.

Example 5-4. BankAccount: an account object that isn't transaction-ready

```
public class BankAccount : System.Web.Services.WebService
{

    float Balance;

    [WebMethod(EnableSession = true)]
    public void Withdraw(float amount)
    {
        // Modify the balance and store it in state.
    }

    [WebMethod(EnableSession = true)]
    public void Deposit(float amount)
    {
        // Modify the balance and store it in state.
    }

    [WebMethod(EnableSession = true)]
    public void Update()
    {
        // Update the database with the new Balance value.
    }

}
```

One problem with this design is that it's easy to leave an account object in an inconsistent state. For example, for a client to perform a transaction, two operations are required—a withdrawal on one bank account and a deposit to another. Both accounts will need to be accessed through separate proxy classes to ensure separate sessions and the separation of state data. It's quite possible that one of these methods could succeed, while the other fails, perhaps due to network difficulty or a server problem. This isn't acceptable in a real-world application.

To ensure that this sort of bank account transfer is successful, you need to wrap the `Withdraw()` and `Balance()` methods into one transaction: a withdrawal for one account object and a deposit for another. A web service, however, can participate only as the root of a COM+ transaction. This means you can't include more than one web method in a single transaction, and there's no way to ensure that withdrawals and deposits are bound together.

To support transactions, you must model your web service as a stateless utility class and specify account information in parameters as primitive data types or structures, as demonstrated in Example 5-5.

Example 5-5. TransactionalAccountUtility: a transactional utility service

```
public class TransactionalAccountUtility : System.Web.Services.WebService
{

    [WebMethod(TransactionOption = Required)]
    public void Transfer(float amount, int accountFrom, int accountTo)
    {
        // Retrieve and update the corresponding database records.
    }

}
```

This works because the entire transaction is contained inside a single web method. When the `Transfer` method is invoked in Example 5-5, a new COM+ transaction is started automatically. If an unhandled exception occurs inside the `Transfer()` method, the transaction is automatically rolled back. Otherwise, the transaction is committed as soon as the method ends (unless any other transactional components have voted to roll it back). You can explicitly vote to commit or roll back the current transaction using the `SetComplete()` or `SetAbort()` methods of the `System.EnterpriseServices.ContextUtil` class.

Keep in mind that COM+ transactions don't represent the only way to implement a transaction inside a web service. It's probably far more likely that the web service will start a database transaction using ADO.NET (or call a stored procedure that encapsulates multiple database operations and a transaction). COM+ is best suited to distributed transactions that need to manage more than one data source. That's because all the code in a transactional web method is automatically bound together into a single transaction, even if it deals with multiple data sources. The only requirement is that the data sources (technically known as *resource managers*) must support the OLE Transactions standard. Many enterprise data sources—including SQL Server (from version 6.5 up), Oracle 8*i*, Microsoft Message Queuing, and IBM DB2—meet these requirements.

Because web methods must always be the root in a transaction, the Required and RequiresNew values for TransactionOption are equivalent. Similarly, Disabled, NotSupported, and Supported all disable transactions for the web method, despite what their names may suggest.

State Management Scenarios

One of the most common reasons for using state is to create a web service that exposes information from a data source. Consider, for example, a web service that provides information about callers in a customer support database. There are at least three ways to model this service, each with its own trade-offs, as described in the following sections.

Thin Layer Design

The *thin layer design* consists of simple methods, each of which wraps a single operation. For example, in a typical thin layer design each method might correspond to a single stored procedure in a database. This allows the database to follow optimized query paths. It also encourages the calling application to retrieve only the information that is needed. Information is never stored in any type of state. This design is modeled in Example 5-6.

Example 5-6. CustomerThinLayer: a thin layer design

```
// This class provides a thin layer over a support database
// that lists registered customers and logs calls to technical support.
public class CustomerThinLayer : System.Web.Services.WebService
{
    [WebMethod]
    public int GetTotalCalls(string customerName)
    {
        // Perform DB search and return total number of calls.
    }

    [WebMethod]
    public int GetAverageCallLength(string customerName)
    {
        // Perform DB search and return average call length.
    }

    [WebMethod]
    public string[] GetProductsOwned(string customerName)
    {
        // Perform DB search and return list of products owned by a customer.
    }

}
```

The disadvantages of thin layer design are more subtle than its obvious advantages:

- A relatively sophisticated client may need to make numerous calls to the web service and perform numerous similar searches to retrieve all the information it requires. This may slow down the application with unnecessary repeated database access, especially in a high-use scenario.

- .NET web services do not support method overloading. This means that you may need to use awkward method names like GetCallsByCustomerName() and GetCallsByDate(). If you are supporting several different client applications, the web service can quickly become a hodgepodge of miscellaneous, poorly organized methods.

- The thin layer design tends to model the database that it accesses quite closely. Often, each of its server-side methods directly correlates to an existing stored procedure. If the database design changes, it might be difficult to change the web service without creating a new, incompatible version.

Stateful Design

A *stateful design*, as demonstrated in Example 5-7, uses state to simplify its design and provide a more convenient access model for the client, while avoiding the problems of property procedures noted earlier.

Example 5-7. CustomerState: a stateful design

```
public class CustomerState : System.Web.Services.WebService
{
    [WebMethod(EnableSession = true)]
    public void Populate(string customerName)
    {
        // Perform DB search and store information in a temporary state store.
        // This method must be called first.
    }

    [WebMethod(EnableSession = true)]
    public int GetTotalCalls()
    {
        // Retrieve information from state and return total number of calls.
    }

    [WebMethod(EnableSession = true)]
    public int GetAverageCallLength()
    {
        // Retrieve information from state and return average call length.
    }

    [WebMethod(EnableSession = true)]
    public string[] GetProductsOwned()
    {
```

Example 5-7. CustomerState: a stateful design (continued)

```
        // Retrieve information from state and return list of products.
    }

}
```

Some of the potential problems in stateful design include:

- Even if a client needs to access only one method, the same `Populate()` method must be used to retrieve all the related information, potentially imposing an unnecessary toll on the database.

- If most of the information that is retrieved from the database is stored in server-side state, a significant amount of server memory could be used. This type of application tends to work perfectly when first deployed and become a victim of its own success—faltering as more clients start to use it.

 Using a `Populate()` method reduces the number of database queries but increases the amount of information that each query returns. The performance effect depends on client usage patterns: if only one or two methods are typically used before the class is discarded, the memory required to store the additional, unused information would reduce performance. If, on the other hand, the `Populate()` method retrieves a large amount of information from several different tables, aggregates this information, and then provides the summary data through other methods, a substantial performance *increase* is possible. This pattern might be found in a web service that provides data mining.

This chapter examines different ways to implement a stateful web service like that shown in Example 5-7. These solutions demonstrate common stateful design that can be useful, as long as you understand the potential pitfalls. Interestingly, these designs can become much more scalable when state is replaced by a combination of persistent storage (for example, a database) and data caching. This approach is demonstrated in Chapter 7.

Aggregate Design

The *aggregate design*, shown in Example 5-8, extends the thin layer design by combining (or aggregating) several pieces of information into a custom structure. In order to implement this design efficiently, you usually need to have a precise idea of the information clients will want to retrieve. Nevertheless, there are several compelling benefits: the number of web method calls is reduced, no state is held between calls, and a database query can be reduced to a summary or an aggregation of data before it is returned, lowering the transmission cost. The client can then perform additional processing with the `CallInfo` structure returned by `CustomerAggregate`.

Example 5-8. CustomerAggregate: an aggregate stateless design

```
public class CustomerAggregate : System.Web.Services.WebService
{
    [WebMethod]
    public CallInfo GetCallInfo(string callerName)
    {
        // Perform DB search, fill a CallInfo object, and return it.
    }
}

public struct CallInfo
{
    public int TotalCalls;
    public int AverageCallLength;
    public string[] ProductsOwned;
}
```

Microsoft generally advocates aggregate design in its platform examples.* It's an elegant solution, but it can waste bandwidth with irrelevant data (for example, if a client simply needs the total number of calls). This could be particularly inconvenient for a non-.NET client or a thin client (like a mobile phone) that needs to retrieve only a single piece of information.

ASP.NET's Session State Facility

ASP.NET's session state is the easiest way to add sophisticated state management to an application, because the infrastructure is already built. ASP.NET's session state works almost identically for web services as for ASP.NET web forms. With session state, each user that accesses a web service (and, in fact, each individual proxy class) has access to its own collection of state information. This information is stored in a weakly typed key/value collection that can include simple data types or instances of .NET objects.

Session state is ideal for sensitive data (like credit card numbers), because it is stored exclusively on the server and never transmitted to the client. It is also well suited for complex data (like recordsets or even COM objects) that cannot be easily serialized to a client-side cookie.

The Session Cookie

ASP.NET identifies and tracks sessions with a unique 120-bit session ID string. ASP.NET generates this value and stores it in a special session cookie (named `ASP.NET_SessionId`), which it sends with the response. When the client presents this cookie on subsequent requests, ASP.NET worker processes retrieve the serialized data associated

---

* Primarily the IBuySpy case studies, which are available for download from *http://www.ibuyspy.com/*.

with the session ID from the state server as a binary stream, convert it into live objects, and place these objects into the session state collection. Session ID values are created and managed automatically by the ASP.NET Framework using an algorithm that guarantees uniqueness and randomness, so that they can't be interpreted or regenerated by a malicious user.

In ASP.NET web form applications, you can also choose to transmit session IDs using a cookieless mode, which embeds the session ID directly into the URL page request. With web services, this approach is not an option. This means that ASP.NET session state requires the use of a cookie and is thus inherently tied to the HTTP protocol. While this is generally not a problem, it limits your ability to communicate with the web service using SOAP messages over another protocol (for example, SMTP) in which cookies are not supported.

Using Session State

As you saw earlier in Example 5-3, you can use the session state features of ASP.NET by setting the EnableSession property of the WebMethod attribute to true:

```
[WebMethod(EnableSession = true)]
```

Access to the session collection is enabled on a method-by-method basis, rather than for an entire class. This fine-grained control is designed to optimize performance. Even if the session collection is empty, it takes time for ASP.NET to examine the session ID cookie and look up the corresponding session. For that reason, session support is disabled by default. Note that the EnableSession property configures whether session objects are *available* in a given method, but it does not create or destroy the session collection. You can safely call a session-enabled method followed by a session-restricted method without clearing or abandoning the current session.

The System.Web.SessionState.HttpSessionState class provides access to session information. You can access the current session collection through the built-in Session object, provided your web service inherits from the System.Web.Services.WebService class. Alternatively, you can use the static System.Web.HttpContext.Current property:

```
System.Web.SessionState.HttpSessionState session;
session = System.Web.HttpContext.Current.Session;
session["name"] = value;
```

The Items Collection

The HttpSessionState class contains two state collections: Items and StaticObjects. The StaticObjects collection contains state objects that are defined in the *global.asax* file with <object runat="server"> tags. This collection is immutable and is generally more useful for web form applications than web services (and thus won't be discussed in this book). The Items collection contains objects added through code at runtime and is the default indexer for the HttpSessionState class. Each item in the collection is identified with a unique string key that you choose. Unlike many other .NET collection types, this string key is *not* case-sensitive.

You can add an object to the collection using the Add() method or by simply assigning it to the HttpSessionState class with a new key:

```
// If there is no object in state with the key "name", one will be created.
// If there is a "name" object, it will be replaced.
Session["name"] = "Bill";

// Any type of object can be stored in session state.
DataSet dsSales = new DataSet("Sales");
Session["Sales"] = dsSales;
```

You can remove an item from session state with the Remove() method or by replacing the object with a null reference.

```
Session["Sales"] = null;
```

Session state items are stored as the base System.Object type. This means that any .NET object can be stored in session state (because all .NET objects can be downcast to the System.Object type). It also means that you need to cast an object when you retrieve it from session state:

```
String name = (string)Session["Bill"];
DataSet dsSales = (DataSet)Session["Sales"];
```

Accessing Stateful Services

To use a web service that uses ASP.NET's cookie-based session state, a client must take some additional steps. The proxy class inherits a number of useful properties from the SoapHttpClientProtocol class in the System.Web.Services.Protocols namespace. One of these is CookieContainer, which contains all the cookies sent and received with each web service request.

By default, CookieContainer provides a null reference, and sessions are not supported. To enable session support, you need to supply a new System.Net. CookieContainer instance:

```
// Create the web service proxy class.
localhost.SessionTest test = new localhost.SessionTest();

// Create and assign the empty cookie collection.
test.CookieContainer = new System.Net.CookieContainer();
```

In some cases, you might want (or need) to release the reference to the proxy class but continue to access the session state collection. In this case, you can store either the entire CookieContainer collection or the relevant session cookie. You can retrieve the session cookie using its name and the web service address:

```
// Create web service proxy class.
localhost.SessionTest test = new localhost.SessionTest();

// Create a System.Uri object representing the web service location.
```

```
Uri uri = new Uri("http://localhost");

// Retrieve the cookie collection from the proxy class.
System.Net.CookieCollection cookies = test.CookieContainer.GetCookies(uri);

// Retrieve the session ID cookie.
System.Net.Cookie cookie = cookies["ASP.NET_SessionId"];
```

Once you have retrieved the session cookie, you can store it and use it to access the session at a later time, provided the session has not timed out. You can even pass it to another class or component that needs to use the same web service. This chapter provides a full example of storing and retrieving a session ID cookie in a later example (Example 5-13).

 Generally, each web service class uses its own session, with its own cookie. Alternatively, you could use the same cookie for more than one web service, which would allow the web services to share data (provided they were in the same web application). However, this technique is discouraged because it adds additional (and sometimes murky) interdependencies between web services.

Session State Configuration

Session state, like many other ASP.NET services, can be configured through the *machine.config* file or a *web.config* file in the appropriate virtual directory where the *.asmx* file is hosted. See Example 5-9 for a sample file with session state settings. The configuration file allows you to set the timeout and the other advanced options that govern how session state is stored. If you create your web service as a Visual Studio .NET project, it will include an automatically generated *web.config* file.

Example 5-9. Sample web.config settings for session state

```
<?xml version="1.0" encoding="utf-8" ?>
<configuration>
    <system.web>
        <!-- Other settings omitted for clarity. -->

        <sessionState
            mode="InProc"
            stateConnectionString="tcpip=127.0.0.1:42424"
            sqlConnectionString="data source=127.0.0.1;user id=sa;password="
            cookieless="false"
            timeout="20"
        />

    </system.web>
</configuration>
```

The default *web.config* file provides a sample `sqlConnectionString` and `state-ConnectionString`, even though these values will not be used as long as the mode is set to `InProc`.

Remember, configuration files apply to all the web services and web forms in the current virtual directory. In order to provide distinct settings for web services and web forms, you should place the corresponding *.asmx* and *.aspx* files in different virtual directories (which is a good organizational approach anyway).

Mode

The Mode attribute provides for options, as listed in Table 5-1.

Table 5-1. Session mode options

Mode	Description
InProc	This is the default option. It instructs ASP.NET to store session items in the IIS process, which is faster (no cross-process communication is required to serialize and retrieve information).
Off	This setting disables session state management for every web service and web method.
StateServer	This setting instructs ASP.NET to use a separate Windows service for state management, as identified by the stateConnectionString attribute.
SqlServer	This setting instructs ASP.NET to use an SQL Server database to store session information, as identified by the sqlConnectionString attribute. This is the most resilient state store, but also the slowest by far.

Out-of-Process State Servers

ASP.NET provides out-of-process state services to overcome some common problems:

- In-process session state is bound to a single web server. That means that it is not shared in a web farm scenario, which can cause a client to lose state information when a request is routed to a different server.
- In-process session state is lost if the ASP.NET worker process crashes and a server restart is required.

The two out-of-process state options (StateServer and SqlServer) overcome these problems. Of course, they have their own drawbacks, including access times that are typically much slower. In general, if you aren't using a web farm to balance server load over multiple computers, you should stick to the in-process state store.

Using a Windows Service for State

The easiest way to configure the ASP.NET State Service (see Figure 5-1) is to use the Microsoft Management Console snap-in included with the ASP.NET Framework (select Start → Programs → Administrative Tools → Computer Management on the web server). Select the Services and Applications → Services node.

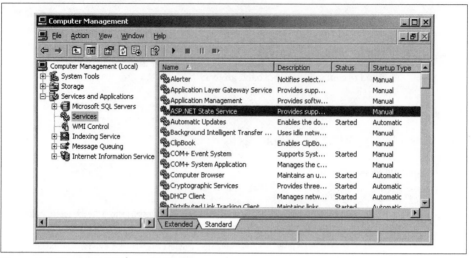

Figure 5-1. The ASP.NET State Service

From the console, you can manually stop and start the service and configure Windows to automatically start the service on startup. You cannot, however, configure the port used for configuration. This port (42424 by default) can be changed using *regedit.exe*. Modify the Port value in the key:

```
HKEY_LOCAL_MACHINE → System → CurrentControlSet → Services → aspnet_state →
Parameters
```

To use the ASP.NET State Service in a web service or web application, you need to specify the TCP/IP address of the server and port in the corresponding *web.config* file:

```
<!-- This example specifies the address 127.0.0.1 and port 42424 -->
<sessionState
    mode="StateServer"
    stateConnectionString="tcpip=127.0.0.1:42424"
```

In a web farm scenario, you will also need to configure the machine key so that it is the same for each server. The machine key is used to encrypt session data with a server-specific key that is generated automatically. In order to successfully share state across computers, each server must be able to interpret the state information, and thus each server must have the same hardcoded machine key.

The machine key is specified in the *machine.config* configuration file on each web server (typically found in the *\WINNT\Microsoft.NET\Framework\[version]\CONFIG* directory). The default machineKey setting is as follows:

```
<machineKey validationKey="AutoGenerate"
            decryptionKey="AutoGenerate"
            validation="SHA1"
```

The validationKey and decryptionKey keys can each be set manually using 40–128 hexadecimal (0–f) characters. The following example shows a hardcoded machineKey that might be used in a web farm scenario (the actual key values have no significance, and are used only to encrypt or hash data):

```
<machineKey validationKey="1234567890abcdef1234567890abcdef1234567890abcdef"
            decryptionKey="abcdef1234567890abcdef1234567890abcdef1234567890"
            validation="SHA1"
```

For some additional information about ASP.NET web farm settings, see *ASP.NET in a Nutshell*, by Duthie and MacDonald (O'Reilly, 2002) and *Programming ASP.NET*, by Liberty and Hurwitz (O'Reilly, 2002).

Using a SQL Server Database for State

The SQL Server state facility provides the greatest reliability, but the slowest performance. It uses stored procedures to serialize and retrieve session data to and from the *tempdb* database. To use SQL Server state management, you must install the stored procedures. The ASP.NET Framework includes a special Transact-SQL script for this purpose; it is called *InstallSqlState.sql* and is typically found in the *\WINNT\ Microsoft.NET\Framework\[version]* directory. You can run this script using a utility like *OSQL.exe*.

To use SQL Server state management, specify a connection string with a valid user account and the SQL Server location:

```
<!-- This example specifies user "sa" and location 127.0.0.1 -->
<sessionState
    mode="SqlServer"
    sqlConnectionString="data source=127.0.0.1;
                         user id=sa;password=opensesame"
```

Timeout

One significant drawback to session state is that it isn't tied to the lifetime of the class or application. Essentially, session state sets aside a piece of live memory on the web server in the hopes that a client will return and use it later.

If this approach were used without any checks or boundaries, the web server would quickly use up all of its available memory. To avoid this problem, session state is typically removed if no requests are received within the number of minutes specified by the timeout attribute. In the following sample setting, the session will expire after 20 minutes:

```
<sessionState
    timeout="20"
```

This is the main trade-off of session state storage: you must choose a time frame short enough to allow valuable memory to be reclaimed on the server, but long enough to allow a user to be able to continue a session after a short delay.

Designing Session-Friendly Classes

Following good design practices with your web service can improve the situation. However, there is no way to create a web service that automatically clears the session collection when you are finished using it. It might occur to you to use the web service's Dispose() method for this purpose. Unfortunately, the Dispose() method is called automatically after every method call, making it unsuitable. Instead, you must create an additional web method:

```
[WebMethod(EnableSession = true)]
public void ReleaseSession()
{
    // Time out the session immediately.
    Session.Abandon();
}
```

The client should then call this method before releasing the reference to the proxy class:

```
private void StateTest(object sender, System.EventArgs e)
{
    // Create the CustomerState web service.
    localhost.CustomerState customer = new localhost.CustomerState();

    // (Add code to use the web service.)

    // Release the session before customer goes out of scope.
    customer.ReleaseSession();
}
```

There is no way to force clients to use this method. In other words, you must still set a session timeout to protect your web server from clients that don't perform the appropriate cleanup or don't release their references soon enough.

 If you share sessions between web services, each web service should explicitly remove its subset of objects from the state collection in the ReleaseSession() method, rather than abandon the whole session. To remove a specific object, use the HttpSessionState.Remove() method.

Example: Managing Session State

The code in Example 5-10 expands on Example 5-7 by making use of ASP.NET session state. This example uses the following methods:

Populate()

Creates a DataTable and stores it in session state. In this example, the table is filled with a random list of calls. Each call has two fields: one identifies the name of the caller and the other identifies the length of the call.

Sample GetTotalCallLength() *and* GetCallers() *methods*

Return partial information from the DataTable. The former iterates through the DataTable, adds up the length of each call, and returns the total. The latter creates an array of strings and copies the names of the callers into this array.

ReleaseSession()

Releases all the session data automatically.

GetSessionID()

Shows what session is assigned.

Example 5-10. CustomerState: a stateful data access service

```
public class CustomerState : System.Web.Services.WebService
{
    [WebMethod(EnableSession=true)]
    public int Populate()
    {
        // Instead of using lookup code, this method creates a DataTable
        // and fills it with dummy information.
        DataTable calls = new DataTable();

        // Define two columns for this table.
        calls.Columns.Add("Customer", typeof(System.String));
        calls.Columns.Add("Minutes", typeof(System.Int32));

        // Add some random information into the table.
        Random rand = new Random();
        int count = rand.Next(200) + 1;
        string[] customers = {"Bill", "Mary", "Yefim", "Sara", "Sadaeo"};

        for (int i = 0; i < count; i++)
        {
            DataRow newRow = calls.NewRow();
            newRow["Customer"] = customers[rand.Next(5)];
            newRow["Minutes"] = rand.Next(60);
            calls.Rows.Add(newRow);
        }

        // Store the DataTable.
        Session["Calls"] = calls;

        return calls.Rows.Count;
    }

    [WebMethod(EnableSession=true)]
    public int GetTotalCallLength()
    {
        DataTable calls = (DataTable)Session["Calls"];
        int totalLength = 0;
```

Example 5-10. CustomerState: a stateful data access service (continued)

```
        foreach (DataRow row in calls.Rows)
        {
            totalLength += (int)row["Minutes"];
        }

        return totalLength;
    }

    [WebMethod(EnableSession=true)]
    public string[] GetCallers()
    {
        DataTable calls = (DataTable)Session["Calls"];
        string[] callers = new string[calls.Rows.Count];

        for (int i = 0; i < calls.Rows.Count; i++)
        {
            callers[i] = (string)calls.Rows[i]["Customer"];
        }
        return callers;
    }

    [WebMethod(EnableSession=true)]
    public void ReleaseSession()
    {
        // Time out the session immediately.
        Session.Abandon();
    }

    [WebMethod(EnableSession=true)]
    public string GetSessionID()
    {
        return Session.SessionID;
    }

}
```

The client code shown in Example 5-11 is an ASP.NET web forms page (Figure 5-2) that provides three buttons: one (Populate) that repopulates the session information and two (QueryLength and QueryCallers) that use the other web methods to retrieve and display the available information the service exposes.

In order to maintain the correct web service session, the client page stores the session cookie in view state before every postback (view state encodes information in a special hidden field in an individual web page).

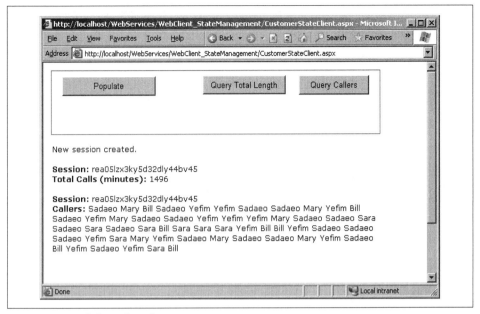

Figure 5-2. A web form client for CustomerState

Example 5-11. CustomerStateClient: a web form client for the CustomerState service

```
using System;
using System.Data;
using System.Net;

namespace StateManagement
{
    public class CustomerStateClient : System.Web.UI.Page
    {
        protected System.Web.UI.WebControls.Button Populate;
        protected System.Web.UI.WebControls.Button QueryLength;
        protected System.Web.UI.WebControls.Button QueryCallers;
        protected System.Web.UI.WebControls.Label Results;

        // The automatically generated code that links the button events
        // to the appropriate methods has been ommitted for clarity.

        private void Populate_Click(object sender, System.EventArgs e)
        {
            // You could just create a new proxy instance, but that would leave
            // any previous session's information in memory until it times out.
            localhost.CustomerState proxy = GetProxy();
            proxy.ReleaseSession();
            proxy.Populate();
            StoreCookie(proxy);
            Results.Text = "New session created.";
```

```csharp
    }

    private void QueryLength_Click(object sender, System.EventArgs e)
    {
        localhost.CustomerState proxy = GetProxy();
        Results.Text = "<b>Session:</b> " + proxy.GetSessionID() + "<br>";
        Results.Text += "<b>Total Calls:</b> " + proxy.GetTotalCallLength();
        StoreCookie(proxy);
    }

    private void QueryCallers_Click(object sender, System.EventArgs e)
    {
        localhost.CustomerState proxy = GetProxy();
        Results.Text = "<b>Session:</b> " + proxy.GetSessionID() + "<br>";
        Results.Text += "<b>Callers:</b> ";
        string[] callers = proxy.GetCallers();
        foreach (string caller in callers)
        {
        Results.Text += caller + " ";
        }
        StoreCookie(proxy);
    }

    private localhost.CustomerState GetProxy()
    {
        // Create the web service proxy.
        localhost.CustomerState proxy = new localhost.CustomerState();

        // Prepare the proxy to hold a session cookie.
        proxy.CookieContainer = new CookieContainer();

        // Try to retrieve the cookie from view state.
        Cookie sessionCookie = (Cookie)ViewState["cookie"];
        if (sessionCookie != null)
        {
            // Apply the previous session cookie.
            proxy.CookieContainer.Add(sessionCookie);
        }

        return proxy;
    }

    private void StoreCookie(localhost.CustomerState proxy)
    {
        // Retrieve and store the current cookie for next time.
        Uri uri = new Uri("http://localhost");
        CookieCollection cookies = proxy.CookieContainer.GetCookies(uri);
        ViewState["cookie"] = cookies["ASP.NET_SessionId"];
    }

    }
}
```

Is this an ideal use of session state? In general, it's best to avoid storing a large DataSet in server memory. However, it the client requires little more than simple aggregate information (like the total of all calls) and releases the session properly when complete, this design can work. However, it's usually better to replace it with dedicated methods. In this case, you might want to substitute a stateless web service that used an SQL Sum query to retrieve the number of calls directly from the data source.

Application State

ASP.NET also provides global in-memory storage that all clients can access through the System.Web.HttpApplicationState class. Unlike with session storage, you don't need to explicitly enable access to application state; it's always available through the built-in Application object of the web service proxy class (or through the current HttpContext).

Programmatically, you access application state the same way that you access session state: by using a weakly typed name/value collection of objects. Unlike session state, however, application state is less common and less useful. Part of the problem is that the HttpApplicationState class is not thread-safe, and you must explicitly lock the entire collection before changing a value, which can impede performance. Objects in application state that might be used simultaneously must also be designed to be thread-safe.

The web service in Example 5-12 is a canonical example that uses application state to manage a global counter.

Example 5-12. GlobalCounter: using application state to manage a global counter

```
public class GlobalCounter : System.Web.Services.WebService
{
    [WebMethod]
    public void Increment()
    {
        Application.Lock();
        if (Application["counter"] == null)
        {
            Application["counter"] = 0;
        }
        else
        {
            Application["counter"] = (int)Application["counter"] + 1;
        }
        Application.UnLock();
    }

    [WebMethod]
    public int Value()
```

```
    {
        return (int)Application["counter"];
    }

}
```

Chapter 6 provides a complete example that demonstrates how you can use application state to host a component.

Custom Cookies

The examples so far have revolved around how to store specific client-related information that will be used in several different methods. Maintaining this information in server-side memory is one approach. Another option is to let the client track and resubmit this information with every request. There are two tools with this option: the relatively primitive (but simple) cookies, and the more sophisticated SOAP headers. First, we'll consider cookies.

While session state is an all-purpose powerhouse that can store complex .NET objects, cookies are an extremely simple form of storage that can retain only string information. Cookies are also stored on the client in a plain text format and sent back and forth across the Internet, making them very insecure.

Before using a cookie in a web service, you should consider a few details:

- Like session state, custom cookies restrict web services to the HTTP protocol.
- Cookies are insecure and limited to string information.
- The client does not control when cookies are being sent. In fact, the application may not even be aware that the web service is retrieving additional information from a cookie, which can cause confusion when identical method calls return different results.

In other words, a web service should never require a cookie, and a cookie should never be used for critical information. Instead, cookies could be used as a quick path to retrieve a small portion of information. If the cookie retrieval fails, you could then perform the required slower operation (like a database lookup). Cookies could also be used to set some external preferences that may or may not be taken into consideration in a web method, or they could be used to send a state token that allows your web service to look up information you have manually stored in a database.

To use a custom cookie, follow these four steps:

1. Create a cookie object for your web service's URL.
2. Insert the required information into the cookie.

3. Add the cookie to the web server response (using the Response object). The cookie will be sent back to the server with every request from the same proxy class (provided the proxy class has enabled cookies by creating a new, empty CookieContainer).

4. On a subsequent web method call, retrieve the cookie (using the Request object) and examine its value.

 Custom cookies are handled slightly differently on the web service side than they are on the client side. This is because the proxy class uses types in the System.Net namespace (like the Cookie and Cookie-Container classes), while the Response and Request objects use types in the System.Web namespace that provide better backward compatibility with legacy ASP code (like HttpCookie and HttpCookieCollection).

Example 5-13 uses a custom cookie to provide a different return value from a web method depending on the client's language. (In a more traditional web service design, you would handle this by creating distinct versions of a method for different languages or by requiring the user to specify a value from a language enumeration in a method parameter. However, using cookies could simplify programming on the client side because some details are handled transparently.)

Example 5-13. CookieTest: using a cookie to indicate a language preference

```
public class CookieTest : System.Web.Services.WebService
{

    [WebMethod]
    public void SetLanguagePreference(string language)
    {
        // Create and attach the cookie.
        HttpCookie cookie = new HttpCookie("preferences");
        cookie.Values.Add("Language", language);
        Context.Response.AppendCookie(cookie);
    }

    [WebMethod]
    public string GetGreeting()
    {
        // Attempt to retrieve a cookie preference.
        try
        {
            HttpCookie cookie = Context.Response.Cookies["preferences"] ;
            if (cookie.Values["Language"] == "french")
            {
                return GetGreetingFrench();
            }
            else
            {
                return GetGreetingEnglish();
```

```
        }
    }
    catch e as Exception
    {
        return GetGreetingEnglish();
    }
}

private string GetGreetingFrench()
{
    return "Bonjour";
}
private string GetGreetingEnglish()
{
    return "Hello";
}

}
```

Remember, the client must explicitly choose to support cookies by initializing the `CookieContainer` property on the proxy class with a new, empty `CookieContainer` object.

Stateless Web Services and Tickets

One of the problems with stateless web services is that they typically require a lot of repetitive information sent in the parameters of each method call. Often, this solution includes information for authentication or session support that is not directly related to the method or the information it returns. Two examples include:

- A custom authentication system, which might require a user ID and password before providing any information. (Or, more commonly, a custom authentication system would issue a time-limited key that would need to be supplied with all future method calls.)

- A custom state management system. For example, you might store state information in a temporary record in a database. This is similar to ASP.NET's session state facility (in SQL Server mode), but you might choose to do it on your own for greater control, for longer-term storage, or to remove the reliance on the session cookie.

Both of these approaches require some sort of ticket (or token) to be supplied to each method. Implementing these designs can make for some cumbersome coding. For example, it could change this method:

```
public int GetTotalCallsByCustomer(string firstName, string LastName)
{
    // Perform calculations/database lookup and return the result.
}
```

into this:

```
public int GetTotalCallsByCustomer(string firstName, string LastName,
                                   int SecurityKey, int SessionID)
{
    // Call a verification routine with the SecurityKey.
    // Retrieve state information from a database with the SessionID.
    // Perform calculations/database lookup and return the result.
}
```

Clearly, if you have a web service that requires these tokens, the coding becomes a little less elegant and a lot more awkward. Not only can the method signature grow to include seemingly unrelated parameters, but also the client has to track this information and submit it with every call.

The previous cookie example hinted at a way that you could maintain and send this information automatically. Unfortunately, cookies have a number of drawbacks. They are awkward for the client to create or manipulate, and they can make a web service's operation less transparent, because the client never sees the information in the cookies.

Another option is to use SOAP headers. SOAP headers supply additional information that is added outside of the main body of the SOAP message and are automatically provided with every web method request.

SOAP Headers

A SOAP message can have three parts: envelope, header, and body. While the SOAP specification requires that a SOAP message have an envelope and body, the header is not required and in many cases is not used. For example, when data is returned in a SOAP message, it is usually placed in its body, not its header. The result is a SOAP message that will likely resemble that in Example 5-14.

Example 5-14. A SOAP message that might be returned by a GetTotalCallLength method

```
<?xml version="1.0" encoding="utf-8"?>

<soap:Envelope>

  <soap:Body>
    <GetTotalCallLengthResponse xmlns="http://tempuri.org/">
      <GetTotalCallLengthResult>472</GetTotalCallLengthResult>
    </GetTotalCallLengthResponse>
  </soap:Body>

</soap:Envelope>
```

The outermost element, `<soap:Envelope>`, contains the `<soap:Body>` element, which in turn contains our data. The soap envelope namespace is defined by the XSD located at *http://schemas.xmlsoap.org/soap/envelope/*, which outlines the three message parts and all of the other elements and attributes found in the SOAP language. This is where the rules for creating SOAP messages are laid out.

Until now, all of our examples have used messages of this format, leaving out the header element. However, the header element can be very useful for passing data *out-of-band*, or separate from the data passed back and forth as part of the web service. Example 5-15 adds a SOAP header that passes a value of 102.

Example 5-15. A SOAP sent to GetTotalCallLength with headers

```
<?xml version="1.0" encoding="utf-8"?>

<soap:Envelope>
  <soap:Header>
    <IDHeader xmlns="http://tempuri.org/" />
      <value>102</value>
  </soap:Header>

  <soap:Body>
    <GetTotalCallLength xmlns="http://tempuri.org/" />
  </soap:Body>
</soap:Envelope>
```

The SOAP header is usually set by the client and retrieved by a web service method. Additional method parameters aren't required.

Defining a SOAP Header

The first step when using a SOAP header is defining a custom data class to hold the header information. This class must derive from the SoapHeader class in the System. Web.Services.Protocols namespace and can be defined in the web service *.asmx* file.

```
using System.Web.Services.Protocols;
```

The following custom SoapHeader class adds a public field to store an authentication key:

```
public class SecurityHeader : System.Web.Services.Protocols.SoapHeader
{
    public string AuthenticationKey;
}
```

The next step is to create a field in the web service to store an instance of the custom SOAP header. This field must also be public.

```
public class HeaderService : System.Web.Services.WebService
{
    public SecurityHeader CurrentUser;

    // (Other web service code omitted.)
}
```

At this point, you have a web service that can receive a SOAP header with any method call. However, nothing happens until you explicitly flag a method with the SoapHeader attribute, as shown for the DoSomething() method of HeaderService in Example 5-16. The SoapHeader attribute names the web service member variable that corresponds to the SOAP header that the method wants to process. This name is provided as a string, rather than a reference, indicating that .NET performs reflection to determine the appropriate class member.

Example 5-16. HeaderService: a web service that can receive a custom SOAP header

```
public class HeaderService : System.Web.Services.WebService
{
    public SecurityHeader CurrentUser;

    [WebMethod, SoapHeader("CurrentUser")]
    public string DoSomething()
    {
        if (Authenticate(CurrentUser.AuthenticationKey))
        {
            return CurrentUser.AuthenticationKey.ToString() + " is allowed";
        }
        else
        {
            return CurrentUser.AuthenticationKey.ToString() + " is denied";
        }
    }

    private bool Authenticate(string key)
    {
        // Perform some authentication.
        return true;
    }

    [WebMethod]
    public string Login(string user, string password)
    {
        // Perform some authentication.
        // Then, return a GUID and store with an expiration time
        // in memory or in a database.
        return Guid.NewGuid().ToString();
    }
}

public class SecurityHeader : System.Web.Services.Protocols.SoapHeader
{
    public string AuthenticationKey;
}
```

In Example 5-16, the DoSomething() method of HeaderService indicates that it wants to process the custom SecurityHeader. When the client invokes this method, the header object is provided through the CurrentUser member variable. You can use multiple SoapHeader attributes to process more than one header in a given method. You'll notice in this example that the web service doesn't actually store the ticket or perform any authentication. Chapter 9 presents a more sophisticated caching example that does fill in these details. For now, it's instructive to consider just how a SOAP header value is submitted and tracked.

The Proxy Class

A couple of interesting details turn up in the proxy class. A slightly shortened version is shown in Example 5-17.

Example 5-17. SimpleHeaderService: a proxy class that incorporates custom SOAP headers

```
using System;
using System.Web.Services;
using System.Web.Services.Protocols;

[WebServiceBinding(Name="SimpleHeaderServiceSoap")]
public class SimpleHeaderService : SoapHttpClientProtocol
{
    public SecurityHeader SecurityHeaderValue;

    public SimpleHeaderService()
    {
        this.Url = "http://localhost/SoapHeaders/SimpleHeaderService.asmx";
    }

    [SoapHeader("SecurityHeaderValue")]
    [SoapDocumentMethod(...)]
    public string DoSomething() {
        object[] results = this.Invoke("DoSomething", new object[0]);
        return ((string)(results[0]));
    }

    // (Login method omitted.)

}

[System.Xml.Serialization.XmlRootAttribute(...)]
public class SecurityHeader : SoapHeader
{
    public string AuthenticationKey;
}
```

A member variable is automatically added to the proxy class for the custom header. By default, this header has the same name as the custom SoapHeader class, with the word Value added on the end. The client can set this variable at any point, but no actual web service communication will take place.

The specific proxy method that requires the header (DoSomething) uses a SoapHeader attribute that names the corresponding SecurityHeaderValue member variable. In other words, when the client calls this method, .NET automatically examines the SecurityHeaderValue property and inserts a corresponding SOAP header into the request. On the web service side, this header is transformed back into a Security-Header object and placed into the corresponding member variable in the web service.

Using SOAP Headers

The previous few sections provided a technical blow-by-blow description of how .NET handles SOAP headers. On the client side, the process reduces to the following straightforward steps:

1. The client creates an instance of the custom SoapHeader class defined in the web service and sets it values as needed.

2. The client assigns the object to the corresponding proxy class member variable. (At this point, no actual communication with the web service takes place.)

3. The client invokes a web method. If the web method is flagged in the proxy class as requiring the SOAP header, it is transmitted along with the SOAP body.

This example bypasses the Login() method and sets a ticket value manually. This allows you to easily verify that the information in the SOAP header is being transmitted to the service.

```
// Create an instance of the custom header class.
localhost.SecurityHeader header = new localhost.SecurityHeader();

// Set a known GUID.
string key = Guid.NewGuid().ToString();
header.AuthenticationKey = key;

// Create the service, and assign the header.
localhost.SimpleHeaderService service = new localhost.SimpleHeaderService();
service.SecurityHeaderValue = header;

// Invoke a web method, and display the result.
MessageBox.Show("Sent: " + key + "\n\nReceived: " + service.DoSomething(),
                "Result");
```

The DoSomething() method returns a value from the header, as shown in Figure 5-3.

Figure 5-3. The result of DoSomething()

The next time you call DoSomething(), or any other method that uses the same SOAP header, the header will be transmitted automatically. This ability (set once, use many times) makes SOAP headers extremely convenient for sending information that's required in many different methods. It can also give your web service the illusion of state. From the client's perspective, the SOAP header is applied only once. In reality, it is the proxy class that is maintaining the header and resending it with every web method invocation.

SOAP headers are ideal for sending tokens (like keys or IDs that refer to a specific state database record or user). In practice, you can use a SOAP header for any type of information that can be serialized to SOAP (including primitive data types, arrays, and structures). The only drawback to using SOAP in this way is that it adds a somewhat proprietary interface to your web service. In other words, it may not be immediately obvious what web methods require a specific use of SOAP headers, because this information isn't provided in the Internet Explorer test page or the WSDL document. It's a good idea to add this information using the WebMethod attribute:

```
[WebMethod(Description = "Requires custom SOAP header SecurityHeader")]
```

Required headers

By default, when a web method defines a SoapHeader attribute, the client must supply the corresponding header. If it doesn't, the .NET Framework will throw a SoapHeaderException (if your web method has trouble interpreting the SoapHeader, you can also throw this exception manually).

To change this behavior and make a SOAP header optional, you can use the Required property:

```
[SoapHeader("CurrentUser", Required = false)]
```

If you make a SOAP header optional, you should test the corresponding member variable to see if it holds a null reference before you try to use it.

Output headers

You can use the Direction option to send information in a web service's SOAP response as well as the client's SOAP request. Example 5-18 shows a different security pattern that uses this technique. In this web service, clients log in with a username and password and receive a key that they can use to access other methods. Presumably, this key is stored in some kind of cache or in server memory so that key validation is quicker than the database lookup.

Example 5-18. A bidirectional header

```
public class SimpleHeaderService : System.Web.Services.WebService
{

    public SecurityHeader CurrentUser;
```

Example 5-18. A bidirectional header (continued)

```
[WebMethod]
[SoapHeader("CurrentUser", Direction = SoapHeaderDirection.InOut)]
public void DoSomething()
{
    if (Authenticate(CurrentUser))
    {
        // Perform the task.
    }
    else
    {
        // User is not allowed.
        return;
    }
}

private bool Authenticate(SecurityHeader user)
{
    if (CurrentUser.AuthenticationKey == "")
    {
        // Perform a database lookup. If a valid user is found,
        // assign a key value and store it somewhere.
        user.AuthenticationKey = Guid.NewGuid().ToString();
    }

    // Check the current key, and return true or false if it
    // can be authenticated.
    return true;
}

}

public class SecurityHeader : System.Web.Services.Protocols.SoapHeader
{
    public string UserName;
    public string Password;
    public string AuthenticationKey = "";
}
```

The interesting thing about this web service is that the authentication is performed seamlessly when needed. The client does not need to know how often the credentials are being checked or worry about calling a Login() method. Instead, the SOAP headers handle the security layer automatically. Table 5-2 lists the possible values for the Direction property.

Table 5-2. Values for the Direction property

Value	Result
SoapDirection.In	The header is sent one way: from the proxy class to the web service.
SoapDirection.Out	The header is sent one way: from the web service to the proxy class.
SoapDirection.InOut	The header is sent both ways: to the web service with the request and back to the proxy class with the response.

Problems with the Ticket System

The ticket system presented here has one potential security flaw: the user ID and password information is passed with every request in clear text, making it easy prey for Internet eavesdropping. Your only option is to use SSL to protect every method call, whereas the earlier example really requires SSL for only the first call to the Login() method. Another way to get around this is to make all parameters bidirectional and erase the password and user ID information as soon as a ticket is generated. However, this process is not necessarily intuitive to the client, which may not realize why a request is denied when the ticket expires.

All this hints at one of the key drawbacks with custom ticket systems: the client must know the details of the authentication process ahead of time. Without a widely accepted standard authentication process flow, this will result in many unique authentication implementations that cannot be automatically accessed, defeating one of the goals of web services: automation. Standards such as XLANG, WSCL, WSFL, and WS-Security attempt to address some of these issues; however, as of yet, none is widely accepted.

Unknown headers

In some cases, a client may define the class for a SOAP header rather than the web service. In fact, the web service may not even natively recognize the header. In this case, the web service can still retrieve and examine its data as a block of raw XML. To do this, the web service needs to define a SoapUnknownHeader member variable. Ideally, you should use an array to retrieve all the unrecognized headers:

```
public class HeaderService : System.Web.Services.WebService
{
    public SoapUnknownHeader[] unknownHeaders;
}
```

You can then retrieve the unknown headers in a specific web method by using the SoapHeader attribute. The following example is a web method that iterates through all the unknown headers and examines the XmlElement object that represents the header:

```
[WebMethod]
[SoapHeader("unknownHeaders", Required=false)]
public string DoSomething()
{
    string combinedXml = "";
    if ( unknownHeaders != null )
    {
        foreach (SoapUnknownHeader header in unknownHeaders)
        {
            combinedXml += header.Element.InnerText;
        }
    }
    return combinedXml;
}
```

With a .NET client, the only times you are likely to encounter an unknown header are when the client is using a different SOAP header definition (perhaps from a previous version of the web service) or the proxy class has been manually modified. The unknown header might also indicate an error, particularly if the SOAP message was constructed manually by a non-.NET client.

All custom `SoapHeader` objects inherit two important properties that are designed to let the client know if a header was recognized:

MustUnderstand

> This means the recipient must be able to interpret the header or a `SoapHeaderException` will be thrown. `MustUnderstand` is set by the sender and is true by default.

DidUnderstand

> This indicates whether the header was successfully processed. It is set by the receiver.

 Remember, the web service and the client can act as either a recipient or a sender. Typically, SOAP headers are sent with the request from the proxy class to a web service, but depending on the Direction property of the SoapHeader attribute, you can also send a header back to the client.

By default, .NET assumes that if the recipient defines the custom SOAP header class, it understands it. It then sets the default value for `DidUnderstand` to true. For instance, in our early examples, a `SecurityHeader` was defined in the web service. This means that `DidUnderstand` defaults to true for any web methods in that web service. Similarly, because the class definition is copied into the proxy class, the `DidUnderstand` property defaults to true for any header that is sent in a response back to the client.

With unknown headers, the situation is a little different. Because they are not defined in the web service, `DidUnderstand` defaults to false. The web service must explicitly change `DidUnderstand` to true, or a `SoapHeaderException` is thrown when the method ends. Alternatively, the client can set `MustUnderstand` to false before sending the SOAP message, relieving the web service of the responsibility.

```
[WebMethod]
[SoapHeader("unknownHeaders", Required=false)]
public string DoSomething()
{
string combinedXml = "";

    if ( unknownHeaders != null )
    {
      foreach (SoapUnknownHeader header in unknownHeaders)
      {
        combinedXml += header.Element.InnerText;
```

```
    // Check whether this is a known header.
    if (header.Element.Name == "SecurityHeader")
    {
        header.DidUnderstand = true;
        // Do something with the element.
    }
    else
    {
        header.DidUnderstand = false;
        // If this header has MustUnderstand set to true,
        // a SoapException will occur at the end of this method.
    }
  }
 }
 return combinedXml;
}
```

SOAP Header Issues

One of the greatest disadvantages of SOAP headers is that they work only if you're using SOAP as the access method. HTTP GET and POST obviously don't support SOAP headers. This is fine for most cases; however, being tied to SOAP as an access protocol may cause problems down the line, depending on the client type. This is not to say that you couldn't have two versions of a web method—one that supports SOAP headers and one that doesn't—but maintaining two code bases is an entirely new can of worms.

The other disadvantage to using SOAP headers is one of incompatibilities. In a perfect world, all of the SOAP implementations would be able to talk to one another in complete harmony. This is unfortunately not the case, as incompatibilities exist between the Microsoft SOAP implementation and other SOAP toolkits. When sending messages with SOAP headers between .NET and other SOAP toolkits, you're more likely to run into these types of incompatibility problems because, in some cases, SOAP toolkit vendors have only recently added support for SOAP headers. It might take a little additional work in some situations to overcome these communication barriers, as we'll see in Chapter 11. Potential incompatibilities aside, SOAP headers can be a very elegant way of providing custom authentication and state management to your web services.

Asynchronous Services

With .NET, you can invoke a web method just as easily as you call a method on a local class. In professional web service development, this syntactical similarity can be misleading, and might even encourage you to use web services inefficiently, adding unnecessary delays to your client applications.

The truth is, though web service calls look like ordinary method calls, they can't always be treated the same. Even the simplest web method takes a nontrivial amount of time to return, due to the time required to transmit information over the Internet. One of the ways to deal with web service delays is to call web methods asynchronously.

As you've learned already, calling a web service involves an exchange of messages. The automatically generated proxy class sends a request and waits for the web service response message. The majority of this chapter concentrates on how you can use the features of the .NET platform to exploit this fact and create true asynchronous consumers that carry on with useful work while the proxy class waits.

Toward the end of the chapter, we'll look at how you can create an asynchronous service using separate components. This technique allows you to create web services that work on their own and can report information about the status of long-running operations.

Asynchronous Consumption

In essence, an asynchronous consumer submits a request for a given method and returns to pick up the result at a later point. This is the natural behavior of a web service, which is masked by the proxy class layer (see Figure 6-1).

Some operations are more suited to asynchronous use than others. For example, if your application needs a given piece of information before it can continue, there is often no reason to use asynchronous access (unless you want to make the application more responsive and allow the user to cancel the operation). On the other hand, if you are starting a long-running task that will eventually update the display with new information, asynchronous consumption may be ideal.

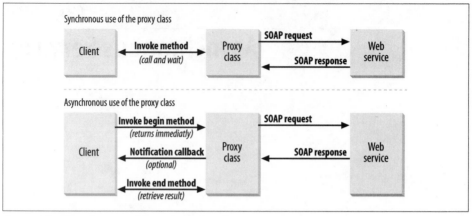

Figure 6-1. Using the proxy class asynchronously

 Web services do not need to be specially designed in order to support asynchronous use. Web service communication is intrinsically asynchronous because it is based on an exchange of SOAP messages. Using the proxy class layer, you can call any web method synchronously or asynchronously.

The BeginInvoke and EndInvoke methods

The automatically generated proxy class has the basic features that you need to call any method asynchronously. Consider the simple web service shown in the following example, which waits for a period of time (a random number of seconds from 5 to 10). The return value is the number of seconds it waited.

```
using System;
using System.Web.Services;
using System.Web.Services.Protocols;

public class TimeDelay : System.Web.Services.WebService
{
    [WebMethod]
    public int Delay()
    {
        DateTime start = DateTime.Now;
        Random rand = new Random();
        TimeSpan delay = new TimeSpan(0, 0, rand.Next(5, 10));
        while (DateTime.Now < start.Add(delay))
        {}
        return delay.Seconds;
    }
}
```

The automatically generated proxy class for this service actually contains three methods.

```
public int Delay()
{
    object[] results = this.Invoke("Delay", new object[0]);
    return ((int)(results[0]));
}

public System.IAsyncResult BeginDelay(System.AsyncCallback callback,
                                      object asyncState)
{
    return this.BeginInvoke("Delay", new object[0], callback, asyncState);
}

public int EndDelay(System.IAsyncResult asyncResult)
{
    object[] results = this.EndInvoke(asyncResult);
    return ((int)(results[0]));
}
```

The first method takes the same name as the original web service method. This is the method you use to call a web service method and wait for it to return. The proxy class uses the derived SoapHttpClientProtocol.Invoke() method to make the remote call.

The other two methods, BeginDelay() and EndDelay(), are provided for asynchronous interaction. They use the SoapHttpClientProtocol.BeginInvoke() and SoapHttp-ClientProtocol.EndInvoke() methods to call a web service without waiting for the response.

 BeginXXX methods always provide two extra parameters. For example, if the Delay web method required two parameters, BeginDelay would have four. The first two would correspond to the web method parameters, and the last two would be special synchronization ingredients, discussed in this chapter. The corresponding EndXXX method always requires one parameter.

Polling Asynchronous Requests

To call a web method asynchronously, start by calling the corresponding BeginXXX method in the proxy class. The BeginXXX method returns a special IAsyncState object that allows you to determine when the method is complete.

The following example is part of an asynchronous Windows consumer. It defines two form-level variables to hold a reference to the proxy class and track the state of the asynchronous method. The web method is invoked when a button is clicked.

```
IAsyncResult handle;
localhost.TimeDelay ws = new localhost.TimeDelay();

private void cmdStart_Click(object sender, System.EventArgs e)
{
    // Don't allow a method to be started again while it is in progress.
    cmdStart.Enabled = false;
```

```
    handle = ws.BeginDelay(null, null);
    lblStatus.Text = "Operation started";
}
```

BeginDelay() returns immediately, often giving you the chance to perform additional actions before the proxy class has even sent the SOAP request message.

One crude way to retrieve the result is by polling (checking periodically) the IAsyncState.IsComplete property. When this value is true, the SOAP response message has been received, and the client can retrieve the result by calling the EndDelay method with the IAsyncState object as a parameter.

In the Windows client example, you can allow the user to check for a result by clicking a different button:

```
private void cmdCheck_Click(object sender, System.EventArgs e)
{
    if (handle == null)
    {
        lblStatus.Text = "Not started yet; handle is null";
    }
    else if (handle.IsCompleted)
    {
        int result = ws.EndDelay(handle);
        lblStatus.Text = "Finished, and returned a delay of " +
                        result + " seconds";

        // Reenable the Start button.
        cmdStart.Enabled = true;

        // Clear the IAsyncState object to prevent calling
        // EndDelay twice (which causes an exception).
        handle = null;
    }
    else
    {
        lblStatus.Text = "Not ready yet";
    }
}
```

Every time the user clicks the Check button, the current status is displayed in a label control. Figure 6-2 shows the result of clicking the Check button once the asynchronous operation is complete.

> Before checking the IAsyncState.IsComplete property, you should check that IAsyncState does not contain a null reference. The BeginXXX method returns immediately, making it possible for a client to attempt to use IAsyncState before it has been initialized. You can verify this in the sample project by clicking the Start and Check buttons in quick succession.

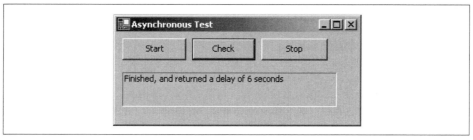

Figure 6-2. A simple asynchronous Windows client

The final step is to perform the minimum required amount of cleanup. This includes a cancel button that allows the operation to be halted immediately. Similarly, if the user closes the form, any outstanding operations should be canceled to prevent an exception. In order to cancel a request, you must explicitly cast the IAsyncState object to a System.Web.Services.Protocols.WebClientAsyncResult object, which provides an Abort() method.

```
private void cmdStop_Click(object sender, System.EventArgs e)
{
    Abort();
    cmdStart.Enabled = true;
}

private void TestForm_Closing(object sender,
                              System.ComponentModel.CancelEventArgs e)
{
    Abort();
}

private void Abort()
{
    if (handle != null)
    {
        if (handle.IsCompleted == false)
        {
            WebClientAsyncResult webHandle = (WebClientAsyncResult)handle;
            webHandle.Abort();
        }
        handle = null;
    }
}
```

Incidentally, if you wish to make an asynchronous method synchronous, you can call the EndXXX method immediately. This method won't return until the operation is complete.

```
localhost.TimeDelay ws = new localhost.TimeDelay();

// Give the web service method a head start.
IAsyncResult handle = ws.BeginDelay(null, null);
```

```
// (Perform some other time-consuming tasks.)

// Retrieve the result. If it isn't ready, wait.
int result = ws.EndDelay(handle);
```

Calling Several Methods Simultaneously

One of the nice things about asynchronous consumption is that you can call multiple methods at once or the same method multiple times. .NET is able to distinguish the different calls, because each one uses a different IAsyncResult handle. As long as you present the correct IAsyncResult handle to the EndXXX method, you will be provided with the corresponding return value.

```
localhost.TimeDelay ws = new localhost.TimeDelay();

// Call the same method three times.
IAsyncResult handle1 = ws.BeginDelay(null, null);
IAsyncResult handle2 = ws.BeginDelay(null, null);
IAsyncResult handle3 = ws.BeginDelay(null, null);

// Retrieve the three results, in order.
int result1 = ws.EndDelay(handle1);
int result2 = ws.EndDelay(handle2);
int result3 = ws.EndDelay(handle3);
```

The next example rewrites our simple form tester so that it supports multiple method calls. A System.Collections.ArrayList object is used to hold the collection of IAsyncResult objects. It all works like this:

1. Every time the user clicks the Start button, a new method call is made and the corresponding IAsyncResult object is added to the ArrayList.

2. Every time the user clicks the Check button, the code iterates through the ArrayList and reports on the contents.

3. A little bit of additional functionality is needed to handle completed results, because the EndDelay() method can't be called more than once. Whenever a completed request is found, the IAsyncResult item is replaced in the ArrayList by an Int32 object that holds the actual result. This approach works because ArrayList objects are generic Object collections that can hold any type. The code checks for this change when it iterates through the ArrayList, determining whether each item is an Int32 or IAsynResult object.

The end result is shown in Figure 6-3.

```
public class SimultaneousCalls : System.Windows.Forms.Form
{
    // (Windows designer code omitted.)
    ArrayList requests = new ArrayList();
    private void cmdStart_Click(object sender, System.EventArgs e)
    {
        IAsyncResult handle = ws.BeginDelay(null, null);
```

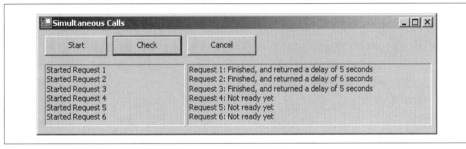

Figure 6-3. Calling web methods concurrently

```
        requests.Add(handle);
        lblReport.Text += "Started Request " + requests.Count + "\n";
    }

    private void cmdCheck_Click(object sender, System.EventArgs e)
    {
        lblStatus.Text = "";

        for (int i = 0; i < requests.Count; i++)
        {
            lblStatus.Text += "Request " + (i+1).ToString() + ": ";

            if (requests[i] == null)
            {
                lblStatus.Text += "Not started yet";
            }
            else if (requests[i] is IAsyncResult)
            {
                IAsyncResult handle = (IAsyncResult)requests[i];
                if (handle.IsCompleted)
                {
                    int result = ws.EndDelay(handle);
                    lblStatus.Text += "Finished, and returned a delay of " +
                                    result + " seconds";
                    requests[i] = result;
                }
                else
                {

                    lblStatus.Text += "Not ready yet";
                }
            }
            else if (requests[i] is Int32)
            {
                lblStatus.Text += "Finished, and returned a delay of " +
                                requests[i].ToString() + " seconds";
            }
            lblStatus.Text += "\n";
        }
    }
}
```

In addition, adding some sort of cleanup code in case the operation is canceled before it is complete is probably a good idea:

```
private void cmdCancel_Click(object sender, System.EventArgs e)
{
    lblStatus.Text = "";
    lblReport.Text = "";
    Abort();

}
private void SimultaneousCalls_Closing(object sender, _
            System.ComponentModel.CancelEventArgs e)
{
    Abort();
}

private void Abort()
{
    for (int i = 0; i < requests.Count; i++)
    {
        if (requests[i] is IAsyncResult)
        {
            IAsyncResult handle = (IAsyncResult)requests[i];
            if (!handle.IsCompleted)
    {
                WebClientAsyncResult webHandle = (WebClientAsyncResult)handle;
                webHandle.Abort();
            }
        }
    }
    requests.Clear();
}
```

Using a WaitHandle

You can also interact with an asynchronous request using a System.Threading. WaitHandle object. The WaitHandle gives you the freedom to submit a batch of requests and wait for any one request (or every request) to complete before continuing. The simplest way to do this is to use the IAsyncResult.AsyncHandle property, which returns a synchronization object you can use.

For example, the following statement blocks your code until the proxy class returns a result:

```
localhost.TimeDelay ws = new localhost.TimeDelay();
IAsyncResult handle = ws.BeginDelay(null, null);

// Wait for the result.
handle.AsyncWaitHandle.WaitOne();
```

You can also use an overloaded WaitOne() method or a TimeSpan object to specify a maximum wait period as a number of milliseconds.

```
// Wait 100 milliseconds or until the method returns (whichever comes first).
handle.AsyncWaitHandle.WaitOne(100, false);

// The same statement with a TimeSpan object.
handle.AsyncWaitHandle.WaitOne(new TimeSpan(0,0,0,0,100), false);
```

The WaitHandle class also provides two useful static methods: WaitAll() and
WaitAny(). The WaitAll() method accepts an array of WaitHandle objects and waits
until the operations on each handle are complete. This provides a useful way to manage multiple web method calls.

```
// Wait for all the calls to finish.
WaitHandle.WaitAll(waitHandleArray);
```

For example, consider a scenario in which you need to make multiple independent
web method calls. Before your application can continue, you must complete all of
these calls. However, to increase performance, you can execute all of the calls at
once. You could manage this scenario with some inelegant code (for example, a loop
that continuously polls all the IAsyncResult objects). A better solution is to use the
WaitHandle.WaitAll() method.

To test this technique, you can create a program that makes three web method calls
synchronously or asynchronously, depending on which button the user clicks. The
program is shown in action in Figure 6-4.

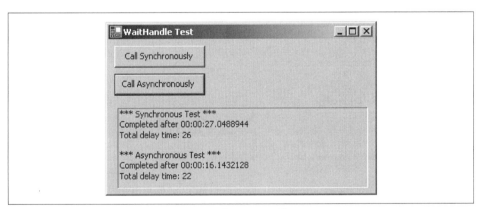

Figure 6-4. Managing concurrent requests with WaitHandles

```
public class WaitHandleTest : System.Windows.Forms.Form
{
    // (Windows designer code omitted.)

    localhost.TimeDelay ws = new localhost.TimeDelay();

    private void cmdCallAsynchronously_Click(object sender, System.EventArgs e)
    {
```

```
    // Indicate that tasks are taking place.
    this.Cursor = Cursors.WaitCursor;

    // Keep track of the elapsed time.
    DateTime startDate = DateTime.Now;

    // Call three methods asynchronously.
    IAsyncResult handle1 = ws.BeginDelay(null, null);
    IAsyncResult handle2 = ws.BeginDelay(null, null);
    IAsyncResult handle3 = ws.BeginDelay(null, null);

    WaitHandle[] waitHandle = {handle1.AsyncWaitHandle,
                handle2.AsyncWaitHandle, handle3.AsyncWaitHandle};

    // Wait for all the calls to finish.
    WaitHandle.WaitAll(waitHandle);
    int totalDelay = ws.EndDelay(handle1) + ws.EndDelay(handle2) +
                ws.EndDelay(handle3);
    TimeSpan elapsedTime = DateTime.Now - startDate;

    lblResult.Text += "*** Asynchronous Test ***\n;
    lblResult.Text += "Completed after " + elapsedTime.ToString() + "\n";
    lblResult.Text += "Total delay time: " + totalDelay.ToString() + "\n\n";

    this.Cursor = Cursors.Default;
}

private void cmdCallSynchronously_Click(object sender, System.EventArgs e)
{
    // Indicate that tasks are taking place.
    this.Cursor = Cursors.WaitCursor;

    // Keep track of the elapsed time.
    DateTime startDate = DateTime.Now;

    // Execute three methods synchronously. These will
    // be performed one after another, in the order they appear.
    int totalDelay = ws.Delay() + ws.Delay() + ws.Delay();

    TimeSpan elapsedTime = DateTime.Now - startDate;
    lblResult.Text += "*** Synchronous Test ***\n";
    lblResult.Text += "Completed after " + elapsedTime.ToString() + "\n";
    lblResult.Text += "Total delay time: " + totalDelay.ToString() + "\n\n";

    this.Cursor = Cursors.Default;
}
}
```

The results are telling. Even performing the test on a local computer that doesn't
provide multithreading, the wait times are reduced when the methods are called
simultaneously and asynchronously. Typically, a total wait time of 22 seconds is
reduced to about 16.

The example uses multiple calls to the same method. You could substitute this with multiple calls to different methods, without changing the underlying concept. The only important detail is that all the methods must be independent. If you need to retrieve a result from one method and supply it as a parameter to another, you must perform these steps synchronously, in order.

You can also use the WaitHandle.WaitAny() method with an array of wait handles. This method returns when any one of the web service methods has completed. The method returns an integer that specifies the array index of the IAsyncResult instance that satisfied the wait. It is now complete (although it is possible that multiple operations will complete in quick succession).

Using Callbacks

Wait handles and polling are useful if your application needs to wait for information from a web service before it can continue. However, if your application has useful work to do that doesn't depend on this information, these techniques are inefficient (and inconvenient). They often require that some code be dedicated to periodically checking the IAsyncResult state, which reduces performance, adds complexity, and potentially ties up the main thread of execution, preventing other important code from being executed. The examples we've considered so far have handled this by polling only at the user's request. This technique works well for a demonstration program but would be unworkable in most professional applications.

Fortunately, .NET provides another approach to interacting with asynchronous web method calls: callbacks. Callbacks allow you to submit a delegate that identifies a specific method in your code. When the web method is complete, this delegate is invoked and passed the appropriate IAsyncResult object.

The method you create to receive the callback must use the signature defined by the System.AsyncCallback delegate:

```
public void Callback(IAsyncResult handle)
{ }
```

To attach a callback, you create an AsyncCallback delegate variable that points to your method. Then, you pass this variable to the BeginXXX method.

```
// Create the delegate variable cb.
// cb is essentially a function pointer to the Callback method.
AsyncCallback cb = new AsyncCallback(Callback);

// Start the method asynchronously, with the callback.
ws.BeginDelay(cb, null);
```

Your callback method simply retrieves the result. It has no way of knowing what request originated the response, unless you use a different callback method for every web method request. To circumvent this problem, .NET allows you to send some additional information that will be provided with the result object in the IAsyncResult.AsyncState property. This information can consist of any object and is specified in the second special parameter of the BeginXXX method.

```
ws.BeginDelay(cb, requestNumber);
```

In our examples, we use a form-level variable to keep track of the current proxy class instance. If you do not use this technique, or you use several different proxy class instances, you must pass the proxy class instance in the asyncState parameter:

```
ws.BeginDelay(cb, ws);
```

You can then retrieve it and cast it to the appropriate type in the callback procedure:

```
public void Callback(IAsyncResult handle)
{
    localhost.TimeDelay ws = (localhost.TimeDelay)handle.AsyncState;
    int result = ws.EndDelay(handle);
}
```

Using these callback techniques, you can rewrite the earlier example of multiple asynchronous calls with a client that automatically reports when a task is finished (see Figure 6-5).

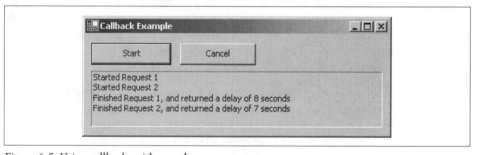

Figure 6-5. Using callbacks with asynchronous requests

Notice in this example that requests that take the shortest amount of time don't necessarily finish first. The reason for this apparent discrepancy is the fact that sending a request to start the web method can take several seconds, adding extra time before the proxy class method returns. If you adjust the Delay web method to use a much longer delay (like one between 10 and 30 seconds), this discrepancy will disappear, and you will see that the method calls with the least delay finish first.

```
public class CallbackExample : System.Windows.Forms.Form
{
    // (Windows designer code omitted.)

    int requestCount = 0;
    localhost.TimeDelay ws = new localhost.TimeDelay();

    private void cmdStart_Click(object sender, System.EventArgs e)
```

```
{
    requestCount += 1;
    lblReport.Text += "Started Request " + requestCount.ToString() + "\n";
    AsyncCallback cb = new AsyncCallback(Callback);
    ws.BeginDelay(cb, requestCount);
}

public void Callback(IAsyncResult handle)
{
    int result = ws.EndDelay(handle);
    lblReport.Text += "Finished Request " + handle.AsyncState.ToString() +
                    ", and returned a delay of " + result + " seconds\n";
}

}
```

There is one potential oversight in the previous example. The callback method will not execute on the same thread as the calling code. This means that it may execute at the same time another part of your application is executing. To prevent potential problems, you should use synchronization (like the lock statement) when accessing objects that could be in use by other parts of your program.

Controls follow slightly different rules—it's never appropriate to try to lock a control for exclusive access, as this can cause problems with various system calls. Instead, you should always use the Invoke() method to marshal control method calls operations to the user interface thread. In order to do so, you'll need to create a helper class that performs the update:

```
public class Updater
{
    private string addText;
    private Control control;

    public Updater(string text, Control control)
    {
        this.addText = text;
        this.control = control;
    }

    public void Update()
    {
        this.control.Text += addText;
    }
}
```

You must then rewrite the code that handles the callback:

```
public void Callback(IAsyncResult handle)
{
    int result = ws.EndDelay(handle);
    string text ="Finished Request "+ handle.AsyncState.ToString() +
        ", and returned a delay of " + result + "seconds \n";
```

```
    Updater updater = new Updater(text, lblReport);

    // Marshal the code to the user interface thread.
    lblReport.Invoke(new MethodInvoker(updater.Update));
}
```

Clearly, multithreaded programming can get a little sticky, especially when dealing with user interface and shared resources. Unfortunately, we can't cover every aspect in a single chapter. For more information, you may want to consult the MSDN or a dedicated book about .NET threading.

Using a Complete Threading Class

The examples so far are ideal for executing independent web methods. However, they aren't much help if you need to perform several methods in a specific order. For example, imagine you have two web methods you want to call, and the second web method requires information returned from the first. You can't invoke both of these methods asynchronously and still control the order in which they execute.

To solve this problem, you must create your own threading class. This technique bypasses the features built into the proxy class, but it's an ideal solution in many cases.

The threading class calls all the web service methods you need synchronously, in the appropriate order. However, this task is performed on a different thread, so it doesn't tie up your application. When it's completed its tasks, it calls back to your application by raising an event.

```
public class ServiceThread
{
    public int Result1;
    public int Result2;

    public event EventHandler OperationComplete;
    public void Start()
    {
        localhost.TimeDelay ws = new localhost.TimeDelay();
        Result1 = ws.Delay();
        Result2 = ws.Delay();
        OperationComplete(this, new EventArgs());
    }
}
```

The ServiceThread class defines two member variables to store the results of its operations. Alternatively, you can pass this information to your application in a custom EventArgs object with the event.

The calling code creates an instance of the ServiceThread class on a new thread. It also assigns an event handler for the OperationComplete event and then continues with its normal operation.

```
private void cmdStart_Click(object sender, System.EventArgs e)
{
    // Create the thread.
    ServiceThread st = new ServiceThread();
    Thread thread = new Thread(new ThreadStart(st.Start));

    // Connect an event handler.
    st.OperationComplete += new EventHandler(this.OperationComplete);

    // Start the thread.
    thread.Start();

    cmdStart.Enabled = false;
}
```

The OperationComplete event handler updates the form when it receives the event
(see Figure 6-6).

```
private void OperationComplete(object sender, System.EventArgs e)
{
    ServiceThread st = (ServiceThread)sender;
    lblStatus.Text = "Finished, and returned a delay of "
                    + st.Result1.ToString() + " and "
                    + st.Result2.ToString() + " seconds.";
    cmdStart.Enabled = true;
}
```

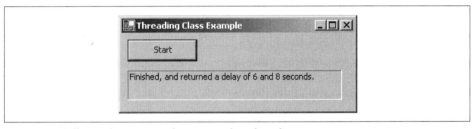

Figure 6-6. Calling web services with a custom threading class

The OperationComplete event occurs on the new thread you created, not on the user
interface thread. Thus, to make this code safe, you need to use the Control.Invoke()
method, as shown earlier.

Asynchronous Services

As you've seen, web service communication is completely asynchronous. However,
the typical web method is not. For example, our Delay() method runs from start to
finish on the same ASP.NET worker thread.

This lack becomes a bit of an issue if you want to add enhanced features to your web
services. For example, new web service developers commonly ask how they can create a web method that returns progress information. That way, a progress bar could

be displayed on the client side, indicating the status of a long-running operation. While this is theoretically possible with SOAP, it's not the way .NET web services are designed. A web method can't return any information until it finishes its task. This is a limitation compared to other Remote Method Invocation techniques, which allow the client to receive events or callbacks.

OneWay Methods

One interesting approach is to use a "fire-and-forget" web method. You can mark a web method for this style of execution by adding a SoapRpcMethod attribute (from the System.Web.Services.Protocols namespace) with the OneWay property set to true.

```
using System.Web.Services;
using System.Web.Services.Protocols;

public class AsynchronousService: WebService {

    [SoapRpcMethod(OneWay = true)]
    [WebMethod]
    public void StartLongOperation()
    {
        // Begin a process that takes a long time to complete.
    }

}
```

In this case, the client returns immediately, cannot receive a return value, and will not be notified about any exceptions that are thrown. The web method will continue to execute asynchronously. If you need to store a result that the client needs to access later, you will probably place it in some sort of persistent storage, such as a database. The database record will need to incorporate some piece of user identification (such as a user ID) in order to identify who it is for. There is no way to return a unique ticket to the client, and so this approach isn't as flexible as the one we'll consider next.

Asynchronous Services with Components

You can also implement a sophisticated asynchronous web service using separate components. For example, you could create a service that reports its progress by dividing the service into several different web methods. One method would start the operation, another would retrieve a progress update, and a third would retrieve the final result. This approach is much more complex and can pose scalability challenges, but it does have interesting uses as well. We'll examine this design for the remainder of this chapter.

In order to use this pattern, the actual task must be completed on a different thread than the one that serves the client. This result is achieved via a separate component.

In the example in the next section, there are three classes (not including the client): the web service class, a service monitor class, and the actual service class. The details of the arrangement are diagrammed in Figure 6-7.

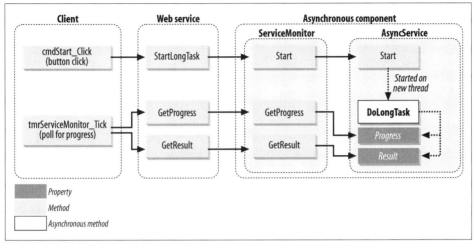

Figure 6-7. A model for an asynchronous service

The first step is to start with the innermost layer and create the component, as explained in the following section.

The Service class

The component contains two classes. The first of these, Service (called AsyncService in this example), performs the actual operation. It contains two member variables, one for tracking the progress (as an integer representing the percent complete) and one for holding the final result.

```
using System;
using System.Threading;

public class AsyncService
{
    public int Progress;
    public int Result;

    public void Start()
    {
        Thread asyncThread = new Thread(new ThreadStart(DoLongTask));
        asyncThread.Start();
    }

    private void DoLongTask()
    {
        DateTime start = DateTime.Now;
        TimeSpan delay = new TimeSpan(0, 0, new Random().Next(30, 59));
```

```
        while (DateTime.Now < start.Add(delay))
        {
            Progress = (int)(Math.Round((DateTime.Now.Subtract(start).TotalSeconds
                                    / delay.TotalSeconds) * 100));
        }
        Result = delay.Seconds;
    }
}
```

The method DoLongTask() contains the logic that would usually be contained in the web service method. All it does is loop for a random number of seconds (between 30 and 59). Each time it passes through the loop, it updates the Progress member variable. When the loop is finished, it sets the Result member variable.

Note that the DoLongTask() method is private. The ServiceMonitor class simply calls the public Start() method, which creates a new thread to work on. If this extra step hadn't been taken, the Start() and DoLongTask() methods would have executed synchronously, and the ServiceMonitor wouldn't regain control until everything was complete.

The AsyncService Class and Thread Pooling

There is one potential weakness that you could improve upon in the AsyncService class. Currently, it creates a thread for every new client. However, in a web service situation, it's possible that you might have dozens or hundreds of simultaneous client requests. If you create a thread for each client, the server will quickly become bogged down just tracking and scheduling all these threads, and performance will be adversely affected. A better approach would be to use some sort of thread pooling (perhaps through the .NET System.Threading.ThreadPool class).

With the ThreadPool class, you "work items" with complete abandon. The .NET runtime decides whether to execute this work item with a currently available thread, a new thread, or simply queue it until an existing thread is free. By default, the ThreadPool class allows only 25 threads per CPU (with one additional thread for monitoring).

Here's the rewritten code that would use a thread pool instead of a dedicated thread. Note that QueueUserWorkItem() is a static method—the thread pool is a shared, system-wide resource.

```
public void Start()
{
    WaitCallback work = new WaitCallback(DoLongTask);
    ThreadPool.QueueUserWorkItem(work);
}
```

The ServiceMonitor class

The ServiceMonitor class is the second part of the component. It provides an intermediate layer between the "real" web service and the AsyncService class. You could

---

use ServiceMonitor to manage more than one asynchronous web service class, but it's best to divide the work. If multiple clients are trying to access the same object at once, there will be an inevitable wait for some of them.

```
using System;
using System.Collections;

public class ServiceMonitor
{
    Hashtable clients = new Hashtable();

    public string Start()
    {
        // Generate a new unique key.
        // The key is a relatively unique string of numbers that combines
        // the current time and a random number from 0 to 999.
        // Alternatively, you could use a GUID.
        string key;
        Random rand = new Random();
        key = DateTime.Now.Ticks.ToString() + rand.Next(1000).ToString();

        AsyncService serviceInstance = new AsyncService();
        serviceInstance.Start();

        clients.Add(key, serviceInstance);

        return key;
    }

    public int GetProgress(string key)
    {
        try
        {
            return ((AsyncService)clients[key]).Progress;
        }
        catch
        {
            // It would be better to return a custom error.
            return 0;
        }
    }

    public object GetResult(string key)
    {
        try
        {
            Object obj = ((AsyncService)clients[key]).Result;
            release(key);
            return obj;
        }
        catch
        {
            // It would be better to return a custom error.
```

```
        return 0;
      }
    }

    private void release(string key)
    {
        clients[key] = null;
    }
  }
```

The ServiceMonitor class uses a Hashtable to store a collection of multiple requests. The Hashtable is similar to an ArrayList but is optimized for fast lookup using a key. Each time a new request is received, a unique key is generated using the current date, the current time, and a random number from 0 to 999. A new instance of the AsyncService is created, added to the Hashtable with the appropriate key, and started. The key is returned to the client, which uses it to retrieve the progress or the result.

The client can query information about a current request, using the key and the GetProgress() and GetResult() methods. Notice that GetResult() returns a weakly typed object. This way it is more loosely coupled, because it does not make any assumption about the return value. Another interesting point is that, as soon as the result is retrieved, the AsyncService instance is destroyed. This automatic cleanup is a design decision. Another approach might be to have the client call Release() manually (assuming an environment of considerate clients).

 If an error occurs (whether it is the result of an invalid key, a service that hasn't started yet, or some other problem), it is caught and ignored. A better design choice might be to return a custom error, which the calling web service could then translate into a custom SOAP error. For more information about error handling, refer to Chapter 8.

Compiling the component

Before you can use this component with a web service, you must compile it to a DLL. This DLL is then placed in the \bin subdirectory of the appropriate ASP.NET application. When ASP.NET starts this application (which it does automatically in response to any web service or web page request), it automatically references all the assemblies in the \bin directory and makes them available to all web pages and web services in the application.

To compile the DLL, you can use Visual Studio .NET to add a project reference or you can use the csc command-line utility. If you use the latter, remember to specify the /t:library parameter to indicate that it is a DLL:

```
csc /t:library AsyncComponent.cs
```

The web service

The topmost level is the web service itself. The web service does little more than forward requests on to the custom component. However, the web service has the additional task of creating, storing, and locating the component instance, which is shared between all clients and used for all requests. To allow for this, the component is stored in Application state, which was discussed in detail in Chapter 5. Using the global Application collection means that the ServiceMonitor component has to support multiple threads. This is because all ASP.NET requests will share the same ServiceMonitor component, and multiple requests may be executed at the same time on separate ASP.NET worker threads.

```
using System;
using System.Web;
using System.Web.Services;

using AsyncComponent;
public class AsyncWebService : System.Web.Services.WebService
{
    AsyncComponent.ServiceMonitor c;

    [WebMethod]
    public string StartLongTask()
    {
        if (Application["AsyncComponent"] == null)
        {
            c = new ServiceMonitor();
            Application["AsyncComponent"] = c;
        }
        else
        {
            c = (ServiceMonitor)(Application["AsyncComponent"]);
        }

        return c.Start();
    }

    [WebMethod]
    public int GetProgress(string key)
    {
        c = (ServiceMonitor)(Application["AsyncComponent"]);
        return c.GetProgress(key);
    }

    [WebMethod]
    public object GetResult(string key)
    {
        c = (ServiceMonitor)(Application["AsyncComponent"]);
        return c.GetResult(key);
    }

}
```

The client starts the asynchronous web service by calling the StartLongTask() web method. This method checks whether the appropriate application-level instance of the component exists. If not, it creates it. The GetProgress() and GetResult() methods call the corresponding methods in the component.

The client

The client's job is extremely easy. In fact, it's easier for the client to interact with an asynchronous web service than interact asynchronously with the proxy class.

In this case, we use a simple Windows form that displays a single window. A timer is used to automatically query the GetProgress() web service method every four seconds.

```
public class ClientForm : System.Windows.Forms.Form
{

    // (Windows designer code omitted.)

    localhost.AsyncWebService ws = new localhost.AsyncWebService();
    string key;

    private void cmdStart_Click(object sender, System.EventArgs e)
    {
        key = ws.StartLongTask();
        tmrServiceMonitor.Enabled = true;
    }

    private void tmrServiceMonitor_Tick(object sender, System.EventArgs e)
    {
        int progress = ws.GetProgress(key);
        lblResult.Text = progress.ToString() + "% done";

        // The following line is optional. It configures a ProgressBar control.
        progressBar.Value = progress;

        if (progress == 100)
        {
            tmrServiceMonitor.Enabled = false;
            lblResult.Text = "Returned after ";
            lblResult.Text += ws.GetResult(key).ToString() + " seconds";
        }
    }

}
```

 You may have already realized that one of the drawbacks to this approach is the possibility that clients will overuse the GetProgress() method. This additional polling can exact a significant extra performance burden on your web server and shouldn't be taken lightly.

The result is an asynchronous service that reports its progress, as shown in Figure 6-8.

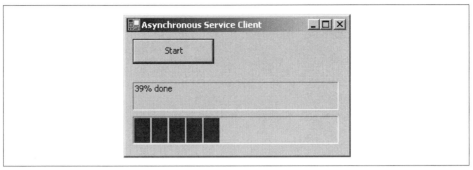

Figure 6-8. The asynchronous web service client

Threading safely

Before this component is robust enough to tackle multiple concurrent clients, we need to add some rudimentary locking. For example, under this system, a single ServiceMonitor object may quite possibly create and track hundreds of AsyncService instances, each one performing a task for a different client. As these clients check these services, some will probably call methods like GetResult() and GetProgress() at the same time. These simultaneous calls could lead to quirky behavior or mysterious errors under the right circumstances. To remedy the situation, you must use locking to obtain brief exclusive access to the resource. This will slow performance (because concurrent clients will have to wait their turn), but it will ensure safe threading.

With the asynchronous web service example, we can implement locking in one of two places: the web service (by locking access to the component before calling a method) or in the component itself. In this case, it makes sense to give this responsibility to the component, to eliminate repetitive code and ensure safety if it is used in a different scenario (for example, through .NET remoting) or another web service. The most important change is to lock the Hashtable whenever it is used (for adding a client, changing a value, or just enumerating through it).

Here's a more defensive rewriting of the ServiceMonitor class. The changes are highlighted in bold.

```
public class ServiceMonitor
{
    Hashtable clients = new Hashtable();

    public string Start()
    {
        string key;
        Random rand = new Random();
        key = DateTime.Now.Ticks.ToString() + rand.Next(1000).ToString();

        AsyncService serviceInstance = new AsyncService();
        serviceInstance.Start();
```

```
        lock (clients)
        {
            clients.Add(key, serviceInstance);
        }

        return key;
    }

    public int GetProgress(string key)
    {
        try
        {
            AsyncService client = (AsyncService)clients[key];
            lock (client)
            {
                return client.Progress;
            }
        }
        catch
        {
            return 0;
        }
    }

    public object GetResult(string key)
    {
        try
        {
            AsyncService client = (AsyncService)clients[key];
            lock (client)
            {
                object result = client.Progress;
            }
            release(key);
            return obj;
        }
        catch
        {
            // It would be better to return a custom error.
            return 0;
        }
    }

    void release(string key)
    {
        lock (clients)
        {
            clients[key] = null;
        }
    }
}
```

Note that the AsyncService instance is locked before the GetResult() or
GetProgress() method is called, even though only one client will be accessing a

specific task at a time. This is because the asynchronous service could be updating the progress or result information at the same time that the web service is attempting to read the information.

One minor change is required to the web service to ensure that the component can't be accidentally created twice if two clients discover at the same time that it doesn't exist:

```
[WebMethod]
public string StartLongTask()
{
    // Ensure that the component is not created at the same time
    // by multiple clients.
    Application.Lock();

    if (Application["AsyncComponent"] == null)
    {
        c = new ServiceMonitor();
        Application["AsyncComponent"] = c;
    }
    else
    {
        c = (ServiceMonitor)(Application["AsyncComponent"]);
    }
    Application.UnLock();

    return c.Start();
}
```

This method locks the Application collection, which can hamper performance if you use this collection for other purposes. In this case, it's probably better to write a *global.asax* file for the ASP.NET application that handles the Application_Start event and automatically creates the required component. In Visual Studio .NET, a *global.asax* file is provided as part of your web service project.

```
using System;
using System.Web;
using AsyncComponent;

public class Global : System.Web.HttpApplication
{
    protected void Application_Start(Object sender, EventArgs e)
    {
        ServiceMonitor c = new ServiceMonitor();
        Application["AsyncComponent"] = c;
    }
}
```

You should then remove the object creation code from the StartLongTask() method.

Other Approaches to Asynchronous Services

Our example used a backend component hosted by ASP.NET to provide asynchronous work. However, there are other possible approaches. One example is to use an out-of-process component, perhaps even one running on another computer. To communicate with this component, the web service has several options: it could use .NET remoting, or rely on a dedicated messaging service like Microsoft Message Queuing or even email. These approaches feature slower communication, because the overhead in communicating out-of-process or through an intermediary is greater than communicating with the in-memory ASP.NET Application collection. However, they may not require multithreaded code, and can thus offer an easier programming model.

When creating a web service, you'll need to think carefully about these issues. The component-based asynchronous service is a sophisticated design that adds complexity and requires careful testing. If you don't need to use it, you'll find that it's much easier to work with the asynchronous proxy class layer.

CHAPTER 7

Caching and Profiling

Caching is one of the most frequently neglected aspects of web programming. Often, developers start to think about caching after every other aspect of a project is complete, rather than considering it from the start. When done right, caching can be a small miracle, boosting the performance of code dramatically, circumventing other bottlenecks, and requiring nothing more that a little straightforward code and planning ahead. In web service programming, caching can also transform stateful designs into scalable server-friendly code.

This chapter explains how to use output and data caching in a web service and provides a design pattern that substitutes caching for session state. You'll also learn details about cache dependencies, policies, and priorities that give you a fine-grained level of control over ASP.NET's caching service. Toward the end of the chapter, we'll consider the tools that let you determine how well your web service performs and assess the effect of different caching strategies.

ASP.NET Caching

Caching is another service (like session state management) that is provided as a part of ASP.NET. ASP.NET's caching features go far beyond what traditional ASP could offer. In fact, there are actually two different types of ASP.NET caching that a web service can use:

Output caching
> Stores the result from a web method invocation and reuses it for other clients that supply the same parameters, within a set amount of time. Output caching happens automatically when you enable it, requires no real web service code, and provides only a coarse level of control.

Data caching
> Works through your web service code. With data caching, you store specific objects in the cache, with the expiration policy and dependencies that you specify. You can then retrieve the information later, but the process is entirely manual.

These two types of caching are complimentary. There's no reason you shouldn't mix both in the same web service (or even in the same web method). While data caching offers more control, neither method of caching can be considered *better* than the other. Microsoft's platform samples often use output caching exclusively because it doesn't cloud the code and it's extremely simple to implement and remove at will.

Figures 7-1 and 7-2 show a high-level comparison of the two different types of ASP. NET caching.

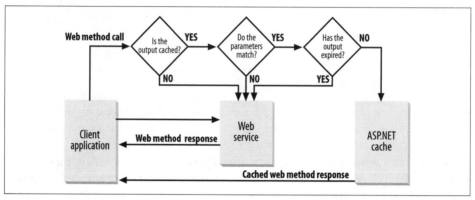

Figure 7-1. ASP.NET output caching

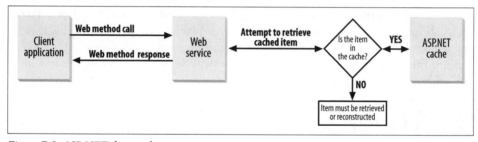

Figure 7-2. ASP.NET data caching

The Purpose of Caching

Both data caching and output caching operate on the same principle: store expensive (time-consuming) information to create so it can be automatically reused. For example, if a web method result requires a complex calculation, output caching may save processing time, speeding up the response rate for the client and lessening the burden on the web server's CPU. However, caching is much more commonly used to save a trip to a data source (like an SQL Server database). Data access is typically the slowest part of any web service and (because connections are finite) the first scalability bottleneck encountered. Whether you are reading from a file or connecting to a database, access can be provided to only a set number of simultaneous users.

Both data caching and output caching store information in an in-memory cache. ASP.NET manages this cache automatically, removing items when they expire or if server memory becomes scarce. This is the most important benefit of caching; ASP. NET monitors it and disposes of unneeded resources automatically, allowing you to put information into the cache without worrying about crippling the server.

 Caching is programmer-friendly: if you make a mistake and enter too much information into the cache, ASP.NET just throws out some of the excess. This is different than session state, when the information remains until it times out, or application state, when the information remains for the life of the application. However, overfilling the cache is not without its own penalties. By doing so, you'll probably force out other, more important information, reducing the efficiency and performance of caching in other parts of your application.

Testing with Cached Web Services

Testing a web service that uses caching can be confusing. For example, if you use data caching, and then solve a problem that was corrupting the cached data, your new code may end up using the original cached data until it expires. This behavior occurs even if you recompile your web service and even if you are using Visual Studio .NET to test your application.

Here are some tips for working with a cached web service:

- If you are using output caching, ASP.NET automatically adds dependency links to the original source files. Recompile your web service to flush out any cached responses.

- In Visual Studio .NET, you can always set breakpoints in your code. If a web method's breakpoints are not triggered when you invoke it, either you are not compiling with the debug symbols for the web service (see Chapter 8 for more information) or the code is not actually being executed because the code is cached.

- Often, you may have a piece of information that is cached for a long amount of time, but you want to force your code to bypass this information and retrieve or recalculate the information. To accomplish this, you can use the Task Manager to find and terminate the ASP.NET worked process (*aspnet_wp.exe*). The next time you run your application, the web service will be restarted with an empty cache.

- A slightly quicker way to empty the cache is to open the *web.config* file in the web service application directory and save it (even if no changes have been made). ASP.NET automatically creates a new application domain to serve new requests and uses the settings from the new *web.config* file in this domain. The cache in the new application domain will be empty. (If you are using Visual Studio .NET, you can modify and save the *web.config* file in the IDE at runtime. Unlike your code files, the *web.config* file will not be read-only.)

Simple Output Caching

Earlier chapters in this book explained the basics of output caching. In order to enable it, all you need to do is specify the `CacheDuration` property with the `WebMethod` attribute. Output caching is always specified as a number of seconds and is applied individually on a per-method basis.

The canonical example for testing caching is to create a method that returns the current time. In the following code listing, the first time the method is requested, the code runs, and the current date is retrieved and returned from the function. The next time the code is run, the cached result will be automatically returned (as long as fewer than 60 seconds have elapsed since the first method call).

```
[WebMethod(CacheDuration=60)]
public string GetDateTime()
{
    return System.DateTime.Now.ToString();
}
```

As you can see, you don't actually insert any caching code into the web method itself. ASP.NET manages the output cache automatically.

One of the most useful features of output caching with a web service is that a response is reused only when the list of supplied method parameters is exactly the same. Consider the following example:

```
[WebMethod(CacheDuration=60)]
public string GetDateTime(bool UTC)
{
    if (UTC == true)
    {
        return System.DateTime.Now.ToUniversalTime().ToString();
    }
    else
    {
        return System.DateTime.Now.ToString();
    }
}
```

This version of the `GetDateTime()` method accepts a single Boolean parameter. If set to `true`, the returned date and time are automatically converted to universal coordinated time (UTC, also known as Greenwich Mean Time, or GMT) according to the web server's time zone. You can run this example through the Internet Explorer test page to verify that ASP.NET actually caches two responses and reuses the one that matches the supplied parameters, provided it has not expired. That means that users requesting UTC time always receive the cached UTC time response, while other users always receive the cached local time response. If ASP.NET did not provide this behavior, output caching would be useless in most scenarios.

In typical application use with the GetDateTime example, you would see only two different cached responses. However, more are possible. For example, if the client invoked the method using HTTP GET from the test page, the parameter could be entered in several different ways, as differentiated by case:

```
http://localhost/OutputCaching.asmx/GetDateTime?UTC=False
http://localhost/OutputCaching.asmx/GetDateTime?UTC=false
http://localhost/OutputCaching.asmx/GetDateTime?UTC=FaLsE
```

Each one of these would be interpreted as a different request and cause a separate copy of the result to be cached.

You can also enable output caching by adding an `<%@ OutputCache %>` directive in the *.asmx* portion of the web service (not the code-behind file or script block). However, this technique is discouraged, because the standard `OutputCache` attributes are not all supported in a web service. Also, Visual Studio .NET does not allow you to modify the *.asmx* file directly.

You *cannot* enable output caching using the `HttpCachePolicy` class and the built-in `Response.Cache` object, as you can with ASP.NET web pages. These methods are not supported for web services. Also, unlike with web pages, web service output caching is always done based on an absolute expiration time. To set a sliding expiration or use advanced caching policies, you need data caching, explained later in this chapter.

Disabling the Cache

When working with caching, you may want to wait until your code is perfected before enabling it and then test your web service caching separate from the main integrity testing, to ensure that you won't be frustrated by ASP.NET's caching behavior.

In order to do this, you could remove the `CacheDuration` property from every `WebMethod` attribute for development testing and then add them back when the web service is about to be released. This approach, however, is likely to lead to error, or at least consume unnecessary time. Instead, you can use an easier undocumented approach.

Your first option is to disable ASP.NET's output caching service directly from the *machine.config* file (found in the *C:\[WindowsDir]\Microsoft.NET\[version]\Config* directory), which specifies the base set of settings used by ASP.NET and inherited for all applications. Search for the word "cache," and you'll find the following settings under the `<httpModules>` configuration section:

```
<add name="OutputCache" type="System.Web.Caching.OutputCacheModule" />
```

To disable caching, you can remove the output caching module by enclosing the following instruction inside an XML comment.

```
<!-- <add name="OutputCache" type="System.Web.Caching.OutputCacheModule" /> -->
```

Now, the CacheDuration property will be harmlessly ignored without any error. Every time you call a method, the code will run and the cache will always remain empty.

Another approach is to disable output caching just for a specific application. To do this, edit the *web.config* file for your web service and add a new instruction that removes the output cache module (you may also have to add the <httpModules> configuration section):

```
<?xml version="1.0" encoding="utf-8" ?>
<configuration>
  <system.web>

    <httpModules>
      <remove name="OutputCache" />
    </httpModules>

    <!-- Other configuration sections left out. -->

  </system.web>
</configuration>
```

You can't combine both methods, however, or you will receive an error warning that you have attempted to remove an httpModule that doesn't exist!

 The OutputCacheModule class handles output caching only. Unfortunately, there is no equivalent way to disable data caching. To test without data caching, you must make your data caching code conditional or comment out the appropriate lines in your code.

Candidates for Output Caching

Caching is, in one respect, competition between different pieces of data in ASP. NET's cache. Those that are deemed invalid, oldest, or least important are evicted first. The art of caching is making sure that the information stored in the cache is being used. If you cache too much or store unimportant information, you compromise your caching strategy and potentially force out other important information.

Another important caching consideration is the significance of stale data. In other words, if you cache information from a database and the database changes, is it acceptable for your data to be temporarily out-of-date until the next cache update? In many cases, this delay is harmless. For example, if the price of an item changes on an e-commerce site, it's acceptable for this change to be phased in as the cache is updated. However, it might be less convenient if you need exact inventory information to make up-to-the-minute ordering decisions.

In order to perfect output caching, you need to decide what web methods make good caching candidates. The following tips outline the basic guidelines.

Cache methods that take time. If your web method does little more than perform some trivial calculations, there's really no reason to cache. In this case, the client would probably not notice any saved time, because the longest part of the web method invocation is spent sending the request and response messages over the Internet.

Cache methods that access a limited resource. If your web method reads data from a file or database, it automatically becomes a good candidate for caching. These resources are usually the bottleneck of most small- or mid-sized web applications, because the number of simultaneous database connections and file handles is limited. Even if output caching doesn't provide a noticeable speed increase for the client, it allows your web service to perform much better under high-user loads.

Cache methods that return a relatively small set of possible outputs. The internationalized GetDateTime() example, shown a couple of sections back, is an ideal web method, because there are only two possible ways to invoke it: with the UTC parameter set to false or true. For best results, you should cache methods like this that allow only a limited amount of flexibility.

On the other hand, consider the following method, which accepts two numbers and adds them together:

```
[WebMethod]
public float AddTwoNumbers(float numberOne, float numberTwo)
{
    return (numberOne + numberTwo);
}
```

This type of method is generally not worth caching, because there is virtually an unlimited number of possible requests. Even if some duplicate requests are found and the output can be occasionally reused, the output cache will be filled up with a large amount of unimportant information. And remember, when you add unimportant information to the cache, you could force out other valuable data.

Most web methods fall somewhere in between these two extremes. For example, consider this GetProductInfo() method:

```
[WebMethod]
public ProductInfo GetProductInfo(int ID)
{ ... }
```

It makes sense to assume that the maximum number of different cached responses corresponds to the number of different products in the corresponding database table (assuming clients never attempt to retrieve information for a nonexistent product). For a large e-commerce company, the likelihood of receiving requests for identical products in a short amount of time might be very small. On the other hand, a company that is creating or marketing its own products would have a much smaller set of data and provide a smaller set of possible responses. In this case, the GetProductInfo() method could be an ideal candidate for output caching.

Don't cache methods that depend on other objects. With output caching, the assumption is that the only variable that can affect the result is the list of supplied parameters. If your web method makes use of other built-in objects, this may not be the case. For example, if you retrieve specific user information from the User property or retrieve previously stored data from the Session collection, your method is probably not suitable for output caching because there are hidden dependencies. In other words, a response might be reused, even when it doesn't apply. As discussed later in this chapter, you can manually invalidate a cached object, but setting up sophisticated dependencies can be complicated.

Don't cache methods that have other side effects. Successful output caching effectively circumvents your code. For example, if your web method includes some code used to log the request for future usage study, it won't be executed when a cached response is served. Similarly, if your code needs to update a built-in object (like the Session collection) or perform any other task that can't be skipped, you can't use output caching. In this case, the better solution is to use data caching.

Don't cache methods that provide data in different ways. Many methods use essentially the same data but don't return the same result. For example, consider this function:

```
enum Currencies
{
    US,
    Euros,
    Canadian,
}

[WebMethod]
public DataSet GetProductList(Currencies currency)
{
    // (Code to retrieve data from database goes here.)

    // Find out the type of currency using the Currencies enumeration.

    if (currency == Currencies.US)
    {
        // (Modify prices with current exchange rate.)
    }
    else if (currency == Currencies.Euros)
    {
        // (Modify prices with current exchange rate.)
    }

    // And so on...
}
```

This web method always deals with the same data: a list of products. However, depending on the supplied currency, a DataSet with different values is returned. This may seem like an ideal candidate for output caching because the Currencies enumeration provides only a limited set of possible options. However, output caching is still less efficient than it could be.

The problem is that output caching saves a separate copy of essentially the same data for each currency. A better design would use data caching to retrieve the common product list DataSet, regardless of the price. The web method code could *then* modify the prices and return the final DataSet. This technique is demonstrated a little later in this chapter.

Caching Times

So how do you know exactly how long to cache a web method result? Unfortunately, there is no obvious rule. In a high-volume web site, you might gain a significant performance increase by storing a result for a few seconds. On the other hand, if you know that information is not likely to change, and you know that it won't take much space in the cache (for example, perhaps the method doesn't accept any parameters), you can store the information for hours! Consider the following GetProductCategories() web method, which caches its result for 100 minutes:

```
[WebMethod(CacheDuration=6000)]
public DataSet GetProductCategories()
{}
```

Information stored for this long is at the mercy of ASP.NET, which uses its own algorithms to determine whether cached information is being used and may unexpectedly remove information when needed. Though ASP.NET will attempt to remove the least-used items first, the overall behavior is impossible to predict.

Data Caching

Output caching stores only the result from a web service method. Data caching, on the other hand, can store any type of information. With data caching, you can add the specific data you want to the cache and retrieve it any point. You can even specify cache dependencies and expiration policies. The disadvantage of data caching is that you need to write code in your web method to take advantage of it. With careful organization, however, you can separate this code from the main body of your web methods.

The basis for data caching is a simple dictionary collection called Cache (an instance of the System.Web.Caching.Cache class) that works in almost the exact same way as the Session and Application collections detailed in Chapter 5. For example, the Cache collection indexes every item using a descriptive string and can accommodate any .NET object, including custom data or business objects. Like the Application collection, the Cache collection is global to your application. In fact, in traditional ASP development, it was common to use the Application collection to simulate a crude form of caching.

There are two fundamental differences in how the Cache collection works, compared to the Application collection:

- ASP.NET manages the Cache, and removes items when they expire or if memory becomes scarce. This means that you must always check whether a cached object exists before you try to use it. Otherwise, you could end up with the infamous null-reference exception. This also means that you don't need to worry about performing cache cleanup on your own.

- The Cache object is thread-safe. This means that you don't have to use methods like Lock() and Unlock() when adding or removing items (remember, the Application collection requires you to manage user concurrency). Of course, you could still run into concurrency problems if you store an object that isn't thread-safe in the cache and more than one client attempts to change or use this object at once. Depending on the situation, you might be able to circumvent this problem by just making a temporary duplicate copy of the item in the cache and using the copy in the web method.

To access the Cache collection in a web service, you need to use the Context.Cache property if your web service inherits from the base System.Web.Services.WebService class and the HttpContent.Current.Cache property if it doesn't.

 The Context.Cache object is an instance of the System.Web.Caching. Cache class. Don't confuse it with the Context.Response.Cache property, which references an instance of the System.Web.HttpCachePolicy class. The HttpCachePolicy configures output caching for a web page but is useless for web services.

Inserting Items into the Cache

As with the Application and Session collections, you can add an item to the Cache collection just by assigning to a new key name:

```
Context.Cache["key"] = dsProducts
```

However, with this method, you give up the opportunity to specify an expiration policy. Instead, it's much more common to use one of the overloaded versions of the Insert() method. The four Insert() versions are:

Context.Cache.Insert(*key, value*);
    Inserts an item into the cache under the specified key name and using the default priority and expiration. This is the same as using the indexer-based collection syntax and assigning to a new key name.

Context.Cache.Insert(*key, value, dependencies*);
    Inserts an item into the cache under the specified key name and using the default priority and expiration. The last parameter contains a CacheDependency object that links to other files or cached items and allows the cached item to be invalidated when these change.

```
Context.Cache.Insert(key, value, dependencies, absoluteExpiration,
slidingExpiration);
```

Inserts an item into the cache under the specified key name using the default priority and the indicated sliding or absolute expiration policy (you cannot set both at once). This is the most commonly used version of the Insert() method.

```
Context.Cache.Insert(key, value, dependencies, absoluteExpiration,
slidingExpiration, priority, onRemoveCallback);
```

Allows you to configure every aspect of the cache policy for the item, including expiration, dependencies, and priority. In addition, you can submit a delegate that points to a method you want invoked when the item is removed.

 The Cache collection is global to your entire web application. If you insert an item in a web service, you can retrieve it from a web page in the same application and vice versa. If you are developing a web application that provides similar functionality through web services and web pages, data caching provides you with an easy way to reuse resources. However, keep in mind that the Cache object is application- and machine-specific, which means that each server in a web farm will have its own local cache.

Absolute Expiration Versus Sliding Expiration

With data caching, you have two choices for specifying an expiration policy. One of these is *absolute expiration*, which invalidates cache items after a fixed period of time (as with output caching). Absolute expiration is a sort of "best before" date and works best when you know that data can be considered valid for only a specific amount of time. For example, you could use absolute expiration to keep a stock quote for 10 seconds or a product catalog for one hour.

With *sliding expiration*, the other choice, ASP.NET waits for a set period of inactivity to dispose of a neglected cache item. For example, if you use a sliding expiration period of 10 minutes, the item will be removed only if it is not used over a 10-minute period. The item could be invalidated in as little as 10 minutes or kept indefinitely if it is in continuous demand. Sliding expiration works well when you have information that is always valid but may not be in high demand. For example, a lookup service might retrieve historical data, like a census report or newspaper document that doesn't expire because it's no longer valid, but shouldn't be kept in the cache if it isn't doing any good.

To use absolute expiration, set the slidingExpiration parameter to TimeSpan.Zero. The following example caches an object for 10 seconds, with no dependencies:

```
Context.Cache.Insert("key", obj, null, DateTime.Now.AddSeconds(10),
                      TimeSpan.Zero);
```

To use a sliding expiration policy, set the `absoluteExpiration` parameter to `DateTime.Max`. The following example stores an item until the value has been idle for 10 minutes:

```
Context.Cache.Insert("key", obj, null, DateTime.MaxValue,
                     TimeSpan.FromMinutes(10));
```

 Even though the `Cache.Insert()` method provides parameters for both a sliding expiration and an absolute expiration date, you cannot set both of them at once. If you attempt to do so, you will receive an `ArgumentException`.

Other Cache Members

The `Insert()` method is the key to using the `Cache`. The `Cache` object provides relatively few other members (shown in Table 7-1).

Table 7-1. Other members of the Cache class

Member	Description
Count	Returns the number of items stored in the cache. Primarily useful when monitoring the performance of an application or debugging.
Item	Allows you to enumerate through every item in the collection. Items in the cache are cast to the generic `System.Object` type.
Add()	Works the exact same as the fourth version of the `Insert()` method, except that it fails if you attempt to add an item under a key that already exists.
Remove()	Removes the item with the specified key name.

There's no method for clearing the entire data cache, but you can enumerate through the collection using the `DictionaryEntry` class. Doing this gives you a chance to retrieve the key for each item and provides an easy way to empty the collection:

```
private void ClearCache()
{
    foreach(DictionaryEntry objItem in Context.Cache)
    {
        Context.Cache.Remove(objItem.Key.ToString());
    }
}
```

Or you can retrieve a list of cached items in much the same way:

```
private string GetAllItems()
{
    string itemList = "";
    foreach(DictionaryEntry objItem in Context.Cache)
    {
        itemList += objItem.Key.ToString() + " ";
    }
```

```
    // itemList includes the key for every cached item.
    return itemList;
}
```

This code would be rarely used in a deployed application but is extremely useful while testing your caching strategies (as you'll see with the examples later in this chapter).

Cache Priorities

Depending on the version of the Insert() method that you choose to use, your cached item may be given the default priority, or you may choose to assign a specific priority using one of the values listed in Table 7-2. The priority is important for cache scavenging. When ASP.NET detects that the server is low on memory, it will selectively delete items that are underused and have the lowest priority.

Table 7-2. CachePriority values

Value	Description
AboveNormal	These items are less likely to be deleted than Normal priority items.
BelowNormal	These items are more likely to be deleted than Normal priority items.
Normal	These items are likely to be deleted from the cache as the server frees system memory only after Low or BelowNormal priority items have been removed. This is the default.
High	These items are the least likely to be deleted from the cache when the server frees system memory.
Low	These items are the most likely to be deleted from the cache when the server frees system memory.
NotRemovable	These items will ordinarily not be deleted from the cache.

A Simple Data Caching Example

The next example solves the problem posed by the multicurrency GetProductList() method. It splits the code for the method into two procedures: the public GetProductList() method and the private GetProductListDataSet() method, which performs the actual data retrieval. This is the step that will be skipped if the required information is found in the Cache collection:

```
enum Currencies
{
    US,
    Euros,
    Canadian,
}

[WebMethod]
public DataSet GetProductList(Currencies currency)
{
    // Check the cache for the product DataSet.
```

```
    // If it is found, retrieve it. If it is not, create it with the
    // GetProductListDataSet function and add it to the cache.
    DataSet dsProducts;
    if (Context.Cache["ProductList"] == null)
    {
        dsProducts = GetProductListDataSet();
        Context.Cache.Insert("ProductList", dsProducts, null,
                        DateTime.Now.AddSeconds(60), TimeSpan.Zero);
    }
    else
    {
        dsProducts = (DataSet)Context.Cache["ProductList"];
    }
    // (Find out the type of currency using the Currencies enumeration,
    // and modify the DataSet accordingly. This code is left out for clarity.)

    return dsProducts;
}

private DataSet GetProductListDataSet()
{
    // Code to retrieve data from database goes here.
    // Uncomment the following line for a simple test.
    // return new DataSet("Products");
}
```

This example introduces one new problem. As written, the GetProductList() method works directly with the DataSet in the cache. Even when the item is assigned to the dsProducts variable, the memory reference is copied only, and not the actual object.

This means that if more than one user accesses the GetProductList() method at once, both instances may try to access and modify the same object (the cached DataSet) at the same time. Even worse, when the code modifies the DataSet to have the appropriate prices, the cached copy of the DataSet is also being changed!

To solve the multiuser concurrency problem, your GetProductList() method can use the lock statement to obtain exclusive access to the object in the cache. In this case, however, what the code really needs is a duplicate copy of the object that it can tailor for the appropriate currency. Luckily, DataSets support this use with two built-in methods: Clone(), which copies the schema information but no data, and Copy(), which makes an exact replication of the DataSet.

Here's a rewritten version that uses responsible caching by creating a duplicate DataSet:

```
[WebMethod]
public DataSet GetProductList(Currencies currency)
{
    // Check the cache for the product DataSet.
    // If it is found, retrieve it. If it is not, create it with the
    // GetProductListDataSet function and add it to the cache.
    DataSet dsProducts;
```

```
if (Context.Cache["ProductList"] == null)
{
    dsProducts = GetProdcutListDataSet();
    Context.Cache.Insert("ProductList", dsProducts, null,
                    DateTime.Now.AddSeconds(60), TimeSpan.Zero);
}
else
{
    dsProducts = (DataSet)Context.Cache["ProductList"];
}
dsProducts = dsProducts.Copy();

// (Find out the type of currency using the Currencies enumeration
// and modify the DataSet accordingly. This code is left out for clarity.)
return dsProducts;

}
```

 Unlike many .NET objects, the DataSet's Clone() method does not create an exact copy. Instead, it copies the schema information (for example, the table and column information), but not the data. To copy both the schema information and the data, you must use the Copy() method instead.

Cloning

The modification problem discussed previously with the DataSet occurs with any reference type that you need to modify without affecting the cache. However, it's not always as easy to resolve, because not all objects provide a Clone() or Copy() method. In this section, we'll take a quick look at how cloning works in .NET and how you can add support for it to your custom data and business objects.

Table 7-3 summarizes the common data types in the .NET platform. Value types don't need support for cloning, because assigning from one value type to another automatically copies the contents, not an object reference.

Table 7-3. Value and reference types

Type	Includes
Value types	Int32, Single, Double, Decimal, DateTime, TimeSpan, Char, Byte, Boolean, simple structures, and all other basic numeric types
Reference types	Array, DataSet, and just about every .NET object that isn't a simple structure
Reference types that behave like value types	String

Many .NET reference types implement the ICloneable interface and provide a Clone() method for copying (the Array is one such example). In your own data class, you can add cloning support by implementing the ICloneable interface. This interface includes one method—Clone()—that returns a duplicate copy of the object (as a loosely typed System.Object).

The code you write in the Clone() method can make use of a special protected method called MemberwiseClone(), which every class inherits from the base System. Object class. This method is available only to code inside the class, not to code using the class, because it does not always produce the desired results for more complex objects. The next two examples show why.

First, consider the following data class:

```
public class ProductInfo
{
    public string Name;
    public decimal Price;
}
```

Making this object cloneable is easy:

```
public class ProductInfo: ICloneable
{
    public string Name;
    public decimal Price;
    public object Clone()
    {
        return this.MemberwiseClone();
    }
}
```

The only trick is that the client calling the Clone() method needs to cast the returned object to the appropriate ProductInfo type.

The second example introduces a new wrinkle:

```
public class ProductList
{
    public string CategoryName;
    public ProductInfo[] Products;
}
```

The ProductList class includes an array of ProductInfo objects. If we use the same strategy shown in the previous example, we'll end up with two objects that refer to the same array. If we explicitly clone the array in the custom Clone() method, we'll get a little closer—we'll have two ProductList objects and two arrays, but both will still hold the same collection of the ProductInfo objects. This subtlety is why the MemberwiseClone() method is not exposed directly. It's just too easy to unwittingly misuse it.

Here's the full cloning logic implemented correctly:

```
public class ProductList
{
    public string CategoryName;
    public ProductInfo[] Products;
```

```
public object Clone()
{
    // Create a shallow copy of the ProductList object.
    ProductList prodCopy = (ProductList)this.MemberwiseClone();

    // Copy the array.
    prodCopy.Products = (ProductList)prodCopy.Products.Clone();

    // Duplicate the objects referenced in the array.
    for (int i = 0; i < prodCopy.Products.Length; i++)
    {
        prodCopy.Products[i] = (ProductList)prodCopy.Products[i].Clone();
    }

    return prodCopy;
}

}
```

The ProductList class is now easy to use and modify when incorporated in a web service caching strategy. Note that this example works only with the cloneable version of the ProductInfo class.

 If a prebuilt object doesn't provide a Clone() or Copy() method, there is no easy way to copy it. Instead, you need to create a new object and assign each property from the first object to the second. (In this case, it probably makes sense to derive a custom cloneable version of the object and add a Clone() method that does exactly that.)

Cache Dependencies

You've already seen that cached items can be removed for several reasons:

- They expire according to a set sliding or absolute expiration policy.
- You remove them manually with the Cache.Remove() method.
- ASP.NET removes them to free up needed server memory.

You can also create cache dependencies, which provides another way for cached items to be invalidated. When an item like a file or cached object is changed, ASP. NET will automatically remove any dependent cached items.

Cache dependencies are encapsulated by the CacheDependency object (in the System. Web.Cache namespace). The basic pattern for dependencies works like this:

1. Create a CacheDependency object. ASP.NET begins monitoring the underlying file or cached object immediately.
2. Add an item to the cache, using the overloaded Insert() method that allows you to specify a CacheDependency object.
3. If the resource referenced by the CacheDependency object changes, ASP.NET removes the dependent cached item.

The CacheDependency class provides eight different constructors (shown in Table 7-4).

Table 7-4. CacheDependency constructors

Parameters	Description
filenames	Monitors a single file or directory for changes.
filenames[]	Monitors an array of files and directories for changes.
filenames, startTime	Monitors a single file or directory for changes. Monitoring begins at the specified time.
filenames[], startTime	Monitors an array of files and directories for changes. Monitoring begins at the specified time.
filenames[], cachekeys[]	Monitors an array of files and directories for changes and an array of other cache items.
filenames[], cachekeys[], dependency	Monitors an array of files and directories for changes and an array of other cache items. This dependency is also dependent on another CacheDependency object.
filenames[], cachekeys[], startTime	Monitors an array of files and directories for changes and an array of other cache items. Monitoring for the file items begins at the specified time.
filenames[], cachekeys[], dependency, startTime	Monitors an array of files and directories for changes and an array of other cache items. Monitoring for the file items begins at the specified time. This dependency is also dependent on another CacheDependency object.

Creating File Dependencies

When you use file dependencies, you link a cached item to a specific file or directory (or more than one file or directory). Windows monitors these resources automatically and invalidates the cached item when any of the following happen:

- The file or directory is deleted.
- The file or directory is created (if it didn't already exist).
- The file is modified (written to disk with a new last-access time).
- A file is added or removed from a monitored directory.

Creating a dependency is easy. Just remember that the CacheDependency constructor requires absolute paths. If you want to use a file that is in the same directory as the web service, you can use the Server.MapPath() method to determine the full physical path.

To create the next example, we need to revisit the simple ProductInfo class created earlier (the noncloneable version is fine):

```
public class ProductInfo
{
    public string Name;
    public decimal Price;
}
```

The following two web service methods allow you to create a cached `ProductInfo` object that is dependent on the file *products.xml*. You can test this caching by manually deleting, adding, or changing the *products.xml* file and calling the `CheckDependentItem()` method:

```
[WebMethod]
public void SetFileDependency()
{
    ProductInfo list = new ProductInfo();

    CacheDependency dependency = new
        CacheDependency(Server.MapPath("products.xml"));

    Context.Cache.Insert("ProductList", list, dependency);
}

[WebMethod]
public string CheckDependentItem()
{
    if (Context.Cache["ProductList"] == null)
    {
        return "Item has been removed.";
    }
    else
    {
        return "Item is still present.";
    }
}
```

You can also use the `ChangeFile()` method shown next, which programmatically modifies the XML file (in order to use it as written, you must import the `System.IO` namespace). If you call `ChangeFile()` followed by `CheckDependentItem()`, you will find that the cached item has been removed:

```
[WebMethod]
public void ChangeFile()
{
    StreamWriter w = File.CreateText(Server.MapPath("products.xml"));
    w.Flush();
    w.Close();
}
```

A simple console client can test this behavior using the following pattern:

```
// Create the proxy class.
DependencyService proxy = newDependencyService();

// Cache the item and set the dependency on products.xml.
proxy.SetFileDependency();

// Check whether the item is still present.
string message = proxy.CheckDependentItem();
Console.WriteLine(message);
```

```
// Modify the products.xml file through another web method.
Console.WriteLine("Modifying products.xml ...")
proxy.ChangeFile();

// Check whether the item is still present.
message = proxy.CheckDependentItem();
Console.WriteLine(message);
```

The output for this application is as follows:

```
Item is still present.
Modifying products.xml ...
Item has been removed.
```

ASP.NET begins to monitor a dependent item for changes as soon as you create a CacheDependency object (unless you use one of the CacheDependency constructors that accepts a start time parameter). That way, if the file changes before you add the dependent item to the cache, the item is invalidated automatically when it is added.

 It is possible to extend caching dependencies by using ASP.NET file-system monitoring. For example, you could create an SQL Server database with a TRIGGER that automatically writes an empty file when a specific table is changed. This way, a dependent DataSet in the cache could be invalidated as soon as changes are made. This technique is best with information that is stored for long periods and changed infrequently. Otherwise, the overhead of writing files on the web server may hamper performance.

Creating Dependencies on Other Cache Items

You can link cache items together in such a way that, as soon as one is removed from the cache for any reason, other related items are removed as well. This magic is performed by creating a CacheDependency object that points to one or more cached items. The dependency is invalidated if:

- The item is removed with the Cache.Remove() method.
- The item is replaced with the Cache.Insert() method or by assigning a new value to the key.

The dependency is *not* invalidated if an item is changed by modifying one of its properties.

The next example caches three DataTable objects, representing a list of products, product categories, and product prices. The product list DataTable is dependent on the product categories and product prices DataTable objects; if either of these items is removed, the product list will be removed as well.

```
[WebMethod]
public string LinkedInvalidationTest()
{
    ClearCache();
```

```
    // Create all three objects.
    DataTable prices = new DataTable("Prices");
    DataTable categories = new DataTable("Categories");
    DataTable list = new DataTable("Products");

    // (Code to fill the DataTables goes here.)

    // Add the first two objects.
    Context.Cache.Insert("Prices", prices);
    Context.Cache.Insert("Categories", categories);

    // Create a dependency for the third object, then add it.
    string[] keys = {"Prices", "Categories"};
    CacheDependency dependency = new CacheDependency(null, keys);
    Context.Cache.Insert("ProductList", list, dependency);

    // Remove the Categories item. The dependent ProductList item
    // will be removed automatically.
    Context.Cache.Remove("Categories");

    return "Cache contains: " + GetAllItems();
}
```

To test this behavior, the code then removes the Categories DataTable, and returns the list of items in the cache (which will contain only the Prices item). The code makes use of two private helper functions, ClearCache() and GetAllItems() (introduced earlier in the chapter), to empty the cache and report the items in it. You can test this web method by triggering it through the Internet Explorer test page. The result will be "Cache contains: Prices."

When creating cache item dependencies, you must always create the Cache-Dependency object after the item it references is added to the cache. This design poses one problem: there is no way to create two items that are interdependent. The following example shows one such failure.

The FailedInterdependentTest() web method creates two ProductInfo objects and tries to make the first one dependent on the second and the second one dependent on the first. Because the dependencies are created before the objects are in the cache, both items are invalidated immediately when they are added.

```
[WebMethod]
public string FailedInterdependentTest()
{
    ClearCache();

    ProductInfo prod1 = new ProductInfo();
    ProductInfo prod2 = new ProductInfo();

    string[] keys1 = {"prod2"};
    string[] keys2 = {"prod1"};

    CacheDependency dependency1 = new CacheDependency(null, keys1);
    CacheDependency dependency2 = new CacheDependency(null, keys2);
```

```
    // Attempt to add both items. However, they are invalidated immediately.
    Context.Cache.Insert("prod1", prod1, dependency1);
    Context.Cache.Insert("prod2", prod2, dependency2);

    return GetAllItems();
}
```

To solve this problem, you need to either change your caching plans or make use of callbacks.

The Item Removed Callback

The Cache.Insert() method gives you the opportunity to submit a delegate that identifies a procedure that will be called when the given item is removed from the cache. This code could happen at any point and won't be tied to any particular web method invocation. It also will run on a different thread than your web service (and thus won't be able to easily communicate with it). Generally, this callback is used to perform cleanup (by deleting related resources for the removed item) or some sort of tracking/diagnostics.

One way to use the item removed callback is to create two mutually dependent cache items. These items won't need a CacheDependency—instead, your code will programmatically decide whether to remove other items.

Here's the code for the successful version of the interdependent item test. It returns a string that informs the user what the cache contained before and after the first item was removed:

```
[WebMethod]
public string SuccessfullInterdependentTest()
{
    ClearCache();

    ProductInfo prod1 = new ProductInfo();
    ProductInfo prod2 = new ProductInfo();

    CacheItemRemovedCallback callback = new
        CacheItemRemovedCallback(ItemRemovedCallback);

    Context.Cache.Insert("prod1", prod1, null, DateTime.MaxValue, TimeSpan.Zero,
        CacheItemPriority.Normal, callback);
    Context.Cache.Insert("prod2", prod2, null, DateTime.MaxValue, TimeSpan.Zero,
        CacheItemPriority.Normal, callback);

    string report = "Before: " + GetAllItems();
    Context.Cache.Remove("prod1");
    report += "After: " + GetAllItems();

    return report;
}
```

This code depends on the callback shown next. This code causes reentrancy (the callback is called again before it is complete, when an item is removed), and it attempts to remove items that could have already been removed. Both of these characteristics are completely harmless.

```
public void ItemRemovedCallback(string key, object value,
        CacheItemRemovedReason reason)
{
    if (key == "prod1" || key == "prod2")
    {
        Context.Cache.Remove("prod1");
        Context.Cache.Remove("prod2");
    }
}
```

Once again, you can easily test this web method through the Internet Explorer test page. Figures 7-3 shows the returned report information and process.

Figure 7-3. Running the SuccessfulInterdependentTest()

The callback also provides your code with additional information, including the removed item (which could be added back to the cache programmatically if desired) and the reason it was removed. Possible reasons are shown in Table 7-5.

Table 7-5. CacheItemRemovedReason values

Value	Description
DependencyChanged	Removed because a file or key dependency changed
Expired	Removed because it expired (according to its sliding or absolute expiration policy)
Removed	Removed programmatically by a Remove() method call or by an Insert() method call that specified the same key
Underused	Removed because ASP.NET decided it wasn't important enough and wanted to free memory.

Replacing Stateful Design with Caching

In Chapter 5, you learned how you can replace stateful designs with a ticket system that places information in a temporary database table with a unique ID. (The user must then submit the appropriate ID, or it can be stored in session state, a cookie, or provided in a SOAP header.)

This design performs reliably for large amounts of data and large numbers of users but much more slowly for small sets of users because of the additional overhead needed to retrieve information from the database. In order to solve this problem, you can add caching to store information in server memory, as long as it's available. Your code can then check the cache first and turn to the database as a last resort, allowing multiple subsequent web method invocations to work more quickly.

Figure 7-4 shows how this technique works with a web service that uses state to track authentication. Essentially, the strategy is to bypass the database as often as possible by retrieving information from the cache instead.

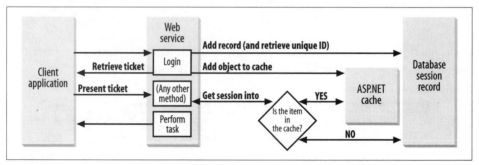

Figure 7-4. ASP.NET output caching

The example here defines a database with two tables: Users (which contains the user ID and password information) and Sessions (which tracks the currently logged-on users). The structure for these tables is shown in Figure 7-5. (If you want to test this example without manually creating the tables, you can download the SQL Server table creation script from *http://www.prosetech.com/*.)

Users					Sessions		
Column Name	Data Type	Length	▲		Column Name	Data Type	Length	▲
🔑 ID	int	4			🔑 GUID	uniqueidentifie	16
UserName	varchar	50			SecurityLevel	smallint	2
Password	varchar	50					

Figure 7-5. Users and Sessions tables

Note that the Sessions table uses a globally unique identifier (GUID), not a unique identity field. This makes it impossible for a user to "hijack" another user's session (by guessing the identification number). You'll also note that the Sessions table retains no user information, for increased privacy. It simply tracks issued sessions and the authorized security level.

The database also includes a NewSession stored procedure that creates a session and returns the generated GUID:

```
CREATE PROCEDURE NewSession
(
    @SecurityLevel int,
    @GUID uniqueidentifier OUTPUT
)
 AS
  SET @GUID = NEWID()
  INSERT INTO Sessions (GUID, SecurityLevel) VALUES (@GUID, @SecurityLevel)
```

It is possible to create a simpler version of this design that relies exclusively on the output cache and doesn't enter any session information into the database. However, the approach developed here allows the most freedom. For example, it gives you the freedom to run an hourly database script to delete old sessions or allow them to remain for weeks. These extremely old sessions would time out and would be removed from the output cache but would then remain in the database. The user could then return to the web service, supply an old session key, and resume working with the previous set of data, which your web service would then add back to the database. (This design is best if you don't need to enforce strict security and aren't worried about a user trying to gain access to another user's session).

To implement this design in a web service, start by creating a class that encapsulates the session information you want to retain. In the example we'll consider, this is just a user authentication level, as shown in this SessionInfo class:

```
public class SessionInfo
{
    public UserLevel SecurityLevel;

    public SessionInfo(UserLevel securityLevel)
    {
        SecurityLevel = securityLevel;
    }
}

enum UserLevel
{
    Admin = 1,
    Normal = 0,
    Guest = 2,
    Denied = -1
}
```

When adding the session information, the web service simultaneously adds it to the database and the ASP.NET cache. In this case, the session is created in the dedicated Login() method of a web service. Here the user is authenticated, and the session is created with the appropriate authentication level. The session record is added to the database and then the output cache, indexed with the GUID as a key.

Unlike the previous examples, we've included all the ADO.NET database code required to create a concrete implementation of this design pattern. If you're familiar with ADO.NET or its predecessor, ADO, you'll recognize familiar objects like the SqlConnection and SqlCommand in the following example.

```csharp
public class CachedSecureService : System.Web.Services.WebService
{
    private string connectionString = "Data Source=localhost;" +
        "Initial Catalog=OReilly;Integrated Security=SSPI";

    [WebMethod]
    public string Login(string userName, string password)
    {
        // Validate user against a database.
        // In a production-level service, this would
        // probably use a stored procedure.
        SqlConnection con = new SqlConnection(connectionString);

        // Define command for checking the user.
        string SQL = "SELECT UserName From Users " +
                    "WHERE UserName='" + userName +
                    "' AND Password='" + password + "'";
        SqlCommand GetUser = new SqlCommand(SQL, con);

        // Define command for creating the session.
        // (We default the user level to admin, but typically this
        // information would be read from the user database.)
        userLevel UserLevel = UserLevel.Admin;
        SqlCommand AddSession = new SqlCommand("NewSession", con);
        AddSession.CommandType = CommandType.StoredProcedure;
        SqlParameter param;
        param = AddSession.Parameters.Add("@GUID", SqlDbType.UniqueIdentifier);
        param.Direction = ParameterDirection.Output;
        param = AddSession.Parameters.Add("@SecurityLevel", SqlDbType.SmallInt);
        param.Value = userLevel;

        string ticket;

        try
        {
            con.Open();
            string databaseUserName = GetUser.ExecuteScalar().ToString();
            if (userName != databaseUserName)
            {
                throw new SecurityException();
            }

            // Add the session to a database, and retrieve the
            // unique row ID into a string variable named ticket.
            AddSession.ExecuteScalar();
            ticket = AddSession.Parameters["@GUID"].Value.ToString();

            con.Close();
        }
        catch (Exception e)
        {
            con.Close();
            // Throw an exception without any database details
            // (for security reasons).
```

```
            throw new SecurityException("Cannot authenticate");
        }

        // Construct the sessionInfo object.
        SessionInfo sessionInfo = new SessionInfo(userLevel);
        // Add the sessionInfo object to the cache, keeping it valid for
        // 20 minutes of disuse (just like ASP.NET's session state),
        // and using the database row unique ID.
        Context.Cache.Insert(ticket, sessionInfo, null,
            DateTime.MaxValue, TimeSpan.FromMinutes(20));

        // Return the ticket.
        return ticket;
    }

    // (Other web methods omitted.)
}
```

Now, all the other web methods will require the GUID ticket as a parameter. (Alternatively, you could implement a design using a cookie or SOAP header system.) Using that ticket, methods can verify whether the security level is appropriate by checking the output cache first and then the database (if needed). This authentication is handled through a dedicated private method. Ideally, database access will be concentrated in the Login() method and won't be required for any other method, although in practice you may need to tweak the cache timeout to get the best performance.

```
[WebMethod]
public string DoSomething(string ticket)
{
    if (AuthenticateUser(ticket) == UserLevel.Admin)
    {
        // Put method-specific code here.
        // For a test, we return the string "Authenticated".
        return "Authenticated";
    }
    else
    {
        return "Denied";
    }
}

private UserLevel AuthenticateUser(string ticket)
{
    SessionInfo session = (SessionInfo)Context.Cache[ticket];
    if (session != null)
    {
        return session.SecurityLevel;
    }
    else
    {
        // Look for ticket record in DB. If found, return the security level,
        // and add the session back to the cache.
```

```
            // For our test, we always deny the user.
            return UserLevel.Denied;
        }
    }
```

The client would use the following access pattern:

```
CachedSecureService proxy = new CachedSecureService();
string ticket = proxy.Login("[userID]", "[password]");
string result = proxy.DoSomething(ticket);
```

When used properly, this technique can produce extremely high performance web services. Microsoft uses a variant of this model in its Favorites web service platform example, which is documented on the MSDN site (*http://msdn.microsoft.com*), although the source code is not provided. In the Favorites service, the session ticket is actually a string with two parts. The first part is the GUID ticket, as used in the previous example. The second portion is the result of hashing the session ticket with a secret value. When a user calls another method, the Favorites web service recreates the hash and checks that the supplied hash is correct. If it's not, the key is immediately identified as invalid. This saves an extra database trip and defends the site from crude denial-of-service attacks (in which a malicious user repeatedly calls a method with an invalid session key).

Profiling Your Web Service

In an ideal world, you could devise a caching strategy and then immediately tell how well it works. Unfortunately, web services, like all Internet applications, are not so ideal. To start with, it's difficult to simulate a realistic user load and retrieve quantitative information about how well a web service is performing. To further complicate matters, caching strategies might perform well only in specific usage scenarios—and some caching strategies might actually perform best when the user load is artificially high! As an example of the latter, consider a cached item with a sliding expiration policy. If repeated requests are received in a short amount of time, the item will be kept alive and in the in-memory cache. If only a few occasional requests are received, the object might have to be reconstructed from a database on each occasion—a much slower prospect.

There are no easy answers when profiling web services—like all forms of statistics, it often seems that the way you form the question (i.e., structure the test) helps to predetermine the result. Quite simply, performance testing is an art in itself, one that could merit a book of its own.

Of course, you don't need to operate completely in the dark. There are some ways to get a basic picture about how your web services are working. Most of these are based on Windows Performance Counters, which provide you with a great deal of important information about the performance of your web application. In addition, you can use a more comprehensive testing tool like Application Center Test (included with enterprise versions of Visual Studio .NET) or Web Application Stress Tool (the longtime favorite of ASP developers, available for free download at *http://webtool.rte. microsoft.com*). With Visual Studio .NET, you can add an Application Center Test project directly to your solution and enter a list of VBScript commands that correspond to web page requests. Be warned, however, neither of these tools is customized to work as easily when testing a web service as when testing a web page. More targeted tools are still to come.

The Testing Environment

Microsoft makes several recommendations about the ideal environment for performance testing:

- The test environment should contain only the development web server and the clients that will be testing it.
- All network activity unrelated to the test should be minimized.
- All the web service requests should come from dedicated clients. Ideally, the logging is also performed on a separate computer. If you attempt to run a stress-testing tool with the client and web service on the same computer, the results will probably be compromised.
- Use fast network components and avoid using HTTP proxy servers.
- Create enough load to bring the web server's processor use to at least 80 percent. The fundamental idea behind stress testing is that you increase the stress level until the web service (or some resource it relies on) becomes a bottleneck and prevent further increases. If any other part of the system is slower than the web server or web service, it becomes the first, limiting bottleneck, and it will be impossible to measure the maximum capacity of your code or profile its limitations.

Performance Counters

When performing a stress test, you have two challenges. You must be able to simulate the appropriate load (either by creating your own fake "robot" client application or using a dedicated tool), and you need some way to record the performance. Fortunately, the Windows operating system provides an ideal tool for measuring all aspects of performance

You can use generic counters that track the overall health of your web server and counters that are specifically targeted to report ASP.NET information (like the number of concurrent requests being served). You can even create your own performance counters to record application-specific data (like the number of transactions per hour).

Stress testing tools like the Microsoft Web Application Stress Tool use performance counters as well. They record the information and can provide various types of summary reports.

To add a counter that tracks web server performance, choose Settings → Control Panel from the Start menu, and then choose Administrative Tools → Performance. Ideally, you'll perform this step from another computer so that you can track the web server performance without needing to actually use the web server (and possibly impose some additional overhead). See Figure 7-6.

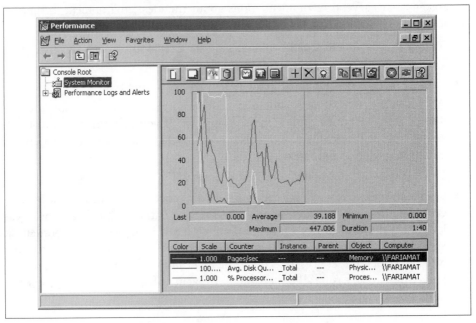

Figure 7-6. Active performance counters

By default, you'll only see a few standard performance counters, like those for measuring the current computer's CPU and disk drive use. To add more useful counters, right-click on the counter list and choose Properties. Select the Data tab, remove the default counters, and click Add to choose more useful ones. See Figure 7-7.

To add a new counter, follow these steps:

1. Specify the web server computer.

2. Choose the Performance Object—the category of performance counter. A list of some of the most important categories is provided in Table 7-6. Many of these counters are installed with the .NET Framework.

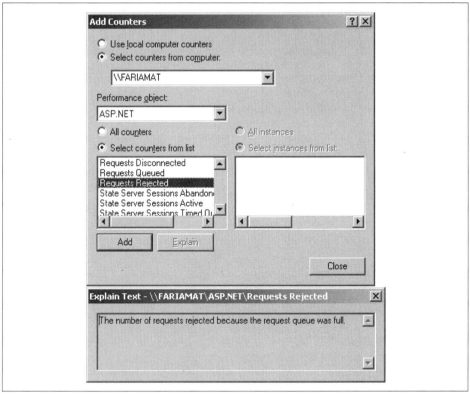

Figure 7-7. Adding a new performance counter

3. Choose a specific counter from the list. For information about what information the counter provides, click the Explain button, which pops up another window with a short description about the counter.

4. Click Add to add the counter you want.

Table 7-6. Performance categories

Category	Description
.NET CLR Data	Provides information about SQLClient connections, connection errors, and connection and pooling.
.NET CLR Exceptions	Provides information about the total number of exceptions that have been thrown and their rate. Exceptions (even when dealt with by exception handling code) can slow down an application.
.NET CLR LocksAndThreads	Provides information about thread contention (when more than one thread is trying to obtain exclusive access to the same resource). This is possible if you are using the lock statement with components in application state or data caching and can significantly reduce performance.
.NET CLR Memory	Provides a great deal of information about garbage collection.

Table 7-6. Performance categories (continued)

Category	Description
ASP.NET	Provides information about the performance of the ASP.NET service. This includes information like the total number of applications running, the number of queued requests, the current sessions, and the number of times the worker process has been restarted (due either to automatic recycling, as determined by the settings in the *machine.config* file, or to application error).
ASP.NET Applications	Provides information about a single specific web application. Remember, a web application is defined as a virtual directory where you host web services (and, optionally, ASP.NET web pages). Each web application has its own memory space for storing session and application state and its own *web.config* settings.
Processor	Provides information about the web server CPU load.
System	Provides information about context switches, file operations, total processes, and other basic system health benchmarks.

 You will also see two additional categories: ASP.NET [version] and ASP.NET Applications [version]. These are exactly the same as the corresponding ASP.NET and ASP.NET Applications categories. The difference is that if you have more than one version of ASP.NET installed, there will be multiple ASP.NET [version] categories, and the ASP.NET and ASP.NET Applications categories will automatically map to the most recent version. This allows you to use performance counters with web services running on different versions of the .NET Framework at the same time.

Important ASP.NET Counters

Generally, you should start testing with a modest load and gradually increase the load until a bottleneck is found. If the CPU usage is at 85 percent, it is generally the bottleneck. If the maximum number of simultaneous requests is reached before this point, there is likely a different bottleneck, which may be discoverable through a different counter. Here are some rules of thumb:

- Start with the % CPU Utilization counter from the Processor category. If this remains consistently low regardless of the load, another resource is likely holding your application up. For example, your web service code might be waiting for a database connection or a lock on a shared object.

- Look at the Requests Queued in the ASP.NET category to determine the number of requests waiting to be processed and get an idea about the maximum load your web server can support. You can also use Requests/Sec in the ASP.NET Applications category to determine the throughput of your web application.

- You can study the success of your caching strategies with a host of counters in the ASP.NET Applications category. For example, profile data caching with Cache API Hits, Cache API Misses, Cache API Hit Ratio, and Cache API Turnover Rate. Examine output caching with Output Cache Hits, Output Cache Misses, and OutputCache Turnover Ratio.

- Look for potential signs of trouble. For example, you might see the number of .NET exceptions climbing or notice an increase in one of the ASP.NET general health/distress counters, like Application Restarts or Worker Process Restarts. Keep in mind that ASP.NET restarts don't always indicate a problem—the worker process may be periodically recycled according to settings specified in the web server's *machine.config* file.

- If you are using session state, pay particular attention to counters in the ASP. NET Applications category like Sessions Active, Sessions Abandoned (programmatically), and Sessions Timed Out. These counters can give you an idea about how successful your session state management really is.

CHAPTER 8

Debugging, Tracing, and Logging

So far, the chapters in this book have concentrated on ways to design and build a professional web service. But what happens if something goes wrong? In this chapter, you'll learn a few key techniques that can help you guard against errors and reign in misbehaving web services. Some of these techniques include:

- Using Visual Studio .NET's integrated debugger, with its celebrated single-step execution.
- Handling web service exceptions and taking control of the SoapException class to provide additional information about errors.
- Using .NET Framework services for logging and tracing.
- Using SOAP extensions to peer beneath .NET's object layer and examine actual SOAP messages.
- Creating a generic SOAP extension for automatic logging.

These techniques cover almost every aspect of web service development, including coding, development testing, and troubleshooting in the field. Fortunately, the built-in services in Visual Studio .NET and the .NET Framework make it easy to track and resolve web service problems.

Debugging in Visual Studio .NET

Visual Studio .NET's integrated debugger is the favorite tool of many developers. It allows you to step through code line-by-line and monitor the current state of your application's data while it's running. You can use these debugging tools in web services as easily as in local code, provided you set up your Visual Studio .NET solution correctly, as demonstrated in the following sections.

Creating a Web Service-Client Solution in VS.NET

Before you can start debugging a web service, you must first create a solution that contains both the web service and the client application. To add a new project to a solution, right-click on the solution in the Solution Explorer and select Add → New Project (see Figure 8-1).

Figure 8-1. A solution with a web service and client project

A solution can contain any combination of different projects. That means that you can add a Windows Forms project, an ASP.NET project, or even a console project as a client. You can even add multiple clients to the same solution. To configure which client you want to use at the moment (i.e., which client will be built and executed when you click the Start button), just right-click on the project and select Set as StartUp Project.

 Even though the web service and client are in the same solution, you still have to add the web reference to every client project. Remember, before you can add a web reference, you must have compiled the web service.

When testing a client project, you can single-step into web methods exactly the same way that you would single-step into local methods (with slightly more latency due to the HTTP communication). In the example in Figure 8-2, the current point of execution is on a web method statement. When the Step Into key (typically F11 or F8) is pressed, the execution point jumps to the start of the web service code.

You can also use all the other debugging tools, like watches and the Immediate window, in both the client and the web service project.

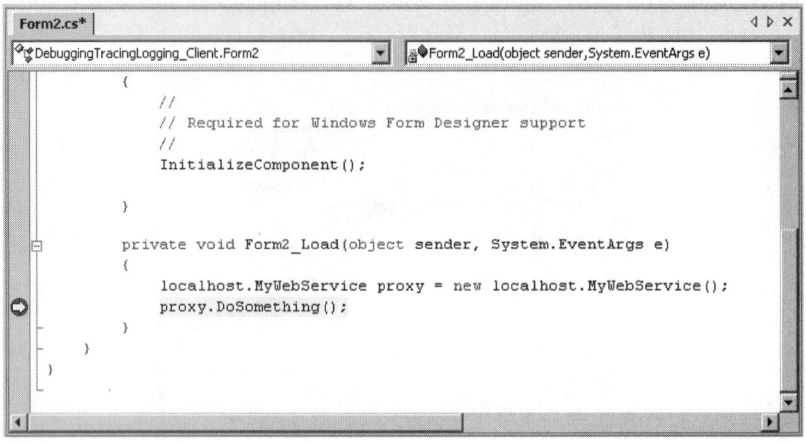

```
  Form2.cs*                                                                    ◀ ▷ ✕
  🔧 DebuggingTracingLogging_Client.Form2          ▼   🔷 Form2_Load(object sender,System.EventArgs e)  ▼
              {                                                                      ▲
                  //
                  // Required for Windows Form Designer support
                  //
                  InitializeComponent();

              }

              private void Form2_Load(object sender, System.EventArgs e)
              {
                  localhost.MyWebService proxy = new localhost.MyWebService();
  ➡             proxy.DoSomething();
              }
          }
      }
                                                                                     ▼
  ◀                                                                               ▶
```

Figure 8-2. Single-stepping into a web service

Setting Web Service Breakpoints

After you've worked with the previous configuration for a while, you might notice one problem: while you can single-step from the client code into the web service, VS. NET ignores any breakpoints you set directly in the web service code. These breakpoints are flagged with question marks when you run the client project. See Figure 8-3.

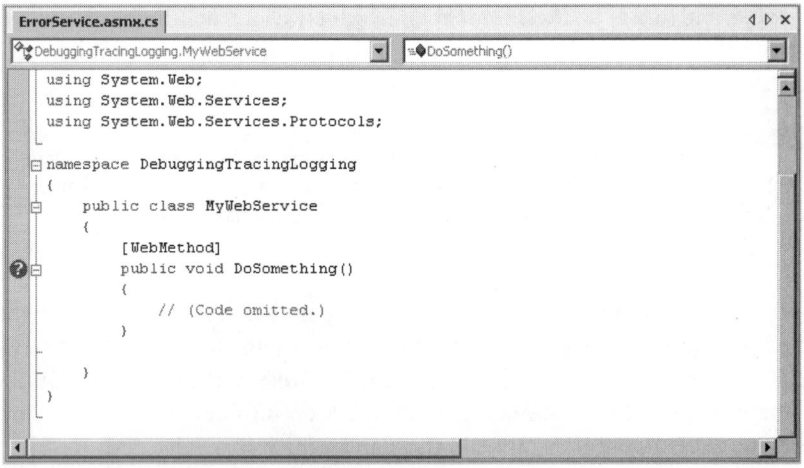

```
  ErrorService.asmx.cs                                                          ◀ ▷ ✕
  🔧 DebuggingTracingLogging.MyWebService          ▼   ≡🔷 DoSomething()              ▼
      using System.Web;                                                              ▲
      using System.Web.Services;
      using System.Web.Services.Protocols;

      namespace DebuggingTracingLogging
      {
          public class MyWebService
          {
              [WebMethod]
  ❓          public void DoSomething()
              {
                  // (Code omitted.)
              }

          }
      }
                                                                                     ▼
  ◀                                                                               ▶
```

Figure 8-3. The mystery of the missing breakpoints

The problem is that VS.NET does not, by default, compile the web service and load its debug symbols. In order to fix this problem, you need to tweak a few settings.

First, right-click on the web service project in the Solution Explorer and select Properties. Browse to the Configuration Properties → Debugging Settings (Figure 8-4).

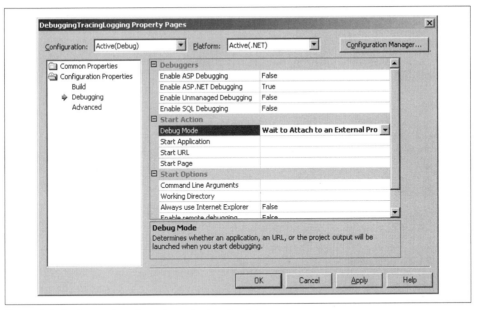

Figure 8-4. Project settings for web service breakpoints

Under Debug Mode (in the Start Action group), select Wait to attach to an external process. Now, whenever you start the web service, it is rebuilt and loaded into memory, but the test page is not displayed. Click OK to accept these changes.

You must also configure a solution-wide setting. Right-click on the solution in the Solution Explorer and select Properties. Browse to the Common Properties → Startup Project settings (Figure 8-5).

Select the Multiple Startup Projects option. Set both your client project and the web service to have the action start and click OK to accept your changes. Now, whenever you run your solution, both projects will be started according to their Start Action options. The client project runs as usual, but the debugging information is loaded for both projects, allowing you to set and use breakpoints at any location.

Using Exceptions

As in any .NET code, web service methods can and should raise exceptions. Generally, .NET design guidelines discourage returning error information in return codes (and discourage using exceptions to indicate anything other than an unrecoverable error). Exceptions should be thrown whenever a problem that would affect the result occurs. If an exception occurs in the web method but can be safely handled without affecting the outcome, an exception is not required.

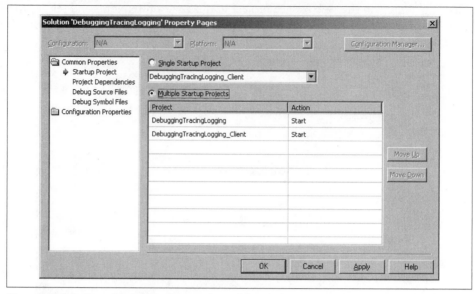

Figure 8-5. Solution settings for web service testing

Unfortunately, web service exceptions are not delivered to the client in their original form. To see the problem in action, consider the following web service:

```
public class ErrorService : System.Web.Services.WebService
{
    [WebMethod]
    public void GenerateError()
    {
        int X = 0;
        int Y = 1 / X;
    }
}
```

When executed, you might expect this segment of code to generate a System. DivideByZero exception. If you catch the error in your web service code, that's exactly what you'll find. In your client, however, the reality is a little different.

To try it out, you can use the following client code, which catches a generic exception and displays some basic information:

```
private void CallError_Click(object sender, System.EventArgs e)
{
    localhost.ErrorService proxy = new localhost.ErrorService();
    try
    {
        proxy.GenerateError();
    }
    catch (Exception err)
    {
        string message = "Exception Type: " + err.GetType().ToString();
```

```
        message += "\r\n\r\n";
        message += "*** Message ***\r\n" + err.Message + "\r\n\r\n";
        message += "*** Stack Trace ***\r\n " + err.StackTrace;

        MessageBox.Show(this, message);
    }
}
```

When this code executes, the message box shown in Figure 8-6 is displayed.

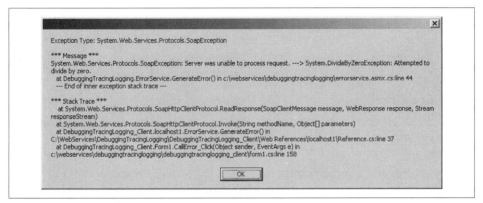

Figure 8-6. The DivideByZero exception at the client

Clearly, the client does not receive the original DivideByZero exception. Instead, this exception is caught by ASP.NET Framework services on the server and wrapped into a generic (and much less helpful) SoapException object.

The Message Property

The origin of the error isn't a complete mystery. Some additional information about the DivideByZero error is inserted as text into the SoapException.Message property, including its original type and the web method where the problem occurred.

```
System.Web.Services.Protocols.SoapException:
Server was unable to process request. ---> System.DivideByZeroException: Attempted to
divide by zero.
   at DebuggingTracingLogging.ErrorService.GenerateError()
```

Because this information is provided as a single long text string, it's not easy to evaluate it and determine the root cause of the error in code. Sadly, the InnerException property is not used at all for SoapException objects.

The StackTrace Property

The Message property indicates the web method where the error occurred. The StackTrace property, however, hints at a slightly different story.

```
   at System.Web.Services.Protocols.SoapHttpClientProtocol.ReadResponse
(SoapClientMessage message, WebResponse response, Stream responseStream)
```

```
    at System.Web.Services.Protocols.SoapHttpClientProtocol.Invoke
(String methodName, Object[] parameters)

    at DebuggingTracingLogging_Client.localhost.ErrorService.GenerateError()
in D:\DebuggingTracingLogging\DebuggingTracingLogging_Client\Web References\
localhost\ErrorService.cs:line 30

    at DebuggingTracingLogging_Client.Form1.CallError_Click
(Object sender, EventArgs e)
in d:\debuggingtracinglogging\debuggingtracinglogging_client\form1.cs:line 107"
```

The error the client detects actually occurs in the `SoapHttpClientProtocol.ReadResponse` method. The proxy class uses this method when it attempts to read the SOAP response message. The process unfolds in several steps:

1. An error occurs in the web service.

2. .NET catches the error.

3. .NET writes error information into the SOAP response message, according to the SOAP standard.

4. When the client reads the SOAP response, it signals the error by throwing a `SoapException`. This `SoapException` encapsulates all the information in the SOAP error message.

In other words, there's no direct way to throw and catch a .NET exception over the boundaries of SOAP communication. Every unhandled exception becomes a generic `System.Web.Services.Protocols.SoapException` (or a `SoapHeaderException` if the error occurs while processing a SOAP header).

This also means that there is little point in deriving special exception classes to throw from your web service. To acquire more control over exception information, you need to create an intermediary layer and work with—not against—the `SoapException` class.

Creating Enlightened Exceptions

SOAP exceptions do allow for some extensibility. For example, you can add custom XML information to indicate the problem. This information is provided in the `Detail` and `OtherElements` properties of the `SoapException` class, as listed in Table 8-1.

Table 8-1. SoapException additional properties

Property	Description
Message	The text error message. By default, this message contains information about the original exception type.
Code	Indicates one of four predefined SOAP fault codes, which are provided as static read-only fields of the `SoapException` class. They include `ClientFaultCode` (there was a problem with the client's SOAP request), `MustUnderstandFaultCode` (a required part of the SOAP message was not recognized), `ServerFaultCode` (an error occurred on the server), and `VersionMismatchFaultCode` (an invalid namespace was found). The default is `ServerFaultCode`.

Table 8-1. SoapException additional properties (continued)

Property	Description
Actor	Indicates the code that caused the error. By convention (and by default), this is set to the URL of the web service that generated the error.
Detail	Contains application-specific error information as a block of XML. By default, it is null. Typically, this property is used if the problem is the result of invalid information submitted by the client.
OtherElements	Contains additional information about the error that is not directly related to the client's SOAP request (like a problem in other components or a network issue). By default, it is null.

When an error occurs in your web service, you can use these properties to provide more information to the client or to provide information in a more structured, consistent format. To do this, you need to intercept the original exception and throw a new, customized SOAP exception.

The following example shows another problematic web method. This method catches its own errors and creates the appropriate reporting information in an XML markup format:

```
using System;
using System.Web;
using System.Web.Services;
using System.Web.Services.Protocols;
using System.Xml;

public class ErrorService : System.Web.Services.WebService
{
    [WebMethod]
    public void ThrowException(int divisor)
    {
        try
        {
            int Y = 1 / divisor;
        }
        catch (Exception err)
        {
            // Create the detail information.
            XmlDocument doc = new XmlDocument();
            XmlNode node = doc.CreateNode(
                XmlNodeType.Element, SoapException.DetailElementName.Name,
                SoapException.DetailElementName.Namespace);
            XmlNode child = doc.CreateNode(
                XmlNodeType.Element, "OriginalException",
                SoapException.DetailElementName.Namespace);
            child.InnerText = err.GetType().ToString();
            node.AppendChild(child);

            // Create the custom SoapException.
            SoapException soapErr = new SoapException(
                err.Message, SoapException.ServerFaultCode,
                Context.Request.Url.AbsoluteUri, node);
```

```
            // Throw the SoapException.
            throw soapErr;
        }
    }
}
```

This example wraps the actual web service code in a try/catch block. The DivideByZeroException is then intercepted, and a SoapException is created instead. The SoapException is given the message from the original exception, and the Actor and Code properties are set with the recommended values. Unfortunately, this is unavoidably tedious code. There is no way to use the XML serialization features of the .NET platform to help you out, because the SoapException class can accommodate only an XML fragment, not a complete XML document.

The interesting part is the SoapException.Detail property, which is filled using an XmlNode. An XmlNode represents a portion of an XML document, and it can contain elements and subelements. When creating the XmlNode object, the example makes use of the static read-only field DetailElementName, provided by the SoapException class. This field provides an error-proof way to set the basic namespace and name information for your XmlNode so that it matches the SOAP standard.

 For more information about the XmlNode object and the ways you can use it, refer to the class library reference. Like most XML objects, XmlNode is found in the System.Xml namespace.

The custom XML information consists of a single <OriginalException> tag, although it could contain any combination of XML tags, attributes, and values. In this example web service, <OriginalException> is used to identify the type name of the intercepted exception. The client code can make use of this additional information, provided it specifically catches a SoapException (rather than a generic exception):

```
private void CallException_Click(object sender, System.EventArgs e)
{
    localhost.ErrorService proxy = new localhost.ErrorService();
    try
    {
        proxy.ThrowException(0);
    }
    catch (SoapException err)
    {
        string message = "Type: " + err.GetType().ToString() + "\r\n\r\n";
        message += "*** Message ***\r\n" + err.Message + "\r\n\r\n";

        // SoapException-specific properties.
        message += "*** Actor: ***\r\n" + err.Actor + "\r\n\r\n";
        message += "*** Code: ***\r\n" + err.Code + "\r\n\r\n";
        message += "*** Detail: ***\r\n" + err.Detail.OuterXml;
```

```
        MessageBox.Show(this, message);

    }
}
```

The message box shows the combined information (see Figure 8-7).

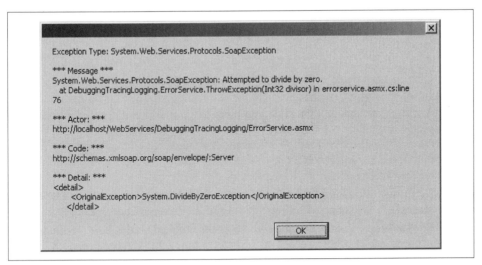

Figure 8-7. The enlightened exception

The most important aspect of this example is that by adding this XML content, it becomes possible to pass exception information to the client in a structured way, so that this information can be evaluated in code. Here's an example that checks to see if a SoapException was caused DivideByZeroException, using some simple XML navigation with .NET's XmlNode class:

```
// Determine the original exception, by examining the <OrginalException> element.

XmlNode node = err.Detail.SelectSingleNode("OriginalException");

if (node.InnerText == typeof(DivideByZeroException).ToString())
{
    MessageBox.Show(this, "Identified the original exception.");
}
```

Clearly, this is much more reliable than trying to parse the Message string and look for specific snippets of text.

Logging Errors with .NET

The examples up to this point have assumed a high degree of interaction between the client and web service developers. In many cases, however, a developer creates a web service and makes it available to a wide range of clients. These clients don't have access to the web service code. Conversely, the web service developers can't always identify or may not even be aware of errors on the client side.

For these reasons, it becomes important to create a web service that looks after itself. Depending on your needs, a respectable web service should log errors and activities so that problems or problematic behavior can be identified later on. The .NET Framework provides many tools that can help you with this task.

Log Types

There are actually several distinct types of information you might want to log:

- Performance-related information that helps you assess usage patterns, as discussed in Chapter 7.
- Auditing information that helps you track usage and identify potential security problems. Auditing is a business requirement and doesn't present any new technical challenges. (For a sample Microsoft case study, read the online documentation of the Favorites web service—search for "Favorites Service" at *http://msdn.microsoft.com*.)
- Diagnostic information that allows you to analyze unusual behavior. The custom SOAP extension demonstrated later in this chapter is a good example.
- Error information that identifies problems encountered on the server and may be symptomatic of other issues. This is the type of logging we examine in the first part of this chapter.

Depending on your requirements, you may need to perform all or only some of these types of logging. For example, you may already be using a third-party tool to monitor performance. Or you may be using the web service internally, in which case you don't need to log user actions and create an audit trail. But unless you are able to write invulnerable code, you should always perform some basic error logging for any unusual or unexpected errors.

Logging with the Application Log

.NET provides easy access to the system event logs through the `EventLog` class. These logs contain central repositories that can store application, system, and security events and are accessed through the `System.Diagnostics` namespace. It's helpful to import this namespace so you can use it without fully qualifying type names:

```
using System.Diagnostics;
```

The following example writes exception information into the application log:

```
[WebMethod]
public void GenerateLoggedError()
{
    try
    {
        int X = 0;
        int Y = 1 / X;
    }
```

```
    catch (Exception err)
    {
        EventLog log = new EventLog();
        log.Source = "ErrorService";
        log.WriteEntry(err.Message, EventLogEntryType.Error);
    }
}
```

 By default, this code will generate an exception if the ASP.NET worker process does not have access rights to the registry. One solution is to set the username attribute of the processModel element in the *machine.config* file to SYSTEM. Of course, this gives the web service a new responsibility—authenticating the client before allowing the return of potentially sensitive log information (which could be used to devise web service attacks).

The Source property identifies the application (in this example, the ErrorService web service). Events can be entered as Error, Warning, or Information types, depending on the value you use from the EventLogEntryType.

To read the event log, choose Administrative Tools → Event Viewer from the Control Panel (see Figure 8-8). Select the Application log. You can double-click for specific information about an event, as shown in Figure 8-9.

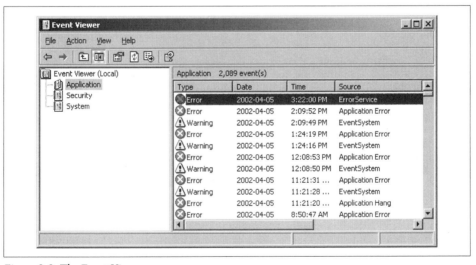

Figure 8-8. The Event Viewer

Be warned: event logs can be deleted and, by default, are automatically overwritten when the maximum size is reached (typically only half a megabyte), as long as they are at least a certain age (typically seven days). That means that application logs aren't suited for important information that needs to be retained (for example, productivity/usage information you want to keep to generate performance reports).

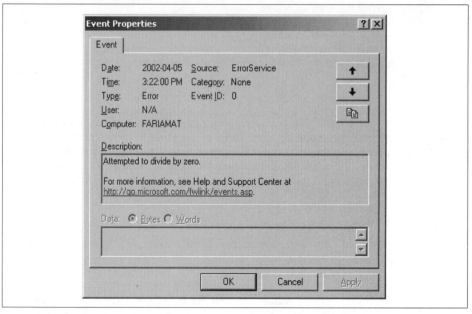

Figure 8-9. The ErrorService event log entry

 To configure log settings, right-click on the Application log and select Properties. You can use other commands from the context menu to clear the events in the log, save log entries, or open an external log file.

Event logging also consumes disk space, processor time, and other system resources. You should be careful not to try and store superfluous information or large quantities of data. If you have such specific logging requirements, use the functionality in the System.IO or System.Data namespace to create files or database records. For example, some web services use database records to create an audit trail that tracks every action a client makes.

Retrieving Logs

Rather than rely on an on-site user to review the appropriate logs, it generally makes sense to create a companion web method that extracts the important information and returns it to you using an array, custom collection object, or DataSet. This allows you to retrieve error log information from any other computer whenever you need to check on the web service.

```
[WebMethod]
public DataSet GetErrorLog()
{
    EventLog log = new EventLog("Application");

    // Create a table to store the event information.
```

```
DataTable dt = new DataTable();
dt.Columns.Add("Type", typeof(string));
dt.Columns.Add("Message", typeof(string));
dt.Columns.Add("Time", typeof(DateTime));

foreach (EventLogEntry entry in log.Entries)
{
    if (entry.Source == "ErrorService")
    {
        // Populate the table.
        DataRow drNew = dt.NewRow();
        drNew["Type"] = entry.EntryType.ToString();
        drNew["Message"] = entry.Message;
        drNew["Time"] = entry.TimeGenerated;
        dt.Rows.Add(drNew);
    }
}

// A DataTable on its own is not a supported web service type.
DataSet ds = new DataSet();
ds.Tables.Add(dt);
return ds;
}
```

This web method automatically looks up all the corresponding entries and returns them in a DataSet. The client application can easily create a simple display or event log browser with a minimal amount of code. The following example uses data binding with a DataGrid control:

```
localhost.ErrorService proxy = new localhost.ErrorService();
dgEvents.DataSource = proxy.GetErrorLog().Tables[0];
```

Figure 8-10 shows the retrieved error log information in the client. If you have several web services, you could create an entirely separate utility web service for this type of function. You could then send the name of the web service (or use an enumerated value) as a parameter when calling the GetErrorLog() method. The GetErrorLog() method would then retrieve all the event log entries that pertain to this web service. You could even create additional web service methods that clear the current log entries or archive them to another file. Even better, by separating the web service from its logging functionality, you ensure that clients won't accidentally use the logging and error-tracking web methods.

Of course, as it stands, this approach has a significant drawback: it's unprotected from potentially malicious clients. You should add some type of authentication strategy to your web service, as described in Chapter 9. In fact, in this case, integrated Windows security may make a lot of sense, because the administrator is likely to be a known user authenticated by a Windows domain server on the same network.

Logging by Email

When you create a log, you also create the requirement that someone (or some application) must regularly review the log and extract important information. You could

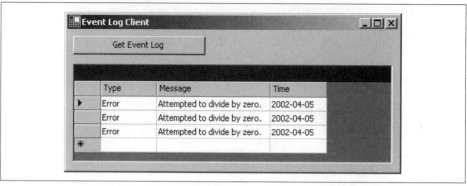

Figure 8-10. Retrieving the event log in a custom client

also use other parts of the .NET Framework for a more customized solution. A common technique is to alert a system administrator about a critical server error (like a problem caused by lack of disk space) by email. In a .NET web service, you can accomplish this interaction using the System.Web.Mail namespace. To get started, import the namespace:

```
using System.Web.Mail;
```

This namespace contains two useful classes: the MailMessage class, which represents an individual email message, and the SmtpMail class, which contains the static Send() method that allows you to mail it. These mailing features use the built-in SMTP service included with IIS, which is similar to the CDO component often used in traditional ASP development.

```
[WebMethod]
public void GenerateLoggedError()
{
    try
    {
        int X = 0;
        int Y = 1 / X;
    }
    catch (Exception err)
    {
        MailMessage message = new MailMessage();

        message.To = "admin@mycompany.com";
        message.From = "ErrorService Web Service";
        message.Subject = "Application Exception: " + err.GetType().ToString();
        message.Body = err.Message;

        SmtpMail.SmtpServer = "localhost";
        SmtpMail.Send(message);
    }
}
```

A great deal of exception information can be entered in a simple email message. You might want to use additional information identifying the web service, the time the problem occurred, and the client. To handle these details, you would probably create a generic private method in your web service class that sends the preformatted email.

 Note that in order to send email from a web service, you need to have a properly configured SMTP server. You can find the appropriate settings in IIS Manager under Default SMTP Server. (Right-click and select Properties. Most of the important configuration details are under the Delivery tab.) SMTP server configuration is beyond the scope of this book, but Microsoft provides an introduction to Internet email and mail servers (with some traditional ASP code thrown in for good measure) at *http://www.microsoft.com/TechNet/prodtechnol/iis/ deploy/config/mail.asp*. Incidentally, you should use error handling when invoking the Send() message, because many errors are possible (for example, if the SMTP service is unresponsive or not found).

Tracing and Assertions

As mentioned before, there's no shortage of tools in the .NET library for accessing files and databases. One interesting technique uses the Trace class in the System. Diagnostics namespace. The Trace class is handy because it can work as a debugging tool that outputs information to the Output window in debug mode and as a logging tool that records the same information to a log file in release mode.

There are three essential static methods in the Trace class: Assert(), Fail(), and WriteLine(). Assert() tests a condition. If the condition evaluates to false, the assertion has failed, and a special error message with a stack trace is outputted to the Trace's output stream:

```
Trace.Assert(returnCode == 0);
```

If you are running your web service in debug mode and the returnCode variable has a value other than zero, the message shown in Figure 8-11 appears in the Debug view of the Output window.

You can also output a message with a stack trace using the Trace.Fail() method:

```
catch (Exception err)
{
    Trace.Fail(err.Message);
    // You could also specify a short and long message.
    // Trace.Fail(err.GetType().ToString(), err.Message);
}
```

Last, the WriteLine() method outputs text directly:

```
Trace.WriteLine("GetAccount() was executed without a valid customer object.");
```

```
Output                                                                    ⊠
Debug                                                                     ⯆
  ---- DEBUG ASSERTION FAILED ----                                        ▲
  ---- Assert Short Message ----

  ---- Assert Long Message ----


      at ErrorService.GenerateError()  c:\webservices\debuggingtracinglogging\errorservice.a
      at RuntimeMethodInfo.InternalInvoke(Object obj, BindingFlags invokeAttr, Binder binder
      at RuntimeMethodInfo.InternalInvoke(Object obj, BindingFlags invokeAttr, Binder binder
      at RuntimeMethodInfo.Invoke(Object obj, BindingFlags invokeAttr, Binder binder, Object
      at MethodBase.Invoke(Object obj, Object[] parameters)
      at LogicalMethodInfo.Invoke(Object target, Object[] values)
      at WebServiceHandler.Invoke()
      at WebServiceHandler.CoreProcessRequest()
      at SyncSessionlessHandler.ProcessRequest(HttpContext context)
      at CallHandlerExecutionStep.Execute()
      at HttpApplication.ExecuteStep(IExecutionStep step, Boolean& completedSynchronously)
      at HttpApplication.ResumeSteps(Exception error)
      at HttpApplication.System.Web.IHttpAsyncHandler.BeginProcessRequest(HttpContext contex
      at HttpRuntime.ProcessRequestInternal(HttpWorkerRequest wr)
      at HttpRuntime.ProcessRequest(HttpWorkerRequest wr)
      at ISAPIRuntime.ProcessRequest(IntPtr ecb, Int32 iWRType)
                                                                          ▼
◄                                                                     ►
```

Figure 8-11. A failed web service assertion

> In order to use tracing from your web service, you must have the debug symbols loaded. Make sure you configure your web service to start automatically with the client project and wait, as described in the "Debugging in Visual Studio .NET" section earlier in this chapter.

The interesting detail is how easily you can convert debug tracing to logging and capture the results. All you need to do is add a TextWriterTraceListener:

```
// Assume that you generate a unique filename (fileName).
// Typically, you would use a combination of user and date information.
Trace.Listeners.Add(new TextWriterTraceListener(File.Create(fileName)));
Trace.AutoFlush = true;
```

On the downside, you need to explicitly enable the listener in every web method. You also need to make sure your tracing code is included in the compiled web service (by adding the /d:TRACE flag to the compiler command line when you compile your code or /d:TRACE=True for VB.NET code). Visual Studio .NET enables tracing by default for compilation, and you can make changes through the Project Properties window.

Even with these restrictions, tracing provides a short path to basic logging features. It's particularly useful when testing in the field before the full deployment of a finished service. It's also extremely simple, which means it's likely to work when other logging methods might not (for example, you will probably have trouble logging database connection problems).

SOAP Extensions

Sometimes it's useful to have the ability to record lower-level logging information. For example, you might want to track the actual SOAP messages that are exchanged between the server and client. You can do this by creating a custom SOAP extension.

You might wonder what value there is in diving down below the .NET web service abstraction into the actual SOAP messages. When working with web services, it's easy to forget that the class-based syntax you use to call a web method and return a result is a programming abstraction on top of a framework of .NET services. These services handle the underlying reality: the exchange of SOAP request and response messages. Part of the reason .NET web services are so remarkable is that they hide this lower level. For example, even though SOAP messages are simple XML, .NET allows you to use strongly typed values. Even though a web method call involves the exchange of a request and response message, .NET allows you to invoke it through a proxy as though the web method were a local function.

Like all abstractions, the .NET web service model has its limits. The most obvious problems occur when you are working with non-Microsoft web services or web clients. These applications don't have the benefit of the .NET services and probably need to create or process SOAP messages manually. When communication breaks down in this type of scenario, you often need to look at the underlying SOAP to determine whether the problem was a syntactical one (invalid formatting of the SOAP message) or an application error (incorrect client data or a server-side error or timeout).

With .NET, you can access the underlying SOAP by using SOAP extensions. SOAP extensions are an extensibility mechanism that lets you add functionality at a different stage in the request/response cycle, as shown in Figure 8-12.

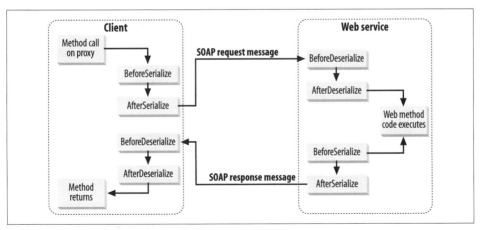

Figure 8-12. Stages in processing a SOAP message

SOAP extensions have a chance to process a SOAP message just before it is sent or immediately after it is received. They can work on the client end or the server side.

SOAP extensions have a wide variety of uses, including compression, encryption, and logging. In this section, we explore the last of these. While this provides an excellent introduction, you should keep in mind that SOAP extensions are actually limited only by your imagination. The only drawback is that they are unashamedly SOAP-specific. That means they won't work if you want to communicate with a web service through other methods like HTTP GET.

The SOAP Extension Classes

Two classes—SoapExtension and SoapExtensionAttribute—are used for creating SOAP extensions. Both of these classes are found in the System.Web.Services. Protocols namespace.

To create a SOAP extension, you follow a few straightforward steps:

1. Create a class that derives from SoapExtension. Implement the basic infrastructure (override the abstract methods) and add your own functionality.

2. Create a class that derives from SoapExtensionAttribute, and modify it to point to your custom SoapExtension class.

3. Apply the SoapExtensionAttribute to a web method or proxy class method.

Remember, SOAP extension work on a per-method basis. You can apply a SOAP extension to as many web or proxy class methods as you want (and you can apply multiple extensions to the same method).

Creating the SoapExtension Class

The first step in creating a SOAP extension is to create a custom SoapExtension class. SoapExtension includes several methods that you must override:

```
public class CustomExtension : SoapExtension
{
    public override object GetInitializer(
      LogicalMethodInfo methodInfo, SoapExtensionAttribute attribute)
    {}

    public override object GetInitializer(Type serviceType)
    {}

    public override void Initialize(object initializer)
    {}

    public override void ProcessMessage(SoapMessage message)
    {}
}
```

The first three methods are used to optimize initialization. For a simple extension that doesn't need to set up any additional data, you can code your methods as follows:

```
public override object GetInitializer(
  LogicalMethodInfo methodInfo, SoapExtensionAttribute attribute)
{ return null; }

public override object GetInitializer(Type serviceType)
{ return null; }

public override void Initialize(object initializer)
{}
```

Processing the Message

The ProcessMessage() method is the heart of your SOAP extension. This method is called automatically by .NET at four different stages during the processing of a SOAP message. These stages are represented by the SoapMessageStage enumeration, and occur in the following order:

1. The client calls a proxy class method.
2. The SoapMessageStage.BeforeSerialize stage occurs. .NET calls the Process-Request() method for any local extensions on the proxy class method.
3. The .NET data is serialized to a SOAP message.
4. The SoapMessageStage.AfterSerialize stage occurs. .NET calls the Process-Request() method for any local extensions on the proxy class method.
5. The SOAP message is sent over the network to the web server.
6. The web server receives the SOAP message.
7. The SoapMessageStage.BeforeDeserialize stage occurs. .NET calls the Process-Request() method for any extensions on the web method.
8. The SOAP message is deserialized to .NET data.
9. The SoapMessageStage.AfterDeserialize stage occurs. .NET calls the Process-Request() method for any extensions on the web method.
10. The web server receives the supplied method parameters.

When the web server returns a SOAP response, the same stages occur in the same order, but the client becomes the recipient and the web server is the sender:

1. The web method finishes processing and returns a result.
2. The SoapMessageStage.BeforeSerialize stage occurs. .NET calls the Process-Request() method for any extensions on the web method.
3. The .NET data is serialized to a SOAP message.

4. The `SoapMessageStage.AfterSerialize` stage occurs. .NET calls the `Process-Request()` method for any extensions on the web method.

5. The SOAP message is sent over the network to the client.

6. The client proxy class receives the SOAP message.

7. The `SoapMessageStage.BeforeDeserialize` stage occurs. .NET calls the `Process-Request()` method for any local extensions on the proxy class method.

8. The SOAP message is deserialized to .NET data.

9. The `SoapMessageStage.AfterDeserialize` stage occurs. .NET calls the `Process-Request()` method for any local extensions on the proxy class method.

10. The client receives the return value.

The `ProcessMessage()` method receives a `SoapMessage` object. This object contains information about the SOAP message and its current stage. The following example uses the `SoapMessage` object to write information to a log file every time a new stage occurs, thereby creating a crude logging tool:

```
public override void ProcessMessage(SoapMessage message)
{
    FileStream fs = new FileStream("c:\\test.log", FileMode.Append,
                                   FileAccess.Write);
    StreamWriter w = new StreamWriter(fs);
    w.Write("Message in: " + message.Stage.ToString());
    w.WriteLine(" at: " + DateTime.Now);
    w.Close();
    fs.Close();
}
```

If you apply this extension to a web method and invoke it once, an output file with the following information will be created (or appended to itself, if it already exists):

```
Message in: BeforeDeserialize at: 2001-09-26 12:59:28 PM
Message in: AfterDeserialize at: 2001-09-26 12:59:28 PM
Message in: BeforeSerialize at: 2001-09-26 12:59:29 PM
Message in: AfterSerialize at: 2001-09-26 12:59:29 PM
```

In order to bind the extension to a web method, however, you need to create and apply a custom `SoapExtensionAttribute`.

Creating the SoapExtensionAttribute

The next step is to create a custom attribute. As a C# programmer, you probably already use attributes regularly (one obvious example is the `WebMethod` attribute that precedes every web service method, as described in Chapter 2). However, you may not have not created your own attribute. To create a custom attribute, simply code a class that derives from another attribute type (in this case, we use the `Soap-ExtensionAttribute` attribute).

The SoapExtensionAttribute has three purposes: to identify your extension, set its priority relative to other extensions, and funnel any additional data you need through custom properties. At its simplest, a custom SoapExtensionAttribute looks like this:

```
// Specify that this attribute can be used only on methods.
[AttributeUsage(AttributeTargets.Method)]
public class CustomExtensionAttribute : SoapExtensionAttribute
{

    public override Type ExtensionType
    {
        get { return typeof(CustomExtension); }
    }

    public override int Priority
    {
        get { return 0; }
        set {}
    }

}
```

These three property methods (two get methods and one set) are abstract and must be overridden in your custom attribute class. The most important property is ExtensionType, which returns the type of your custom SoapExtension class. The other methods allow you to configure a priority.

You can now apply the custom attribute to a method:

```
[WebMethod]
[CustomExtension]            // Equivalent to [CustomExtensionAttribute]
public void TestMethod()
{ }
```

Note that, as always, when you specify the attribute, you can leave out the final part of its name (Attribute). This name should not be confused with the name of the actual SoapExtension class, even though it may be the same.

A Simple Logging Extension

The next example integrates everything described so far to create a rudimentary logging extension. We start with the extension class:

```
public class SimpleTraceExtension : SoapExtension
{
    public override object GetInitializer(LogicalMethodInfo methodInfo,
                                          SoapExtensionAttribute attribute)
    { return null; }

    public override object GetInitializer(Type serviceType)
    { return null; }

public override void Initialize(object initializer)
```

```
{ }

    public override void ProcessMessage(SoapMessage message)
    {
        FileStream fs = new FileStream("c:\\simple.log", FileMode.Append,
                                       FileAccess.Write);
        StreamWriter w = new StreamWriter(fs);
        w.Write("--------------------------------- ");
        w.WriteLine("Message in: " + message.Stage.ToString());
        w.WriteLine("Action: " + message.Action);
        w.WriteLine("URL: " + message.Url);
        w.WriteLine(DateTime.Now);

        if (message.Stage == SoapMessageStage.BeforeDeserialize)
        {
            StreamReader r = new StreamReader(message.Stream);
            w.WriteLine();
            w.WriteLine(r.ReadToEnd());
            message.Stream.Position = 0;
        }

        w.WriteLine();
        w.Close();
        fs.Close();
    }

}
```

A few interesting points arise:

- Various properties of the SoapMessage class are used to retrieve information. The most useful property is Stream, which contains the actual SOAP message.

- The SoapMessage.Stream property can be accessed only in the BeforeDeserialize stage. In the AfterDeserialize stage, the stream has been read and is empty. In the AfterSerialize stage, the stream is writable, but not readable. In the BeforeSerialize stage, the stream can't be accessed at all.

- After reading the stream, you need to reset its position. Otherwise, the CLR attempts to read starting at the end, is unable to deserialize the message, and throws an exception.

The next ingredient is the custom attribute:

```
[AttributeUsage(AttributeTargets.Method)]
public class SimpleTraceExtensionAttribute : SoapExtensionAttribute
{

    private int priority;

    public override Type ExtensionType
    {
        get { return typeof(SimpleTraceExtension); }
    }
```

```csharp
    public override int Priority
    {
        get { return priority; }
        set { priority = value; }
    }

}
```

Note that an `AttributeUsageAttribute` is applied to the class definition. This indicates that the attribute is valid only on a method definition.

The following is a web service that uses the extension:

```csharp
public class SoapExtensionService : System.Web.Services.WebService
{
    [WebMethod]
    [SimpleTraceExtension]
    public string TestMethod(int number)
    {
        return "You supplied: " + number.ToString();
    }
}
```

When a client calls this method, the following log file is generated:

```
------------------------------- Message in: BeforeDeserialize
Action: http://tempuri.org/TestMethod
URL: http://localhost/DebuggingTracingLogging/SoapExtensionService.asmx
2001-09-26 2:54:12 PM

<?xml version="1.0" encoding="utf-8"?>
<soap:Envelope xmlns:soap="http://schemas.xmlsoap.org/soap/envelope/" xmlns:
xsi="http://www.w3.org/2001/XMLSchema-instance" xmlns:xsd="http://www.w3.org/2001/
XMLSchema">
  <soap:Body>
    <TestMethod xmlns="http://tempuri.org/">
      <number>4</number>
    </TestMethod>
  </soap:Body>
</soap:Envelope>

------------------------------- Message in: AfterDeserialize
Action: http://tempuri.org/TestMethod
URL: http://localhost/DebuggingTracingLogging/SoapExtensionService.asmx
2001-09-26 2:54:12 PM

------------------------------- Message in: BeforeSerialize
Action: http://tempuri.org/TestMethod
URL: http://localhost/DebuggingTracingLogging/SoapExtensionService.asmx
2001-09-26 2:54:12 PM

------------------------------- Message in: AfterSerialize
Action: http://tempuri.org/TestMethod
URL: http://localhost/DebuggingTracingLogging/SoapExtensionService.asmx
2001-09-26 2:54:12 PM
```

Advanced SOAP Extensions

The earlier logging example suffers from a few problems. First of all, the filename is hardcoded, making it useless if you want to use the same extension for multiple methods. Another limitation is that the log file records only the received request, not the response. Though the extension is triggered at the appropriate stage (in this case, AfterSerialize), the SoapMessage.Stream is write-only at that moment. To solve both of these problems, you need to delve a little deeper into SOAP extensions.

In the next two sections, you'll learn how to create an initializer to allow the web service programmer to set a different log filename for each method and how to use the ChainStream() method to access the SOAP message even when the SoapMessage. Stream property is not accessible.

Initializing Data

The SoapExtension class provides two methods—Initialize() and Get-Initializer()—that work in tandem to provide some initial information to your SoapExtension class. The GetInitializer() method is called only once: the first time your extension is used for a particular method. It gives you the chance to construct and store additional information. Store this information by wrapping it into an object and returning it from the GetInitializer() method. This object will then be provided to the Initialize() method every time the extension is invoked for the same method.

In other words, if you need to look up information from a database or perform some other time-consuming tasks, the GetInitializer() method allows you to do it with a one-time performance hit. If you don't need any special information, you must still override the GetInitializer() method, but you should just return null.

```
public override object GetInitializer(
   LogicalMethodInfo methodInfo, SoapExtensionAttribute attribute)
{
    // Look up data here and build a DataSet.
    // Now store the DataSet.
    return dsInfo;
}

public override void Initialize(object initializer)
{
    // The DataSet is provided as the initializer parameter.
    // You can store the DataSet in a member variable to use in this pass.
    this.dsInfo = (DataSet) initializer;
}
```

You may need to do a little work with the debugger before you really understand how these two methods work. When your web service is loaded into memory, .NET will execute the GetInitializer() method of every extension. This method is invoked independently for each method (meaning you will have one initializer in memory for each SoapExtensionAttribute in your service). GetInitializer() is not invoked again unless the web service is recompiled.

Make sure you distinguish between the two versions of the GetInitializer() method. One allows you to set the initializer object. The other is used to retrieve the type of initializer object:

```
public override object GetInitializer(Type serviceType)
{
    return typeof(DataSet);    // dsInfo.GetType() is equivalent
}
```

One other interesting point is the information that GetInitializer() provides in its parameters: a LogicalMethodInfo object that describes the method where the trace extension is applied and the SoapExtensionAttribute that is applied to it. Typically, the SoapExtensionAttribute is the most useful. For example, you could define an additional property in your custom SoapExtensionAttribute class, set it in the attribute definition, and then retrieve it in your SoapExtension class. You'll see an example of this trick later in this chapter.

LogicalMethodInfo allows you to retrieve metadata information about the method, such as its name and the data types of its parameters and return value. Some of its properties allow you to continue your investigation with the reflection types ParameterInfo and MethodInfo from the System.Reflection namespace.

 The LogicalMethodInfo class provides access to a method's metadata. You cannot access other pieces of information like the supplied parameter values. (In fact, they wouldn't be useful because the initializer object you construct will be used every time the method is invoked, regardless of parameter values.)

The ChainStream() Method

The ChainStream() method provides another way to access the SOAP stream. ChainStream() allows you to directly access the memory buffer with the SOAP message. The drawback is that you inherit the responsibility for retrieving and forwarding the memory stream. If you fail to do so, other SOAP extensions may not receive the message, or (more likely) the SOAP message will be lost and an error will occur.

The basic implementation for an extension with ChainStream() is:

```
public class CustomExtension : SoapExtension
{
    // Code for the initialize functions omitted.

    Stream oldStream;
    Stream newStream;

    // Save the stream into a local memory buffer.
```

```csharp
public override Stream ChainStream( Stream stream )
{
    oldStream = stream;
    newStream = new MemoryStream();
    return newStream;
}

// If the stream contains the SOAP message, forward it along.
public override void ProcessMessage(SoapMessage message)
{
    if (message.Stage == SoapMessageStage.AfterSerialize)
    {
        newStream.Position = 0;
        CopyStream(newStream, oldStream);
    }
    else if (message.Stage == SoapMessageStage.BeforeDeserialize)
    {
        CopyStream(oldStream, newStream);
        newStream.Position = 0;
    }
}

void CopyStream(Stream from, Stream to)
{
    TextReader reader = new StreamReader(from);
    TextWriter writer = new StreamWriter(to);
    writer.WriteLine(reader.ReadToEnd());
    writer.Flush();
}
}
```

This represents a fair bit of infrastructure code. However, as long as you follow this pattern, your extension will run smoothly, and it will have the opportunity to access and modify the SOAP stream. You'll see how this can help create a better logger in the next section.

A More Advanced Logging Extension

Using ChainStream() and the initialization features, it's possible to create a more sophisticated logging extension that overcomes some of the shortcomings of the last example.

The initialization features provide an easy way to make the log filename configurable on a per-method basis. The first ingredient is a special SoapExtensionAttribute that has a Filename property.

```csharp
[AttributeUsage(AttributeTargets.Method)]
public class AdvancedTraceExtensionAttribute : SoapExtensionAttribute
{

    private string filename = "c:\\defaultlog.txt";
    private int priority;
```

```csharp
    public override Type ExtensionType
    {
        get { return typeof(AdvancedTraceExtension); }
    }

    public override int Priority
    {
        get { return priority; }
        set { priority = value; }
    }
    public string Filename
    {
        get { return filename; }
        set { filename = value; }
    }
}
```

The Filename property can be specified when the custom attribute is applied:

```csharp
public class SoapExtensionService : System.Web.Services.WebService
{
    [WebMethod]
    [AdvancedTraceExtension(Filename="c:\TestMethod.log")]
    public string TestMethod(int number)
    {
        return "You supplied: " + number.ToString();
    }
}
```

The web service retrieves the filename setting from the attribute class in the GetInitializer() method and stores it in the initializer object. The initializer is converted into a valid member variable each time the Initialize() method is called.

```csharp
public class TraceExtension : SoapExtension
{
    Stream oldStream;
    Stream newStream;
    string filename;

    public override object GetInitializer(LogicalMethodInfo methodInfo,
                                          SoapExtensionAttribute attribute)
    {
        return ((AdvancedTraceExtensionAttribute) attribute).Filename;
    }

    public override object GetInitializer(Type serviceType)
    {
        return filename.GetType();
    }

    public override void Initialize(object initializer)
    {
        filename = (string) initializer;
    }
```

```csharp
public override void ProcessMessage(SoapMessage message)
{
    FileStream fs = new FileStream(filename, FileMode.Append,
                                   FileAccess.Write);
    StreamWriter w = new StreamWriter(fs);
    w.Write("------------------------------- ");
    w.WriteLine("Message in: " + message.Stage.ToString());
    w.WriteLine("Action: " + message.Action);
    w.WriteLine("URL: " + message.Url);
    w.WriteLine(DateTime.Now);
    w.WriteLine();

    // We have to flush the file-to-date before streaming to it.
    w.Flush();

    if (message.Stage == SoapMessageStage.AfterSerialize)
    {
        // Store the SOAP reponse message in the file.

        newStream.Position = 0;
        CopyStream(newStream, fs);
        newStream.Position = 0;
        CopyStream(newStream, oldStream);
    }
    else if (message.Stage == SoapMessageStage.BeforeDeserialize)
    {
        CopyStream(oldStream, newStream);

        // Store the SOAP request message in the file.
        newStream.Position = 0;
        CopyStream(newStream, fs);

        newStream.Position = 0;
    }
    fs.Close();
}

public override Stream ChainStream( Stream stream )
{
    oldStream = stream;
    newStream = new MemoryStream();
    return newStream;
}

void CopyStream(Stream from, Stream to)
{
    TextReader reader = new StreamReader(from);
    TextWriter writer = new StreamWriter(to);
    writer.WriteLine(reader.ReadToEnd());
    writer.Flush();
}
}
```

This extension uses `ChainStream` to write both the SOAP request and response to the log file. Here is the log file that is generated when `TestMethod()` is invoked once, with the parameter number set to 4:

```
------------------------------ Message in: BeforeDeserialize
Action: http://tempuri.org/TestMethod
URL: http://localhost/DebuggingTracingLogging/SoapExtensionService.asmx

2001-09-27 12:28:45 PM
<?xml version="1.0" encoding="utf-8"?>
<soap:Envelope xmlns:soap="http://schemas.xmlsoap.org/soap/envelope/" xmlns:
xsi="http://www.w3.org/2001/XMLSchema-instance" xmlns:xsd="http://www.w3.org/2001/
XMLSchema">
  <soap:Body>
    <TestMethod xmlns="http://tempuri.org/">
      <number>4</number>
    </TestMethod>
  </soap:Body>
</soap:Envelope>

------------------------------ Message in: AfterDeserialize
Action: http://tempuri.org/TestMethod
URL: http://localhost/DebuggingTracingLogging/SoapExtensionService.asmx
2001-09-27 12:28:45 PM

------------------------------ Message in: BeforeSerialize
Action: http://tempuri.org/TestMethod
URL: http://localhost/DebuggingTracingLogging/SoapExtensionService.asmx
2001-09-27 12:28:45 PM

------------------------------ Message in: AfterSerialize
Action: http://tempuri.org/TestMethod
URL: http://localhost/DebuggingTracingLogging/SoapExtensionService.asmx
2001-09-27 12:28:45 PM

<?xml version="1.0" encoding="utf-8"?>
<soap:Envelope xmlns:soap="http://schemas.xmlsoap.org/soap/envelope/" xmlns:
xsi="http://www.w3.org/2001/XMLSchema-instance" xmlns:xsd="http://www.w3.org/2001/
XMLSchema">
  <soap:Body>
    <TestMethodResponse xmlns="http://tempuri.org/">
      <TestMethodResult>You supplied: 4</TestMethodResult>
    </TestMethodResponse>
  </soap:Body>
</soap:Envelope>
```

You could easily convert this example to use a different log store, including a database.

Proxy Extensions

The logging examples in this chapter have focused single-mindedly on web service extensions. However, web service extensions are of little use if you want to view the

SOAP messages sent between your application and a third-party web service. Even if the web service on the other end is based on the .NET platform, you won't have access to the source code, and you won't be able to make the modifications needed to apply the extension.

In this situation, there are several possible solutions. You could create a web service of your own and use it as a proxy. It could log the messages just before it forwards them to the "real" web service. This is the approach taken by some third-party products. Fortunately, an easier method is available. You can develop a local trace extension and apply it to the appropriate methods in your proxy class:

```
[System.Diagnostics.DebuggerStepThroughAttribute()]
[SoapDocumentMethodAttribute("http://tempuri.org/TestMethod",
  Use=SoapBindingUse.Literal, ParameterStyle= SoapParameterStyle.Wrapped)]
[AdvancedTraceExtension(Filename="c:\TestMethod.log")]
public string TestMethod(int number)
{
    object[] results = this.Invoke("TestMethod", new object[] {number});
    return ((string)(results[0]));
}
```

This works equally as well, because the AdvancedTraceExtension extension displays both SOAP responses and requests. The order of stages will be slightly different, however:

```
-------------------------------- Message in: BeforeSerialize
Action: http://tempuri.org/TestMethod
URL: http://localhost/DebuggingTracingLogging/SoapExtensionService.asmx
2001/09/27 1:10:33 PM

-------------------------------- Message in: AfterSerialize
Action: http://tempuri.org/TestMethod
URL: http://localhost/DebuggingTracingLogging/SoapExtensionService.asmx
2001/09/27 1:10:34 PM

<?xml version="1.0" encoding="utf-8"?>
<soap:Envelope xmlns:soap="http://schemas.xmlsoap.org/soap/envelope/" xmlns:
xsi="http://www.w3.org/2001/XMLSchema-instance" xmlns:xsd="http://www.w3.org/2001/
XMLSchema">
  <soap:Body>
    <TestMethod xmlns="http://tempuri.org/">
      <number>4</number>
    </TestMethod>
  </soap:Body>
</soap:Envelope>

-------------------------------- Message in: BeforeDeserialize
Action: http://tempuri.org/TestMethod
URL: http://localhost/DebuggingTracingLogging/SoapExtensionService.asmx
2001/09/27 1:10:36 PM

<?xml version="1.0" encoding="utf-8"?>
```

```
<soap:Envelope xmlns:soap="http://schemas.xmlsoap.org/soap/envelope/" xmlns:
xsi="http://www.w3.org/2001/XMLSchema-instance" xmlns:xsd="http://www.w3.org/2001/
XMLSchema">
  <soap:Body>
    <TestMethodResponse xmlns="http://tempuri.org/">
      <TestMethodResult>You supplied: 4</TestMethodResult>
    </TestMethodResponse>
  </soap:Body>
</soap:Envelope>

------------------------------ Message in: AfterDeserialize
Action: http://tempuri.org/TestMethod
URL: http://localhost/DebuggingTracingLogging/SoapExtensionService.asmx
2001/09/27 1:10:36 PM
```

 To edit the proxy class in Visual Studio .NET, select Project → Show All Files. Unfortunately, any changes you make are lost when you regenerate the proxy class.

Remember, logging and SOAP extensions can impose a performance penalty, particularly if you use database access. As with every aspect of web service design, you need to keep in mind that web services may serve hundreds of users and have to operate quickly to compensate for network delays.

CHAPTER 9

Security and Authentication

Potential security risks are an unfortunate fact of life. Since the rollout of the first Bulletin Board System (BBS), crackers of all types, from so-called script kiddies to white hats, have been pounding away at just about anything with an IP address. One of the most important defenses available to a web administrator is to follow the myriad of hotfixes and patches regularly posted by Microsoft. Although these frequent releases might make you feel like Lucille Ball in the chocolate factory (a famous episode in her equally famous 50's TV sitcom), installation of these fixes is a necessary step in keeping your system secure.

Following Microsoft's system documentation is important, but there's much more you can do to protect your web services. In this chapter, we discuss some of the common vulnerabilities exposed by the web service applications, as well as the security techniques you can use to plug them.

Potential Vulnerabilities

One of the important things to realize as you consider how to secure a web service is that your system is only as secure as its weakest point. You can have a failover cluster of CheckPoint firewalls running on Sun UltraSparcs working as server guard dogs, but if IIS isn't correctly patched or if your application is poorly written, the firewalls provide about as much protection as a flowerpot on your doorstep. This is why the security of the network, the operating system, and the application are important, as well as that of the system as a whole. By looking at the whole web service system and identifying its security-related components, you can effectively plan for security. With that in mind, the focus of this chapter is web service security; a full discussion of the intricacies of system security are outside the scope of this book. We'll take a brief look at the security components of a typical web service system before moving on to consider .NET web service security specifically.

Let's take a look at a generic web service system, paying attention to the entire call process—from receipt of an initial request message to the running of a server process to the sending of a response message—including events that occur from the moment a request message is generated on the client to the moment the response is received from the web service. Figure 9-1 shows the elements involved in a typical web service call and response.

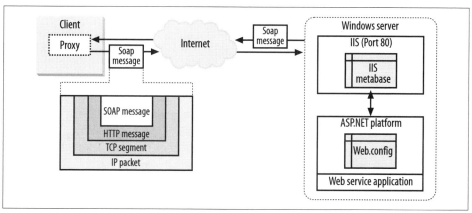

Figure 9-1. Web service request/response process

A web service call begins at the client. Using a proxy object, the client makes a request, in the form of a SOAP message, to the web method. If this communication occurs over the Internet, as shown in the diagram, the SOAP message is encapsulated into a network packet or broken into multiple packets. This packet is routed to the web server that hosts the web method, which is usually listening on port 80. The web server then looks at the URL to determine which server process should handle the request and passes the request on to the appropriate process, which, in the case of a web method, is the ASP.NET worker process (*aspnet_wp.exe*, *aspnet_ewp.exe*, or similar). The worker process executes the request using the .NET Framework and web service application, returning the resulting SOAP message back along the chain.

The five components present during the execution of most web services are:

Network
> The communication medium between the client and service.

Operating system
> The operating system hosting the web service application. The operating system connects to the network via a network card.

Web server
> An application that runs on top of the operating system, listening for HTTP traffic, usually on port 80. In the case of ASP.NET, the IIS web server interacts directly with .NET via an ISAPI DLL called *aspnet_isapi.dll*. Versions 4.0 and 5.0 of the IIS web server also use an internal data storage mechanism called the *metabase* to store configuration and security information.

ASP.NET platform
    An application that runs as a process hosted by the operating system. This .NET
    worker process receives requests for web methods from the web server and then
    uses a custom application to process them.

Web service application
    Runs within the .NET worker process.

Each of these components has a specific way of interacting with the others, and most
security issues exist at the interfaces between them. In addition, while security considerations for the last two components (the .NET platform and the web service
application) are clearly central to web service security, some of the security considerations for the first three are not. We're not going to talk about operating system or
network security considerations, but they're just as critical as internal considerations. We recommend you pick up a good book on security, such as O'Reilly's
Securing Windows NT/2000 Servers for the Internet by Stephen Norberg (2000) to
learn more about network security and hardening the Windows operating system.

Web Service Authentication

Authentication is the process of determining the identity of a user, confirming that a
user is the person or process he claims to be. The approach to authentication in a
web service is pretty much the same as that for an ASP.NET web site. The difference
is that instead of authenticating users, you're usually authenticating computers.
However, from the point of view of the web service, whether the calling party is a
user or a computer is irrelevant. You can use the authentication capabilities of the
operating system, web server, .NET platform, and application to create a layered
authentication model. Conceptually, the components of this security model look like
those in Figure 9-2.

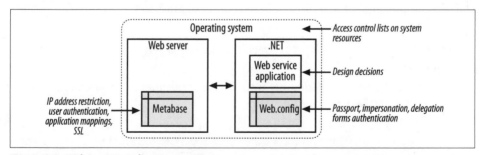

Figure 9-2. Web service authentication system

Figure 9-2 shows the relationship between the Windows operating system, the IIS
web server, the .NET platform, and a web service application. Each of the four components has its own set of features for configuring authentication. Each of the four
components has a persistence mechanism for storing configuration information. Windows can use either an NT Domain or Active Directory to store information about

user accounts, group membership, and other metadata. The IIS web server uses a database called the *metabase* to store IIS configuration settings. The .NET platform uses a hierarchical configuration structure including a *machine.config* file for storing global configuration information; the web service application, part of .NET, uses a *web.config* file for storing configuration information. As you'll see, for the most part, the configuration settings in a web service's *web.config* file override the global settings of the *machine.config* file.

Each of these components plays a different role in the authentication process, and it's important to understand the relationship between them, particularly between IIS and .NET, in order to configure an authentication method that meets your security, performance, and reliability requirements. We're going to focus on the authentication features of the .NET platform, but in order to do so, we'll first review some of the security features provided by IIS.

IIS Security Features

The IIS web server provides a rich set of security features that you can use to manage access to your server. The configuration of these features plays an important role in the security model of a web service application. IIS allows you to configure four basic types of security:

- User authentication methods (including client certificates)
- IP address and domain name restrictions
- Server certificates (SSL)
- Application mappings

These security features can be configured using the Internet Services Manager and are stored in the IIS metabase.

User Authentication and Client Certificates

User authentication is a process in which user credentials are requested and then compared against the list of valid domains of local user accounts. These lists are stored either on a domain controller, in Active Directory, or on the local machine. In a non–web service application, these credentials can be supplied by the user via a pop-up login box or by the client machine using the built-in Windows security features. The user authentication options available in IIS 5.0 are as follows:

Anonymous Access
    No username or password is required from the user. IIS runs in the security context of the user account specified as the Anonymous User Account in ISM. The default account is the `IUSR_SERVERNAME` account, created by IIS upon installation. This option is the obvious choice for publicly available sites.

Basic Authentication

When using this authentication method for a web site, the user is prompted to enter a username, a password, and possibly a domain name. This information is then passed as part of the HTTP request to the server and is encoded using Base64 encoding. (We use the term "encoded" lightly. Considering the ease with which Base64 can be deciphered, it is virtually equivalent to plain text, which is why this method is often referred to as "clear text authentication.") IIS allows the request to go through only if the username/password combination matches a valid domain or local user account. Because of its lack of real security, basic authentication is often used in conjunction with SSL.

Digest Authentication

This method is available only in Windows 2000 and IIS 5.0. It operates in a similar fashion to Basic Authentication; however, it encrypts the user's password information using a hashing mechanism called MD5. MD5, which stands for Message Digest 5, is an algorithm developed by RSA. Unlike Basic Authentication, which is supported by most browsers and web service clients, *Digest Authentication works only with clients running .NET or with IE 5.x or later*. In addition, Digest Authentication requires that a user account be stored in Active Directory.

Integrated Windows Authentication

This method uses HTML challenge/response or Kerberos to authenticate a user with a Windows NT Domain or Active Directory account. This authentication method is highly secure, in part because unlike Basic or Digest Authentication, the password is never sent across the network. However, this method is best suited for an intranet environment in which the client and server are part of the same domain, since it does not work over a firewall or proxy server. In addition, reliance on Active Directory or a Windows Domain for user authentication can severely limit scalability. This method is not recommended for use with non-.NET clients.

Client Certificates

Each client must have a valid digital certificate, which is presented to the server as part of the authentication process. The client certificate can be mapped to a Windows account on the server. This method is not currently in widespread use, mainly because of the overhead involved in creating, distributing, and managing certificates. Each certificate must be distributed to the client on which it will be used.

The security and performance level are often the two determining factors when choosing the appropriate authentication method for a web application. The chart in Figure 9-3 compares several authentication methods on the basis of performance and security.

This chart is merely a guide. In reality, the level of security and performance depend on a number of factors. The security level of a client certificate, for example, is very

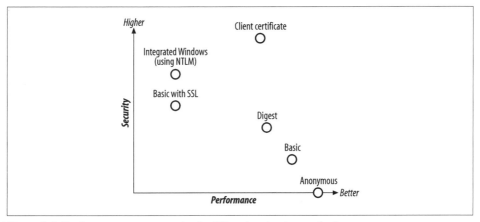

Figure 9-3. Performance versus security for IIS authentication methods

much dependent on how secure the certificate distribution process is. Likewise, the performance of Integrated Windows security depends on your network architecture and the number of users in the domain or directory.

Security Risks of Basic Authentication

When you choose Basic Authentication, your username and password are sent using Base64 encoding. This encoding provides virtually no security and can easily be intercepted. To make matters worse, it will most likely be sent by your client along with every SOAP message, further exposing you to any risk posed by sniffers. For these reasons, basic authentication should be used in conjunction with transport layer security such as SSL. Here is an example of the SOAP message sent by the client when using basic authentication:

```
POST /securityservices/windowauth.asmx HTTP/1.1
User-Agent: Mozilla/4.0 (compatible; MSIE 6.0; MS Web Services Client Protocol
1.0.2914.16)
Content-Type: text/xml; charset=utf-8
SOAPAction: "http://tempuri.org/GetPrincipalInfo"
Authorization: Basic eLKJsdfjleijfLKJvbw==
Content-Length: 312
Expect: 100-continue
Host: localhost
```

Basic Authentication and SSL

Another security method is Basic Authentication with asymmetric SSL encryption, which is perhaps the most common secure access method on the Internet today. This method is particularly well suited for web services because both Basic Authentication and SSL are widely recognized security features. Obviously, the security level of SSL is very much dependent on the key size used, and the relative protection it provides compared to a method like Digest Authentication can be difficult to compare, because each is vulnerable to a different type of attack.

IP Address and Domain Name Restriction

Another security tool is IP address and domain name restriction, in which access to server resources is limited based on the IP address, network address, or domain name of the client. This restriction—which in IIS is set using the Directory Security tab in the Internet Services Manager—is the first test applied to each HTTP request, preceding all of the other security rules. If the HTTP request originates from an IP address or domain name that is part of the restricted list, a 403.6 error: "Forbidden: IP Address Restricted" is returned, and none of the other authentication processes is attempted.

Domain name restriction is determined using a reverse DNS lookup on the IP address. This can be a very slow process and can severely limit your web server's performance. For this reason, it's a rarely used feature.

Application Mappings Restrictions

Application mappings are used by IIS to determine which program should handle a page request, based on the file extension of the requested URL. For example, requests for web service applications, with the extension *.asmx*, are handled by *aspnet_isapi.dll*. You can view the full list of mappings in the Internet Services Manager, by clicking on the properties of your web server, editing the master properties of the WWW Service, and pressing the Configuration button on the Home Directory tab. The screen should look something like Figure 9-4.

This screen lists the extension, the associated program (an ISAPI DLL), and the HTTP verbs that are accepted by this application. In addition to modifying the master application mappings, which adds or removes mappings from all web sites on the server, you can also modify the mappings for each individual web site. If no application mapping exists in the metabase, IIS simply returns the file.

IIS Security Flow

The IIS security features that we've mentioned are applied in the following order for both regular HTTP and SSL-encrypted HTTP:

1. IP address and domain name restriction
2. Application mapping (HTTP verb) restriction
3. User authentication

This process is displayed in Figure 9-5.

Any attempted access that is denied by IIS results in the familiar 40X set of error messages (e.g., 404, 403.6, etc.) The user authentication process is actually

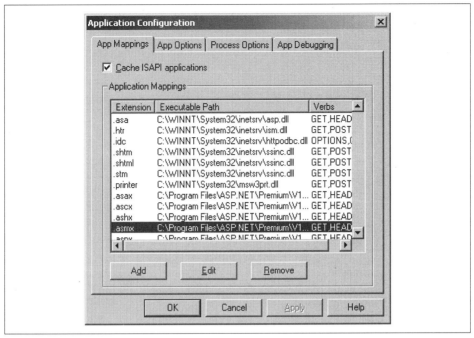

Figure 9-4. IIS master application mappings

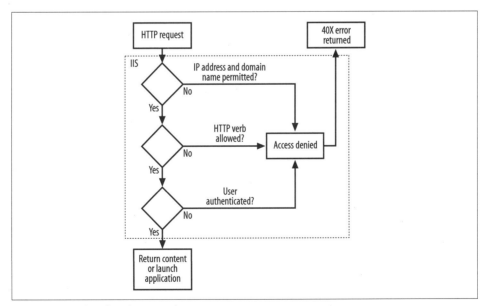

Figure 9-5. Order of application of IIS security processes

performed by the operating system. As we've mentioned, if anonymous access is enabled, the web server operates under the default user security context (e.g., IUSR_MYSERVER). Otherwise, the security context of the authenticated user is used (note that this may not be the case when the site content is retrieved over the network from a file share).

If the user request meets all of the authentication criteria, either content is returned or the request is passed to another application via an ISAPI DLL as defined in the IIS application mappings configuration. In the case of a web service, the request is passed to the involved ASP.NET process. This is where .NET security comes into play. In the next section, we take a look at some of the ASP.NET security features and how they interact with IIS.

ASP.NET Security

In ASP 3.0, security was handled either by IIS and Windows or by the ASP application itself. If you chose to use the built-in features of IIS and Windows, you could set up the proper user accounts either using the MMC or programmatically with ADSI and configure IIS security to use those accounts. If you chose to implement security only in the application, you could set IIS to allow anonymous access and then use a custom forms-based authentication method usually involving an SQL database. Use of ASP.NET provides another security layer that increases your choices of the proper security model for your application. In this section, we discuss the ASP.NET security model and how it interacts with Windows and IIS.

The machine.config and web.config Files

We've already seen that .NET provides a hierarchical approach to configuration. The two configuration files discussed so far, *machine.config* and *web.config*, use an XML format to store configuration information. The *machine.config* file is called the *server* or *root* configuration file and is in the *[WinNT]\Microsoft.NET\Framework\[version]\ CONFIG* folder. This file allows you to make configuration settings at the platform level. Configuration done in the *machine.config* file is applied globally to all .NET applications running on the server.

The *web.config* file is the application configuration file and is stored in the directory containing your ASP.NET or web service application. While there is only one *machine.config* file per server, each web application can have multiple *web.config* files, stored in any directory of the web application. *web.config* sets configuration options at both the application and directory level. For most configuration options, the settings in the *web.config* file closest to the .NET resource being called override the settings in any other configuration file. This means that you can specify a default configuration for the server using the *machine.config* file, another configuration for a web service application on the server using a *web.config* file in the root folder (which overrides *machine.config*), and then override both of these configuration settings using another *web.config* file in a subdirectory of this application.

In addition, each *web.config* file applies configuration settings to its own directory and all child directories (that lack a *web.config* file) below it. Of course, there are some caveats to this: settings in the higher-level configuration files can be locked using the <allowOverride> directive, which is useful in hosting scenarios in which the system administrator wants to limit system access or security. A locked higher-level configuration cannot be overridden by the settings in a *web.config* file.

At runtime, .NET gathers each of the *web.config* files for the application and compiles a list of configuration settings for each application resource. This list is cached in memory for quick access by each request. .NET also monitors the state of each configuration file and regenerates the cached list if one of them changes. By default, all web requests to configuration files are blocked and return a 403 (forbidden) error.

ASP.NET Authentication Providers

The ASP.NET security layer allows you to optionally use one of three authentication providers. These providers are code modules that can verify user credentials and perform other security management tasks such as cookie management, something that had to be done manually in ASP 3.0. By "code module," we mean that each of the authentication providers is implemented by a class that implements the System.Web. IHttpModule interface. This interface allows the class to interact with the HTTP runtime. The authentication provider classes are sealed, so you can't inherit from them; however, each provides a means for interacting with the authentication process (for attaching a custom IPrincipal object) through a special authentication event supported by the *global.asax*. We'll discuss this in a bit.

Since a web service application uses the same HTTP pipeline as an ASP.NET application, you can use the ASP.NET authentication providers for your web service applications. Bear in mind, however, that these providers were designed to work with user-centric ASP.NET applications, and as a result, they may not be appropriate for use in your web service applications. The three supported providers, along with descriptions and limitations, are listed in Table 9-1.

Table 9-1. ASP.NET authentication providers

Authentication provider	Description	Design considerations
Windows Authentication	Authentication is performed by IIS using basic, digest, or Windows (NTLM, Kerberos), and requests are made using the security context of the authenticated user. You can use *web.config* to further allow or deny the accounts on a per-directory basis.	Good choice for authentication in systems with low to moderate load when you want security with a minimum of coding. Simple logon process provides good compatibility with non-MS services; still requires a cookie.
Forms Authentication	Unauthenticated requests are redirected to HTML form using HTTP client-side redirection. If the request is authenticated, the server returns a cookie that the client can use for subsequent access. This is pretty much the same process that was manually coded in many ASP 3.0 applications but is now part of the architecture.	Similar to ASP 3.0 authentication style. Can support moderate to high load depending on form/submission design. Requires clients to accept HTTP redirects and know how to process resulting form, which is not good for web service scenarios.

Table 9-1. ASP.NET authentication providers (continued)

Authentication provider	Description	Design considerations
Passport Authentication	This provider allows you to use the highly touted Passport authentication services offered by Microsoft. This service, which is designed more for consumer access, provides users with single-logon access to Passport-enabled sites. The service gives the site user profile services through the `PassportIdentity` class.	This option is inappropriate for most web service applications. User credentials cannot be fully verified due to the intermediary client.

In addition to the three providers described in Table 9-1, you can opt out of using a provider entirely. In this case, resources are accessed under the context of either the local ASP.NET process or the IUSR account if impersonation is enabled.

To configure our web service to support an ASP.NET authentication provider, add the following lines to the *web.config* file:

```
<configuration>
  <system.web>
    ...
    <authentication mode= "[Windows/Forms/Passport/None]">
      <!-- Authentication Options -->
    </authentication>
    <authorization>
    <!-- Permit or deny users -->
    </authorization>
    <identity impersonate="true|false"
      [username="username" password="password"]/>
    ...
  </system.web>
</configuration>
```

The `<authentication>` element specifies the authentication provider. Depending on the method chosen (e.g., `Windows`, `Forms`, `Passport`, or `None`), several authentication options can be specified as well. Note that there can be only one authentication method per application, which must be stored in the *web.config* file in the application root directory. You can still set other resource restrictions using *web.config* files in child directories, but if you try to set authentication in one of these files, an exception will be thrown.

The `<authorization>` element explicitly permits or denies access to Windows users and groups or restricts access based on HTTP verbs such as GET and POST. Finally, the `<identity>` section enables or disables impersonation.

Using Windows Authentication in Web Services

Because the .NET Windows authentication provider works in conjunction with IIS authentication, it's best suited for intranet scenarios or for Internet scenarios in which the expected load is moderate to low. This is because Windows authentication, which performs user authentication against a domain controller or Active Directory, is inherently less scalable than performing authentication against a SQL database or XML file. In addition, you must set up user accounts and passwords for each user using the appropriate Windows NT or 2000 console (or programmatically through something like ADSI). As mentioned, it's also important to choose your IIS authentication method carefully when operating in an Internet environment if you want to ensure compatibility with clients on non-Windows platforms.

Configuring Windows authentication

In order to configure Windows authentication for your application, you must specify it as the authentication mode in your application's *web.config* file as follows:

```
<configuration>
  <system.web>
    <authentication mode= "Windows" />
    <identity impersonate="true" />
  </system.web>
</configuration>
```

The <identity> section, also important, enables or disables impersonation. Setting impersonate to true results in clients operating under the security context of the user account with which they logged into IIS. For example, if we set our web service client to present a credentials object with username alex and password whatever, the client will then access server resources in the context of the user alex. If user alex is permitted to access (via an access control list, or ACL) a given *.asmx* web service, it will be executed. If, however, impersonate is set to false, this same situation will result in the client's access being done using the security context of the default IIS account (e.g., IUSR_MyServer).

> If you do not enable impersonation, all web service code will run under a special account (called ASPNET) that is created when you install the framework. The goal of this account is to grant only permissions required for a web request processing, and make it more difficult for a malicious user to exploit code permissions to attack a web server. You can instruct ASP.NET to use a different account by modifying the *machine.config* file, as described at the end of this chapter.

Two important things to note regarding the <identity> element are that it can be set only in the root *web.config* file for your application. If you try to set it in more than one place in your application, an exception will be thrown. Also, it can be used only in conjunction with Windows authentication.

Restricting access by user and group

You can also use the <authorization> section to restrict access based on NT/2000 user and group by using the subsections called <allow> and <deny>. The format for these sections is as follows:

```
<authorization>

  <allow users="comma-separated list of users"
     roles="comma-separated list of roles"
```

```
        verbs="comma-separated list of verbs" />

    <deny users="comma-separated list of users"
        roles="comma-separated list of roles"
        verbs="comma-separated list of verbs" />

</authorization>
```

This format allows you to permit or deny access based on user account, group membership, or HTTP verb. In addition to the comma-separated list, you can also use two wildcards as follows:

Asterisk
> To allow every member of the type (user, role, or verb)

Question mark
> To allow the anonymous user (cannot be used with role or verb)

To put this into perspective, here are a couple of examples:

```
<authorization>
    <allow users="lmullen, devans, aclayton, MyDomain\phewson" />
    <deny users="bstreisand, MyDomain\bmanilow" />
<authorization>
```

Using a section like this allows access to the first four users and denies access to the second two (bstreisand and bmanilow). The use of the domain names for the last two users in each row is important. By default, .NET will look for the user on the local server—not in the local domain as is the behavior of IIS authentication. You must include the domain name or the restriction won't be implemented properly.

The following example uses both roles and users:

```
<authorization>
    <allow users="lmullen, devans, aclayton, MyDomain\phewson"
            roles="MyDomain\Accounting" />
    <deny users="lmullen, MyDomain\bmanilow" />
<authorization>
```

This scenario is a bit more complicated. Here, the same users are allowed, along with all members of the Accounting group in the domain MyDomain. Two users are also denied, one of which—lmullen—is permitted as well. So does lmullen get allowed or denied? Furthermore, what if bmanilow is a member of the Accounting group? The answer is that the rules are applied in order, so that the first rule takes precedence. In this case, user lmullen would be allowed since the <allow> rule appears before the <deny> rule.

By default, .NET is configured to allow all users. Remember that the configuration files are interpreted in a hierarchical manner. If no configuration setting exists in the folder or application *web.config* file, .NET checks the *machine.config* file. Notice that this root configuration file contains the following entry:

```
<allow users="*"/>
```

which grants access to all users.

Restricting access by HTTP verb

We showed earlier that IIS is capable of restricting access to resources based on the HTTP verb, such as GET or POST, using the Application Mappings section of the IIS management console. Similar restrictions at the .NET security layer can be achieved by using the <authentication> section of the configuration file; you can go one step further by limiting HTTP verb access by user or role. This more granular level of restriction allows you to permit HTTP GETs and POSTs to some users, while restricting other features such as DELETEs to different users. For web service applications, this tactic is particularly useful, because it allows us to limit the type of consumer allowed on a per-user basis. For example, you could deny HTTP GET access to external clients, forcing them to use HTTP POST/SOAP, while allowing internal development staff to consume the service using GET. The following is an example of this type of scenario:

```
<configuration>
  <system.web>
    <authentication mode="Windows" />
    <authorization>
      <allow verbs="GET" users="MyDomain\alex, MyDomain\matthew" />
      <deny verbs="GET" users="*" />
    </authorization>
  </system.web>
</configuration>
```

This configuration file prevents any user other than alex and matthew from using the GET HTTP method to access the contents of the directory (and any subdirectories without their own *web.config* file).

There may also be some cases in which you want to restrict access at the file level rather than the directory level. This restriction can be achieved using the <location> element. For example, if you just wanted to restrict HTTP GET access to a specific web service, you could use something like the following.

```
<configuration>
  <location path="MyPublicService.asmx">
    <system.web>
      <authentication mode="Windows" />
      <authorization>
        <allow verbs="GET" users="MyDomain\alex, MyDomain\matthew" />
        <deny verbs="GET" users="*" />
      </authorization>
    </system.web>
  </location>
</configuration>
```

This configuration prevents any user other than alex or matthew from using the HTTP GET method to access the *MyPublicService.asmx* web service.

Configuring explicit impersonation

You can also explicitly specify the account that you'd like .NET to impersonate, using the <identity> element:

```
<configuration>
  <system.web>
    <identity impersonate="true" name="MyDomain\aferrara"
password="mypass" />
  </system.web>
</configuration>
```

This configuration forces .NET to access resources using the specified aferrara account in the domain MyDomain. Unfortunately, the password must also be supplied in clear text, adding considerable risk to this feature.

IIS and the Windows authentication provider

The Windows authentication provider works in conjunction with IIS security. In many cases, this is a nice feature, since it gives you a much greater level of control than does ASP 3.0. In addition, in a server farm environment, implementing user restrictions at the .NET level is much more manageable than doing it at the IIS level, because .NET's configurations are stored in the *web.config* file, which can be replicated across however many servers you may have. The IIS metabase, on the other hand, contains machine-specific information, and, as a result, the metabase from one machine cannot be installed to another machine. In addition, the metabase is much slower to configure than the XML-based *web.config* file.

These advantages come at a price. The additional security layer adds more complexity to the security system. With it, you must make sure that not only the ACLs and IIS security settings but also the *web.config* file(s) and *machine.config* file are properly configured. It's not difficult to see why so many security vulnerabilities are due to improperly configured security systems. With so many "moving parts," it makes sense to spend some time designing your security architecture instead of rushing in and trying to create one on the fly. The flowchart in Figure 9-6 displays IIS and .NET security interactions.

The top part of the flow chart in Figure 9-6 is the IIS authentication flow discussed previously. The bottom part is the .NET authentication process. First, .NET checks whether impersonation is enabled. As we've mentioned, if this is not the case, all requests will be made using the security context of the local ASP.NET worker process account. If impersonation is enabled, .NET runs under the context of the authenticated user, or the IIS service account if IIS has been configured for anonymous access. At this point, any access to server resources is checked against the authorization list in the configuration files, and the server's Access Control List (for NTFS). If the user is not permitted to access a given resource, a .NET error is returned. For this reason, we've included two "denied" states in the figure. The first state in the IIS part of the diagram represents an HTTP error such as a 403 (forbidden) error. The second state represents a .NET error, which has a noticeably

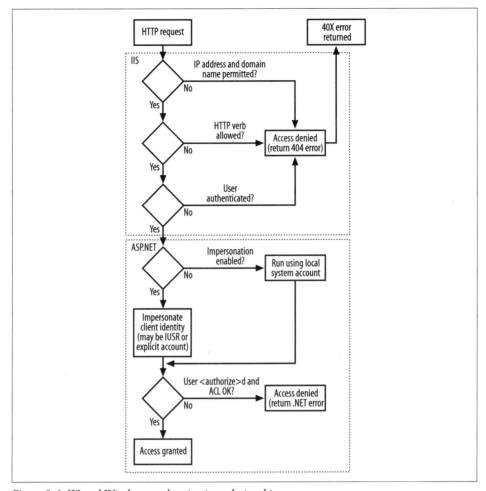

Figure 9-6. IIS and Windows authentication relationship

different (and customizable) appearance. Recognizing the difference between these two error states can be very useful for troubleshooting your web service applications.

 Only resources that have been mapped to ASP.NET in IIS are subject to ASP.NET security. This means that images, text files, ASP 3.0 pages, and the like that do not have ISAPI mappings to ASP.NET are not affected by any of the ASP.NET security settings we've been discussing. Setting a restriction in a *web.config* file restricts only applications that are processed by ASP.NET.

Avoiding Forms Authentication

With ASP.NET forms authentication, Microsoft has implemented a common authentication schema found in most ASP 3.0 and earlier applications. This involves using a cookie to determine whether the user is authenticated. When a client attempts to access a server resource, the server checks to see whether the client has an access cookie. If not, the server returns an HTTP redirect to an ASP.NET page, or, in this case, a web service, that performs the authentication and sets an access cookie. Using this cookie, the client is then authorized to access server resources. In earlier versions of ASP, most of this logic needed to be manually coded. This typically involved creating a database structure to keep track of "session" cookies and making a call to an authentication function (perhaps stored in an include file) each time an ASP page was accessed.

One obvious drawback to the preceding scenario is that if you forget to include this authenticating function in a page, it becomes open to public access (assuming IIS security is set to anonymous). Fortunately this authentication scheme is built into .NET, which can be a real boon to ASP.NET applications. The forms authentication provider is a sealed class that exposes several static (shared) methods that can be used in ASP.NET applications to perform common tasks such as authenticating, setting cookies, or expiring cookies (in effect, logging out the user). Unfortunately, however, this authentication provider is not a suitable solution for a web service application.

There are several reasons you *cannot* use forms authentication with a web service. The practical reason is that it just doesn't work well, and if you attempt to implement it, you'll be met with the frustrations analogous to trying to fit a square peg in a round hole. In short, forms authentication is designed for user access, not for arbitrary client access. In theory, this makes a good deal of sense as well, since forms authentication makes use of cookies, HTTP redirection, and HTTP GET. The result is that if you were to use forms authentication, you would not be able to use SOAP as the access protocol, but would instead be restricted to HTTP GET. We've already seen how this severely limits web service functionality. In addition, forms authentication's reliance on HTTP redirects not only can confuse clients that don't support redirection, but also can result in mismatched-parameters errors. If, for example, an unauthenticated client were to make a call to a method that took an integer as a parameter and was redirected to a login page with a different method signature, an error would result.

Avoiding Passport Authentication

Passport is the authentication component of Microsoft's MyServices consumer web services initiative, which has undergone some changes since its original announcement in October of 2001. Passport's original goal was to provide a single sign-on authentication service that would be maintained and brokered by Microsoft. Some believe that the growing popularity of a competing online authentication service, called the Liberty Alliance Project (of which Microsoft is not a member), in addition to the reluctance of businesses to outsource customer identity services, was one of the reasons Microsoft has since announced a shift in its My Services strategy. The new strategy focuses on licensing the My Service technology to companies so that they can manage the identities of their clients. Fortunately, the technical implementation details are similar regardless of the business strategy.

The initial idea behind Passport was simple. Anyone with a Hotmail or MSN account is automatically a member of this service and is able to access any Passport-enabled site using a single logon. For example, a Hotmail user could log in to Passport using Hotmail and then access any Passport-enabled site—such as Amazon or eBay—without having to log on again manually.

When a user signs in, the Passport service sets an encrypted cookie that is active until the user closes the browser or explicitly requests a logoff. The great part about this setup is the ease with which Passport users can access sites via a single login. No more remembering a different username and password for each site. The potentially risky part of this was that your personal user information would be brokered by one company—Microsoft. In addition, user profile information, specified by the user, is made available to member sites. Under Microsoft's new plan, this is not the case. Instead, a company (or a trusted third party) can implement the Passport identity directory, and your personal information is then brokered by the company (or third party) with whom you do business. We can only hope that some agreement will come about between Microsoft and the Liberty Alliance to allow interoperability between these two identity management services.

Using Passport authentication in .NET is done through an `IIdentity`-derived class called `PassportIdentity`, which is part of the `System.Web.Security` namespace.

Web sites can implement Passport by downloading and installing the Passport SDK available from *http://www.passport.com/business/*. Be aware that the Passport service is not free, and you'll need to register and pay a fee in order to even download the SDK. After setting up an account with Microsoft and installing the SDK, you can take advantage of Passport authentication on your site by adding the following to the *web.config* file:

```
<configuration>
  <system.web>
    <authentication mode="Passport">
    </authentication>
  </system.web>
</configuration>
```

Passport is essentially a forms-based authentication mechanism, which means that it suffers from the same drawbacks as .NET forms authentication. The default, out-of-the-box installation is designed to make use of HTTP GET, cookies, and HTTP redirects to authenticate users, which severely limits (or possibly even destroys) its potential use as an authentication process for a web service application. However, the Passport SDK does provide an API that can be used to programmatically access the Passport service, opening the door to potential use in web service applications of the future.

Passport authentication requires that nonauthentication clients be redirected to an external Passport server, making it a poor choice for web service authentication.

It's also worth noting that the Passport SDK includes a set of UI components that you can use to implement a variety of Passport-connected account management and e-commerce (through Express Purchase) functions in your site.

Programmatic Security

In addition to implementing security at the operating system, web server, and .NET platform level, you can also control access programmatically in your web service applications. Implementing security at the application level allows for more fine-grained security, since most web service applications can be stored in one *.asmx* file but will then have multiple web methods, each possibly requiring different access levels. In order to restrict access at the method level using the techniques we've discussed so far, you'd have to put each method into its own *.asmx* file and then configure Windows, IIS, and/or .NET security to allow the appropriate access level on the file. In addition, the error message returned to the client would be one of the standard HTTP error messages (e.g., 403) and would not be customizable on a per–web method basis.

In order to restrict access at the method level or provide custom SOAP exceptions, you need to be able to programmatically set access restrictions. This means you need to be able to programmatically access information about the client such as the username and perhaps Windows group membership.

Fortunately, the .NET platform exposes several objects that you can use to programmatically access this type of information. Of course, if you choose to forgo the Windows authentication provider and instead configure IIS to allow anonymous access, several techniques are available for restricting access in your web services. Some of those techniques, or design patterns, are discussed in the next section. There we explore the facilities available for programmatically accessing client information for clients that have been authenticated via the Windows authentication provider.

Identities, Roles, and Principals

Many enterprise-level systems (Windows included) implement a *role-based* access model. In this model, each user of the system, whether a real person or a service, is mapped to a user account, and each user account is made a member of zero or more roles (sometimes called *groups*). Security is then managed at the role level, so that all of the members of a given role are granted (or denied) access based on the security settings for the role. This scheme makes managing access more convenient, because, rather than setting access for many individual users, you can set it for a role and then add or remove users from the role as necessary. Since the Windows operating system uses this type of security model, it's no surprise that .NET includes classes that are analogs to users and roles.

Identity objects are conceptually similar to user accounts, encapsulating information about the user or client being authenticated. However, in addition to containing information such as the user's name, the identity object can also contain information about the IIS authentication type used—NTLM, Basic, or custom. .NET defines two identity objects; GenericIdentity and WindowsIdentity, and you can create custom identity objects by implementing the IIdentity interface, which can incorporate custom identity information. The WindowsIdentity class, which we'll discuss later in this chapter, is a member of the System.Security.Principal namespace and represents a Windows NT/2000 user account (and security token).

A Principal object is an encapsulation of an Identity object and associated role information, collectively providing the security context under which the current thread is running. As it does with the Identity object, .NET provides two types of Principals and the ability to create custom Principal classes. The GenericPrincipal object is a basic implementation of the IPrincipal interface, which all Principal objects must implement. The WindowsPrincipal object represents a Windows NT/2000 identity/role entity; it checks the Windows membership for the currently logged-in user. Web service applications that implement Windows authentication can use an instance of this object to query the security context of the current client.

Understanding the WindowsPrincipal and WindowsIdentity Objects

If no authentication is enabled, the HttpContext object by default includes a reference to an object instance of type GenericPrincipal through the User property. As mentioned earlier, this property encapsulates the security context of the calling client. Depending on your choice of authentication provider for your ASP.NET application, this GenericPrincipal might be automatically replaced with a provider-specific security principal. In the case of IIS authentication and the Windows authentication provider, an instance of a WindowsPrincipal object will be attached to the HttpContext in place of the GenericPrincipal. This object contains security information that maps to your NT/2000 network security configuration. Perhaps the best way to describe this relationship is by taking a look at the properties and methods exposed by both the WindowsPrincipal and WindowsIdentity classes, as shown in Figure 9-7.

The WindowsPrincipal object

In Figure 9-7, we've removed all of the properties and methods inherited from the root Object class. The structure of the WindowsPrincipal object is very simple, containing one property and one method. The Identity property is a reference to an

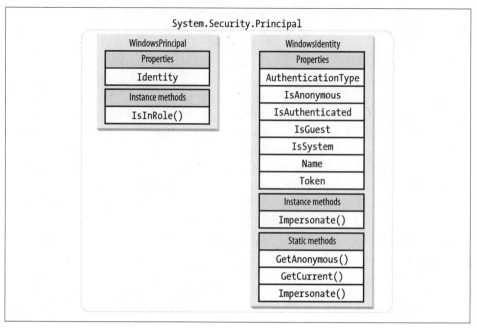

Figure 9-7. WindowsPrincipal and WindowsIdentity classes

object of type WindowsIdentity. The method IsInRole() returns a Boolean value specifying whether the client is a member of a given Windows NT/2000 group, supplied as a method argument. For security reasons, you cannot generate a list of the available NT/2000 groups; however, the System.Security.Principal namespace contains an enumeration of the default or built-in roles available in Windows. These roles are:

- AccountOperator
- Administrator
- BackupOperator
- Guest
- PowerUser
- PrintOperator
- Replicator
- SystemOperator
- User

The roles have an associated internal identifier, which means that, even if you change a role's name in the Windows User or Domain Manager, the mapping to the original role still exists. If you rename the Administrator role to SuperUsers and then query an instance of the WindowsPrincipal object that is a member of the SuperUsers role for "Administrator" rather than "SuperUsers," then the method call returns true.

The WindowsIdentity object

The `WindowsIdentity` object exposes a larger number of properties and methods, including three static methods. Descriptions of these properties and methods are listed in Table 9-2.

Table 9-2. WindowsIdentifier properties and methods

Type	Name	Description
Property	AuthenticationType	Returns the type of authentication used: Basic, NTLM, Kerberos
Property	IsAnonymous	Returns a Boolean value identifying whether the account is anonymous
Property	IsAuthenticated	Returns a Boolean value identifying whether the account is authenticated by Windows
Property	IsGuest	Returns a Boolean value specifying whether the account is identified as a Guest account
Property	IsSystem	Returns a Boolean value specifying whether the account is identified as a System account
Property	Name	Returns the Windows log on name, including the domain if applicable
Property	Token	Returns the Windows account token for the user
Methods (Instance)	Impersonate	Allows code to impersonate a different Windows user
Methods (Static)	GetAnonymous	Returns a WindowsIdentity object representing the anonymous Windows user
Methods (Static)	GetCurrent	Returns a WindowsIdentity object representing the current Windows user
	Impersonate	Allows code to impersonate a different Windows user

Using these properties and methods in conjunction with Windows authentication, you can programmatically restrict access to various web methods, as discussed in the following section.

Using the WindowsPrincipal and WindowsIdentity Objects

We can start by reviewing the output from a simple web method that performs a simple role test and returns the values of the `Identity` object if it is of type `WindowsIdentity`. In the first scenario, we need to *make sure* to set IIS to use either Basic or Windows authentication and then include the following in the *web.config* file to enable the Windows authentication provider.

```
<configuration>
  <system.web>
    <authentication mode="Windows" />
    <identity impersonate="true" />
  </system.web>
</configuration>
```

The web method code is as follows:

```
using System;
using System.Web.Services;
using System.Security.Principal;

public class WindowAuth : System.Web.Services.WebService
{
  public class PrincipalInfo
  {
    public String strType;
    public String Name = "";
    public String AuthenticationType = "";
    public bool IsAdministrator = false;
    public bool IsAuthenticated = false;

    public PrincipalInfo()
    {}
  }

  [WebMethod]
  public PrincipalInfo GetPrincipalInfo()
  {
    PrincipalInfo myPI = new PrincipalInfo();
    //  Get the type of the current Principal object
    myPI.strType = this.User.GetType().ToString();
    //  Test to see if the Principal object is a WindowsPrincipal
    if (this.User.GetType()==
            typeof(System.Security.Principal.WindowsPrincipal)
    {
      WindowsPrincipal winUser = (WindowsPrincipal)this.User;
      //  Test for the Administrator role
      bool IsAdmin = winUser.IsInRole(WindowsBuiltInRole.Administrator);
      myPI.IsAdministrator = IsAdmin;
      myPI.AuthenticationType =
            winUser.Identity.AuthenticationType.ToString();
      myPI.Name = winUser.Identity.Name.ToString();
      myPI.IsAuthenticated = winUser.Identity.IsAuthenticated;
    }
    return myPI;
  }
}
```

This web method uses a custom object called PrincipalInfo to return a structure containing information about the Principal object. We start by checking whether the Principal object is of type WindowsPrincipal. If it is, then we know we can cast it to the appropriate type and access the properties and methods specific to it. The results are returned as a PrincipalInfo object. The code for a sample consumer for this web method is:

```
using System.Web.Services.Protocols;
using System.Net;
using System;
```

```
...
static void Main(string[] args)
{
  string strUser = "";
  string strPass = "";
  string strDomain = "";
  if (args.Length == 3)
  {
    strUser = args[0];
    strPass = args[1];
    strDomain = args[2];
  }
  Proxy.WindowAuth objProxy = new Proxy.WindowAuth();
  System.Net.ICredentials credential = new
              System.Net.NetworkCredential(strUser, strPass, strDomain);
  objProxy.Credentials = credential;
  try
  {
    Proxy.PrincipalInfo objPrincipal = new Proxy.PrincipalInfo();
    objPrincipal = objProxy.GetPrincipalInfo();
    Console.WriteLine("Name: " + objPrincipal.Name +
                ", Type: " + objPrincipal.strType +
                ", Authenticated: " + objPrincipal.IsAuthenticated +
                ", Administrator: " + objPrincipal.IsAdministrator);
  }
  catch(Exception ex)
  {
    Console.WriteLine("Permission Denied: " + ex.Message);
  }
}
...
```

Of course, you must also either add a web reference to your service or reference a compiled proxy DLL.

The previous example uses an instance of the NetworkCredential class to pass the appropriate username, domain, and password. Calling this consumer from the command line returns the following SOAP message:

```
<?xml version="1.0" encoding="utf-8"?>
<soap:Envelope xmlns:soap="http://schemas.xmlsoap.org/soap/envelope/" xmlns:
xsi="http://www.w3.org/2001/XMLSchema-instance" xmlns:xsd="http://www.w3.org/2001/
XMLSchema">
  <soap:Body>
    <GetPrincipalInfoResponse xmlns="http://tempuri.org/">
      <GetPrincipalInfoResult>
        <Name>MyDomain\administrator</Name>
        <AuthenticationType>Basic</AuthenticationType>
        <IsAdministrator>true</IsAdministrator>
        <IsAuthenticated>true</IsAuthenticated>
        <strType>System.Security.Principal.WindowsPrincipal</strType>
      </GetPrincipalInfoResult>
    </GetPrincipalInfoResponse>
  </soap:Body>
</soap:Envelope>
```

The web service is set up to use Windows authentication, since the Principal object was of type WindowsPrincipal. In addition, the administrator user is indeed a member of the administrator group as specified by the result of a query to the IsAdministrator method.

Alternatively, if you disable the Windows authentication provider by changing the authentication mode in the *web.config* file as follows:

```
<authentication mode="None" />
```

you get the following altered resulting SOAP message:

```
<?xml version="1.0" encoding="utf-8"?>
<soap:Envelope xmlns:soap="http://schemas.xmlsoap.org/soap/envelope/" xmlns:
xsi="http://www.w3.org/2001/XMLSchema-instance" xmlns:xsd="http://www.w3.org/2001/
XMLSchema">
  <soap:Body>
    <GetPrincipalInfoResponse xmlns="http://tempuri.org/">
      <GetPrincipalInfoResult>
        <Name />
        <AuthenticationType />
        <IsAdministrator>false</IsAdministrator>
        <IsAuthenticated>false</IsAuthenticated>
        <strType>System.Security.Principal.GenericPrincipal</strType>
      </GetPrincipalInfoResult>
    </GetPrincipalInfoResponse>
  </soap:Body>
</soap:Envelope>
```

This time, the Principal object is of type GenericPrincipal, and that part of the information in the last example is now gone.

Impersonation

In some cases, you may want to use Windows authentication but avoid having to write code to test the group memberships of the Principal object. One way to do so is by using impersonation. By default, impersonation is disabled in the *machine.config* file:

```
<identity impersonate="false"/>
```

However, as we've seen, you can override this setting in the application's root *web.config* file by changing its impersonate attribute to true like this:

```
<authentication mode="Windows" />
<identity impersonate="true" [userName="user" password="pass"] />
```

The optional username and password attributes allow you to explicitly specify the user account under which the application should run. If they are omitted, the application runs under the context of the authenticated user or the IIS anonymous user, depending on the IIS configuration.

When impersonation is enabled, the web service application runs under the security context of the impersonated user. For example, if user Tracy logs in, the application runs under the security context of Tracy's account. If the application attempts to access a resource for which Tracy does not have permissions, an error will result. Implementing security in this fashion allows you to ignore the group membership checks and instead rely on the OS ACLs to restrict access.

Programmatic impersonation

You may have noticed in a previous section that the WindowsIdentity object has an instance method called Impersonate. This method is used to programmatically change the security context of the application at runtime. For example, your web service may need to operate under the default security context part of the time and the context of the client account at other times. The call to impersonate returns a WindowsImpersonationContext object that allows you to "undo" the impersonation as needed. If impersonation is disabled for the application in the *web.config* file, impersonation can be programmatically managed using this method.

The following example of programmatic impersonation uses a text file called *test.txt*, which resides in the root folder of the *C:* drive and is accessible only to a certain user. (Create a text file using Notepad and insert some dummy text.) Set the NTFS permissions by right-clicking on the file and selecting Properties. Using the Security tab, you can set the file so that it is accessible by only one user, as shown in Figure 9-8.

This file is now viewable only to the user xadmin in the domain home.

Remember to make sure the *web.config* file is set to use Windows Authentication (IIS must be configured for this as well) and has impersonation *disabled*:

```
<configuration>
  <system.web>
    <authorization mode="Windows" />
    <identity impersonate="false" />
  </system.web>
</configuration>
```

The following web method uses impersonation to access the contents of *test.txt*, returning its contents as string data. Remember that you must import the System.IO namespace in order to use the File objects:

```
...
using System.IO;
using System.Security.Principal;
...

[WebMethod]
public string GetFile()
{
  string strReturn = "";
```

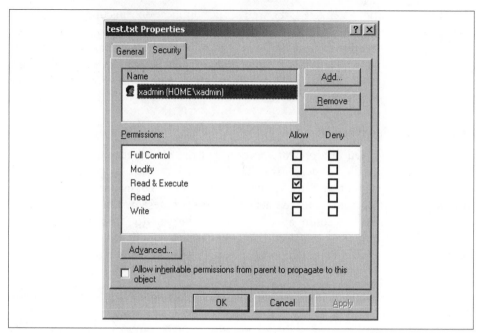

Figure 9-8. Restricting NTFS security on a test file

```
// Test to see whether the Principal object is a WindowsPrincipal
if (this.User.GetType() == typeof(System.Security.Principal.WindowsPrincipal))
{
  // Cast to a WindowsIdentity
  WindowsIdentity winID = (WindowsIdentity)this.User.Identity;
  WindowsImpersonationContext objContext = winID.Impersonate();
  try
  {
    StreamReader re = File.OpenText("c:\\test.txt");
    string input = null;
    while ((input = re.ReadLine()) != null)
    {
      strReturn += input;
    }
    re.Close();
  }
  catch(System.UnauthorizedAccessException e)
  {
    strReturn = e.Message.ToString();
  }
}
return strReturn;
}
```

Without the call to the Impersonate() method of the WindowsIdentity object, the call will fail and return the error message to the client. Using this method, we can force our code to run under the security context of the accessing user, relying on NTFS for restricting access to a file. This works even if impersonation is disabled for the application in the *web.config* file. Note that the Impersonate() method returns a WindowsImpersonationContext object. You can use the WindowsImpersonationContext. Undo() method to end impersonation, and return to life as normal under the default ASP.NET worker process identity.

Impersonation using security tokens

It's also possible to impersonate arbitrary Windows users by using their Windows account token. This account token can be accessed by making a call to the unmanaged LogonUser method, which is part of the unmanaged advapi32.dll. Once you have this account token, you can use it to create a new instance of Windows-ImpersonationContext. A discussion of this process is outside the scope of this text.

Custom Authentication Techniques

We've spent a lot of time talking about the security features built into the .NET platform and how they interact with Windows, IIS, and your web service applications. This integrated approach allows you to leverage the power of Windows security in your web service applications. We realize, however, that the use of Windows security is not appropriate for many web service applications. For example, while Windows Authentication may work very well for a low-to-medium–load web service application, in order for a high-volume multiuser web service to perform well and scale, you would probably want to bypass Windows security. Some of the drawbacks to Windows authentication in this type of environment are as follows:

- User maintenance is difficult to manage.
- Performance can be poor when using network security.
- Scalability is limited for geographically distributed web services (e.g., distributed server farms).

For these reasons, you may often find yourself bypassing IIS and Windows security altogether in favor of a custom security model. This section discusses one of the most commonly used models: using an SQL server to store user information on the server in conjunction with SOAP headers. We'll discuss some of the design considerations you should take into account when implementing this model.

Designing for Performance and Scalability

The .NET authentication providers offer an integrated security solution that leverages well-known Windows security features: user accounts, groups, NTFS, and ACLs. The trade-off for using this fine-grained security model is that its many layers can hamper performance and scalability and its complexity can lead to errors. As an alternative, you can bypass IIS and .NET authentication and implement your own authentication system.

To do this, you must first enable IIS anonymous security in the Internet Services Manager. You might also want to make sure the Authentication provider mode is set to None in your *web.config* file. Assuming you don't want to impersonate the IIS anonymous account, you'll probably want to disable impersonation as well:

```
<authentication mode="None" />
<identity impersonate="false" />
```

Once these two authentication layers are disabled, requests for your *.asmx* service are passed directly to the web service/method and run under the context of the local system account or the account specified in the <processModel> section handler.

Implementing Per-Method Authentication Using SQL

As you might imagine, the simplest way to implement custom authentication in a web service is to use usernames and passwords stored in an SQL Server. You then add username and password arguments to each of your web methods and authenticate the user before executing a method. This type of design is shown in Example 9-1.

Example 9-1. Custom authentication using usernames and passwords

```
using System;
using System.Data;
using System.Web.Services;
using System.Data.SqlClient;

namespace SecurityServices
{
  public class CustomAuth : System.Web.Services.WebService
  {
    public CustomAuth() {}

    [WebMethod(Description="Returns the square of the argument integer i")]
    public int Square(int i, string username, string password)
    {
      // Authenticate the user
      if (!Authenticate(username, password))
      {
        throw new Exception("Invalid Username / Password");
      }
      return i * i;
    }

    private bool Authenticate(String user, String pass)
    {
      bool retAuth = false;
      try
      {
        SqlCommand myCommand = new SqlCommand();
        myCommand.Connection = new
          SqlConnection(
          "server=MySvr;database=pubs;User ID=xxx;password=xxx");
```

```
        myCommand.Connection.Open();
        myCommand.CommandText = "SP_Authenticate" ;
        myCommand.CommandType = CommandType.StoredProcedure ;

        SqlParameter UserName =
          new SqlParameter("@Username", SqlDbType.VarChar, 255);
        UserName.Value =  user.Trim();
        myCommand.Parameters.Add(UserName);

        SqlParameter Password =
          new SqlParameter("@Password",SqlDbType.NVarChar, 255);
        Password.Value = pass.Trim();
        myCommand.Parameters.Add(Password);\

        SqlParameter Valid = new SqlParameter("@Valid",SqlDbType.Int);
        Valid.Direction = ParameterDirection.Output;
        myCommand.Parameters.Add(Valid);
        myCommand.ExecuteNonQuery();

        if (((int)Valid.Value) == 1)
        {
          retAuth =true;
        }
      }
      catch(Exception e) {}
    return retAuth;
    }
  }
}
```

In this example, the Square() method takes an integer argument along with a username and password. First, it calls the private Authenticate method, which validates the username/password combination against an SQL database and returns a Boolean value. If the username/password is invalid, the Square() method throws an exception, which is returned as a SOAP exception to clients using SOAP as an access method. If the client is valid, the method returns the square of the input argument.

The private method Authenticate validates a username/password combination. It calls a stored procedure call—SP_Authenticate—which has three parameters: two input and one output. The two input parameters are for passing the username and password in, and the output parameter returns a code specifying whether the account is valid.

Finally, the SQL stored procedure SP_Authenticate looks like this:

```
create proc SP_Authenticate @username varchar(255), @password varchar(255), @valid
int output
As
...
Validate the username and password
...
select @valid = 0      /* or 1 depending on the outcome */
```

Now we have a simple web service that functions only if called with the proper client credentials. We can manage the list of usernames and passwords very easily, either directly through SQL, through a custom ASP.NET page, or through another web service. We could also just as easily replace the SQL call with a call to a flat file such as an XML document containing a list of acceptable users.

While implementing a custom authentication and authorization scheme like this can involve a considerable amount of effort, you gain an enormous amount of control over how it works. Moreover, with proper design, you can achieve much better performance and scalability than is possible using IIS and Windows authentication against an NT domain. For situations in which you need authentication but expect to have a high load, designing your own authentication and authorization scheme often makes the most sense. However, the key phrase here is "proper design." While you can benefit from increased performance and scalability, you can end up with just the opposite with a poor design. In addition, if you're not careful, you can expose yourself to some serious security risks.

The biggest benefit of the approach shown here is that it implements authentication while maintaining a stateless design. That is, the client doesn't need to store any session information, such as in a cookie. However, it's lacking in two big ways. Two of the problems are as follows:

Client credentials are passed unencrypted with every method call making them susceptible to interception

> Since SOAP messages are by default unencoded (i.e., sent as plain text), the first problem exposes a substantial security risk—anyone who intercepts one of the SOAP requests will be able to see the client's username and password. Since the credentials are passed with each call, n calls to the web method result in passing the credentials in plain text n times. This problem is similar to that of IIS basic authentication, the main difference being that basic authentication uses Base64 encoding to make it *slightly* inconvenient to retrieve the username and password. Of course, you could easily implement Base64 encoding, but as mentioned, it provides virtually no additional security.

Every method call requires a trip to the database

> Another problem with this design is that each call to the web method results in a trip to the database. Since the database is traditionally the least scalable component of a system, a common design goal is to minimize trips to the database. Additionally, since most system architectures place the database on a different physical server from the web or application server, minimizing database trips also helps to reduce network traffic. As the number of requests increases, the database load and network traffic increases as well. You should quickly see that, as a result, this design leaves you open to a denial-of-service attack, because even invalid username/password combinations require a trip to the database. It would be very easy for a malicious user to initiate a large number of calls to GetTicket with invalid credentials. This trick could quickly overload your database.

A better solution is to use some sort of caching in your applications to reduce the number of database trips. One possibility is to store the username and password combination in the ASP.NET Cache object every time the user is successfully validated. Then, on each subsequent request, the application can check the Cache object before making a database trip. This type of design may be appropriate for some situations, but storing the username and password in the Cache object does pose some risks. For one, the cache object is accessible to all of the remaining code in your ASP.NET application and to anyone who gains access to the server, easily compromising it. In the following section, we'll look at a solution to these issues.

Getting Warmer: a Ticket System

One of the ways we can improve the design to avoid the previous problems is to use a *ticket system*. In a ticket system, the client sends credentials only once per session (perhaps through a login method) and is issued a ticket to use for subsequent calls. Generally, a ticket is valid for a set period of time, after which the session expires and the client must request a new ticket.

A *ticket* is an identifier that is locally unique to the session space, meaning that it is unique among all of the currently active and expired sessions. A good choice for a ticket might be a GUID or other large unique number. Using a ticket system maintains authentication, which reduces the number of times client credentials are passed as part of the request.

Rather than request the tickets from SQL for each method call, they can be cached in ASP.NET using the Cache object drastically reducing the number of requests to the database as well as network traffic. Furthermore, since we're storing only a ticket in the Cache object, and not the username and password themselves, this design is more secure than the previous one. Example 9-2 takes a closer look at the code for this type of system.

Example 9-2. Custom authentication using a ticket system

```
using System;
using System.Data;
using System.Web.Services;
using System.Data.SqlClient;

namespace SecurityServices
{
  public class Ticket : System.Web.Services.WebService
  {

    [WebMethod(Description=
    "Ticket gen. method.  Must be called before any other method.")]
    public string GetTicket(string username, string password)
    {
      // Authenticate the user
      if (!Authenticate(username, password))
```

Example 9-2. Custom authentication using a ticket system (continued)

```
    {
      throw new Exception("Invalid Username / Password");
    }
    Guid gTicket = Guid.NewGuid();
    Context.Cache.Insert(gTicket.ToString(), true);
    return gTicket.ToString();
  }

  [WebMethod(Description="Returns the square of the argument integer i")]
  public int Square(int i, string ticket)
  {
    if(!Authenticate(ticket))
    {
      throw new Exception("Invalid Ticket");
    }
    return i * i;
  }

  private bool Authenticate(string ticket)
  {
    bool bRet = false;
    try
    {
      if ((bool)Context.Cache.Get(ticket)) {bRet = true;}
    }
    catch(Exception e){}
    return bRet;
  }

  private bool Authenticate(String user, String pass)
  {
    ...Same as before...
  }
 }
}
```

 As written, this ticket generation system suffers from one possible problem: there is no way to ensure the ticket is not removed from the cache early as memory becomes scarce. Chapter 7 tackles this issue by showing how you can combine caching with a backend database table that stores tickets.

This example adds two methods, GetTicket() and an overloaded Authenticate(). The first one, GetTicket(), must be called by the client with a username and password in order to get a system access ticket. The client can then use this access ticket for authentication when calling other system methods. The GetTicket method calls the same Authenticate method used in Example 9-1 to verify the client credentials against the database. If the client is valid, a new ticket (based on a GUID) is created and a copy of it is stored in the ASP.NET cache for later reference. The Cache object provides a variety of features for item expiration so that the ticket can be set to expire after a specified amount of time.

The `Square` method has not changed much from Example 9-1. The only difference is that it takes a ticket as an argument instead of a username and password. The ticket is then authenticated by the private overloaded `Authenticate` method, which verifies that the ticket is in the application cache. If all is copacetic, the method executes the request and returns the results.

Example 9-2 is meant to provide a basic understanding of how a generic ticket system works. There are, of course, many degrees of freedom in designing this type of system. Some of the design decisions you might find yourself faced with are:

- Where to store the ticket on the server
- When the ticket should expire
- Whether to use cookies to store the ticket on the client
- What action the client should take when the ticket expires

These are just some of the many issues you may find yourself faced with; each can have a drastic effect on your system's performance, scalability, and interoperability with other systems. For example, you've already seen that using cookies for state management can be problematic, because it ties you to the HTTP protocol. The choices you make with respect to these decisions will depend on the requirements for your web service application.

Drawbacks of a ticket system

The biggest disadvantage to a ticket system is that both the server and client must keep track of the ticket. This form of state management can be inconvenient for the client and can limit scalability on the server on which a ticket must be maintained for each client. As the number of clients grows, the amount of server resources used to manage state grows as well. If multiple servers are involved, as in a server farm, it can become difficult to maintain the same state information across servers. One solution is to require client "affinity," in which each client is guaranteed to use the same server for each request, but this can require expensive software or hardware and does not always lead to proper distribution of server load.

Another drawback is that it requires a priori knowledge of how the ticket system works, including the process flow necessary to initially retrieve a ticket. Unfortunately, there are currently no standards for web service security, and WSDL doesn't provide any means of describing the call flow in a structured manner. The goal of specifications such as WS-Security is to establish a standard way of passing credentials and authenticating clients; however; none of these specifications have been widely adopted yet. Some other technologies, such as IBM's Web Service Flow Language (WSFL) and Microsoft's XLANG, attempt to tackle this problem, providing a procedure for describing process flows using XML; however, neither is currently widely accepted.

Opportunities for improvement

From a security perspective, another disadvantage to this system is that a ticket is still passed with every request as plain text. If the ticket expiration is properly managed, the risk of having any harm done can be minimized; however, sending this type of information as plain text is never a good idea. In addition, while this design has reduced the number of times the client's username and password are sent, a risk for interception still exists.

One way to handle the vulnerability of plain text messages is to use SSL to encrypt all of the request traffic. However, this is not a good solution for most systems, because SSL, which is based on asymmetric encryption, is *very* slow. Unfortunately, the SSL capabilities of IIS cannot be selectively applied to the SOAP message, but must rather be applied to the entire communication. For methods that return large amounts of data, the overhead of SSL encryption becomes a limiting factor on performance and server CPU resources.

One option is to use SSL for the GetTicket() method only, ensuring that the user ID and password are hidden. Subsequent requests, which only pass the ticket, will use clear text and be visible. However, if they are intercepted, the damage is limited to a hijacked session rather than to a compromised user account. Finally, you may be able to use the Context.Request.UserHostAddress property in your web service to mitigate even this danger. The UserHostAddress property returns an IP address, and you could theoretically store information about the user's IP address along with the ticket. When validating a ticket, you could first check that the IP address hasn't changed. However, this technique is limited to the standard Internet problems, including cases where the user's IP address is hidden or altered dynamically.

From a pure design perspective, adding arguments to your methods that do not directly relate to the methods' function is inelegant. Whether a username, password, or ticket string, these additional parameters make methods more difficult to maintain and more complicated to call. A better design would be to move control data, such as the authentication information, out of the method signature. One option that should immediately come to mind is the use of a SOAP header as discussed in Chapter 5.

En Fuego: a Custom Authentication Provider

If you've been paying close attention, you'll remember that when we talked about the built-in .NET security providers and the Principal object, we mentioned that you could create your own custom providers. Each of the built-in authentication providers we noted—Forms, Passport, and Windows—is implemented via its own class module. These modules are (respectively):

- FormsAuthenticationModule
- PassportAuthenticationModule
- WindowsAuthenticationModule

All are members of the `System.Web` namespace. Another thing they have in common is they implement the `IHttpModule` interface. This interface has two public instance methods that must be implemented. The first is the `Dispose()` method, which takes no arguments and disposes of any resources used by the implementing module. The second is the `Init()` method, which takes as an argument an instance of an `HttpApplication`. The `Init` method performs any initialization necessary to prepare the module for handling requests.

The `HttpApplication` object defines the methods, properties, and events common to all ASP.NET (and therefore web service) applications. It provides property references to objects such as `Request`, `Response`, `Application`, and `Context`. It also exposes several public instance events, one of which is called `AuthorizeRequest`. This means that by creating a class that implements `IHttpModule`, we can code the `Init` method to bind a custom event handler to the `AuthorizeRequest` event that we can use to execute custom authentication code.

Process Security

We've already discussed several ways in which you can control the security context under which your web service applications execute. By default, ASP.NET runs under a local account that has carefully limited permissions (called `ASPNET`). Unlike the `IUSR_SERVERNAME` account, this account has the required permissions on the directories to compile web service and web page code. However, you can change the account used to execute ASP.NET code, if needed.

This is useful when you need to switch between security contexts in your code. We've also talked about explicitly specifying the security context for an entire web service application by using the `<identity>` element in your *web.config* file as follows:

```
<identity impersonate="true" userName="MyDomain\alex"
password="mypassword"] />
```

As you've seen, you can use the `Impersonate()` method of the `WindowsPrincipal` object to change the security context of the executing thread in your web service applications to the IIS-authenticated user. This setting allows you to control the identity under which each of the requests executes and is useful for setting the security context on either an application level via the application's root *web.config* file or a machinewide level via the *machine.config* file. However, when using impersonation, all threads will start out as the default process (e.g., local system) and assume the context of the specified impersonation account in order to serve requests, reverting back to the default account when they're completed. This means that certain nonrequest events such as `Application_OnStart` and `Application_OnEnd` still run under the default process context. This can be configured in the *machine.config* file using the `<processModel>` section handler. By default, this section handler looks like the following:

```
<processModel
  enable="true" timeout="Infinite"
  idleTimeout="Infinite" shutdownTimeout="0:00:05"
```

```
requestLimit="Infinite" requestQueueLimit="5000"
restartQueueLimit="10"memoryLimit="60" webGarden="false"
cpuMask="0xffffffff" userName="SYSTEM" password="AutoGenerate"
logLevel="Errors"clientConnectedCheck="0:00:05" />
```

You can use this section handler to manage various details related to the ASP.NET worker process. In particular, you can change the account under which the ASP.NET process runs, using the username and password fields to specify a user account. Notice that by default the username is set to SYSTEM and the password to AutoGenerate. This configuration tells .NET to run as a system account for which the password is internally maintained. If impersonation is enabled, however, the impersonation account takes precedence over the process account (unless it is explicitly overridden) and is used to service all requests. Note again that even if impersonation is enabled, the process account is still used to execute Application_ events.

Another special account is the MACHINE account, which should also be configured with AutoGenerate as the password. This is the ASP.NET worker process account that is used by default and is given more limited privileges.

Some of the other attributes for this section handler are described in Table 9-3. The full list is available as part of the .NET Framework General Reference.

Table 9-3. Selected attributes for the <processModel> section handler

Attribute	Value	Description
enable	true/false	Specifies whether the <processsmodel> handler is enabled.
timeout	Number or "Infinite"	Specifies the number of minutes until ASP.NET launches a new worker process to replace the current one. The default is "Infinite".
idleTimeout	Number or "Infinite"	Specifies the number of minutes of inactivity before ASP.NET shuts down the worker process.
shutdownTimeout	Time (HH:MM:SS)	The amount of time the process has to shut itself down before ASP.NET shuts it down. The default is five seconds (00:00:05).
memoryLimit	1–100	The percentage of system memory available for use by the process.

Publishing and Discovery

In most cases, the reason for creating a web service is to expose some sort of business logic in a manner that allows easy, standards-based access by a wide variety of clients. This might involve exposing a freely available service to your clients, such as a package tracking service for goods you sell online, or a fee-based application, such as an API for searching a database of GIS information. Regardless, your service is probably useful only if your customers can find it. Otherwise those late-night Red Bull–induced coding frenzies are all for naught. You'll likely want to make sure that your services are publicly available to anyone who might be interested in them, and also that they're easily discoverable by spiders and other agents. We'll explain how in this chapter. We'll also talk about web service registries, as well as some of the standards that allow you to configure your server to support dynamic discovery.

Publishing

One obvious way to get the word out about your service is to submit it to search engines on the Web, such as Google or Lycos. The big problem with using a search engine is they're designed to index and return unstructured data, such as a consumer web page. Web services, on the other hand, are highly structured (thanks to their roots in XML), and most of them are not meant to be viewed in a web browser. For example, as we've seen, a web service is defined by a WSDL document. This XML-based document defines where the service is located and which protocols are supported, but it doesn't necessarily provide any text description for what the service does or what specific task it accomplishes. In order to allow individuals and computers to search based on that type of information, you must associate additional metadata with the service. What's needed is a special kind of registry that can store the information that's specific to a web service. This is where UDDI comes in.

UDDI

UDDI stands for Universal Description, Discovery, and Integration. As the name suggests, the main goals of the project are providing a standard means for describing businesses and their services, allowing the online discovery of those business and services, and integrating the services in a quick and easy programmatic fashion. This doesn't mean that UDDI can be used only programmatically. As you'll see, the directory can be very valuable in helping people to find businesses and services in much the same way that a search engine works. However, the main purpose of the project was to create a standard infrastructure that could be manipulated programmatically.

History of UDDI

The UDDI standard was proposed by IBM, Microsoft, and Ariba in September 2000. Rather than submit this initial draft to existing standards bodies such as the W3C or the IETF, the three companies decided to create the UDDI project, also known as the UDDI community(*http://www.uddi.org/*) to manage the creation of this standard. In their words, the UDDI project is "a joint initiative of concerned businesses that want to advance Internet-based computing." The organizers of this community currently plan to submit the draft to a standards body after the third draft is complete.

The UDDI community grew quickly from its initial three members to include other industry behemoths such as Sun, HP, and later, SAP. By the time of the second draft release of UDDI (v2.0), the community had several hundred members. You can learn about joining the community at *http://www.uddi.org/community.html*.

Prior to joining UDDI, several community members already offered services that were similar to some of the UDDI functionality. For example, Microsoft's BizTalk server has an online resource (*http://www.biztalk.org/*) that allows users to search, download, and publish XML objects. The OASIS Group has its Registry Information Model (ebRIM), currently in version 2.0, which has failed to be adopted as quickly as many had hoped. In addition, Hewlett-Packard had its E-Services Village, which allowed similar tasks but has since been replaced by UDDI. Many of these services are still in existence; however, most consider UDDI the de facto standard web services registry.

What Is UDDI?

Much of the hype surrounding UDDI's implication for business-to-business (B2B) electronic commerce should be taken with a grain of salt, but the industry support for UDDI does make it the dominant business and service directory standard on the Web. If you plan to publish your business and services, it's important to know what UDDI is and how to take advantage of it. UDDI is:

- A specification for a registry of online business and services
- Designed to take advantage of W3C and IETF standards such as XML, HTTP, DNS, and SOAP

- Governed by the UDDI community
- Free (at least for now)

The first bullet point is particularly important. UDDI in and of itself is merely a specification for the creation of an online business and service registry. This specification incorporates (proposed) standards such as XML, HTTP, and SOAP, and is managed by the UDDI community. Any entity is free to implement the UDDI business registry, which is the goal of the specification. As you'll see, companies such as IBM and Microsoft have created versions of this business registry, which are also free to use for now.

Why UDDI?

We've already talked about the benefits of having a web service directory for publishing and locating services. But what, specifically, makes UDDI such a good candidate for this directory? What is it about UDDI that makes some folks proclaim it to be such a "major advance in B2B" (Meta Group, September 2001, *http://news.com.com/ 2102-1001-245261.html*)? The answers to these questions are revealed as we examine some of the goals of the UDDI standard.

Platform-independence

The UDDI standard defines the framework for a business registry, but it does not dictate any registry implementation details. As a result, the framework can be implemented on any platform (including NT, Linux, Unix, and so on). Microsoft, for example, has a business registry that is developed using .NET on Windows servers. IBM, on the other hand, used its proprietary technologies to develop their business registry.

Open architecture and the freedom to innovate

Not only does the UDDI standard take advantage of open standards such as HTTP, XML, and SOAP, but the UDDI standard itself is also open and free. As long as the standard is adhered to, there are no licensing restrictions on building an additional functionality. And you don't have to pay a licensing fee to implement your own business registry with UDDI.

Wide support

The standard is supported not only by industry megaweights such as Microsoft, IBM, Sun, Oracle, and HP, but also by several hundred other companies. Furthermore, this support is distributed across a variety of industries from Boeing to KPMG Consulting. As the UDDI community phrases it on *http://uddi.org*, UDDI can be used by "any business, of any size, in any industry, in any location, offering any kind of service...." Now before we get too immersed in the warm, fuzzy feeling, it's important to remember that to date the majority of companies either registered with or involved in the project are U.S.-based technology companies. It's also important that you are aware that the majority of the postings to the UDDI registry to date have been improperly formatted junk, making the usefulness of the registry in it's current state minimal at best.

UDDI Business Registries

A UDDI business registry is an implementation of the UDDI standard. This implementation is an online entity with which you can interact either using a browser or via XML messages. As mentioned, there are two major UDDI registries, called *registry nodes*, currently in existence: one is hosted by Microsoft, and the other by IBM. In addition to these two nodes, several others are in the works, with HP the probable next host. Both Microsoft and IBM provide access to these registries free of charge, but in order to access either, you need either a Microsoft Passport or IBM user account.

Each node operator agrees to adhere to the policies and quality-of-service guidelines set forth by the Operator's Council, a committee within the UDDI community. Part of the responsibility of being a node operator is making sure that all registrations are replicated across nodes on a regular basis (currently, every 24 hours). This replication is done over a secure channel, and the result is that each node ends up with a complete set of registered records. The UDDI standard provides a set of processes to ensure integrity and availability of the registry data across nodes. As the size of the directory and number of operator nodes grows, and applications become more dependent on it, the frequency of replication increases.

Operator nodes must conform to the UDDI standard; in the spirit of open XML web services, there is no proprietary requirement. For example, the IBM operator node is implemented using Java, while the Microsoft operator node is implemented as a C# web service using .NET CLR and an SQL Server 2000 backend. In fact, a version of the Microsoft UDDI registry is available as a free download, in case you want to try to set up your own UDDI node for testing. Because they conform to the same WSDL, they behave the same, regardless of the proprietary technology used for implementation.

 The UDDI registry is itself a web service. You can download a developer edition of the service, including source code, from *http://msdn. microsoft.com*.

Conceptually, UDDI is like DNS for businesses. Whereas the DNS system allows you to find a server's address given a hostname, the UDDI registry allows you to find a web service given a company name or line of business. The registry is essentially a searchable database of links to service interfaces (e.g., WSDL, XSD) and implementations (e.g., *.asmx* files).

In addition to these "production" registries, Microsoft provides a "test" registry that can be used as a testing ground for debugging UDDI programs and other interactions without corrupting the real deal. The Microsoft test registry is located at *http://test.uddi.microsoft.com/default.aspx*.

Registry Contents

Each registry contains information about registered businesses and the services they support. As mentioned earlier, unlike a typical search engine, the UDDI registry stores structured data. Business and service information is stored in a structured relational fashion using five broad data types (for UDDI v2.0). Each type has other associated types, some of which we'll discuss. The types and their descriptions are as follows:

businessEntity

This describes the publishing party by a unique identifier, a business name, a short description, some basic contact information, a list of categories identifying the business, and a discovery URL that points to more information about the business.

businessService

Each business entity can have zero or more business services associated with it. A business service entry contains a service description, a list of associated categories for the service, and a list of pointers to references and information about the service. The business service entity represents a logical service representation.

bindingTemplate

A business service can have zero or more binding templates. This contains technical information about a service entry point such as the location or access point in the form of a URL. The business service entity represents a logical service definition, and the binding template represents a physical or concrete service implementation.

publisherAssertion

The publisher assertion entity records relationship information between business entities. Many larger corporations may not be effectively represented by a single business entity. For example, a company like General Electric has multiple subsidiaries operating in a variety of industries. The description and discovery for these subsidiaries is likely to be diverse even though they are all part of a single company. In this case, it makes sense to allow them to publish multiple business entities that are loosely related. The publisherAssertion entity provides this capability.

tModel

The tModel entity is by far the most nebulous, mainly because a tModel contains metadata (data about data). Because of this, a tModel can describe just about anything, but for our purposes the best way to think about tModels is as a source document for determining compatibility. In programming terms, a tModel can be thought of as an abstract class. It's pretty much a recipe for how to construct a service, defining (through WSDL) things such as the methods and bindings for a web service, although not the implementation. As we'll see, this is very useful in the world of UDDI and web services.

The five UDDI entities fit together as shown in Figure 10-1.

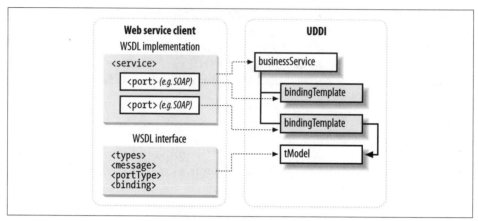

Figure 10-1. Relationships of the five UDDI entities

This relational diagram shows each one-to-many relationship between the business-Entity and businessService and the businessService and bindingTemplate. A similar relationship exists between the bindingTemplate and tModel entities, since a tModel can have multiple associated bindingTemplates.

Documentation on the UDDI data structures is available at *http://www.uddi.org/pubs/DataStructure-V2.00-Open-20010608.pdf*.

Categorization

The ability to assign category information for UDDI registry data was one of the registry's main design goals and is a critical part of the search capabilities exposed. Unlike many online search engines, which assume the burden of categorizing resources, the UDDI registry relies on voluntary categorization. A registered business entity chooses the categories to which it should belong, and the value of using the directory directly as a search engine is reduced because of the potential for inaccurate categorization.

A limiting factor of the UDDI search capabilities is the search does not try to automatically infer category relations. As an example, one of the methods of categorization is the use of the GeoWeb system. This system contains various categories associated with geographical regions. A company categorized as being located in Boston, MA, will be returned in a search for the companies in Boston. However, a search for companies in the category of North America will not return it. The reason is that the UDDI search engine doesn't recognize that Boston is a subcategory of North America. This may at first seem like a severe limitation; however, the goal of the UDDI directory is not to provide extensive search capabilities, but rather a lower-level interface. The task of creating more involved search capabilities has been left to search engines and other upstream users. Since the UDDI registry is expected to grow to contain millions of entities, this plan makes sense, considering the large number of entities that will exist in each category.

Accessing a Registry

The easiest way to access one of the UDDI nodes is through a web browser. The Microsoft UDDI registry is available at *http://uddi.microsoft.com*. The IBM UDDI node can be found at *http://www-3.ibm.com/services/uddi/*. Each of these sites is a full implementation of the UDDI specification and can perform the same tasks. There's no benefit to using one over the other, and as we've mentioned, any changes made in one are replicated to the other.

Registering a Business Entity

The first thing to do is register your business. Remember that these two sites are live production UDDI registries, and any data you add becomes part of the live system. If you're just looking to play around with the capabilities, use one of the UDDI test sites such as *http://test.uddi.microsoft.com*. After clicking the register link on the Microsoft UDDI site and signing in to your Passport account, you'll be presented with a registration screen that looks something like Figure 10-2.

Using this web interface, you can enter the details of your business entity (business name, address, contact person, discovery URL, etc.). Once you've submitted this information, you can use the Administer link to perform other tasks such as adding additional contacts, unique identifiers (e.g., a DUNS number), classifications, services, and tModels:

Contacts
> Each business entity should have at least one contact. The contact information is used by other businesses looking to get in touch with you, and includes information such as name, title, address, phone number, email address, and other pertinent details. Beware: this information is publicly accessible! Many people are aware of the UDDI directory and take advantage of it to create marketing lists. Within three days of signing up, my inbox was clogged with junk mail.

Identifiers
> Identifiers are pieces of data that are unique to a business. Examples of some supported identifiers are DUNS numbers (business identifiers issued by Dun & Bradstreet, Inc.) and RealNames keywords (mappings of words to URLs; see *http://www.realnames.com/*). The UDDI system allows you to specify your own custom identifiers as well.

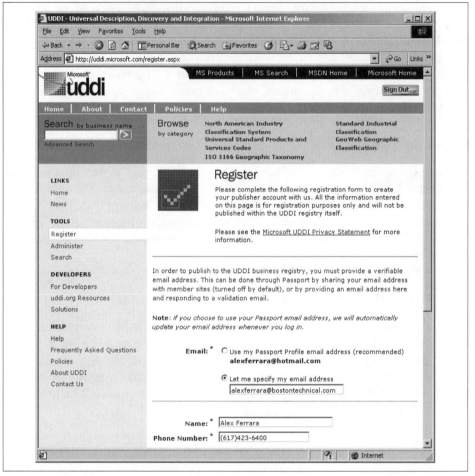

Figure 10-2. Registering your business in the UDDI directory

Classifications

Classifications range from geographical location to industry type. UDDI users can search the directory by entity type and classification, so it's important to make sure your business entity is properly classified. UDDI allows not only business entities but also services to be classified, using the available classification system (as discussed later in this chapter).

Services

These are web services including the WSDL (or other description language) and binding of each service. Services can be categorized and associated with tModels.

tModels

You can associate multiple service templates with both business entities and services.

While these options are important for making sure that your business is properly represented and therefore accessible to UDDI users, you don't have to set up all of the options at once. You can register your business quickly and easily by adding a business name and description. The contact information and classifications are important but not essential to listing your business. Select the Publish option to register your information. See Figure 10-3.

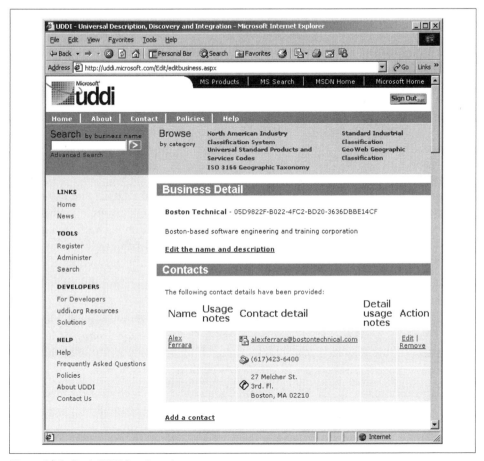

Figure 10-3. Basic UDDI registration

The next step is to make sure your business is properly categorized, as explained in the following section.

The Classification System

Any of the UDDI sites allow you to classify your business using several category types. Some of the supported classifications are listed in Table 10-1.

Table 10-1. UDDI classification systems

Classification	Description	Example(s)
North American Industry Classification System (NAICS)	A government standard business classification system. See *http://www. census.gov/epcd/www/naics.html*. Replaces SIC (see SIC entry).	NAICS 5415: Computer Systems Design and Related Services
Universal Standard Products and Services Codes (UNSPSC)	Classification of products and services. See *http://www.eccma.org/unspsc/*.	81.11.16.01.00: Programming for Visual Basic
ISO 3166 Geographic Taxonomy	Geographical classifications set up by the ISO.	Massachusetts (US-MA)
Standard Industrial Classification (SIC)	Industry classification set up by the U.S. Department of Commerce. This has been replaced by NAICS.	7371: Computer programming services
GeoWeb geographic classification	Classifications based on geographical location.	100013: North America 516499: Boston
UDDI Type taxonomy	UDDI types used for tModels only	Protocol, namespace, WSDL specification

Searches can be done using the advanced search feature of the UDDI site as well as programmatically (as explained later in this chapter). For example, using the Microsoft UDDI Advanced Search page, we can query based on each of the classifications in the table as well as by business name, location, identifier, discovery URL, and tModel name. For example, if you want to find all of the businesses that are located in Boston according to the GeoWeb classification, you might perform a search as shown in Figure 10-4.

Using 516499, the GeoWeb identifier for Boston as the search term yields identical results. Our search returns three results; Churchill Flowers Design Studio, M.L. Martin Consulting, and Boston Technical. If you drill down to any of these businesses, you'll see that each is associated with the GeoWeb Boston classification.

Let's perform another UDDI search, again against the GeoWeb classification, but this time using Massachusetts as the search term. Assuming you spell Massachusetts correctly, the result of this search should look something like Figure 10-5.

The result of this search is much different than that for the previous search. One might expect that the results would include all of the previous results, plus all of the other companies located in Massachusetts cities, but the only company to turn up again is Boston Technical. If you drill down to each of the companies to view their GeoWeb classifications, you'll see why. The UDDI search feature does not infer any logic regarding the relationship of the classification system. A search for Massachusetts returns only entities that have been explicitly assigned the GeoWeb Massachusetts classification. Because neither Churchill Flowers nor M.L. Martin Consulting have been assigned this classification, neither of them appears in the results for this search. On the other hand, Boston Technical, which is classified as both Boston and Massachusetts, appears in both results. Intelligent searching is left to the search

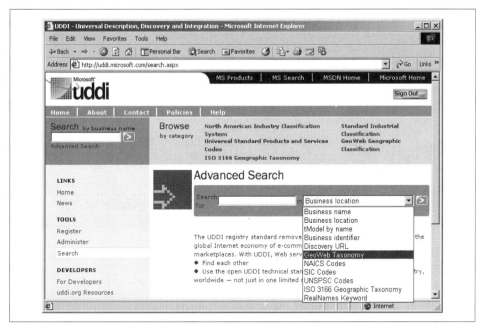

Figure 10-4. UDDI advanced search page

engines that will presumably be built to access the directory and return results to consumers and other clients. Knowing this before you start to write programs to search the directory can save you some time and brain damage. This doesn't mean that you should assign every classification to your business. Doing so would contribute to seriously limiting the utility of the directory and would most likely end up with the removal of your business.

WSDL and UDDI

UDDI provides a framework for the description of businesses and services, along with an extensible mechanism for providing detailed service access information using any service description language—open or proprietary (e.g., WSCL, WSDL, or even simple non-XML text). WSDL is not tightly coupled with the UDDI registry, which makes the UDDI standard more flexible and also makes a lot of sense, considering that WSDL is not yet a standard description language, is likely to continue to change, and may even be surpassed by a more suitable alternative. That said, while the UDDI directory may contain some services described using other languages, WSDL is by far the most common language for describing a web service.

WSDL and the UDDI Data Structures

Earlier in this chapter, we looked at the relationship between several of the primary UDDI data structures. You'll recall that there are three main structures used in the

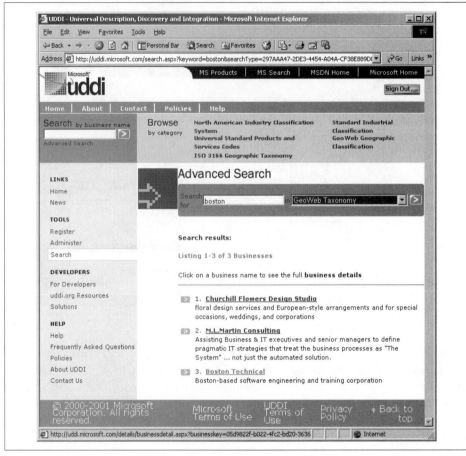

Figure 10-5. UDDI GeoWeb search for Massachusetts

description of a service, each of which has a different purpose. Those three structures are the businessService, bindingTemplate, and tModel, in a relationship shown in Figure 10-6.

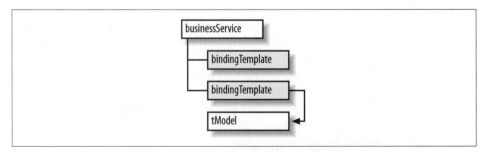

Figure 10-6. UDDI service data structures

We explained in Chapter 3 that the WSDL document consists of several elements used to describe various aspects of a web service, such as the location (<port>), protocol supported (<binding>), message format (<message>), and so on. When the UDDI registry is used for web services, each of the WSDL elements is maintained in the UDDI data structures. The WSDL-to-UDDI mapping is depicted in Figure 10-7.

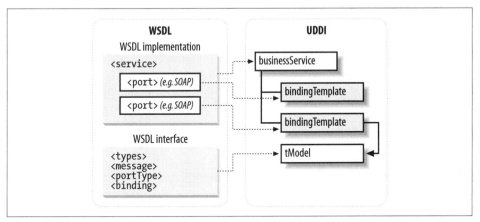

Figure 10-7. Relationship for WSDL-to-UDDI data types

The elements of the WSDL document are stored across the three UDDI data types used to describe a service. Several of the elements map to the tModel data type, while the other two, <service> and <port>, map to the businessService and bindingTemplate types, respectively. Thinking about this split within the context of the UDDI goal of creating a B2B e-commerce exchange should start to make the reason for this clear. The elements of the WSDL document can be categorized as either interface- or implementation-specific. The interface elements—<types>, <message>, <portType>, and <binding>—provide an abstract definition of the web service. They provide information about the message format, protocols supported, and data types used. The other two elements, <service> and <port>, provide implementation-specific information about the service, such as where you can find a particular implementation of a service supporting a given binding (e.g., SOAP).

Abstract and concrete service definitions

One of the strengths of the UDDI specification is that it allows for registration of both abstract and concrete (or instance) service definitions. The abstract definition is accomplished using the tModel, which can reference the service interface for a generic service. This abstract definition does not define any specific service implementation (e.g., there's no URL where you can find the service), but instead provides a signature or conformity rules that instances of the service associated with the tModel should follow.

Conversely, the concrete or instance definition of the service defines instance-specific information, such as the URL where the service can be found. This definition is included in the `bindingTemplate` and `businessService` types (also in another entity called a `tModelInstanceInfo`). Each instance definition can optionally be associated with a `tModel` instance. In this case, the two work together to form the complete picture of the service. The `tModel` describes interface information such as the message structure and bindings supported. The `bindingTemplate` and `businessService` define an implementation of a service that conforms to this `tModel`.

The frictionless marketplace

An important reason for this type of architecture has to do with the way that UDDI is intended to be used. By separating the interface from the implementation, UDDI makes a distinction between consumers and service providers. Using this framework, a consumer in need of a certain service can establish the `tModel` outlining the interface for the required service. Once the consumer has published the `tModel`, service providers can create an implementation of that service (particular to .NET— remember the capability of the *wsdl.exe* tool for generating stub code from WSDL). Once the implementation is complete, the consumer can integrate it. Because the service definition uses a structured format, implementations of the same service should be identical in function. Should one service provider become too expensive or prove unreliable, switching to another is as easy as finding the next service implementation. Alternatively, if the appropriate `tModel` and implementation already exist, the consumer has a set of similar services from which to choose. This type of marketplace, where consumers can choose from a variety of similar services and change providers with minimal cost, is seen as the long-term goal of the UDDI project.

WSDL and tModels

There are several types of `tModels`; when WSDL is used with UDDI, the `tModel` should be of type `wsdlSpec`. This type of `tModel` defines the signature or conformance rules for the service using the WSDL language.

Adding a tModel

Once you've registered a business entity, the next logical step is to start associating web services. After all, the main purpose for using UDDI is the ability to register services with a searchable directory. For this example, we've created a Quote of the Day service that returns a different quote from a historical figure each day. The service contains one method called `GetDailyGeneralQuote` and is located at *http://ws.mydomain.com/services/Service1.asmx* (this is a fictional URL). The code for the service is as follows:

```
using System;
using System.Data;
using System.Web;
```

```csharp
using System.Web.Services;
using System.Data.SqlClient;

namespace services
{
  public class Quote
  {
    public Quote()
    {
      text = "";
      author = "";
      origin = "";
    }
    public string text;
    public string author;
    public string origin;
  }

  [WebService(Namespace="http://www.bostontechnical.com/qotd-interface",
  Description="Quote of the Day Service")]
  public class Service1 : System.Web.Services.WebService
  {

    [WebMethod(Description="Quote of the day generator.", CacheDuration=3600)]
    public Quote GetDailyGeneralQuote()
    {
      SqlConnection conn = new SqlConnection("server=x.x.x.x;database=myDB;user
                          id=Username;password=password");
      SqlDataAdapter myCommand = new SqlDataAdapter("sph_quoteoftheday", conn);
      DataSet ds = new DataSet();
      myCommand.Fill(ds, "Quotes");
      Quote q = new Quote();
      q.text = (string) ds.Tables["Quotes"].Rows[0]["ContentText"];
      q.author = (string) ds.Tables["Quotes"].Rows[0]["Authorname"];
      q.origin = (string) ds.Tables["Quotes"].Rows[0]["origindescription"];
      return q;
    }
  }
}
```

The web service exposes one method called GetDailyGeneralQuote, which hits the database to get the current quote and then returns the content using a custom Quote object. One important thing to notice is the namespace, http://www.bostontechnical.com/qotd-interface. This namespace must be the same one that is registered as part of the tModel; otherwise, you receive errors when you attempt to compile the client application.

Before you register this service, first add a tModel entry, since that's where the abstract WSDL definition is stored. For the published web service to be useful to third parties, they need the service description information stored in the WSDL. In the context of UDDI, this service description information is stored in a tModel with a classification of type `wsdlSpec`. You can add this `tModel` through the UDDI web administration page.

The administration page gives a link to publish a new `tModel`, which allows you to add a new `tModel` UDDI data structure to the registry. Each `tModel` is assigned a unique key called, appropriately enough, the `tModelKey`. This key is a GUID (globally unique identifier) that is automatically generated by the registry when the `tModel` is added. Once the `tModel` is added, this key can be used for programmatic access to the `tModel`. The Initial Add screen should look like Figure 10-8.

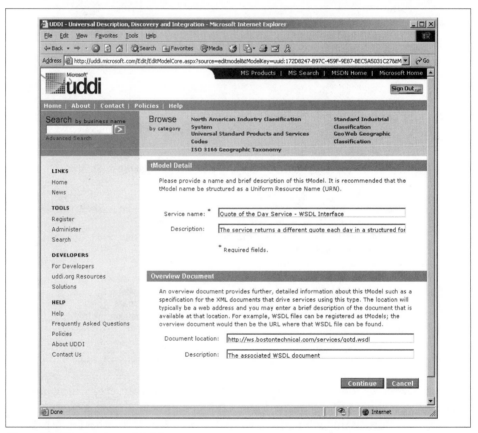

Figure 10-8. Registering a tModel

The service name field is used not only for display but also for `tModel` searches against the UDDI registry, so it's important to be descriptive. The description information is optional and is used for display purposes only.

To fully leverage the capabilities of UDDI and WSDL, the UDDI community recommends that you use only the service interface portion of the WSDL document for your tModel registrations. You can then use the implementation portion of the WSDL document for your service registration using the <import> element to add the WSDL interface. This process is outlined in more detail in the UDDI document titled "Using WSDL in a UDDI Registry" (located at *http://www.uddi.org/ pubs/wsdlbestpractices-V1.05-Open-20010625.pdf*). While the B2B marketplace goals of UDDI make this process advantageous in many situations, making changes to the automatically generated WSDL that .NET generates for your service is guaranteed to bring headaches. The reason for this is that you'll need to manage two separate namespaces, one for the interface and one for the implementation; unless you have a good comprehension of how XML namespaces work, you're guaranteed to run into troubles. Do a quick search for XML Namespace Problem on *http://www.deja.com/*.

An alternative is to avoid using the <import> statement by publishing the interface portion of the WSDL document as a tModel and then publishing the entire WSDL document as part of the bindingTemplate. Registering your service in this way avoids the potential problems associated with namespace conflicts and using the <import> statement, but it leads to another problem: redundant information that can get out of sync. You can also publish the entire WSDL document as your tModel; however, this limits the reusability of the model (which isn't necessarily a bad thing). Our example splits apart the interface and implementation documents so that you can see how the process is supposed to work.

The overview document is where you specify the URL of the WSDL document used for the tModel. Here, we've specified the service interface portion of the WSDL document used for the example Quote of the Day service. The abbreviated WSDL for this example, with binding information for HTTP GET and POST removed, follows. (The full version can be found at *http://ws.bostontechnical.com/services/qotd.wsdl*.)

```
<?xml version="1.0" encoding="utf-8"?>
<definitions name="qotd-interface" xmlns:s="http://www.w3.org/2001/XMLSchema" xmlns:
http="http://schemas.xmlsoap.org/wsdl/http/" xmlns:mime="http://schemas.xmlsoap.org/
wsdl/mime/" xmlns:tm="http://microsoft.com/wsdl/mime/textMatching/" xmlns:soap="http:
//schemas.xmlsoap.org/wsdl/soap/" xmlns:soapenc="http://schemas.xmlsoap.org/soap/
encoding/" xmlns:s0="http://www.bostontechnical.com/qotd-interface"
targetNamespace="http://www.bostontechnical.com/qotd-interface" xmlns="http://
schemas.xmlsoap.org/wsdl/">
  <types>
    <s:schema attributeFormDefault="qualified" elementFormDefault="qualified"
     targetNamespace="http://www.bostontechnical.com/qotd-interface">
      <s:element name="GetDailyGeneralQuote">
        <s:complexType />
      </s:element>
      <s:element name="GetDailyGeneralQuoteResponse">
```

```
      <s:complexType>
        <s:sequence>
          <s:element minOccurs="1" maxOccurs="1"
            name="GetDailyGeneralQuoteResult" nillable="true" type="s0:Quote" />
        </s:sequence>
      </s:complexType>
    </s:element>
    <s:complexType name="Quote">
      <s:sequence>
        <s:element minOccurs="1" maxOccurs="1" name="text" nillable="true"
          type="s:string" />
        <s:element minOccurs="1" maxOccurs="1" name="author" nillable="true"
          type="s:string" />
        <s:element minOccurs="1" maxOccurs="1" name="origin" nillable="true"
          type="s:string" />
      </s:sequence>
    </s:complexType>
    <s:element name="Quote" nillable="true" type="s0:Quote" />
  </s:schema>
</types>
<message name="GetDailyGeneralQuoteSoapIn">
  <part name="parameters" element="s0:GetDailyGeneralQuote" />
</message>
<message name="GetDailyGeneralQuoteSoapOut">
  <part name="parameters" element="s0:GetDailyGeneralQuoteResponse" />
</message>
<portType name="Service1Soap">
  <operation name="GetDailyGeneralQuote">
    <documentation>Quote of the day generator.</documentation>
    <input message="s0:GetDailyGeneralQuoteSoapIn" />
    <output message="s0:GetDailyGeneralQuoteSoapOut" />
  </operation>
</portType>
<binding name="Service1Soap" type="s0:Service1Soap">
  <soap:binding transport="http://schemas.xmlsoap.org/soap/http"
    style="document" />
  <operation name="GetDailyGeneralQuote">
    <soap:operation
  soapAction="http://www.bostontechnical.com/qotd-interface/GetDailyGeneralQuote"
  style="document" />
    <input>
      <soap:body use="literal" />
    </input>
    <output>
      <soap:body use="literal" />
    </output>
  </operation>
</binding>
</definitions>
```

This document is almost identical to what you find when viewing the service's
WSDL by appending the *?wsdl* suffix, with the exception that the <service> element
and child <port> elements information have been removed. We've also added a name
attribute to the definitions to provide more information about the document. When

creating a client against this service, .NET downloads and renames the document according to the value of the name attribute.

Once you've entered this information, the next step is to add a service classification that identifies this tModel as being of type wsdlSpec. You can do this by adding a classification, through UDDI Types Taxonomy → Specification for a Web Service → "Specification for a web service described in WSDL." Once you've done this, you must click the Publish button to publish the addition to the UDDI registry. The resulting screen displaying your tModel should look like Figure 10-9.

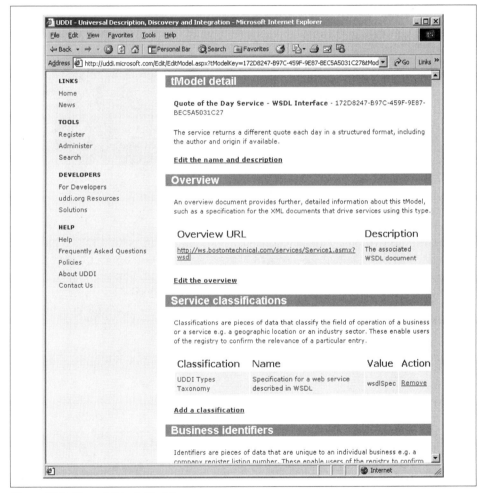

Figure 10-9. The published tModel

Associating a Web Service with Your Business

The UDDI web interface allows you to add and classify services using a forms-driven system. From the Administer page, click the Add a Service link in the Services section. You will be prompted for the name and description for the service. This is the text that gets associated with the businessService entity and returned as part of a search result. For this service, we've added a name and description as shown in Figure 10-10.

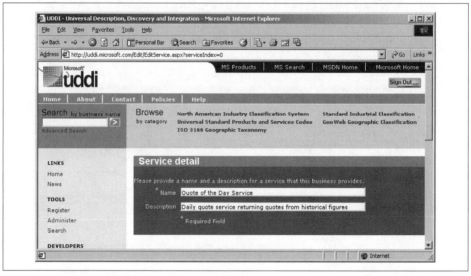

Figure 10-10. Adding a web service—the service detail

The next step is to define a binding for the service. Referring to the UDDI data structure diagram, you'll see that just as each businessEntity structure can have multiple businessService structures associated with it, each businessService can also have multiple bindingTemplates associated with it. The bindingTemplate specifies the technical information about the service entry point such as the URL and access method. Each binding can also refer to the tModel, or service signature, with which the service is in conformance.

By now, you might have realized that the UDDI web site is just a simple wrapper for the directory, providing access to parts of these data structures through a web interface. Each subsequent screen allows you to insert data into another related part of the directory structure. In this case, you can add a binding by clicking the Define New Binding link under the Bindings section on the next screen. The screen should look something like Figure 10-11.

We've provided the endpoint URL of the service along with the URL access type and a brief description. This is part of the information people see when viewing the service in the directory. We've now provided enough information for a person to be able to find the service; however, we'll need to associate it with a published tModel in order for the service to have any significant meaning as a web service.

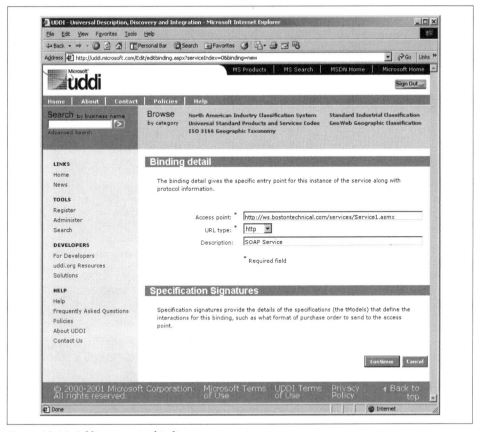

Figure 10-11. Adding a service binding

Associating a Service with a tModel

Just as the Binding Detail section is used to associate the URL for your service implementation, the Specification Signature section is used to reference any tModel to which your service conforms. When you add a tModel specification, you'll be prompted to first search for the tModel by name. If you registered a tModel in the previous step, you should be able to locate it fairly easily. The tModel associated with the Quote of the Day service is called Quote of the Day Service - WSDL Interface. Once you've found the proper tModel, you'll be presented with another edit screen that looks like Figure 10-12.

This screen allows you to specify additional information about your particular implementation of the service defined in the tModel. For example, you can use the Instance Details section to provide a link to any special documentation necessary to use your service. At the bottom of the screen, the Overview Document section allows you to specify the additional information about the tModel. This is where to put the link to

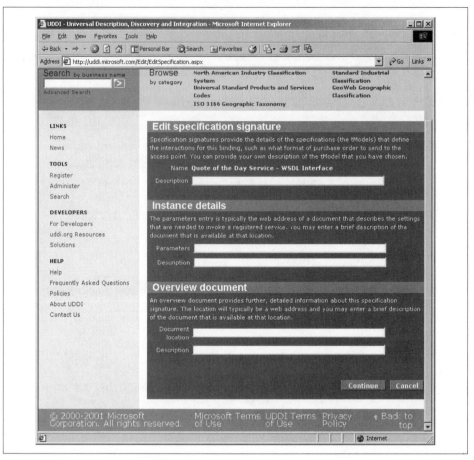

Figure 10-12. Associating a tModel with a service

the WSDL file that contains implementation-specific information. For this example, I've used the following WSDL document:

```
<?xml version="1.0" encoding="utf-8"?>
<definitions name="qotd" xmlns:s="http://www.w3.org/2001/XMLSchema"
xmlns:http="http://schemas.xmlsoap.org/wsdl/http/"
xmlns:mime="http://schemas.xmlsoap.org/wsdl/mime/"
xmlns:tm="http://microsoft.com/wsdl/mime/textMatching/"
xmlns:soap="http://schemas.xmlsoap.org/wsdl/soap/"
xmlns:soapenc="http://schemas.xmlsoap.org/soap/encoding/"
xmlns:interface="http://www.bostontechnical.com/qotd-interface"
targetNamespace="http://www.bostontechnical.com/qotd"
xmlns="http://schemas.xmlsoap.org/wsdl/">
  <documentation>
    This service provides an implementation of a standard quote of the day service.
    The web service uses quotes provided by U-inspire Inc.
  </documentation>
  <import namespace="http://www.bostontechnical.com/qotd-interface"
```

```
         location="http://ws.bostontechnical.com/services/qotd.wsdl" />
      <service name="Service1">
        <documentation>Quote of the Day Service</documentation>
        <port name="Service1Soap" binding="interface:Service1Soap">
          <soap:address
               location="http://ws.bostontechnical.com/services/service1.asmx" />
        </port>
      </service>
    </definitions>
```

This WSDL document, representing the implementation details of the service, is the document from which a proxy is built. The first thing to note is that the targetNamespace for this document is different from that of the interface. To prevent a name collision due to duplicate namespaces, we need to make sure that each of the two WSDL files uses a different namespace.

Here I've used the namespace www.bostontechnical.com/qotd-interface for the WSDL interface document and www.bostontechnical.com/qotd for the implementation document. Chances are, you'll be creating this document from the one that .NET provides automatically; if that's the case, you'll need to be careful to change the namespace in the appropriate locations. Notably, you should make sure that the targetNamespace is set to the namespace for the implementation WSDL (e.g., www. bostontechnical.com/qotd). You'll also need to add a namespace shortcut to the namespace of the interface document so that your bindings will be properly resolved. This appears in the definitions as:

```
    xmlns:interface=http://www.bostontechnical.com/qotd-interface
```

and is referenced later in the document:

```
    <port name="Service1Soap" binding="interface:Service1Soap">
```

Finally, the <import> statement is used to add a reference to the interface document as follows:

```
    <import namespace="http://www.bostontechnical.com/qotd-interface"
      location="http://ws.bostontechnical.com/services/qotd.wsdl" />
```

This completes the implementation WSDL for the example service. On a final note, remember to keep the service namespace the same as the interface namespace since the data types and messages used by the service are presumably defined in the interface WSDL document.

Now we can add this implementation as the overview document and publish the changes to complete the process.

Visual Studio .NET and UDDI

One of the nice capabilities of Visual Studio .NET is that it allows you to easily add a web reference without having to compile a proxy DLL. Furthermore, these references can be easily updated with a click of the mouse. The Add a Web Reference feature has a built-in link to the Microsoft UDDI registry (you can use others as well) that allows you to easily search for and bind to web services. The example service from the previous section can be referenced by selecting Add a Web Reference from the Project menu item and clicking the Microsoft UDDI Directory link. When prompted to enter a business name, in this case, we'd enter **Boston Technical**, since we know the service is associated with that business. The results of our search should look like Figure 10-13

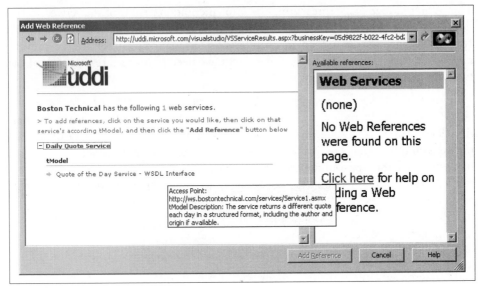

Figure 10-13. Using UDDI through VS.NET

The screen displays each of the tModels associated with the business Boston Technical. Adding a web reference is as trivial as clicking the Quote of the Day tModel link, then clicking Add Reference.

 VS.NET occasionally has difficulty with custom WSDL. As a result, you might need to explicitly add the URL of the service using the Url property of the proxy object.

UDDI Messaging

While manipulating the UDDI registry via a web site like Microsoft's is convenient for some tasks, the real beauty of UDDI is the programmatic API it exposes. Remember that UDDI is really just one large web service; as such, all programmatic interactions with the registry are done using SOAP-formatted messages. Documentation for this API can be found on the UDDI site at *http://uddi.org/pubs/ProgrammersAPI-V2. 00-Open-20010608.pdf*. In truth, two types of APIs are available. The first is a publishing API, which stores or changes registry data. The second is the Inquiry API, which reads items from the registry. Remember that before you are able to add a business entity to the directory via the Microsoft site, you first have to create or log in with a Passport account. This account is necessary not only for access through the web site but also for programmatic access to the Microsoft UDDI registry via the Publisher API. The UDDI specification does not have any relation to Microsoft's Passport, but the specification does have a general requirement for an authentication mechanism, which Microsoft has chosen to fulfill using Passport. The UDDI specification's authentication requirement, in conjunction with the requirement that all Publisher API calls be performed over HTTPS (specifically SSL 3.0), provides a level of security, accountability, and confidentiality to the publishing process.

SOAP and UDDI

The UDDI v2.0 specification makes use of the SOAP 1.1 protocol for messaging. However, not all of the items in the SOAP specification are supported. Some notable exceptions are the following:

SOAP Actors
> The actors feature is not supported. Operator sites will reject any request that arrives with the SOAP Actor attribute in the SOAP header with an E_unsupported error code.

SOAP Encoding
> The SOAP encoding feature (SOAP 1.1 Section 5) is not supported. Operator sites will reject any request that arrives with a SOAP encoding attribute with an E_unsupported error code.

SOAP Headers
> SOAP headers are not supported either. Operator sites will ignore any SOAP headers as long as the must_understand attribute is set to false. Otherwise, a SOAP fault of type MustUnderstand is returned.

The Inquiry API

One of the design goals of the UDDI APIs is simplicity. As a result, there only about 25 or so total functions in the UDDI APIs. The Inquiry API itself contains only 10 functions. These functions can be performed against any operator site using the HTTP protocol. Unlike the Publish API, no authentication is necessary. The functions and their descriptions are as follows:

find_binding
> This searches through the bindings associated with a registered businessService.

find_business
> This locates information about one or more businesses.

find_relatedBusinesses

> Given a unique businessEntity identifier (called a businessKey), this returns information about other related businessEntity entries. The Related Businesses feature manages registration of business units and subsequently relates them based on organizational hierarchies or business partner relationships.

find_service

> Given a businessKey, this searches for specific associated services.

find_tModel

> This finds one or more tModel structures based on name or associated identifiers and classifications.

get_bindingDetails

> Given a bindingKey, this returns binding template information that can be used to make service requests.

get_businessDetail

> Given a businessKey, this returns the full businessEntity information for one or more businesses or organizations.

get_businessDetailExt

> This is similar to get_businessDetail, but returns any extended information associated with the businessEntity. This can occur if the source of the businessEntity is an external (nonhost operator) site.

get_serviceDetail

> Given a serviceKey, this returns businessService details.

get_tModelDetail

> Given a tModelKey, this returns full details about the associated tModel.

As you can see, this set of functions provides basic inquiry services for the UDDI registry. There are no complex querying operations—only what is considered to be a minimal interface for reading data from the registry. We're not going to go into great detail about how to use each of these functions here (you can find full documentation of these functions at the UDDI site: *http://www.uddi.org/*), except to say that each of these functions has an associated XML template that is used when accessing the registry. For example, the syntax for the get_businessDetail function is:

```
<get_businessDetail generic="2.0" xmlns="urn:uddi-org:api_v2" >
<businessKey/> [<businessKey/> ...]
</get_businessDetail>
```

where <businessKey> is the unique identifier for the businessEntity entry. This message would be encapsulated within the body of a SOAP message.

Each of these functions also has a corresponding return message, documented in the UDDI v2.0 Programmer's API. Fortunately, Microsoft has created a freely available .NET UDDI SDK (there's also one available for VB), which is a wrapper for the UDDI messaging process. This SDK provides a layer of abstraction, in the form of .NET classes, on top of the XML messaging API described earlier. We'll talk about where to get and how to use the .NET UDDI SDK in a later section.

The Inquiry API provides three broad forms of query that are commonly recognized patterns traditionally used with registries. These patterns are the browse pattern, the drill-down pattern, and the invocation pattern. Each of the functions described previously are used in one of the patterns, as described in the following sections.

The browse pattern

We're all familiar with the concept of browsing through hierarchical data. Examples include the Active Directory and network browsing features found in Windows domains, which allow you to browse and drill down through different network layers and objects. The UDDI browse pattern is similar, involving the use of search criteria to narrow down a broad set of data to a specific result set. Each of the API functions beginning with the find_ prefix are used for browsing the registry, and all, with the exception of the find_binding function, return a list message of some sort containing information that can be used to browse down to any of the list items.

The drill-down pattern

Once you have a key for one of the four main data types, you can use it to retrieve the full details of the entity. This is done using one of the four following functions:

- get_businessDetail
- get_businessDetailExt
- get_serviceDetail
- get_tModelDetail

Given the appropriate key, each of these functions returns the full details for the associated entity. In this way, you can retrieve all of the information for any of the four main entities.

The invocation pattern

Once you've found the service of interest, the next step will most likely be to invoke the service. This process, called the *invocation pattern*, is implemented through the get_bindingDetails function, which retrieves the binding template data necessary to invoke the service.

The bigger picture

One of the strengths of the UDDI invocation system is it serves as an intermediary between the client and physical service location. This is not unlike the DNS system, which provides mappings of hostnames to physical server addresses. This system solves some of the problems that can arise when the caller and service are tightly coupled, perhaps through hardcoding of the physical service location. In such a case, problems can arise if the location of the service is changed. Because the UDDI system serves as an intermediary brokering service, these types of problems can be easily avoided.

The Publish API

In UDDI v2.0, the publish API consists of a set of 16 functions that perform registry management tasks such as adding, modifying, and deleting instances of the 4 UDDI entities. All of the function calls require the use of SSL (HTTPS) in order to ensure confidentiality and involve the use of some form of authentication as dictated by the host operator to which you wish to publish. The publish API consists of the following functions:

- add_PublisherAssertions
- delete_binding
- delete_business
- delete_publisherAssertions
- delete_service
- delete_tModel
- discard_authToken
- get_assertionStatusReport
- get_authToken
- get_publisherAssertions
- get_registeredInfo
- save_binding
- save_business
- save_service
- save_tModel
- set_publisherAssertion

The functions are fairly self-explanatory. In addition, as we've mentioned, a .NET UDDI SDK encapsulates the UDDI messaging APIs, which are discussed in the next section. For information on how to use the Publish API, check out the Programmer's API reference at *http://uddi.org/pubs/ProgrammersAPI-V2.00-Open-20010608.pdf*.

UDDI Access with .NET

You can interact with a UDDI registry operator using the .NET Framework to send XML-encoded SOAP messages back and forth. In this manner, you can query and manipulate UDDI registry entries; however, this process is not only error-prone but also can be considerably time-consuming. Consider the following example, where we want to use the find_business member function of the Inquiry API to retrieve the business information for our company. The UDDI request for this function in .NET looks like the following:

```
using System;
using System.Web;
using System.Net;
using System.IO;

namespace UDDIAccess
{
  class UDDIQuery
  {
    static void Main(string[] args)
    {
      string result = "";
      // Initialize the WebRequest.
      HttpWebRequest myRequest = (HttpWebRequest)
        WebRequest.Create("http://uddi.microsoft.com/inquire");
      myRequest.Method = "POST";
      myRequest.ContentType = "text/xml";
      myRequest.Headers.Add("SOAPAction", "\"\"");
      string msg = "<?xml version='1.0' encoding='UTF-8'?>
        <Envelope xmlns='http://schemas.xmlsoap.org/soap/envelope/'>
        <Body><find_business generic=\"1.0\"
        xmlns=\"urn:uddi-org:api\">
        <name>Microsoft</name></find_business></Body></Envelope>";
      Byte[] byteMessage = System.Text.Encoding.ASCII.GetBytes(msg.ToCharArray());
      Stream myStream = myRequest.GetRequestStream();
      myStream.Write(byteMessage, 0, byteMessage.Length);
      myStream.Close();
      try
      {
        // Return the response.
        HttpWebResponse myResponse = (HttpWebResponse) myRequest.GetResponse();
        using (StreamReader sr = new StreamReader(myResponse.GetResponseStream()) )
        {
          result = sr.ReadToEnd();
          sr.Close();
        }
        myResponse.Close();
      }
      catch(Exception e) {}
      Console.WriteLine(result);
    }
  }
}
```

Here we use the `HttpWebRequest` class to transmit a SOAP request to the Microsoft UDDI registry. As we've seen, a SOAP message is sent as part of the HTTP header, which means that we must add the following lines to specify that the message is SOAP/XML:

```
myRequest.Method = "POST";
myRequest.ContentType = "text/xml";
myRequest.Headers.Add("SOAPAction", "\"\"");
```

Once you've specified the HTTP method and message type, you can write the XML request message out as part of the request. In this example, we're using the find_business function to get business information about Microsoft. The format of the SOAP message is as follows:

```
<?xml version='1.0' encoding='UTF-8'?>
<Envelope xmlns='http://schemas.xmlsoap.org/soap/envelope/'>
<Body>
<find_business generic="1.0" xmlns="urn:uddi-org:api">
<name>Microsoft</name>
</find_business>
</Body>
</Envelope>
```

In this example, the HTTP request is written to by the GetRequestStream method as follows:

```
string msg = "<?xml version='1.0' encoding='UTF-8'?>
    <Envelope xmlns='http://schemas.xmlsoap.org/soap/envelope/'>
    <Body><find_business generic=\"1.0\"
    xmlns=\"urn:uddi-org:api\">
    <name>Microsoft</name></find_business></Body></Envelope>";
Byte[] byteMessage = System.Text.Encoding.ASCII.GetBytes(msg.ToCharArray());
Stream myStream = myRequest.GetRequestStream();
myStream.Write(byteMessage, 0, byteMessage.Length);
myStream.Close();
```

The resulting SOAP request message is:

```
POST /inquire HTTP/1.1
Content-Type: text/xml
SOAPAction: ""
Content-Length: 214
Expect: 100-continue
Connection: Keep-Alive
Host: 127.0.0.1
<?xml version='1.0' encoding='UTF-8'?><Envelope xmlns='http://schemas.xmlsoap.org/
soap/envelope/'><Body><find_business generic="1.0" xmlns="urn:uddi-org:api"><name>
Microsoft</name></find_business></Body></Envelope>
```

If everything is properly set up, the server responds with the details of the Microsoft business entity in the form of a SOAP response containing an XML document. As you can see, this is a considerable amount of work just to perform a simple query. Having to write this kind of code (or a set of wrapper classes) for each of the functions in the API would be very time-consuming. Fortunately, the majority of the work has been done for us already by the good folks in Redmond.

The .NET UDDI SDK

Microsoft has created a software development kit that encapsulates the messages and logic used to interact with a UDDI registry. The .NET UDDI SDK consists of a set of .NET classes used to query and manipulate the UDDI registry. It's available as a free download from the Microsoft site at *http://uddi.microsoft.com*. Once you download and install the software, you'll be able to use it in your projects by adding a reference to the `Microsoft.UDDI.SDK` assembly, which contains the `Microsoft.UDDI` namespace.

Using the .NET UDDI SDK

The .NET UDDI SDK makes accessing the UDDI registry much more straightforward. Using the SDK, the same `find_business` operation coded earlier can be accomplished in less than 10 lines of code:

```
using Microsoft.Uddi;
...
static void Main(string[] args)
{
  Inquire.Url = "http://uddi.microsoft.com/inquire";
  FindBusiness fb = new FindBusiness();
  fb.Name = "Microsoft";
  BusinessList bl = fb.Send();
  Console.WriteLine(bl.ToString());
}
...
```

As you can see, the UDDI SDK makes this process considerably simpler.

UDDI SDK Usage Patterns

If you take the time to look through the UDDI SDK class hierarchy, you'll notice that most of the classes map to the UDDI request functions and response messages. For example, in order to retrieve details for a business entity named Microsoft, we used a class called `FindBusiness`. We first set the `name` property of this class to `Microsoft` and then called the `send` method. The return value of this call was an instance of a class called `BusinessList`. This is the common usage pattern for the UDDI SDK classes. In general, the steps are:

1. Set authentication if using the Publish API.
2. Create a class instance for the function type you wish to call.
3. Set the appropriate properties that correspond to the variable portions of the message.
4. Call the send method storing the results in the appropriate response instance.

Several examples of how to accomplish basic tasks such as searching and publishing come as part of the SDK download, including a Windows application that you can use to query a UDDI registry. For this reason, we do not cover the SDK usage in any more detail, but you're encouraged to review the samples.

The WS-Inspection Alternative

So far we've spent a great deal of time talking about what UDDI is and how it's used. UDDI is designed to solve the problem of locating and integrating web services when you don't know the provider. However, UDDI is not the best solution for situations in which you already know the party with which you want to interact. In those situations, you'll probably want to avoid making calls to UDDI and instead directly contact the organization providing the service. In order to allow this interaction to occur in a structured fashion, several standards have been proposed, but to date none of them has been widely supported. The closest thing to a common standard is the WS-Inspection specification.

WS-Inspection is a (proposed) specification that provides a means for a consumer to gather information about the web services made available by an entity. Unlike UDDI, which serves as an intermediary for locating services, WS-Inspection allows you to interrogate a company's server directly to find out what services are offered, if any. As you can imagine, this type of process can be very useful for certain scenarios in which you want your services to be known, such as providing a structured method for search engines to spider your server's services.

The specification, for which the initial version was announced in November 2001, is a joint effort between Microsoft and IBM. It is designed to consolidate some of the concepts found in earlier proposals such as Advertising and Discovery Services (ADS) and DISCO, proposed by IBM and Microsoft, respectively. It is also one of a family of five web service specifications put forth by Microsoft in October 2001, the others being WS-License, WS-Referral, WS-Routing, and WS-Security. Interestingly enough, WS-Inspection is the only specification to have evolved as a joint effort. Each of the others (most of which are still in the draft stage) was developed solely by Microsoft employees.

The standard describes an XML format (available at *http://schemas.xmlsoap.org/ws/2001/10/inspection/*) and a set of rules for the creation of a WS-Inspection document. This document contains an aggregation of references to existing WSDL documents describing web services. The following is an example of a WS-Inspection document:

```
<?xml version="1.0"?>
<inspection xmlns="http://schemas.xmlsoap.org/ws/2001/10/inspection/">
  <service>
    <abstract>A Quote of the Day Service</abstract>
    <description referencedNamespace="http://schemas.xmlsoap.org/wsdl/"
                 location="http://ws.bostontechnical.com/services/qotd.wsdl" />
  </service>
</inspection>
```

The first thing to note about the document is that it conforms to the XML Schema located at *http://schemas.xmlsoap.org/ws/2001/10/inspection/*. This schema describes the elements and attributes used in the WS-Inspection document such as `<inspection>`, `<service>`, `<description>`, and a few others. These elements and attributes make up the vocabulary of the WS-Inspection standard. In order to list multiple services in the WS-Inspection document, use additional `<service>` elements using the same structure.

The main purpose of the document is to provide references to service descriptions. In this example, the link is to a WSDL document that describes our Quote of the Day service. This link is provided in the `<description>` element via a referencedNamespace and a location attribute. The referencedNamespace attribute specifies the type of document used for description. This allows the WS-Inspection standard to support multiple description languages, along with multiple versions within a given language, should that be required. In the previous example, the referencedNamespace is the WSDL Schema, specifying that the description document conforms to the WSDL specification. The location attribute is used to specify the URL to the WSDL description. This can be an HTTP link, as in the previous example, or can make use of other access protocols such as HTTPS or FTP. In addition, you can also provide links to description documents residing in the UDDI directory using the serviceKey of the registered service. The following example illustrates this format:

```
<?xml version="1.0"?>
<inspection xmlns="http://schemas.xmlsoap.org/ws/2001/10/inspection/">
  <service>
    <abstract>A Quote of the Day Service</abstract>
    <description referencedNamespace="http://schemas.xmlsoap.org/wsdl/"
                location="http://ws.bostontechnical.com/services/qotd.wsdl" />
    <description referencedNamespace="urn:uddi-org:api">
      <wsiluddi:serviceDescription
                location="http://uddi.microsoft.com/uddi/inquiryapi">
        <wsiluddi:serviceKey>
          c86ebef4-2d48-49bd-8d01-20b1f328013f
        </wsiluddi:serviceKey>
      </wsiluddi:serviceDescription>
    </description>
  </service>
</inspection>
```

Here we've added an additional element called serviceDescription, which provides a link to a UDDI node operator, along with the unique serviceKey, which describes the Quote of the Day service. Using this format, you can add references to the UDDI directory where your services are registered.

Microsoft has created several sample .NET applications that can be used to create and manipulate WS-Inspection documents. The samples include source code and are available from the Microsoft site—search the MSDN online library for WS-Inspection.

IBM has a similar offering as part of the IBM Web Service Toolkit 2.4.1.

By creating a WS-Inspection document for your organization, you provide a structured means for accessing your services. While support for this format is still not very widespread, should things change, you'll soon be able to "register" your site by providing search engines with a link to this document.

Customizing the IE Test Page

In Chapter 3 you learned that an IE test page is automatically generated for a web service by .NET using *DefaultWsdlHelpGenerator.aspx*. The first few lines of source code on a page (following some import directives), contain configuration options you can use to customize the default page.

Setting the showPost value to true changes the type of access used by the test form. The default method is to use HTTP GET.

```
<script language="C#" runat="server">
    // Set this to true if you want to see a POST test form
    // Instead of a GET test form; false is the default
    bool showPost = false;
```

Changing dontFilterXml to true will cause all output XML to be UUEncoded, which can be useful for debugging the format of the XML output. The default is to use no encoding.

```
    // Set this to true if you want to see the raw XML as outputted
    // from the XmlWriter (useful for debugging)
    bool dontFilterXml = false;
```

maxObjectGraphDepth controls the level of depth displayed in the sample messages. If our example used a complex data type represented by multiple levels of XML elements, this setting would determine the number of levels displayed:

```
    // Set maxObjectGraphDepth higher or lower to adjust the depth
    // into your object graph of the sample messages
    int maxObjectGraphDepth = 4;
```

maxArraySize also affects the display of sample messages. By default, only two array items in a sample message are displayed:

```
    // Set maxArraySize higher or lower to adjust the number of array
    // items in sample messages
    int maxArraySize = 2;
```

In addition, it's possible to create a customized version of this help page for your web service by specifying the location in your application's *web.config* file, an XML file that contains its configuration information. This file is not necessary to run an ASP.NET application, but you can use it to specify useful configuration options—such as the authentication method—for your ASP.NET web service applications. In Visual Studio .NET, this file is created automatically when you create a web services project using the web service template. If you're not using Visual Studio .NET, you can create a new file in a text editor and save it as *web.config* to the application root folder. A sample *web.config* file takes the following form:

```
<?xml version="1.0" encoding="utf-8" ?>
<configuration>
  <system.web>
  ... configuration elements & attributes ...
  </system.web>
</configuration>
```

Using this structure, all configuration elements are inserted under the `<system.web>` element. As an example, to tell .NET to use an *.aspx* page other than the *Default-WsdlHelpGenerator.aspx* page, use the following format:

```
<?xml version="1.0" encoding="utf-8" ?>
<configuration>
  <system.web>
    <webServices>
      <wsdlHelpGenerator href="MyGenerator.aspx" />
    </webServices>
  </system.web>
</configuration>
```

In this example, we've specified that the ASP.NET application should use a custom help page called *MyGenerator.aspx*. This file must exist in the root folder of the ASP.NET application.

CHAPTER 11

Interoperability

Much of the difficulty associated with the introduction of new technologies like web services is due to disagreements over standards. Standards documents are frequently subject to interpretation, and different interpretations lead to different implementations. Still, a strong community of users and vendors can work together to remedy this type of situation; for example, despite a plague of initial vendor variations and interoperability problems, Ethernet cards from different vendors can now communicate with one another.

This chapter explores some of the current interoperability issues that exist between current implementations of web services technologies, especially SOAP and WSDL. We also provide some design tips for improving interoperability.

State of the Specifications

Several technologies are core to a web service application. The major ones are SOAP and WSDL, each of which makes use of XML and XML Schema for its grammar (see Chapter 3). In addition, specifications such as UDDI and WS-Inspection play a complementary role in allowing for service discovery and publication (see Chapter 10). The relationships between these six technologies and the .NET Framework are displayed in Figure 11-1.

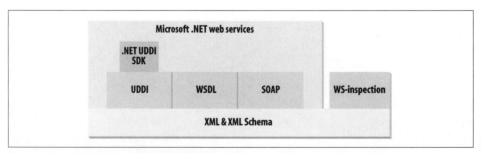

Figure 11-1. .NET web service technologies

UDDI, WSDL, SOAP, and WS-Inspection each depend on XML or the XML Schema for structure. Microsoft .NET web services depend in turn on SOAP, WSDL, and UDDI, but not WS-Inspection for the creation of web service applications.

These XML protocols are by no means the only ones available, but they are the most widely accepted of their kind among many vendors such as SUN, IBM, Oracle, and BEA, and are also the ones used within .NET and most other development tools. (See *http://www.w3.org/2000/03/29-XML-protocol-matrix*, which provides a useful comparison of a number of XML protocols.)

To understand possible interoperability issues, it's important to understand not only the state of each technology but their interdependence. The timeline in Figure 11-2 shows the relative order of events in the evolution of web service technologies.

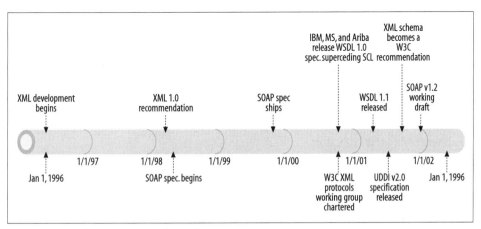

Figure 11-2. Web service protocols timeline

Several web service technologies appeared more or less simultaneously, and the order of their appearance closely mirrors their place on the web service protocol stack (with the exception of XML Schema): XML and SOAP come first, followed by WSDL and UDDI. Table 11-1 lists the state of each at the time this book is being written.

Table 11-1. Web service standards, drafts, and recommendations

Technology	State as of mid-2002
XML	v1.0 W3C Recommendation
XML Schema	W3C Recommendation
SOAP	v1.2 Working Draft v1.1 currently supported by .NET
WSDL	v1.1 specification submitted to W3C v1.2 is a W3C working draft
UDDI	v3.0 managed by UDDI community

Implementation Differences

Throughout this book, our discussions have focused on the default implementations found in the .NET Framework. If you intend to create web services in which the server and client will always be implemented using .NET, interoperability isn't so much of a problem. But you'll probably be using web services to communicate with other platforms as well. In this kind of environment, you can run into several types of problems, most stemming from the still-vague WSDL and SOAP specifications. This vagueness might be intentional: some view web services as a framework for distributed computing based on open standards. Others view them as a standard means for exchanging XML documents. As we examine the details of how messages are formatted, we start to see the implications of each perspective.

SOAP Message Formats

The SOAP specification dictates that the contents of messages sent to and from a web service must be formatted as XML, but doesn't insist on a particular format. Instead, the specification provides support for several message formats, the two most important of which are *document* and *RPC*.

Document style versus RPC style

The document-style message format is the most basic of SOAP message formats and is quickly becoming the default in most development kits, including Microsoft .NET. One camp of users views web services as an opportunity to standardize message-based workflows, considering services to be a communication of XML documents. The document-style message format makes the most sense in this context.

Another group views web services as an opportunity to build a truly open framework for distributed computing. This group views web services as a means of executing remote procedure calls (RPCs) over a network of open protocols. In this scenario, another message format—RPC style—makes more sense. In an RPC-style message, the <soapenv:Body> element contains the name of the method or remote procedure you're invoking, and an element for each parameter of that procedure. This style of message format is defined in Section 7 of the SOAP specification.

The majority of the examples in this book use a synchronous request/response pattern, similar to remote procedure calls, even though the underlying SOAP messages use the "document-style" format. The document-style format is considered to be more flexible than its RPC-style counterpart; that is, everything you can do with RPC style you can also do with document style, but the reverse does not hold true (e.g., RPC style is not well suited for asynchronous services). RPC style was very popular with earlier web services development kits, most likely because some critical pieces were missing from the more general document style approach (e.g., XML Schema); however, all signs from Microsoft suggest that they consider the RPC approach to be on its way out.

All web services created using .NET use the document-style message format by default. Some other web service development kits make use of RPC-style SOAP, including—ironically—the Microsoft SOAP Toolkit v2 (STK). To interoperate with clients and services created with this toolkit, you must use RPC-style SOAP in your .NET applications. Fortunately, *wsdl.exe* automatically takes care of this for you if you're generating a .NET client to access an STK service. The *wsdl.exe* tool is able to generate a proxy that uses the correct message format because information about the message format supported by the service (i.e., RPC or document style) is part of the WSDL document. However, to build an STK client to access a .NET service, you must force .NET to use RPC-style SOAP. Otherwise, the STK client returns an error about not being able to read the WSDL document (of course, you could also change your MS STK client to use document-style SOAP—a trivial change in the more recent versions of the Toolkit).

The SoapDocumentService and SoapRPCService attributes

The SoapDocumentService and SoapRPCService attributes can be applied to the web service to explicitly specify the SOAP message format used by member web methods. Similarly, the SoapDocumentMethod and SoapRPCMethod attributes explicitly specify the SOAP message format at the web method level. To design a .NET service to support RPC-style SOAP, you could use either the SoapRPCService or SoapRPCMethod attributes to change the default document-style SOAP. The difference between the two styles is demonstrated in the following example. Consider the following two web methods, each adding integers and returning the result back to the client:

```
using System.Web.Services.Protocols;
using System.Web.Services.Description;
...
[WebMethod]
[SoapDocumentMethod(
Action="http://ws.bostontechnical.com/AddDocument",
RequestNamespace="http://ws.bostontechnical.com",
ResponseNamespace="http://ws.bostontechnical.com")]
public int AddDocument(int a, int b)
{
  return a + b;
}

[WebMethod]
[SoapRpcMethod(
Action="http://ws.bostontechnical.com/AddRPC",
RequestNamespace="http://ws.bostontechnical.com",
ResponseNamespace="http://ws.bostontechnical.com")]
public int AddRPC(int a, int b)
{
  return a + b;
}
...
```

The first method, AddDocument, has been decorated with the SoapDocumentMethod attribute, which specifies that the WSDL document and SOAP messages should conform to an XSD Schema. The Action property explicitly sets the SOAPAction header of the HTTP POST. The SOAPAction header is a binding-specific (i.e., specific to HTTP) optional header as described by the SOAP spec (see Section 8.5.1). It essentially provides a means of sending information outside the SOAP envelope, which can aid in faster or more efficient processing of the message. You will find that some SOAP implementations support the use of the SOAPAction header, while others do not support it. Regardless, recipients of SOAP messages should not rely on the SOAPAction header—unfortunately, some do, which can result in interoperability problems.

If you skip this property assignment, .NET defaults the Action value to a concatenation of the web service namespace and the method name (i.e., AddDocument). The next two properties, RequestNamespace and ResponseNamespace, explicitly specify the namespace for the method. If left out, this value defaults to the web service's namespace. To understand the differences between each style, take a look at the resulting SOAP request formats in Examples 11-1 and 11-2.

Example 11-1. Document-style request

```
POST /helloworld/Service1.asmx HTTP/1.1
Host: localhost
Content-Type: text/xml; charset=utf-8
Content-Length: 640
SOAPAction: "http://ws.bostontechnical.com/AddDocument"

<?xml version="1.0" encoding="utf-8"?>
<soap:Envelope xmlns:xsi="http://www.w3.org/2001/XMLSchema-instance" xmlns:xsd="http://
www.w3.org/2001/XMLSchema" xmlns:soap="http://schemas.xmlsoap.org/soap/envelope/">
  <soap:Body>
    <AddDocument xmlns="http://ws.bostontechnical.com">
      <a>3</a>
      <b>16</b>
    </AddDocument>
  </soap:Body>
</soap:Envelope>
```

Example 11-2. RPC-style request

```
POST /helloworld/Service1.asmx HTTP/1.1
Host: localhost
Content-Type: text/xml; charset=utf-8
Content-Length: 560
SOAPAction: "http://ws.bostontechnical.com/AddRPC"

<?xml version="1.0" encoding="utf-8"?>
<soap:Envelope xmlns:xsi="http://www.w3.org/2001/XMLSchema-instance" xmlns:xsd="http://
www.w3.org/2001/XMLSchema" xmlns:soapenc="http://schemas.xmlsoap.org/soap/encoding/"
xmlns:tns="http://ws.bostontechnical.com/services" xmlns:types="http://ws.bostontechnical.
com/services/encodedTypes" xmlns:soap="http://schemas.xmlsoap.org/soap/envelope/">
```

Example 11-2. RPC-style request (continued)

```
<soap:Body soap:encodingStyle="http://schemas.xmlsoap.org/soap/encoding/">
  <q1:AddRPC xmlns:q1="http://ws.bostontechnical.com">
    <a xsi:type="xsd:int">3</a>
    <b xsi:type="xsd:int">16</b>
  </q1:AddRPC>
</soap:Body>
</soap:Envelope>
```

The primary difference between the two message formats is that RPC-style request messages include type information for each of the arguments while document-style requests do not. In the RPC-style example (Example 11-2), this is done via the following attributes on both the a and b elements:

```
xsi:type="xsd:int"
```

In the document-style example (Example 11-1), the type information is not included in the SOAP message, but rather in the <types> section of the WSDL document.

SOAP Encoding Formats

In Example 11-2, notice the use of a soap:encodingStyle attribute in the Body element. Another property that you can set for your service or method is the encoding format of the message. The two options are encoded and literal.

In the encoded format, data is formatted according to the encoding rules specified in Section 5 of the SOAP specification, which describes how various data types, including structures, arrays, objects, and object graphs, should be serialized. (If this sounds familiar, it's because Section 5 encoding was designed primarily as a substitute for XML Schema, which had not yet been completed at the time of the SOAP specification.) There are various pros and cons to using the encoded style, which are outside the scope of this text—for more information, see *Programming Web Services with SOAP*, by Snell, Tidwell, and Kulchenko (O'Reilly, 2002). With the approval of the XML Schema standard, this message format has become less common. When using the encoded format, the client and server deal with data in terms of objects, which makes it a natural fit for RPC-style SOAP. In fact, RPC-style SOAP cannot be used with the other message format: literal.

When using the document/literal approach, data is serialized according to an XML Schema and the resulting XML document becomes the payload of the SOAP message (in the <body> element). In this scenario, the payload of the SOAP message is not restricted to any of the SOAP Section 5 encoding rules, but rather the data management is completely left to the application (client and server) instead. The client and server deal with XML messages instead of encoded objects. When building ASP.NET web services using either format, .NET hides these formatting details from the developer.

You can change the encoding style used by your service and method by setting the Use property of the appropriate SOAP message format attribute. The following example shows the previous `SoapDocumentMethod` attribute modified to use the `Encoded` message format.

```
[SoapDocumentMethod(
Action="http://ws.bostontechnical.com/AddDocument",
RequestNamespace="http://ws.bostontechnical.com",
ResponseNamespace="http://ws.bostontechnical.com",
Use=SoapBindingUse.Encoded)]
```

SOAP Interoperability

Dozens of SOAP implementations are on the market today. For a fairly comprehensive list of the SOAP toolkits available, check out the SOAP::Lite site (*http://www.soaplite.com/#Toolkits/*) maintained by Paul Kulchenko. You'll see that Microsoft .NET is only one of more than 80 SOAP toolkits offered by a variety of vendors and individuals. You've already learned that using the two widely used Microsoft SOAP implementations, .NET and the SOAP SDK v2.0, can lead to interoperability problems as a result of differences in the SOAP message format each uses. It should come as no surprise that interoperability between SOAP implementations from different vendors can be a significant problem as well.

Common SOAP Interoperability Issues

The majority of web service developers use SOAP toolkits like the one included with .NET to provide a more manageable layer of abstraction on top of the SOAP messaging framework. These toolkits are expected to take care of the communication details associated with SOAP communication by managing the creation and processing of SOAP envelopes. Of course, when different toolkits make different decisions about how to create and process these messages, problems can occur. Some of the more common interoperability issues seen with SOAP are:

- SOAP versions may be incompatible. While SOAP v1.1 is the current standard, many implementations are starting to add features being brought about in the Working Draft version 1.2 of SOAP.

- The SOAP specification describes two primary messaging formats: document/literal and RPC/encoded. Most recent toolkits support both approaches, but some do not. It's important to make sure that both the client and server use the same messaging format.

- The SOAP specification contains some ambiguous language that has spawned different but still orthodox implementations.

- SOAP relies on XML Schema to interpret XML data. For this reason, it's important that parties attempting to communicate successfully use the same revision of XML Schema. This is less of a problem these days, as the XML Schema specification is stable, but as XML Schema continues to evolve, this will no doubt continue to be a potential pitfall.

- When SOAP is used with HTTP as a transport, it requires the SOAPAction header. The value of this header must be enclosed in quotes. (This is a much more specific type of the issue than the others but has caused many problems.)

- SOAP supports Unicode characters; however, some toolkit implementations have had interoperability problems with Unicode representation.

A list of additional issues can be found at *http://www.xmethods.net/soapbuilders/ interop.html*. In addition, the majority of the SOAP toolkits available are version 1.0 products and suffer from the usual bugs found in new software. Fortunately, a great deal is being done to ensure that SOAP implementations are able to communicate properly. If you have interoperability problems with a specific vendor's implementation of SOAP, the first thing to do is check for documentation of known interoperability problems.

SOAP Builders

The vague sections of the SOAP specification made it clear early on that interoperability would be an issue. Recognizing that interoperability was critical to the success of SOAP and web services as an open distributed computing protocol, many of the early implementers formed a group aimed at identifying and resolving interoperability issues. The group's membership includes big-name companies like IBM and Microsoft as well as individuals and small organizations. Members communicate via the SOAPBuilders Yahoo Group (*http://groups.yahoo.com/group/soapbuilders/*). A review of the archives and associated bookmarks will provide you with the history and current state of SOAP interoperability testing. The group deals with SOAP as well as closely linked WSDL interoperability problems. The bookmarks area (*http:// groups.yahoo.com/group/soapbuilders/links/*) contains links to a variety of useful sites such as the following:

SOAPBuilders Testing Interfaces
  A specification for a service interface that SOAP implementers can publish in order to take part in interoperability testing

SOAPBuilders Interop Lab
  Lists of endpoints that implement the test interface

SOAP Interop Issues
  A collection of known SOAP interoperability issues and test results

The test results can be particularly useful when troubleshooting a SOAP interoperability problem.

The SOAP Interoperability Test

The SOAP interoperability test specification is a service definition that allows creators of SOAP implementations to test out their products. The good folks at

Xmethods have put together the specification, located at *http://www.xmethods.net/ soapbuilders/proposal.html*. The service consists of 11 methods, each of which returns a basic data type. The included methods are:

```
echoString
echoStringArray
echoInteger
echoIntegerArray
echoFloat
echoFloatArray
echoStruct
echoStructArray
echoVoid
echoBase64
echoDate
```

Example request and response messages for the echoString method are at *http:// www.xmethods.net/soapbuilders/proposal.html#echoString*. The service implementation does not require a WSDL document, but sample WSDL is available to make service creation easier for some toolkits.

The interoperability service tests the ability of a server to parse a client's SOAP envelope, deserialize the data type contained in the body, and return a valid response document that the client can also parse and deserialize. The results of tests against various platforms can be found at Jake's SOAP Journal (*http://jake.soapware.org/*).

To date, the interoperability test has been a major boon to the state of SOAP operability. Future plans for the test include adding the full set of data types supported in the recently approved XML Schema standard, as well as support for WSDL testing.

WSDL Interoperability

The .NET Framework does a great job of hiding the WSDL details from developers who don't want to be bothered by them. You can use either the Add a Web Reference function in Visual Studio .NET (as discussed in Chapter 3) or *wsdl.exe* (in conjunction with the compiler) to create proxy classes without knowing WSDL. (That is, until something goes wrong and the automatic creation fails.)

At the time of this writing, the current version of the WSDL specification is 1.1. This is the version supported with the *wsdl.exe* tool that is provided as part of Visual Studio .NET. It's important to realize that this tool and the Add a Web Reference feature of VS.NET work only with WSDL documents that follow version 1.1. Earlier versions, including SCL documents (a predecessor to WSDL), are not supported. This means that any WSDL document created with Beta 1 of the .NET Framework is not convertible using the current tools.

Since it's become common for SOAP toolkits to provide automatic WSDL generators, the problem of WSDL interoperability has become more manageable. As mentioned in the previous section, the same groups that manage SOAP interoperability testing manage WSDL testing as well.

HTTP Interoperability and M-Post

Most web service applications use SOAP over HTTP as a binding. HTTP is a mature technology but was never intended to be used in the manner in which the SOAP specification specifies. Specifically, SOAP data is passed in the HTTP header portion of the message using a special header called SOAPAction (see previous sections), which marks the message as SOAP. This header has a variety of additional uses, such as traffic content filtering.

In an effort to extend the ability of the HTTP protocol to support new headers (such as SOAPAction), a new Internet Draft has been created: the HTTP Extension Framework, which defines a mechanism for a new form of HTTP verb. The verb takes the form M-*XXXX*, where *XXXX* represents the name of a verb. Some clients have begun to support the M-POST mechanism, resulting in interoperability problems with servers that do not support it. For instance, by default, IIS is configured to map the *.aspx* file extension to allow only GET, HEAD, and POST. As a result, an IIS instance receiving an M-POST header returns a 403 error message. You can configure IIS to support arbitrary HTTP verbs (including M-POST) using the IIS MMC. Edit the properties of the site that you wish to modify and click the Configuration button on the Home directory tab. Here you can add M-POST to the list of HTTP verbs supported by *.aspx* files.

Known Interoperability Problems

As of this writing, several known interoperability issues have been identified between some of the more popular development toolkits. Fortunately, most vendors of these toolkits have been diligent about rectifying known problems; however, even if the problem is readily fixed, lengthy product development life cycles can delay fixes. In this section, we mention some of the more frequent interoperability problems currently plaguing the web service landscape as well as sites that provide more in-depth information.

Apache SOAP v2.2

Most developers know the Apache foundation for its popular open source web server, which (according to the Netcraft survey, at *http://www.netcraft.com/survey/*) is used by more than half of web sites in existence today. In addition, the Apache foundation supports numerous open source development toolkits, notably the Xerces

XML parser and the Apache SOAP implementation. The Apache SOAP project has its roots in the IBM SOAP Toolkit, whose source code was given to Apache by IBM. Details and links for these products are at *http://xml.apache.org*. Several interoperability issues currently exist with the Apache SOAP implementation.

SOAP level: SOAPAction header dispatch

A common use of the SOAPAction header is to route incoming (server-bound) SOAP messages to the target service that processes it. Apache SOAP does not support this use of the SOAPAction header, and instead uses the namespace URI of the SOAP body element (first child element), which can cause interoperability problems in clients that are unaware of this limitation.

XML level: byte order mark (BOM)

Most Apache SOAP implementations use the Xerces XML parser to parse incoming SOAP messages. One issue with the Xerces XML parser involves UTF-8 encoded SOAP requests (the default in .NET) that make use of a byte order mark that .NET does not insert by default. A byte order mark is a special set of characters that may be used to signify the beginning of a data stream. This problem should not occur with the built-in SOAP features of .NET, but it can be an issue if you circumvent the .NET capabilities in favor of a custom SOAP implementation.

SOAP level: xsi:type dependency

When using RPC-style SOAP, Apache SOAP requires that every SOAP envelope be self-describing in terms of types. This means that every typed value must be explicitly described using the xsi:type attribute:

```
<soap:Envelope xmlns:xsi="http://www.w3.org/2001/XMLSchema-instance" xmlns:xsd="http:
//www.w3.org/2001/XMLSchema" xmlns:soapenc="http://schemas.xmlsoap.org/soap/encoding/
" xmlns:tns="http://ws.bostontechnical.com/services" xmlns:types="http://ws.
bostontechnical.com/services/encodedTypes" xmlns:soap="http://schemas.xmlsoap.org/
soap/envelope/">
  <soap:Body soap:encodingStyle="http://schemas.xmlsoap.org/soap/encoding/">
    <tns:GetCircle>
      <i xsi:type="xsd:int">2</i>
    </tns:GetCircle>
  </soap:Body>
</soap:Envelope>
```

Issues can arise since use of xsi:type is not required by the SOAP spec—a problem with the current Apache SOAP implementation (v2.2), because it is not WSDL-aware; as a result it requires a workaround to function properly (available since v2.1) if self-describing type definitions are not included (see *http://xml.apache.org/soap/docs/guide/interop* for details). .NET automatically includes the self-describing type information, so this should not normally be a problem.

Additional potential issues

The Apache SOAP implementation suffers from the following additional potential problems:

No support for `MustUnderstand`
> The `MustUnderstand` header is ignored by the Apache SOAP implementation.

No header access via default provider
> The default RPC provider in Apache SOAP does not provide access to any headers in the SOAP envelope. As you've seen in earlier chapters, SOAP headers are very useful for things like authentication and session state, so this is a problem.

Full details about the current state of Apache SOAP interopability are at *http://xml.apache.org/soap/docs/guide/interop/*. In addition, a good article on integrating Apache SOAP and .NET XML web services is at *http://support.microsoft.com/directory/article.asp?id=q308466&sd=msdn*.

SOAP::Lite 0.51

The SOAP::Lite Toolkit is a popular SOAP implementation for Perl. This Perl module can be downloaded from the Comprehensive Perl Archive Network (CPAN) at *http://www.cpan.org/*. It requires Perl version 5.00503 or later.

Due to incompatibilities between the .NET WSDL automatic generator and the SOAP::Lite WSDL reader, creating SOAP::Lite clients for .NET web services requires some manual editing of the .NET WSDL. Specifically, the SOAP::Lite WSDL reader expects type information to be in a namespace called xsd rather than the default of s used by .NET.

The modification is simple: save the WSDL file that is automatically generated by .NET and then edit it with a text editor. Change this line:

```
xmlns:s="http://www.w3.org/2001/XMLSchema"
```

to the following:

```
xmlns:xsd=http://www.w3.org/2001/XMLSchema
```

Make sure that all references to the s shorthand in the WSDL document are changed to xsd instead. Remember that WSDL is case-sensitive.

It's also a good idea to remove all of the references to the HTTP GET and HTTP POST bindings. If you haven't already done this by modifying the *web.config* file, remember to remove the portTypes and service ports sections of the WSDL as well.

MS SOAP Toolkit v3.0

Before the release of .NET, chances are you used the Microsoft SOAP Toolkit to develop web services using ASP. This toolkit is essentially a COM component that encapsulates many of the common features needed to read and write SOAP. The toolkit includes:

- A high-level interface that hides the details of SOAP
- A low-level interface that gives knowledgeable programmers more control over SOAP messages
- Support for WSDL 1.1

In addition, the toolkit and associated samples are available as a free download from the Microsoft site. As one might expect of a Microsoft product, the SOAP Toolkit works well with the .NET implementation. One thing to note, however, is that the SOAP Toolkit defaults to using RPC-style SOAP, while .NET defaults to document/literal style. The reason for this choice is that the SOAP Toolkit is designed as a tool for leveraging existing COM components as a web service, making RPC-style SOAP a natural fit.

Maximizing Interoperability

Getting .NET web services to work with clients developed with other toolkits should be fairly straightforward. In most cases, you shouldn't have a problem; however, minor differences in implementations can cause hours of hair-pulling frustration. Here are some tips to design services for maximum interoperability:

Use RPC/encoded SOAP
> Some SOAP toolkits, notably Apache SOAP, have difficulty with the document/literal style of SOAP. To make your services as interoperable as possible, use RPC-style–encoded SOAP. As we've seen, this is very easy to implement using the SoapRpcService and SoapRpcMethod attributes as follows:
> ```
> [System.Web.Services.Protocols.SoapRpcService]
> public class Service1 : System.Web.Services.WebService
> ```

Avoid SOAP headers
> For all of their power and functionality, SOAP headers can be more trouble than they're worth. Some implementations have trouble with attributes such as Actor and MustUnderstand. Other implementations don't pass the header information to the application layer at all. Support for SOAP header attributes is improving but is still not as widespread as you might hope.

Disable non-SOAP bindings
> Simplifying the problem is often the best form of troubleshooting. If you don't plan to support HTTP GET and POST in your web services, remove them from the WSDL. By doing so, you'll also prevent problems that can arise from automatic proxy generators that don't understand non-SOAP bindings. Making this change in .NET is as easy as modifying your *web.config* file as follows:
> ```
> <webServices>
>     <protocols>
> ```

```
        <remove name="HttpPost" />
        <remove name="HttpGet" />
    </protocols>
</webServices>
```

This change prevents the HTTP GET and POST bindings from appearing in the automatically generated WSDL document.

Check for proper XML Schema

A common interoperability issue until late 2001 involved XML Schema versions. Some implementations, notably Apache SOAP and the IBM Web Service Toolkit 2.4.1, used an older version of the XML Schema that caused problems between implementations (such as .NET) that used the 2001 version. Make sure the client and service use the same version—probably the 2001 version, available at *http://www.w3.org/2001/XMLSchema/*.

Additional interoperability issues

As interoperability issues continue to surface, your best weapon is a healthy set of browser bookmarks. Sites like the Microsoft support page (*http://support.microsoft.com*), the VS.NET beta test site (*http://beta.visualstudio.net*), the ASPNG mailing lists (*http://aspng.com*) maintained by Charles Carroll, and others can prove to be your best resources.

Namespace Quick Reference

The System.Web.Services Namespace

The System.Web.Services namespace is the starting point for creating web services. It contains a WebService class that custom web services can inherit from in order to gain access to ASP.NET intrinsics and the WebMethodAttribute and WebServiceAttribute, which are used to mark web service classes and methods and add additional information. Most of the types in other web service namespaces are used seamlessly by the .NET Framework and are not used directly by the .NET programmer.

WebMethodAttribute

System.Web.Services (system.web.services.dll)   sealed class

Use the WebMethodAttribute to mark all the methods that should be made available to web service clients. All methods marked with this attribute will be automatically accessible and will be included in the WSDL document that .NET generates (and the proxy class). Methods that are not marked with this attribute will not be visible or usable, even if they are public.

You can set various properties when you use this attribute. For example, the Description property is used to add a string of information about a web method that is used by the automatically generated WSDL description document and the Internet Explorer test page. CacheDuration specifies (in seconds) how long a response will be cached and reused for web method requests with identical parameter values. (For detailed information about caching, refer to Chapter 7.) EnableSession allows you to configure whether session support is enabled for your web method. (For detailed information about using session state, refer to Chapter 5.) By default, a web service method will not be cached at all, and session support will not be enabled.

The MessageName property is used to add an alias to a method. This is most commonly used with polymorphic (overloaded) methods, which must be given unique names, or "disambiguated" before you can use them as web methods. When adding overloaded methods, the original method should retain its name for compatibility with existing clients.

The TransactionOption property allows a web method to take part in a COM+ transaction. Due to the stateless nature of the HTTP protocol, web service methods can only participate as the root object in a transaction. This means that both System.EnterpriseServices.TransactionOption. RequiresNew and System.EnterpriseServices.TransactionOption.Required will have the same effect, causing the web method to start a new transaction when it is invoked. Other COM objects that require transactions can then be created and used by the web method. A transaction started in this way is automatically committed when the method ends, unless the method explicitly calls System.EnterpriseServices.ContextUtil.SetAbort() or an unhandled exception occurs.

To set a property of the WebMethodAttribute, specify it by name in the attribute declaration (as in [WebMethod(EnableSession = true)]).

```
public sealed class WebMethodAttribute : Attribute {
// Public Constructors
   public WebMethodAttribute();
   public WebMethodAttribute(bool enableSession);
   public WebMethodAttribute(bool enableSession, System.EnterpriseServices.TransactionOption transactionOption);
   public WebMethodAttribute(bool enableSession, System.EnterpriseServices.TransactionOption transactionOption, int cacheDuration);
   public WebMethodAttribute(bool enableSession, System.EnterpriseServices.TransactionOption transactionOption, int cacheDuration,
                             bool bufferResponse);
// Public Instance Properties
   public bool BufferResponse{set; get; }
   public int CacheDuration{set; get; }
   public string Description{set; get; }
   public bool EnableSession{set; get; }
   public string MessageName{set; get; }
   public TransactionOption TransactionOption{set; get; }
}
```

Hierarchy   System.Object→ System.Attribute→ WebMethodAttribute

Valid On   Method

WebService   disposable

System.Web.Services (system.web.services.dll)   class

When creating a web service, you can inherit from this class to gain access to the built-in ASP.NET objects Application (the current System.Web.HttpApplicationState collection), Server, Session, User, and Context (which provides access to the built-in Request and Response objects). If you don't need to access these objects (or you choose to go through the System.Web.HttpContext. Context property), you don't need to derive your web service from this class.

When creating a web service class, all web methods must be marked with the WebMethodAttribute. You should also add the WebServiceAttribute to the class declaration to configure additional properties.

```
public class WebService : System.ComponentModel.MarshalByValueComponent {
// Public Constructors
   public WebService();
```

```
// Public Instance Properties
  public HttpApplicationState Application{get; }
  public HttpContext Context{get; }
  public HttpServerUtility Server{get; }
  public HttpSessionState Session{get; }
  public IPrincipal User{get; }
}
```

Hierarchy   System.Object→System.ComponentModel.MarshalByValueComponent(System.Component-
                   Model.IComponent, System.IDisposable, System.IServiceProvider)→WebService

WebServiceAttribute

System.Web.Services (system.web.services.dll)   sealed class

This attribute is not required to create a web service, but it should be used before a web service is deployed to specify a unique XML namespace and allow clients to distinguish your web service from others on the Web. By default, if you do not use this attribute, the default namespace http://tempuri.org/ is used. XML namespaces look like URLs, but they do not actually need to correspond to valid locations on the Web. In a web service, the XML namespace is used to uniquely identify parts of the Service Description (WSDL) file that specifically pertain to the web service. The Name property identifies the local portion of the XML-qualified name, which will be the web service class name by default. Elements of the WSDL contract that are specific to WSDL use the http://schemas.xmlsoap.org/wsdl/ namespace.

Ideally, you should use a namespace that you control, such as your company's web site address. This XML namespace should not be confused with the .NET namespace used programmatically by clients. For more information on XML qualified names, see *http://www.w3.org/TR/REC-xml-names/*.

You can also set a Description property, which contains information about your web service that will be displayed in automatically generated description documents and the Internet Explorer test page.

```
public sealed class WebServiceAttribute : Attribute {
// Public Constructors
  public WebServiceAttribute();
// Public Static Fields
  public const field string DefaultNamespace;                          // =http://tempuri.org/
// Public Instance Properties
  public string Description{set; get; }
  public string Name{set; get; }
  public string Namespace{set; get; }
}
```

Hierarchy   System.Object→System.Attribute→WebServiceAttribute

Valid On   Class

WebServiceBindingAttribute

System.Web.Services (system.web.services.dll)   sealed class

This attribute is used to mark the class declaration of the proxy class that allows communication between a client and a web service. It defines a WSDL (Web Service Description Language) binding. The Name and the Namespace properties must be set to the name and XML namespace of the web service. An example is [WebServiceBinding(Name = "StockQuote", Namespace = "http://www.mysite.com/MyServices")]. These properties match the corresponding properties in the WebServiceAttribute.

Note that you must also use a System.Web.Services.Protocols.SoapDocumentMethodAttribute or System.Web. Services.Protocols.SoapRpcMethodAttribute to describe the binding for each individual web service method represented in the proxy class. This code is generated automatically in the proxy class by adding a Visual Studio .NET web reference or using the *WSDL.exe* utility included with ASP.NET.

```
public sealed class WebServiceBindingAttribute : Attribute {
// Public Constructors
   public WebServiceBindingAttribute();
   public WebServiceBindingAttribute(string name);
   public WebServiceBindingAttribute(string name, string ns);
   public WebServiceBindingAttribute(string name, string ns, string location);
// Public Instance Properties
   public string Location{set; get; }
   public string Name{set; get; }
   public string Namespace{set; get; }
}
```

Hierarchy   System.Object→ System.Attribute→ WebServiceBindingAttribute

Valid On   Class

The System.Web.Services.Protocols Namespace

The System.Web.Services.Protocols namespace contains types used to support communication between a client and a web service. These types define the protocols used to encode and transmit data across an Internet connection, including HTTP GET, HTTP POST, and SOAP.

The primary use of these types is to support the proxy class that manages the communication between web service and client. You can create this proxy class automatically using the Visual Studio .NET IDE or the *WSDL.exe* command-line utility, or you can code it by hand. This class will inherit from HttpGetClientProtocol, HttpPostClientProtocol, or SoapHttpClientProtocol (which is the most common choice, and the default for automatically generated proxy classes). Other important types in this namespace include the attributes that you use to set the encoding for SOAP request and response messages, such as SoapDocumentMethodAttribute.

This class also provides types you can use to create SOAP extensions. Typically, SOAP extensions are used to directly access the SOAP messages exchanged between web services and clients, before they are sent or deserialized into objects. The SoapExtension class and SoapExtensionAttribute are the basic building blocks for SOAP extensions. You can also use SoapHeader and SoapHeaderAttribute classes to create custom SOAP headers for your message. You can then create web service methods that require specific custom SOAP headers.

AnyReturnReader

System.Web.Services.Protocols (system.web.services.dll)   class

This class supports the .NET Framework infrastructure. You do not need to use it directly in your code.

```
public class AnyReturnReader : MimeReturnReader {
// Public Constructors
  public AnyReturnReader();
// Public Instance Methods
  public override method object GetInitializer(LogicalMethodInfo methodInfo);        // overrides MimeFormatter
  public override method void Initialize(object o);                                  // overrides MimeFormatter
  public override method object Read(System.Net.WebResponse response,
                        System.IO.Stream responseStream);                            // overrides MimeReturnReader
}
```

Hierarchy   System.Object→ MimeFormatter→ MimeReturnReader→ AnyReturnReader

HtmlFormParameterReader

System.Web.Services.Protocols (system.web.services.dll)   class

This class supports the .NET Framework infrastructure. You do not need to use it directly in your code.

```
public class HtmlFormParameterReader : ValueCollectionParameterReader {
// Public Constructors
  public HtmlFormParameterReader();
// Public Instance Methods
  public override method object[] Read(System.Web.HttpRequest request);             // overrides MimeParameterReader
}
```

Hierarchy   System.Object→ MimeFormatter→ MimeParameterReader→ ValueCollectionParameter-
                       Reader→ HtmlFormParameterReader

HtmlFormParameterWriter

System.Web.Services.Protocols (system.web.services.dll)   class

This class supports the .NET Framework infrastructure. You do not need to use it directly in your code.

```
public class HtmlFormParameterWriter : UrlEncodedParameterWriter {
// Public Constructors
  public HtmlFormParameterWriter();
// Public Instance Properties
  public override field bool UsesWriteRequest{get; }                                    // overrides MimeParameterWriter
// Public Instance Methods
  public override method void InitializeRequest(System.Net.WebRequest request, object[] values);    // overrides MimeParameterWriter
  public override method void WriteRequest(System.IO.Stream requestStream, object[] values);        // overrides MimeParameterWriter
}
```

Hierarchy   System.Object→MimeFormatter→MimeParameterWriter→UrlEncodedParameterWriter→ HtmlFormParameterWriter

HttpGetClientProtocol   marshal by reference, disposable

System.Web.Services.Protocols (system.web.services.dll)   class

You can inherit from this class to create a proxy class that communicates using the HTTP GET protocol, which sends parameters in the query string portion of the URL. When using this class, you must use the corresponding HttpMethodAttribute to bind proxy class methods to web service methods.

```
public class HttpGetClientProtocol : HttpSimpleClientProtocol {
// Public Constructors
  public HttpGetClientProtocol();
// Protected Instance Methods
  protected override method WebRequest GetWebRequest(Uri uri);                           // overrides HttpWebClientProtocol
}
```

Hierarchy   System.Object→System.MarshalByRefObject→System.ComponentModel.Component(System. ComponentModel.IComponent, System.IDisposable)→WebClientProtocol→HttpWebClientProto- col→HttpSimpleClientProtocol→HttpGetClientProtocol

HttpMethodAttribute

System.Web.Services.Protocols (system.web.services.dll)   sealed class

This attribute is used to bind methods in an HttpGetClientProtocol or HttpPostClientProtocol proxy class to web service methods.

The ParameterFormatter property specifies how the proxy encodes parameters before sending them to a web service method. The ReturnFormatter property specifies how the proxy class decodes the web method's return value. Both of these values must be set, as there is no default value. Set ReturnFormatter to the UrlParameterWriter type if you are using HTTP GET, or the HtmlFormParameterWriter type if you are using HTTP POST. Always set ParameterFormatter to the XmlReturnReader type. An example attribute declaration for HTTP GET is [HttpMethodAttribute(typeof(XmlReturnReader), typeof(UrlParameterWriter))].

```
public sealed class HttpMethodAttribute : Attribute {
// Public Constructors
  public HttpMethodAttribute();
  public HttpMethodAttribute(Type returnFormatter, Type parameterFormatter);
// Public Instance Properties
  public Type ParameterFormatter{set; get; }
  public Type ReturnFormatter{set; get; }
}
```

Hierarchy System.Object→ System.Attribute→ HttpMethodAttribute

Valid On Method

HttpPostClientProtocol

marshal by reference, disposable

System.Web.Services.Protocols (system.web.services.dll)   class

You can inherit from this class to create a proxy class that communicates using the HTTP POST protocol, which encodes parameters in the body of the HTTP request. When using this class, you must use the corresponding HttpMethodAttribute to bind proxy class methods to web service methods.

```
public class HttpPostClientProtocol : HttpSimpleClientProtocol {
// Public Constructors
  public HttpPostClientProtocol();
// Protected Instance Methods
  protected override method WebRequest GetWebRequest(Uri uri);              // overrides HttpWebClientProtocol
}
```

Hierarchy System.Object→ System.MarshalByRefObject→ System.ComponentModel.Component(System.
ComponentModel.IComponent, System.IDisposable)→ WebClientProtocol→ HttpWebClientProto-
col→ HttpSimpleClientProtocol→ HttpPostClientProtocol

HttpSimpleClientProtocol

marshal by reference, disposable

System.Web.Services.Protocols (system.web.services.dll)   abstract class

This abstract class provides basic functionality for communicating with a web service over HTTP. This class is inherited by HttpGetClientProtocol and HttpPostClientProtocol, both of which your proxy classes can derive from directly. Parameters for an HTTP proxy are encoded using application/x-www-form-urlencoded content type.

```
public abstract class HttpSimpleClientProtocol : HttpWebClientProtocol {
// Protected Constructors
  protected method HttpSimpleClientProtocol();
// Protected Instance Methods
  protected method IAsyncResult BeginInvoke(string methodName, string requestUrl, object[] parameters, AsyncCallback callback,
                          object asyncState);
```

```
      protected method object EndInvoke(IAsyncResult asyncResult);
      protected method object Invoke(string methodName, string requestUrl, object[] parameters);
}
```

Hierarchy   System.Object→ System.MarshalByRefObject→ System.ComponentModel.Component(System.
ComponentModel.IComponent, System.IDisposable)→ WebClientProtocol→ HttpWebClientProto-
col→ HttpSimpleClientProtocol

HttpWebClientProtocol   marshal by reference, disposable

System.Web.Services.Protocols (system.web.services.dll)   abstract class

This abstract base class provides basic functionality for communication between a web
service and proxy class. The System.Web.Services.Discovery.DiscoveryClientProtocol, HttpSimpleClientProtocol,
and SoapHttpClientProtocol class all inherit from HttpWebClientProtocol. The proxy class inherits from
one of these derived classes, depending on which transmission protocol it is using.

You can use the Proxy property to connect to a web service through a firewall, as in ws.Proxy =
new WebProxy("http://proxyserver:80", true);. This property will override the computer's default
Internet settings. You can also set the AllowAutoRedirect property to allow a client to follow
server redirects. This is false by default for security reasons. The UserAgent property is automatically set to something like "MS web services Client Protocol 1.0.2509.0," where 1.0.
2509.0 is the Common Language Runtime version.

The CookieContainer property is important when connecting to a web service that uses ASP.
NET's session state facility. In order to allow a proxy class to reuse the same session on
subsequent calls, you must explicitly create a new (empty) System.Net.CookieContainer object,
and assign it to the CookieContainer property. This allows the proxy class to store the session
cookie with each call. If you want multiple proxy class instances to access the same session,
or if you want to re-create a proxy class and use a previous session that has not yet timed
out, you must take extra steps to transfer or store the System.Net.CookieContainer object.

```
public abstract class HttpWebClientProtocol : WebClientProtocol {
// Protected Constructors
  protected method HttpWebClientProtocol();
// Public Instance Properties
  public bool AllowAutoRedirect{set; get; }
  public X509CertificateCollection ClientCertificates{get; }
  public CookieContainer CookieContainer{set; get; }
  public IWebProxy Proxy{set; get; }
  public string UserAgent{set; get; }
// Protected Instance Methods
  protected override method WebRequest GetWebRequest(Uri uri);                    // overrides WebClientProtocol
  protected override method WebResponse GetWebResponse(System.Net.WebRequest request);    // overrides WebClientProtocol
  protected override method WebResponse GetWebResponse(System.Net.WebRequest request,
                                       IAsyncResult result);                     // overrides WebClientProtocol
}
```

Hierarchy   System.Object→ System.MarshalByRefObject→ System.ComponentModel.Component(System.
ComponentModel.IComponent, System.IDisposable)→ WebClientProtocol→
HttpWebClientProtocol

LogicalMethodInfo

System.Web.Services.Protocols (system.web.services.dll)   sealed class

A LogicalMethodInfo object is provided to the SoapExtension.GetInitializer() method. This object contains information about the web service or proxy class method where the custom SoapExtensionAttribute is applied.

```
public sealed class LogicalMethodInfo {
// Public Constructors
    public LogicalMethodInfo(System.Reflection.MethodInfo methodInfo);
// Public Instance Properties
    public ParameterInfo AsyncCallbackParameter{get; }
    public ParameterInfo AsyncResultParameter{get; }
    public ParameterInfo AsyncStateParameter{get; }
    public MethodInfo BeginMethodInfo{get; }
    public ICustomAttributeProvider CustomAttributeProvider{get; }
    public Type DeclaringType{get; }
    public MethodInfo EndMethodInfo{get; }
    public ParameterInfo[] InParameters{get; }
    public bool IsAsync{get; }
    public bool IsVoid{get; }
    public MethodInfo MethodInfo{get; }
    public string Name{get; }
    public ParameterInfo[] OutParameters{get; }
    public ParameterInfo[] Parameters{get; }
    public Type ReturnType{get; }
    public ICustomAttributeProvider ReturnTypeCustomAttributeProvider{get; }
// Public Static Methods
    public static method LogicalMethodInfo[] Create(System.Reflection.MethodInfo[] methodInfos);
    public static method LogicalMethodInfo[] Create(System.Reflection.MethodInfo[] methodInfos, LogicalMethodTypes types);
    public static method bool IsBeginMethod(System.Reflection.MethodInfo methodInfo);
    public static method bool IsEndMethod(System.Reflection.MethodInfo methodInfo);
// Public Instance Methods
    public IAsyncResult BeginInvoke(object target, object[] values, AsyncCallback callback, object asyncState);
    public object[] EndInvoke(object target, IAsyncResult asyncResult);
    public object GetCustomAttribute(Type type);
    public object[] GetCustomAttributes(Type type);
    public object[] Invoke(object target, object[] values);
    public override method string ToString();                                  // overrides object
}
```

LogicalMethodTypes   serializable

System.Web.Services.Protocols (system.web.services.dll)   enum

This enumeration specifies whether a web service method was invoked synchronously, or asynchronously with the corresponding Begin method.

```
public enum LogicalMethodTypes {
  Sync = 1,
  Async = 2
}
```

Hierarchy   System.Object→ System.ValueType→ System.Enum(System.IComparable, System.IFormattable,
                     System.IConvertible)→ LogicalMethodTypes

MatchAttribute

System.Web.Services.Protocols (system.web.services.dll)   sealed class

.NET allows you to create screen scraping web services that search the HTML content on a
web page using a regular expression. To create a pattern-matching web service, you need to
create a WSDL document with <match> elements. These elements specify the regular
expression to use when parsing the contents of the page, and how many matches should be
returned. When the client builds the proxy class for a pattern-matching web service, it will
include a MatchAttribute that describes the match elements you added to the WSDL
document.

The Pattern property specifies the regular expression pattern to use when searching the web
page. IgnoreCase specifies whether the regular expression should be run in case-sensitive
mode (the default). MaxRepeats specifies the maximum number of matches that will be
returned (-1, the default, indicates all). Finally, Group specifies a grouping of related matches,
while Capture specifies the index of a match within a group.

```
public sealed class MatchAttribute : Attribute {
// Public Constructors
  public MatchAttribute(string pattern);
// Public Instance Properties
  public int Capture{set; get; }
  public int Group{set; get; }
  public bool IgnoreCase{set; get; }
  public int MaxRepeats{set; get; }
  public string Pattern{set; get; }
}
```

Hierarchy   System.Object→ System.Attribute→ MatchAttribute

Valid On   All

MimeFormatter

System.Web.Services.Protocols (system.web.services.dll)   abstract class

This class supports the .NET Framework infrastructure. You do not need to use it directly
in your code.

```
public abstract class MimeFormatter {
// Protected Constructors
  protected method MimeFormatter();
// Public Static Methods
  public static method MimeFormatter CreateInstance(Type type, object initializer);
  public static method object GetInitializer(Type type, LogicalMethodInfo methodInfo);
  public static method object[] GetInitializers(Type type, LogicalMethodInfo[] methodInfos);
// Public Instance Methods
  public abstract method object GetInitializer(LogicalMethodInfo methodInfo);
  public virtual method object[] GetInitializers(LogicalMethodInfo[] methodInfos);
  public abstract method void Initialize(object initializer);
}
```

MimeParameterReader

System.Web.Services.Protocols (system.web.services.dll)   abstract class

This class supports the .NET Framework infrastructure. You do not need to use it directly in your code.

```
public abstract class MimeParameterReader : MimeFormatter {
// Protected Constructors
  protected method MimeParameterReader();
// Public Instance Methods
  public abstract method object[] Read(System.Web.HttpRequest request);
}
```

Hierarchy   System.Object→MimeFormatter→MimeParameterReader

MimeParameterWriter

System.Web.Services.Protocols (system.web.services.dll)   abstract class

This class supports the .NET Framework infrastructure. You do not need to use it directly in your code.

```
public abstract class MimeParameterWriter : MimeFormatter {
// Protected Constructors
  protected method MimeParameterWriter();
// Public Instance Properties
  public virtual field Encoding RequestEncoding{set; get; }
  public virtual field bool UsesWriteRequest{get; }
// Public Instance Methods
  public virtual method string GetRequestUrl(string url, object[] parameters);
  public virtual method void InitializeRequest(System.Net.WebRequest request, object[] values);
  public virtual method void WriteRequest(System.IO.Stream requestStream, object[] values);
}
```

Hierarchy   System.Object→MimeFormatter→MimeParameterWriter

MimeReturnReader

System.Web.Services.Protocols (system.web.services.dll)   abstract class

This class supports the .NET Framework infrastructure. You do not need to use it directly in your code.

```
public abstract class MimeReturnReader : MimeFormatter {
// Protected Constructors
  protected method MimeReturnReader();
// Public Instance Methods
  public abstract method object Read(System.Net.WebResponse response, System.IO.Stream responseStream);
}
```

Hierarchy   System.Object→ MimeFormatter→ MimeReturnReader

NopReturnReader

System.Web.Services.Protocols (system.web.services.dll)   class

This class supports the .NET Framework infrastructure. You do not need to use it directly in your code.

```
public class NopReturnReader : MimeReturnReader {
// Public Constructors
  public NopReturnReader();
// Public Instance Methods
  public override method object GetInitializer(LogicalMethodInfo methodInfo);       // overrides MimeFormatter
  public override method void Initialize(object initializer);                        // overrides MimeFormatter
  public override method object Read(System.Net.WebResponse response,
                          System.IO.Stream responseStream);                   // overrides MimeReturnReader
}
```

Hierarchy   System.Object→ MimeFormatter→ MimeReturnReader→ NopReturnReader

PatternMatcher

System.Web.Services.Protocols (system.web.services.dll)   sealed class

This class supports the .NET Framework infrastructure. You do not need to use it directly in your code.

```
public sealed class PatternMatcher {
// Public Constructors
  public PatternMatcher(Type type);
// Public Instance Methods
  public object Match(string text);
}
```

SoapClientMessage

System.Web.Services.Protocols (system.web.services.dll)   sealed class

This class represents a SOAP request sent by a proxy client or SOAP response received by a proxy client. It inherits from SoapMessage, which defines most of the functionality used for SOAP messages.

```
public sealed class SoapClientMessage : SoapMessage {
// Public Instance Properties
   public override field string Action{get; }                              // overrides SoapMessage
   public SoapHttpClientProtocol Client{get; }
   public override field LogicalMethodInfo MethodInfo{get; }               // overrides SoapMessage
   public override field bool OneWay{get; }                                // overrides SoapMessage
   public override field string Url{get; }                                 // overrides SoapMessage
// Protected Instance Methods
   protected override method void EnsureInStage();                         // overrides SoapMessage
   protected override method void EnsureOutStage();                        // overrides SoapMessage
}
```

Hierarchy   System.Object→ SoapMessage→ SoapClientMessage

SoapDocumentMethodAttribute

System.Web.Services.Protocols (system.web.services.dll)   sealed class

This attribute is used to specify the encoding for SOAP request and response messages. You can apply this attribute to methods in a web service or in methods in a proxy class that derives from SoapHttpClientProtocol (where it's required to bind the messages to the appropriate web method). You use this attribute, instead of SoapRpcMethodAttribute, when you want to use the Document encoding standard.

There are two options for encoding XML information in a SOAP message: RPC and Document. ASP.NET's default is Document. The Document style specifies that messages are encoded as described in an XSD Schema. When Document style is used, the WSDL document defines the XSD Schemas for SOAP requests and SOAP responses. For more information on the SOAP specification, see *http://www.w3.org/TR/SOAP/* (or see Chapter 4 for more information about SOAP encoding).

One reason you might want to apply this attribute to a web method is to explicitly set the OneWay property. For example, by adding [SoapDocumentMethod(OneWay = true)] before a web method, you ensure that the method will return immediately and can finish processing asynchronously. This ensures that the client doesn't need to wait for the method to return or call it asynchronously. However, this web method will not be able to access the System. Web.HttpContext for the client and will not be able to set a return value. If the client needs to know about the success or result of such a web method, you will have to implement a second method and use some type of ticket-issuing system to keep track of the outstanding request.

```
public sealed class SoapDocumentMethodAttribute : Attribute {
// Public Constructors
  public SoapDocumentMethodAttribute();
  public SoapDocumentMethodAttribute(string action);
// Public Instance Properties
  public string Action{set; get; }
  public string Binding{set; get; }
  public bool OneWay{set; get; }
  public SoapParameterStyle ParameterStyle{set; get; }
  public string RequestElementName{set; get; }
  public string RequestNamespace{set; get; }
  public string ResponseElementName{set; get; }
  public string ResponseNamespace{set; get; }
  public SoapBindingUse Use{set; get; }
}
```

Hierarchy   System.Object→ System.Attribute→ SoapDocumentMethodAttribute

Valid On   Method

SoapDocumentServiceAttribute

System.Web.Services.Protocols (system.web.services.dll)   **sealed class**

This attribute can be applied to a web service's class declaration. It specifies that the default encoding for SOAP request and response messages will be Document. The client can override this default by using the SoapRpcMethodAttribute. This attribute is rarely used, because the default in ASP.NET proxy classes is already Document encoding.

```
public sealed class SoapDocumentServiceAttribute : Attribute {
// Public Constructors
  public SoapDocumentServiceAttribute();
  public SoapDocumentServiceAttribute(System.Web.Services.Description.SoapBindingUse use);
  public SoapDocumentServiceAttribute(System.Web.Services.Description.SoapBindingUse use, SoapParameterStyle paramStyle);
// Public Instance Properties
  public SoapParameterStyle ParameterStyle{set; get; }
  public SoapServiceRoutingStyle RoutingStyle{set; get; }
  public SoapBindingUse Use{set; get; }
}
```

Hierarchy   System.Object→ System.Attribute→ SoapDocumentServiceAttribute

Valid On   Class

SoapException

System.Web.Services.Protocols (system.web.services.dll)   **class**

This is a generic exception for SOAP-related problems. The Common Language Runtime can throw a SoapException when it encounters an incorrectly formatted SOAP message. Also, any error that occurs inside a web service method is caught on the server and returned to the client as a SoapException. ASP.NET will then automatically set the SoapException property (which identifies the web service URL) and the Code property (using one of the fault code fields).

When you are creating your own web methods, you may need to provide more information about exceptions. To do so, catch any server errors and create and throw a corresponding SoapException object. You can specify application-specific details about the error by adding custom XML content to the Detail property. Chapter 8 presents a full example of this technique.

```
public class SoapException : SystemException {
// Public Constructors
    public SoapException(string message, System.Xml.XmlQualifiedName code);
    public SoapException(string message, System.Xml.XmlQualifiedName code, Exception innerException);
    public SoapException(string message, System.Xml.XmlQualifiedName code, string actor);
    public SoapException(string message, System.Xml.XmlQualifiedName code, string actor, Exception innerException);
    public SoapException(string message, System.Xml.XmlQualifiedName code, string actor, System.Xml.XmlNode detail);
    public SoapException(string message, System.Xml.XmlQualifiedName code, string actor, System.Xml.XmlNode detail,
                Exception innerException);
// Public Static Fields
    public static readonly field XmlQualifiedName ClientFaultCode;          // =http://schemas.xmlsoap.org/soap/envelope/:Client
    public static readonly field XmlQualifiedName DetailElementName;        // =detail
    public static readonly field XmlQualifiedName MustUnderstandFaultCode;  // =http://schemas.xmlsoap.org/
                                                                            //  soap/envelope/:MustUnderstand
    public static readonly field XmlQualifiedName ServerFaultCode;          // =http://schemas.xmlsoap.org/soap/envelope/:Server
    public static readonly field XmlQualifiedName VersionMismatchFaultCode; // =http://schemas.xmlsoap.org/
                                                                            //  soap/envelope/:VersionMismatch
// Public Instance Properties
    public string Actor{get; }
    public XmlQualifiedName Code{get; }
    public XmlNode Detail{get; }
}
```

Hierarchy   System.Object→ System.Exception(System.Runtime.Serialization.ISerializable)→ System.SystemException→ SoapException

SoapExtension

System.Web.Services.Protocols (system.web.services.dll)   abstract class

You can inherit from this class to create a custom SOAP extension, which allows you to access and manipulate SOAP messages before they are sent or converted into objects. SOAP extensions can be used to implement additional encryption, compression, or tracing. They can be applied to web services or web service clients. Chapter 8 presents a full example of a SOAP extension that can be used for tracing.

The key to using a derived SoapExtension class is overriding the ProcessMessage() method. This method is called automatically by the ASP.NET Framework at several different SoapMessageStages and provides you with the current SoapMessage object. You also connect your SoapExtension to a proxy class or web service method using a custom SoapExtensionAttribute.

You can initialize a SoapExtension with a constructor method and the Initialize() and GetInitializer() methods. The GetInitializer() method is called only once, the first time a SOAP request is made. It gives you the opportunity to retrieve information about the web service or proxy method (in the methodInfo parameter) and custom SoapExtensionAttribute, and return an appropriate initialization object. This object will be cached and provided to the Initialize() method, which is called every time a SOAP request is made.

```
public abstract class SoapExtension {
// Protected Constructors
  protected method SoapExtension();
// Public Instance Methods
  public virtual method Stream ChainStream(System.IO.Stream stream);
  public abstract method object GetInitializer(LogicalMethodInfo methodInfo, SoapExtensionAttribute attribute);
  public abstract method object GetInitializer(Type serviceType);
  public abstract method void Initialize(object initializer);
  public abstract method void ProcessMessage(SoapMessage message);
}
```

SoapExtensionAttribute

System.Web.Services.Protocols (system.web.services.dll)   abstract class

When using a SoapExtension, you must also derive a custom SoapExtensionAttribute. This attribute is used to "connect" methods in your web service or proxy class to the corresponding extension.

When creating a custom SoapExtensionAttribute, you need to override only the ExtensionType property so that it returns the type of your custom SoapExtension class. You can then use your custom attribute to mark methods in your web service or proxy class. ASP.NET will automatically use the specified SoapExtension when the associated method is invoked.

```
public abstract class SoapExtensionAttribute : Attribute {
// Protected Constructors
  protected method SoapExtensionAttribute();
// Public Instance Properties
  public abstract field Type ExtensionType{get; }
  public abstract field int Priority{set; get; }
}
```

Hierarchy   System.Object→ System.Attribute→ SoapExtensionAttribute

Valid On   All

SoapHeader

System.Web.Services.Protocols (system.web.services.dll)   abstract class

This class allows you to create custom SOAP headers, which are used to send additional information to or from a web service. For example, rather than require an extra security parameter to authenticate every web service method, you could use a custom SoapHeader.

The client could then set a simple property of the proxy class, and the header would be sent automatically with every web method request.

To use a custom SoapHeader, create a class that inherits from SoapHeader and add the member variables you need to contain additional information (in this case, some sort of security credentials). When invoking a method, instantiate your custom SoapHeader, set its properties accordingly, and send it to the web service or proxy class. The web service must provide a member variable to receive the SoapHeader and must indicate which methods will process the custom header. It marks these methods with a SoapHeaderAttribute.

The Actor property is specified by the SOAP standard, and should be set to the URL of the web service. If you set the MustUnderstand property to true, the method in the class receiving the message must set the DidUnderstand property to true, or a SoapHeaderException will be thrown. Note that ASP.NET automatically defaults MustUnderstand to true, and it also automatically defaults DidUnderstand to true as long as the recipient (for example, the web service) contains the custom header class definition. The only time DidUnderstand will not be automatically set to true is when you are explicitly retrieving unknown SOAP headers.

```
public abstract class SoapHeader {
// Protected Constructors
   protected method SoapHeader();
// Public Instance Properties
   public string Actor{set; get; }
   public bool DidUnderstand{set; get; }
   public string EncodedMustUnderstand{set; get; }
   public bool MustUnderstand{set; get; }
}
```

SoapHeaderAttribute

System.Web.Services.Protocols (system.web.services.dll)   sealed class

This attribute is used to receive a custom SoapHeader. Before you can use this attribute, you need to add a member variable of the appropriate SoapHeader type to your web service or proxy class (for example, public MyCustomHeader receivedHeader;). Before invoking a method, the client will set this member to the appropriate header object. You must also add a SoapHeaderAttribute to each method that wants to process the custom header. This declaration specifies the class member that received the custom header object, as in [SoapHeader(MemberName = "ReceivedHeader")].

If a method will process more than one SoapHeader, just add multiple SoapHeaderAttribute declarations. You can also receive all the headers that are not defined in the web service by creating a member array of SoapUnknownHeader objects and using it in the SoapHeaderAttribute declaration.

```
public sealed class SoapHeaderAttribute : Attribute {
// Public Constructors
   public SoapHeaderAttribute(string memberName);
// Public Instance Properties
```

```
  public SoapHeaderDirection Direction{set; get; }
  public string MemberName{set; get; }
  public bool Required{set; get; }
}
```

Hierarchy   System.Object→ System.Attribute→ SoapHeaderAttribute

Valid On   Method

SoapHeaderCollection

System.Web.Services.Protocols (system.web.services.dll)   class

This class contains a collection of SoapHeader objects. It is used for the SoapMessage.Headers property, which contains all the headers in a single SOAP request or response message.

```
public class SoapHeaderCollection : CollectionBase {
// Public Constructors
  public SoapHeaderCollection();
// Public Instance Properties
  public SoapHeader this{set; get; }
// Public Instance Methods
  public int Add(SoapHeader header);
  public bool Contains(SoapHeader header);
  public void CopyTo(SoapHeader[] array, int index);
  public int IndexOf(SoapHeader header);
  public void Insert(int index, SoapHeader header);
  public void Remove(SoapHeader header);
}
```

Hierarchy   System.Object→ System.Collections.CollectionBase(System.Collections.IList, System.Collections.
                   ICollection, System.Collections.IEnumerable)→ SoapHeaderCollection

SoapHeaderDirection   serializable, flag

System.Web.Services.Protocols (system.web.services.dll)   enum

This enumeration is used to set the SoapHeaderAttribute.Direction property. The direction is relative to the receiving method where the attribute is placed. A value of InOut on a web method specifies that the SoapHeader is sent both to the method and back to the client with possible modifications.

```
public enum SoapHeaderDirection {
  In = 0x00000001,
  Out = 0x00000002,
  InOut = 0x00000003
}
```

Hierarchy   System.Object→ System.ValueType→ System.Enum(System.IComparable, System.IFormattable,
                   System.IConvertible)→ SoapHeaderDirection

SoapHeaderException

System.Web.Services.Protocols (system.web.services.dll)   class

This represents an error processing a SoapHeader. Typically, it results when a header with a SoapHeader.MustUnderstand property of true is processed by the receiving method, but the corresponding SoapHeader.DidUnderstand property is not set to true.

```
public class SoapHeaderException : SoapException {
// Public Constructors
    public SoapHeaderException(string message, System.Xml.XmlQualifiedName code);
    public SoapHeaderException(string message, System.Xml.XmlQualifiedName code,Exception innerException);
    public SoapHeaderException(string message, System.Xml.XmlQualifiedName code, string actor);
    public SoapHeaderException(string message, System.Xml.XmlQualifiedName code, string actor, Exception innerException);
}
```

Hierarchy   System.Object→ System.Exception(System.Runtime.Serialization.ISerializable)→ System.System-
                     mException→ SoapException→ SoapHeaderException

SoapHttpClientProtocol   marshal by reference, disposable

System.Web.Services.Protocols (system.web.services.dll)   class

You can inherit from this class to create a proxy class that communicates using the SOAP protocol over HTTP. This is the most commonly used class for creating proxies, and it is the default in proxy classes that .NET generates automatically. When using this class, you must also use the corresponding SoapDocumentMethodAttribute or SoapRpcMethodAttribute to bind a proxy class method to a web service method.

```
public class SoapHttpClientProtocol : HttpWebClientProtocol {
// Public Constructors
    public SoapHttpClientProtocol();
// Public Instance Methods
    public void Discover();
// Protected Instance Methods
    protected method IAsyncResult BeginInvoke(string methodName, object[] parameters, AsyncCallback callback, object asyncState);
    protected method object[] EndInvoke(IAsyncResult asyncResult);
    protected override method WebRequest GetWebRequest(Uri uri);                    // overrides HttpWebClientProtocol
    protected method object[] Invoke(string methodName, object[] parameters);
}
```

Hierarchy   System.Object→ System.MarshalByRefObject→ System.ComponentModel.Component(System.
                     ComponentModel.IComponent, System.IDisposable)→ WebClientProtocol→ HttpWebClientProto-
                     col→ SoapHttpClientProtocol

SoapMessage

System.Web.Services.Protocols (system.web.services.dll)   abstract class

This class represents a SOAP request or SOAP response used to communicate between a web service and proxy class. The SoapMessage class is used primarily for SOAP extensions.

SOAP extensions, which derive from SoapExtension, receive a SoapMessage object at each SoapMessageStage as an argument to the SoapExtension.ProcessMessage() method, which is called automatically by the ASP.NET Framework.

The SoapMessage class provides methods that allow you to retrieve the web service method parameters and the return value encoded in the SOAP message. For a SoapClientMessage, you use the GetInParameterValue() method if the SOAP message is in the SoapMessageStage.BeforeSerialize stage or the GetOutParameterValue() method if it's in the SoapMessageStage.AfterSerialize stage. For a SoapServerMessage, the reverse is true. To verify that the parameters are available, you can use the EnsureInStage() or EnsureOutStage() method (a System.InvalidOperationException will be thrown if the message is not in a compatible stage). Alternatively, you can use the Stage property to determine the state when the SoapMessage was generated.

```
public abstract class SoapMessage {
// Public Instance Properties
    public abstract field string Action{get; }
    public string ContentType{set; get; }
    public SoapException Exception{get; }
    public SoapHeaderCollection Headers{get; }
    public abstract field LogicalMethodInfo MethodInfo{get; }
    public abstract field bool OneWay{get; }
    public SoapMessageStage Stage{get; }
    public Stream Stream{get; }
    public abstract field string Url{get; }
// Public Instance Methods
    public object GetInParameterValue(int index);
    public object GetOutParameterValue(int index);
    public object GetReturnValue();
// Protected Instance Methods
    protected abstract method void EnsureInStage();
    protected abstract method void EnsureOutStage();
    protected method void EnsureStage(SoapMessageStage stage);
}
```

SoapMessageStage   serializable

System.Web.Services.Protocols (system.web.services.dll)   enum

This enumeration indicates the stage that a SoapMessage is in. Messages are serialized into SOAP before they are transmitted over the Internet and deserialized when they are received. Both the web service and the proxy client send and receive messages, and so both participate in the serialization and deserialization process.

```
public enum SoapMessageStage {
    BeforeSerialize = 1,
    AfterSerialize = 2,
    BeforeDeserialize = 4,
    AfterDeserialize = 8
}
```

Hierarchy	System.Object→ System.ValueType→ System.Enum(System.IComparable, System.IFormattable, System.IConvertible)→ SoapMessageStage

SoapParameterStyle   serializable

System.Web.Services.Protocols (system.web.services.dll)   enum

This enumeration is used when applying a SoapDocumentMethodAttribute or SoapDocumentServiceAttribute. It specifies how web service parameter information is encoded in a SOAP message. If you use Bare, parameter information will be placed in multiple elements under the Body element. If you specify Wrapped, all the parameters will be wrapped in a single element beneath the Body element. Default uses the default web service parameter style, which will be Wrapped unless the web service includes a SoapDocumentServiceAttribute in its class declaration that specifies differently.

```
public enum SoapParameterStyle {
  Default = 0,
  Bare = 1,
  Wrapped = 2
}
```

Hierarchy	System.Object→ System.ValueType→ System.Enum(System.IComparable, System.IFormattable, System.IConvertible)→ SoapParameterStyle

SoapRpcMethodAttribute

System.Web.Services.Protocols (system.web.services.dll)   sealed class

This attribute is used to specify the encoding for SOAP request and response messages. You can apply this attribute to methods in a web service or to methods in a proxy class that derives from SoapHttpClientProtocol (where it's required to bind the messages to the appropriate web method). You use this attribute, instead of SoapDocumentMethodAttribute, when you want to use the RPC encoding standard.

There are two options for encoding XML information in a SOAP message: RPC and Document. ASP.NET's default is Document. RPC (found in Section 7 of the SOAP specification) specifies that all method parameters are wrapped in a single element named after the web service method and that each of these elements is named after its respective parameter name. If you apply this attribute to a web method, it will not be able to return objects, because no XSD Schema will be generated.

```
public sealed class SoapRpcMethodAttribute : Attribute {
// Public Constructors
  public SoapRpcMethodAttribute();
  public SoapRpcMethodAttribute(string action);
// Public Instance Properties
  public string Action{set; get; }
  public string Binding{set; get; }
  public bool OneWay{set; get; }
  public string RequestElementName{set; get; }
```

```
public string RequestNamespace{set; get; }
public string ResponseElementName{set; get; }
public string ResponseNamespace{set; get; }
}
```

Hierarchy   System.Object→ System.Attribute→ SoapRpcMethodAttribute

Valid On   Method

SoapRpcServiceAttribute

System.Web.Services.Protocols (system.web.services.dll)   sealed class

This attribute can be applied to a web service's class declaration. It specifies that the default encoding for SOAP request and response messages will be RPC. The client can override this default by using the SoapDocumentMethodAttribute. If you apply this attribute, the web service will not be able to return objects, because no XSD Schema will be generated.

```
public sealed class SoapRpcServiceAttribute : Attribute {
// Public Constructors
  public SoapRpcServiceAttribute();
// Public Instance Properties
  public SoapServiceRoutingStyle RoutingStyle{set; get; }
}
```

Hierarchy   System.Object→ System.Attribute→ SoapRpcServiceAttribute

Valid On   Class

SoapServerMessage

System.Web.Services.Protocols (system.web.services.dll)   sealed class

This class represents a SOAP request sent by a web service or SOAP response received by a web service. It inherits from the SoapMessage class, which contains most of the functionality for SOAP messages.

```
public sealed class SoapServerMessage : SoapMessage {
// Public Instance Properties
  public override field string Action{get; }                                    // overrides SoapMessage
  public override field LogicalMethodInfo MethodInfo{get; }                      // overrides SoapMessage
  public override field bool OneWay{get; }                                       // overrides SoapMessage
  public object Server{get; }
  public override field string Url{get; }                                        // overrides SoapMessage
// Protected Instance Methods
  protected override method void EnsureInStage();                                // overrides SoapMessage
  protected override method void EnsureOutStage();                               // overrides SoapMessage
}
```

Hierarchy   System.Object→ SoapMessage→ SoapServerMessage

SoapServiceRoutingStyle

System.Web.Services.Protocols (system.web.services.dll)   enum

This enumeration is used to specify the SoapDocumentServiceAttribute.RoutingStyle and the SoapRpcServiceAttribute.RoutingStyle properties. Allowed values are RequestElement (the message is routed based on the first child element in the body of the SOAP message) and SoapAction (the SOAP message is routed based on the SOAPAction HTTP header).

```
public enum SoapServiceRoutingStyle {
  SoapAction = 0,
  RequestElement = 1
}
```

Hierarchy   System.Object→ System.ValueType→ System.Enum(System.IComparable, System.IFormattable,
                      System.IConvertible)→ SoapServiceRoutingStyle

SoapUnknownHeader

System.Web.Services.Protocols (system.web.services.dll)   sealed class

This represents a SoapHeader that was not understood by the receiving method in the web service or proxy class. You can receive all unknown headers by creating an array of SoapUnknownHeader objects, and using it with the SoapHeaderAttribute.

```
public sealed class SoapUnknownHeader : SoapHeader {
// Public Constructors
  public SoapUnknownHeader();
// Public Instance Properties
  public XmlElement Element{set; get; }
}
```

Hierarchy   System.Object→ SoapHeader→ SoapUnknownHeader

TextReturnReader

System.Web.Services.Protocols (system.web.services.dll)   class

This class supports the .NET Framework infrastructure. You do not need to use it directly in your code.

```
public class TextReturnReader : MimeReturnReader {
// Public Constructors
  public TextReturnReader();
// Public Instance Methods
  public override method object GetInitializer(LogicalMethodInfo methodInfo);          // overrides MimeFormatter
  public override method void Initialize(object o);                                    // overrides MimeFormatter
  public override method object Read(System.Net.WebResponse response,
                      System.IO.Stream responseStream);                                // overrides MimeReturnReader
}
```

UrlEncodedParameterWriter

System.Web.Services.Protocols (system.web.services.dll)   abstract class

This class supports the .NET Framework infrastructure. You do not need to use it directly in your code.

```
public abstract class UrlEncodedParameterWriter : MimeParameterWriter {
// Protected Constructors
  protected method UrlEncodedParameterWriter();
// Public Instance Properties
  public override field Encoding RequestEncoding{set; get; }                        // overrides MimeParameterWriter
// Public Instance Methods
  public override method object GetInitializer(LogicalMethodInfo methodInfo);              // overrides MimeFormatter
  public override method void Initialize(object initializer);                             // overrides MimeFormatter
// Protected Instance Methods
  protected method void Encode(System.IO.TextWriter writer, object[] values);
  protected method void Encode(System.IO.TextWriter writer, string name, object value);
}
```

Hierarchy   System.Object→ MimeFormatter→ MimeParameterWriter→ UrlEncodedParameterWriter

UrlParameterReader

System.Web.Services.Protocols (system.web.services.dll)   class

This class supports the .NET Framework infrastructure. You do not need to use it directly in your code.

```
public class UrlParameterReader : ValueCollectionParameterReader {
// Public Constructors
  public UrlParameterReader();
// Public Instance Methods
  public override method object[] Read(System.Web.HttpRequest request);              // overrides MimeParameterReader
}
```

Hierarchy   System.Object→ MimeFormatter→ MimeParameterReader→ ValueCollectionParameter-
                  Reader→ UrlParameterReader

UrlParameterWriter

System.Web.Services.Protocols (system.web.services.dll)   class

This class supports the .NET Framework infrastructure. You do not need to use it directly in your code.

```
public class UrlParameterWriter : UrlEncodedParameterWriter {
// Public Constructors
  public UrlParameterWriter();
// Public Instance Methods
  public override method string GetRequestUrl(string url, object[] parameters);        // overrides MimeParameterWriter
}
```

Hierarchy   System.Object→ MimeFormatter→ MimeParameterWriter→ UrlEncodedParameterWriter→
                 UrlParameterWriter

ValueCollectionParameterReader

System.Web.Services.Protocols (system.web.services.dll)   abstract class

This class supports the .NET Framework infrastructure. You do not need to use it directly
in your code.

```
public abstract class ValueCollectionParameterReader : MimeParameterReader {
// Protected Constructors
  protected method ValueCollectionParameterReader();
// Public Static Methods
  public static method bool IsSupported(LogicalMethodInfo methodInfo);
  public static method bool IsSupported(System.Reflection.ParameterInfo paramInfo);
// Public Instance Methods
  public override method object GetInitializer(LogicalMethodInfo methodInfo);        // overrides MimeFormatter
  public override method void Initialize(object o);                                   // overrides MimeFormatter
// Protected Instance Methods
  protected method object[] Read(System.Collections.Specialized.NameValueCollection collection);
}
```

Hierarchy   System.Object→ MimeFormatter→ MimeParameterReader→ ValueCollectionParameterReader

WebClientAsyncResult

System.Web.Services.Protocols (system.web.services.dll)   class

This class is used to return a result when invoking a web service method asynchronously,
through the corresponding Begin and End methods. These method variants are created for
you when you generate a proxy automatically using Visual Studio .NET or WSDL.exe.
Chapter 5 describes how to call web services asynchronously in detail.

```
public class WebClientAsyncResult : IAsyncResult {
// Public Instance Properties
  public object AsyncState{get; }                                                   // implements IAsyncResult
  public WaitHandle AsyncWaitHandle{get; }                                          // implements IAsyncResult
  public bool CompletedSynchronously{get; }                                         // implements IAsyncResult
  public bool IsCompleted{get; }                                                    // implements IAsyncResult
// Public Instance Methods
  public void Abort();
}
```

WebClientProtocol

System.Web.Services.Protocols (system.web.services.dll)   abstract class

This is the base class for all web server proxy classes. It includes basic properties like Url, which is usually set to the appropriate web service address in the proxy class's constructor, and Timeout, which specifies a value in milliseconds. By default, the proxy class uses a Timeout of -1, which represents infinity, although the web server can still time out the request on the server side. The RequestEncoding property is overridden by derived classes to provide the appropriate character encoding.

To set Credentials, you must use a System.Net.ICredentials object like System.Net.NetworkCredential and set the credentials that are specific to the type of authentication you are using. You can also set the PreAuthenticate property to true, which will cause the proxy class to automatically send authentication information with every request.

```
public abstract class WebClientProtocol : System.ComponentModel.Component {
// Protected Constructors
  protected method WebClientProtocol();
// Public Instance Properties
  public string ConnectionGroupName{set; get; }
  public ICredentials Credentials{set; get; }
  public bool PreAuthenticate{set; get; }
  public Encoding RequestEncoding{set; get; }
  public int Timeout{set; get; }
  public string Url{set; get; }
// Protected Static Methods
  protected static method void AddToCache(Type type, object value);
  protected static method object GetFromCache(Type type);
// Public Instance Methods
  public virtual method void Abort();
// Protected Instance Methods
  protected virtual method WebRequest GetWebRequest(Uri uri);
  protected virtual method WebResponse GetWebResponse(System.Net.WebRequest request);
  protected virtual method WebResponse GetWebResponse(System.Net.WebRequest request, IAsyncResult result);
}
```

Hierarchy   System.Object→ System.MarshalByRefObject→ System.ComponentModel.Component(System. ComponentModel.IComponent, System.IDisposable)→ WebClientProtocol

WebServiceHandlerFactory

System.Web.Services.Protocols (system.web.services.dll)   class

This class is used by ASP.NET to instantiate an appropriate HttpHandler for handling web service requests. You do not need to use this class directly in your code.

```
public class WebServiceHandlerFactory : System.Web.IHttpHandlerFactory {
// Public Constructors
  public WebServiceHandlerFactory();
// Public Instance Methods
```

```
 public IHttpHandler GetHandler(System.Web.HttpContext context, string verb,
                                string url, string filePath);         // implements System.Web.IHttpHandlerFactory
 public void ReleaseHandler(System.Web.IHttpHandler handler);         // implements System.Web.IHttpHandlerFactory
}
```

XmlReturnReader

System.Web.Services.Protocols (system.web.services.dll)   class

This class supports the .NET Framework infrastructure. You do not need to use it directly in your code.

```
public class XmlReturnReader : MimeReturnReader {
// Public Constructors
  public XmlReturnReader();
// Public Instance Methods
  public override method object GetInitializer(LogicalMethodInfo methodInfo);      // overrides MimeFormatter
  public override method object[] GetInitializers(LogicalMethodInfo[] methodInfos); // overrides MimeFormatter
  public override method void Initialize(object o);                               // overrides MimeFormatter
  public override method object Read(System.Net.WebResponse response,
                System.IO.Stream responseStream);                               // overrides MimeReturnReader
}
```

Hierarchy   System.Object→ MimeFormatter→ MimeReturnReader→ XmlReturnReader

Web Service Technologies

In this appendix, we provide a categorized list of some of the more commonly used web service technologies, along with a brief description of each. Our categories include transactions, security, description and discovery, routing and process flow, and message encapsulation.

There are many more published standards (both proposed and recommended) in each category, but we've focused on the ones we feel are important to web service development. We've included URLs in case you want to learn more about any of them in particular.

Transactions

XAML (Transaction Authority Markup Language)

URL
   http://www.xaml.org/

Authors
   Bowstreet, Hewlett-Packard, IBM, Oracle, Sun

Description
   A standard allowing coordinated online transaction processing.

Security

XKMS (XML Key Management Service)

URL
   http://www.w3.org/TR/xkms/

Authors

Verisign, Microsoft, webMethods

Description

A protocol for distributing and managing public keys used with XML Signa-tures. As of September 2002, this specification was a W3C Note.

XML Signatures (XML Digital Signatures)

URL

http://www.w3.org/TR/xmldsig-core/

Authors

Microsoft, XMLSec, PureEdge, Accelio

Description

A W3C Recommendation that specifies the syntax and processing rules for digi-tally signing both XML and non-XML data. XML Signatures can be used by a message recipient to ensure data integrity, message authenticity, and signer authenticity.

XML Encryption

Creator

W3C

URL

http://www.w3.org/Encryption/2001/

Authors

IBM, Microsoft, XMLSec

Description

A specification for encrypting arbitrary data and storing the encrypted data (or a reference to the encrypted date) in an XML Encryption element. As of Septem-ber 2002, this specification was a W3C Candidate Recommendation.

SOAP Security Extensions

URLs

http://www.trl.ibm.com/projects/xml/soap/wp/wp.html
http://www.w3.org/Submission/2001/01/

Authors

IBM, Microsoft

Description

A joint effort between IBM and Microsoft, the SOAP Security Extensions are specifications for managing security functions such as authorization, encryption, message integrity verification, and nonrepudiation using XML tags within the header and envelope of a SOAP message. So far only the digital signatures extension has been released to the W3C. The digital signature specification, known as SOAP Security Extensions: Digital Signature, specifies the XML tags and processing rules for including digital signature information in a SOAP header. This specification has been only partially submitted to the W3C and is currently a W3C Note.

WS-Security

URL
  http://msdn.microsoft.com/library/en-us/dnglobspec/html/ws-security.asp

Author
  Microsoft

Description
  A set of enhancements to the SOAP message header that allows for authentication, message integrity verification, and confidentiality, thereby enabling secure interaction between web services.

WS-License

URL
  http://msdn.microsoft.com/library/default.asp?url=/library/en-us/dnglobspec/html/ws-license.asp

Creator
  Microsoft

Description
  A set of XML tags used to describe licensing information within the WS-Security credentials header. This Microsoft specification is an addendum to the WS-Security specification.

Description and Discovery

WSDL

URL
  http://www.w3.org/TR/wsdl/

Authors
  IBM, Microsoft

Description

A specification outlining a format for describing a web service as a set of operations and messages. WSDL supports arbitrary message formats and network protocols; however, the specification explicitly discusses SOAP 1.1, HTTP GET/POST, and MIME. The specification is currently a W3C Note.

UDDI (Universal Description, Discovery, and Integration)

URL

http://www.uddi.org/

Authors

IBM, Microsoft, Ariba

Description

A set of specifications that collectively define message formats and processing rules for publishing, finding, and binding to web services. The specifications define a registry structure, registry operator requirements, and a process for inter-registry replication.

WS-Inspection

URL

http://www-106.ibm.com/developerworks/webservices/library/ws-wsilspec.html

Authors

IBM, Microsoft

Description

A specification for locating web services available at a site. This specification succeeds DISCO and ADS, which were two earlier specifications.

JXTA Search

URL

http://search.jxta.org/protocol.html

Author

Sun

Description

A distributed search protocol that can be used to locate services in a peer-to-peer network.

Routing and Process Flow

WS-Routing

URL

    http://search.jxta.org/protocol.html

Author

    Microsoft

Description

    A protocol specification for routing SOAP messages from a source to a recipient through a set of intermediaries. The protocol works by adding data to the SOAP header. This specification has not been submitted to any standards bodies.

XLANG

URL

    http://www.gotdotnet.com/team/xml_wsspecs/xlang-c/default.htm

Author

    Microsoft

Description

    A specification for describing message exchange behavior among a set of web services. This specification has not yet been submitted to any standards body.

WSCL (Web Services Conversation Language)

URL

    http://www.w3.org/TR/wscl10/

Author

    Hewlett-Packard

Description

    To some extent this specification overlaps with WSDL, providing a different XML syntax for describing web service operations and message flows. However, whereas WSDL can be used to describe protocol bindings and service information (e.g., location), WSCL cannot. Also, whereas WSCL describes the allowable sequencing of document exchanges for a web service, WSDL does not.

WSFL (Web Services Flow Language)

URL

http://www-4.ibm.com/software/solutions/webservices/pdf/WSFL.pdf

Author

IBM

Description

An XML language used for describing usage patterns for web services (e.g., to complete task X, you must use services A followed by B and C) and interaction patterns among web services.

Message Encapsulation

DIME (Direct Internet Message Encapsulation)

URL

http://www.ietf.org/internet-drafts/draft-nielsen-dime-02.txt

Author

Microsoft

Description

A specification describing a lightweight binary message format for encapsulating application-defined data (e.g., file attachments) into a single message. This can be used for sending SOAP messages with attachments as part of the message payload. This specification was submitted as an IETF Draft in February 2002, and expires in December 2002.

Jabber

URL

http://www.jabber.org/

Author

Jeremie Miller

Description

Jabber describes both a transport protocol replacement for HTTP (used primarily for real-time messaging), and an encapsulation format.

Index

We'd like to hear your suggestions for improving our indexes. Send email to *index@oreilly.com*.

AsyncService class, thread pooling and, 188
attributes
    SoapDocumentMethod, 337
    SoapDocumentService, 337
    SoapRPCMethod, 337
    SoapRPCService, 337
    WebMethod, 24, 39
    XML, 115
authentication, 264
    ASP.NET, providers, 271
    custom techniques, 289–297
    forms, ASP.NET, 277
    operating system, 264
    Passport, 278
    per-method, implementation using
        SQL, 290
    providers, custom, 296
    user authentication, IIS, 265
    web server, 264
    web service application, 264
    Windows authentication, 272
        access restriction, 273
        configuration, 273
        impersonation, 276
        provider and, 276

B

B2B (business-to-business), commerce, UDDI
        and, 300
Basic Authentication
    IIS user authentication, 266
    IIS user authentication, security risks, 267
    SSL and, 267
BeginDelay( ) method, 173
BeginGetIPForHostname method, 83
BeginInvoke method, 172
/bin directory
    IIS, 48
    location, 49
binary data, 132
binding, 55
binding declaration, 84
binding element, WSDL, 72
bindingTemplate data entry, UDDI business
        registries, 303
BizTalk Server, 19
boilerplate code, VS.NET web service
        project, 29
BOM (byte order mark), 344
breakpoints, debugging using VS.NET, 232
browse pattern, UDDI Inquiry API, 325

btnUpload_Click method, 134
BufferedResponse property, WebMethod
        attribute, 44
business registries, UDDI, 302
    access, 305
    bindingTemplate data type, 303
    businessEntity data type, 303
    businessService data type, 303
    categories, 304
        classifications, 307
    contents, 303
    entities, registering, 305
    operator nodes, 302
    publisherAssertion, 303
    tModel data type, 303
        association with web services, 319
business-to-business transactions, 3

C

C#
    Console Application template, client
        proxy creation, 79
    data types, converting to XML
        messages, 56
    Hello World type web service, 21
Cache collection, 205
Cache object
    members, 208
    threading, 206
CacheDependency class, constructors, 214
CacheDependency object, 213
CacheDuration property, WebMethod
        attribute, 43, 200
    disabling caching and, 201
CachePriority, 209
Cache.Remove( ) method, 216
caching, 197
    ASP.NET, 197
    cache dependencies, 213, 216
        file dependencies, 214
    callbacks, 218
    cloning and, 211
    data caching, 205
        ASP.NET, 197
        example, 209
    disabling cache, 201
    emptying cache, 199
    in-memory caches, 199
    Insert( ) method, 206
    inserting items in cache, 206
    linking items, 216

output caching
    ASP.NET, 197, 200
    candidates for, 202–205
    profiling web services and, 224–229
    purpose of, 198
    removing items, 218
    stateful design and, 219–224
    time, 205
    VS.NET, 199
    web services, testing, 199
callbacks, asynchronous services and, 181
categories, UDDI registries, 304
    classifications, 307
ChainStream( ) method, 255
CheckDependentItem( ) method, 215
Class attribute, WebService directive, 22
class methods
    serialization and, 117
    as web services, 24
classes
    AsyncService, thread pooling and, 188
    CacheDependency, 214
    definitions, binding declaration, 84
    design, sessions and, 152
    DNSLookupService, 83
    EventLog, 240
    MailMessage, 244
    namespaces, 23
    PassportIdentity, 279
    proxy classes, 78, 86
        HTTPWebClientProtocol, 92
        inheritance, 84
    Service class, 187
    ServiceMonitor, 188
    SmtpMail, 244
    SOAP extensions, 248
    SoapException, 236
    SoapExtension, 248
    SoapExtensionAttribute, 248
    SoapHeader, 162
    System.Web.HttpApplicationState, 157
    System.Web.SessionState.HttpSessionState, 146
    threading classes, 184
    ThreadPool, 188
    Trace, 245
    WindowsIdentity, 281
    XmlSerialization class, 112
    XmlSerializer, 112
client certificates, IIS, 265
    user authentication, 265, 266

client proxies, 78
    creating, 79
        VS.NET, 79
clients, asynchronous services
        components, 192
client/service model, consuming web
        services, 56
Clone( ) method, 211
cloning, caching and, 211
CLR (Common Language Runtime), 103
code sharing, history of web services, 4
CodeBehind attribute, WebService
        directive, 32
code-behind model, VS.NET, 31
COM (Component Object Model), 4
COM objects, screen scraping and, 94
COM+ transactions, 141
command line
    switches, .NET compilers, 52
    typed DataSets, 129
comments in methods, 41
compilers, .NET, 50
complex data types, 110
    as arguments, 119
    serialization, 112
    VideoService web service, 110
complex data types, passing as
        arguments, 122
configuration
    IIS settings, 265
    session state, 148
    VS.NET, web creation and, 25
    Windows authentication, 273
ConsoleSerializer, 113
consumer view, complex data types as
        arguments, 122
ConsumerThinLayer, 142
consuming web services, 54
    asynchronous, 171–185
    binding, 55
    client/service model, 56
    proxies and, 57
    publish/find/bind consumer model, 54
    screen scrapers, 93
CookieContainer, 147
cookies
    critical information and, 158
    session cookies, ASP.NET, 145
    state and custom cookies, 158
CORBA (Common Object Request
        Broker), 4, 7

R

reflection, 34
regex class, RegularExpressions namespace, 95
registries, UDDI (see business registries, UDDI)
registry nodes, UDDI, 302
    operator nodes, 302
regular expressions
    screen scraping and, 95
    WSDL extensions, 96
RegularExpressions namespace, 95
ReleaseSession( ) method, 153
remote hosting, web services, 46
resource managers, 141
response document, XML, 37
REST (REpresentational State Transfer), 69
role-based access models, security, 280
routing standards, 380
RPCs (remote procedure calls), 336
RPC-style messages, SOAP, 336

S

scalability, design and, 289
screen scrapers, 57, 93
    HTML table example, 96–100
    regular expressions and, 95
search engines, 299
security
    ASP.NET, 270
        authentication providers, 271
    design and, 289
    impersonation, 286
    process security, 297
    programmatic, 280
    role-based access models, 280
    standards, 376
    vulnerabilities, 262
    Windows authentication, 272
    WindowsIdentity object, 283
    WindowsPrincipal object, 281
security tokens, impersonation and, 289
serialization, 44, 56, 112
    ConsoleSerializer, 113
    deep serialization, 116
    shallow, 116
    variables and, 116
    XML serialization, 111
        SoapException class and, 238
    XML Shaping and, 114
    XmlSerialization class, 112

Serialize method, XmlSerializer class, 112
server configuration file, 270
    (see also machine.config file)
Service class, asynchronous services and, 187
service consumer model
    proxies, 56
    publish/find/bind process, 55
service description, 34
service element, WSDL, 73
Service Implementation Definition, WSDL, 71
Service Interface Definition, WSDL, 71
service page, VS.NET, 28
service providers, publish/find/bind process, 55
service registry, publish/find/bind process, 55
service view, complex data types as arguments, 120
service1.asmx file, VS.NET, 27, 28
ServiceMonitor class, 188
services, endpoints, 77
session collections, access, 146
session IDs, ASP.NET, 146
Session object, ASP.NET applications, 41
session state
    ASP.NET, 145–148
        session cookies, 145
    configuration, 148
    in-process sesssion state, 149
    machine.config file, 148
    management example, 152
    mode options, 149
    timeouts, 151
    web.config file, 148
sessions, class design and, 152
set method, WebMethod attribute and, 137
SetAbort( ) method, 141
SetComplete( ) method, 141
shallow serialization, 116
simple data types, 101
    structs, 104
Simple Object Access Protocol (see SOAP)
simpleType element, XML, 103
sliding expiration, data caching and, 207
SmtpMail class, 244
SOAP, 63
    encoding formats, interoperability and, 339
    exceptions, 236
    extensions
        advanced, 254–261

string keys, state collections, 147
structs
    namespaces and, 23
    simple data types, 104
Sun ONE (Open Net Environment), 16
system event log, 240
System.Collections namespace, 29
SystemData namespace, 29
System.Data.DataSet namespace, 129
System.Diagnostics namespace, 29, 240, 245
System.DivideByZero exception, 234
System.EnterpriseServices namespace,
    transactions, 44
System.EnterpriseServices.ContextUtil
    class, 141
System.Net namespace, screen scraping
    and, 94
System.Net.Xml.Serialization
    namespace, 114
System.Reflection namespace, 34
System.Web.Cache namespace, 213
System.Web.Caching namespace, web service
    deployment, 45
System.Web.HttpApplicationState class, 157
System.Web.HttpContext.Current
    property, 146
System.Web.Mail namespace, 244
System.Web.Security namespace, 279
System.Web.Services namespace
    aliasing, 22
    WebMethod attribute, 39
    WebService attribute, 37–39
System.Web.Services.Protocols
    namespace, 87, 248
    SoapHeader class, 162
System.Web.SessionState.HttpSessionState
    class, 146
System.Xml.Serialization namespace, 112
    attributes, 115

T

targetNamespace,
        PrimitiveTypesService, 108
Telnet, 59
TemperatureService web service, 117
text editors, 21
    Notepad as, 20
TextWriterTraceListener, 246
thin layer design, state management, 142
thread pooling, AsyncService class and, 188
threading
    asynchronous services, components, 193

threading classes, asynchronous services
        and, 184
ThreadPool class, 188
threads
    Cache object, 206
    HttpApplicationState class, 157
ticket system, design and, 293–296
tickets
    stateless web services, 160
    system problems, 168
Timeout property, WebClientProtocol, 87
timeouts, session state, 151
tModel data type, UDDI registries, 303
    association services with, 319
    WSDL and, 312
Trace class, 245
tracing, 245
TransactionOption property, WebMethod
        attribute, 43
transactions, 43
    ADO.NET, 141
    business-to-business transactions, 3
    COM+, 141
    distributed web service transactions, 44
    methods, 142
    primitive data types and, 141
    root, 142
    standards, 376
    state and, 140
    stateless utility class, 141
    System.EnterpriseServices namespace, 44
types element
    PrimitiveTypesService web service, 108
    WSDL, 71

U

UDDI (Universal Description, Discovery, and
        Integration), 15, 300, 379
    access, .NET and, 326
    browse pattern, 325
    business registries, 302
        access, 305
        categories, 304, 307
        contents, 303
        entity registration, 305
    history of, 300
    Inquiry API, 323
    interoperability and, 334
    messaging, 322
    .NET UDDI SDK, 328
    open architecture, 301
    operator nodes, 302

About the Authors

Alex Ferrara is CTO of Boston Technical, a Boston-based IT consulting firm that specializes in custom application development and systems integration using Microsoft technologies. During his career as a consultant, Alex has had the opportunity to both manage and implement a broad range of technology initiatives for companies including Citigroup, Inc., Titleist, Inc., and Schering-Plough, Inc. He has worked with educational organizations such as Kaplan, Inc. to develop Microsoft Certification courses and has served as a professor in adjunct at Northeastern University. Alex graduated from the University of Pennsylvania with a degree in electrical and computer engineering. He currently lives in New York City with his wife, and is pursuing an MBA at Columbia Business School.

Matthew MacDonald is an author, educator, and MCSD developer. He has written several books about programming with .NET, including *The Book of VB .NET* (No Starch) and *ASP.NET: The Complete Reference* (Osborne McGraw-Hill). He has also been a contributor to several O'Reilly titles, including *C# in a Nutshell, ASP.NET in a Nutshell*, and *ADO.NET in a Nutshell*. In a dimly remembered past life, he studied English literature and theoretical physics.

Colophon

Our look is the result of reader comments, our own experimentation, and feedback from distribution channels. Distinctive covers complement our distinctive approach to technical topics, breathing personality and life into potentially dry subjects.

The animal on the cover of *Programming .NET Web Services* is a boatbill heron. The boatbill heron is native to Central and South America. It is distinguished by its large, wide, flat beak, which is shaped like an upside-down boat. It is a nocturnal creature and does most of its hunting for food in swamplands, but lives in trees. It's diet consists mainly of small fish, snakes, and worms. The boatbill heron is shorter and chunkier than it's heron relatives, and is usually brown or gray, with black markings near the top of its head.

Mary Brady was the production editor and proofreader for *Programming .NET Web Services*. Norma Emory was the copyeditor. Claire Cloutier and Mary Anne Weeks Mayo provided quality control. Johnna Van Hoose Dinse wrote the index. Production support was provided by Derek Di Matteo.

Ellie Volckhausen designed the cover of this book, based on a series design by Edie Freedman. The cover image is a 19th-century engraving from the *Riverside Natural History, Volume IV, Birds*. Emma Colby produced the cover layout with QuarkXPress 4.1 using Adobe's ITC Garamond font.

David Futato designed the interior layout. This book was converted to FrameMaker 5.5.6 with a format conversion tool created by Erik Ray, Jason McIntosh, Neil Walls, and Mike Sierra that uses Perl and XML technologies. The text font is Linotype

Birka; the heading font is Adobe Myriad Condensed; and the code font is Lucas-Font's TheSans Mono Condensed. The illustrations that appear in the book were produced by Robert Romano and Jessamyn Read using Macromedia FreeHand 9 and Adobe Photoshop 6. The tip and warning icons were drawn by Christopher Bing. This colophon was written by Mary Brady.

Other Titles Available from O'Reilly

Microsoft .NET Programming

VB.NET Language in a Nutshell, 2nd Edition

By Steven Roman, Ron Petrusha &
Paul Lomax
2nd Edition May 2002
682 pages, ISBN 0-596-00308-0

The documentation that comes with
VB typically provides only the bare
details for each language element; left
out is the valuable inside information
that a programmer really needs to know in order to solve
programming problems or to use a particular language
element effectively. *VB .NET Language in a Nutshell*, 2nd
Edition documents the undocumented and presents the
kind of wisdom that comes from the authors' many years
of experience with the language. Bonus CD ingegrates
the book's reference section with Visual Studio .NET.

Programming C#, 2nd Edition

By Jesse Liberty
2nd Edition February 2002
650 pages, ISBN 0-596-00309-9

The first part of *Programming C#*, 2nd
Edition introduces C# fundamentals,
then goes on to explain the development of desktop and Internet applications, including Windows Forms, ADO.NET, ASP.NET
(including Web Forms), and Web Services. Next, this
book gets to the heart of the .NET Framework, focusing
on attributes and reflection, remoting, threads and synchronization, streams, and finally, it illustrates how to
interoperate with COM objects.

Programming Visual Basic .NET

By Dave Grudgeiger
1st Edition December 2001
460 pages, ISBN 0-596-00093-6

Programming Visual Basic .NET will
give you an idea of where the various
parts of .NET fit with VB .NET. Ensu-
ing chapters break down and present
the language, the common language runtime, Windows
Forms, ASP.NET and Web Forms, Web Services, and
ADO.NET. The book then moves into topics on developing transactional applications, internationalization, security, and debugging.

Programming ASP.NET

By Jesse Liberty & Dan Hurwitz
1st Edition February 2002
960 pages, ISBN 0-596-00171-1

The ASP.NET technologies are so complete and flexible; your main difficulty
may lie simply in weaving the pieces
together for maximum efficiency.
Programming ASP.NET shows you how to do just that.
Jesse Liberty and Dan Hurwitz teach everything you
need to know to write web applications and web services
using both C# and Visual Basic .NET.

C# in a Nutshell

By Peter Drayton & Ben Albarhari
1st Edition March 2002
856 pages, ISBN 0-596-00181-9

C# is likely to become one of the
most widely used languages for building .NET applications. *C# in a Nutshell* contains a concise introduction
to the language and its syntax, plus
brief tutorials used to accomplish common programming tasks. It also includes O'Reilly's classic-style, quick-
reference material for all the types and members in core
.NET namespaces, including System, System.Text, Sys-
tem.IO, and System.Collections.

ASP.NET in a Nutshell

By G. Andrew Duthie &
Matthew MacDonald
1st Edition June 2002
816 pages, ISBN 0-596-00116-9

As a quick reference and tutorial in
one, *ASP.NET in a Nutshell* goes
beyond the published documentation
to highlight little-known details, stress
practical uses for particular features, and provide real-
world examples that show how features can be used in a
working application. This book covers application and
web service development, custom controls, data access,
security, deployment, and error handling. There is also
an overview of web-related class libraries.

O'REILLY®

To order: 800-998-9938 • order@oreilly.com • www.oreilly.com
Online editions of most O'Reilly titles are available by subscription at *safari.oreilly.com*
Also available at most retail and online bookstores.

How to stay in touch with O'Reilly

1. Visit our award-winning web site

http://www.oreilly.com/

★ "Top 100 Sites on the Web"—PC Magazine
★ CIO Magazine's Web Business 50 Awards

Our web site contains a library of comprehensive product information (including book excerpts and tables of contents), downloadable software, background articles, interviews with technology leaders, links to relevant sites, book cover art, and more. File us in your bookmarks or favorites!

2. Join our email mailing lists

Sign up to get email announcements of new books and conferences, special offers, and O'Reilly Network technology newsletters at:

http://www.elists.oreilly.com

It's easy to customize your free elists subscription so you'll get exactly the O'Reilly news you want.

3. Get examples from our books

To find example files for a book, go to:

http://www.oreilly.com/catalog

select the book, and follow the "Examples" link.

4. Work with us

Check out our web site for current employment opportunities:

http://jobs.oreilly.com/

5. Register your book

Register your book at:

http://register.oreilly.com

6. Contact us

O'Reilly & Associates, Inc.
1005 Gravenstein Hwy North
Sebastopol, CA 95472 USA
TEL: 707-827-7000 or 800-998-9938
    (6am to 5pm PST)
FAX: 707-829-0104

order@oreilly.com
For answers to problems regarding your order or our products. To place a book order online visit:

http://www.oreilly.com/order_new/

catalog@oreilly.com
To request a copy of our latest catalog.

booktech@oreilly.com
For book content technical questions or corrections.

corporate@oreilly.com
For educational, library, and corporate sales.

proposals@oreilly.com
To submit new book proposals to our editors and product managers.

international@oreilly.com
For information about our international distributors or translation queries. For a list of our distributors outside of North America check out:

http://international.oreilly.com/distributors.html

O'REILLY®